THE ULTIMATE
BIBLE
FACT & QUIZ BOOK

THE ULTIMATE
BIBLE
FACT & QUIZ BOOK

RIVER
OAK
PUBLISHING

The Ultimate Bible Fact & Quiz Book
ISBN 1-58919-304-0
Copyright © 2001 by Arcturus Publishing Limited
1-7, Shand Street, London. SE1 2ES

Published by RiverOak Publishing
PO Box 700143
Tulsa, Oklahoma 74170-0143

Cover design by Communiqué
Illustrations by Jim Hansen
Managing Editor, John G. Maxwell

CONTENTS

Foreword

The Bible is one of the world's greatest books. It is a bestseller, has had a far-reaching impact on human civilization, and has encouraged and inspired millions of people throughout history.

The Ultimate Bible Fact & Quiz Book is a new and exciting way to discover the Bible. It can be used in community and church groups, Sunday School classes, family games and devotions, or simply for entertaining reading.

What's unique about this collection of quizzes and facts is its variety. Topics covered include Jesus Christ, important Bible characters, significant events, geography, music, food, love, war, money, gardening, animals, crime, punishment, miracles, angels, dreams … the list is virtually endless!

The quizzes are designed to challenge every age and ability. Some questions may seem easy, such as, *In which town was Jesus born?* or *Who was said to be the wisest king in the Bible?* Others may be a bit more challenging, like *How old was Joash when he began to reign in Judah?* or *What was the name of King David's third son?*

There are hundreds of fascinating facts included. Did you know that one of the words for miracles in the New Testament is *dunamis,* from which we get our word *dynamite?* You'll find this and many more interesting nuggets of information – all about this amazing book called the Bible. Enjoy!

Martin H. Manser

The Light of the World

Quiz # 1

THE LIGHT OF THE WORLD

1. To which bereaved woman did Jesus say, "Don't cry!"?

2. When Dr. Luke described the healing of a man on the Sabbath, he diagnosed the man's illness, using a medical term found nowhere else in the New Testament. What was the illness?

3. Only one of Jesus' miracles is recorded in all four Gospels. Which miracle?

4. What is the Bible reference for the famous verse which begins, "For God so loved the world that he gave his one and only Son…"?

5. After meeting Jesus, who said that he would give away half of his possessions to the poor?

6. Which Gospel starts with the words, "The beginning of the gospel about Jesus Christ, the Son of God"?

7. True or false? Chapter 17 of John's Gospel contains Jesus' longest recorded prayer.

8. To which woman did Jesus say, "Daughter, your faith has healed you. Go in peace and be freed from your suffering"?

9. What was unusual about the place where Jesus healed a little girl who was possessed by an evil spirit?

10. True or false? There is only one mention in the Gospels of a meeting between Jesus and the apostle Paul.

11. Which top Jewish religious leader visited Jesus at night?

12. True or false? A blind beggar kept calling out to Jesus, but the people told him to be quiet.

13. Which Gospel opens with the words, "In the beginning was the Word…"

14. How old was Jesus when his parents took him to the temple in Jerusalem for the Passover?

15. Where did Jesus attend a wedding reception?

---

13. John's Gospel **14.** 12 years old **15.** Cana
10. False. There is no record of such a meeting **11.** Nicodemus **12.** True (Mark 10:47-48)
9. The miracle took place outside Palestine in the region of Tyre and Sidon
7. True **8.** To a woman who had been suffering from bleeding for twelve years
3. The feeding of the 5,000 **4.** John 3:16 **5.** Zacchaeus **6.** Mark's Gospel
1. The widow of Nain who was about to bury her son **2.** Dropsy, which is an accumulation of fluid

Answers

2

Quiz #2

THE LIGHT OF THE WORLD

1. True or false? Jesus prayed in public but it is never recorded that he prayed by himself in private.

2. To which ill woman did Jesus say on the Sabbath, "Woman, you are set free from your infirmity"?

3. When Jesus rode into Jerusalem amid cheering crowds, on what was he riding?

4. Which Old Testament book has a verse in it which is taken as a prophecy about the birth place of Jesus?

5. To whom did Jesus say, "Get up, take your mat and go home"?

6. Which Old Testament book has a verse in it which is taken as a prophecy that Jesus would be born of a virgin?

7. To whom did Jesus say, "Did I not tell you that if you believed you would see the glory of God?"?

8. To which would-be disciple did Jesus say, "Foxes have holes and birds of the air have nests, but the Son of Man has no place to lay his head"?

9. True or false? The last verse in the Bible says, "And surely I am with you always, to the very end of the age."

10. When Jesus told the professional mourners that the ruler's daughter was "not dead but asleep" how did they react?

11. Who asked Jesus, "How is it that we and the Pharisees fast, but your disciples do not fast?"?

12. What did Jesus promise he would give to the weary and burdened if they came to him?

13. True or false? Jesus had half-sisters as well as half-brothers.

14. Jesus had four half-brothers. James and Joseph were two of the brothers. Name one of the other two.

15. Who said, "Where is the one who has been born king of the Jews?"?

Answers

1. False (Matthew 14:23) 2. A woman who had been crippled for 18 years 3. A donkey 4. Micah 5:2 5. To the paralyzed man who had been let down through the roof of a house to reach Jesus 6. Isaiah 7:14 7. Martha 8. A teacher of the law who said, "I will follow you wherever you go." 9. False. This is the last verse of Matthew's Gospel 10. They laughed at Jesus 11. John the Baptist's disciples 12. Rest 13. True (Mark 6:3). 14. Judas and Simon 15. The wise men

Quiz #3

THE LIGHT OF THE WORLD

1. How old was Jesus when he began his ministry?

2. What memorable act did Jesus do immediately before eating the last supper with his disciples on the day we now call Maundy Thursday?

3. True or false? Jesus rebuked a storm on Lake Galilee and it obeyed him.

4. Which Old Testament book has a verse in it which is taken as a Messianic prophecy about the slaughter of the innocents?

5. On what occasion did Jesus say, "I have not found such great faith even in Israel"?

6. True or false? As he looked at the Roman soldiers, Jesus said they were like sheep without a shepherd.

7. To whom did Jesus point and say, "Here are my mother and my brothers"?

8. How old was the daughter of Jairus when Jesus brought her back to life?

9. In which town was Jesus born?

10. What was Jesus' one-word reply to Peter when Peter said, "Tell me to come to you on the water"?

11. When did Jesus say, "Open your eyes and look at the fields! They are ripe for harvest"?

12. When Jesus said to a deaf and dumb man, "Be opened!", what, according to Mark's Gospel, was the actual Aramaic word that Jesus used?

13. Which Old Testament book has a verse in it which is taken as a Messianic prophecy about Jesus being called out of Egypt?

14. To whom did Jesus say, "I was sent only to the lost sheep of Israel"?

15. What had the disciples been arguing about not long before Jesus asked them, "What were you arguing about on the road?"?

---

12. Ephphatha **13.** Hosea 11:1 **14.** The Canaanite woman **15.** About who should be greatest

11. When Jesus' disciples returned to the well and found him talking to a Samaritan woman

8. 12 years old **9.** Bethlehem **10.** Come

6. False. Jesus was talking about the crowds (Matthew 9:36) **7.** His disciples

5. When a centurion asked Jesus to heal his servant, not by visiting his home, but by giving a command.

1. About 30 years old **2.** Jesus washed his disciples' feet **3.** True (Mark 4:39) **4.** Jeremiah 31:15

Answers

4

Quiz #4
THE LIGHT OF THE WORLD

1. True or false? Jesus said to his disciples, "I will not leave you as orphans."

2. About whom was Jesus speaking when he said, "Have I not chosen you, the Twelve? Yet one of you is a devil"?

3. Jesus once healed ten lepers. How many came back to thank him?

4. Which Old Testament book has a verse in it which is taken as a Messianic prophecy about Jesus' ministry being in Galilee?

5. To which group of people did Jesus say, "The harvest is plentiful, but the workers are few"?

6. Who said of Jesus, "You are the Christ, the Son of the living God"?

7. To whom did Jesus say, "Get behind me, Satan"?

8. What did Jesus say is the second greatest commandment?

9. True or false? Immediately after Jesus was baptized he chose his twelve apostles.

10. When did Jesus' clothes become as white as light?

11. What was the name of the devout and righteous man who met Jesus in the temple when he was circumcised?

12. True or false? Jesus regularly attended a synagogue on the Sabbath.

13. Which Old Testament book has a verse in it which is taken as a Messianic prophecy about Jesus riding into Jerusalem on a donkey?

14. About which dead man did Jesus say, "This sickness will not end in death"?

15. True or false? Moses and Elijah were seen at Jesus' ascension.

Answers

1. True (John 14:18) 2. Judas Iscariot 3. 1 4. Isaiah 9:1-2 5. The 72 disciples sent out two by two 6. Peter 7. Peter 8. "Love your neighbor as yourself" 9. False (Matthew 4:1) 10. At the transfiguration 11. Simeon 12. True (Luke 4:44) 13. Zechariah 9:9 14. Lazarus 15. False. They were seen at Jesus' transfiguration (Matthew 17:3)

Quiz #5

THE LIGHT OF THE WORLD

1. When Jesus said that "Elijah has already come", to whom was he referring?

2. To whom did Jesus say, "You are in error because you do not know the Scriptures or the power of God"?

3. True or false? After Jesus spat on a blind man's eyes, the man said he could see people but they all looked tiny, like very young children.

4. Who did Jesus tell that he must be born again?

5. About whom did Jesus say, "Satan has asked to sift you as wheat"?

6. True or false? When Jesus was arrested, Peter helped him to escape.

7. To the nearest five years, which year is it traditionally thought that Jesus started his ministry?

8. True or false? Jesus never married.

9. What are the first recorded words of Jesus in Mark's Gospel?

10. How many different miracles of Jesus do the four Gospels record: to the nearest five?

11. How many different parables of Jesus do the four Gospels record: to the nearest five?

12. About whom did Jesus say, "Take off the grave clothes and let him go"?

13. When Jesus, Mary and Joseph left Egypt, which town did they go to?

14. How many of Jesus' disciples witnessed his transfiguration?

15. Who did Jesus say were like white-washed tombs?

Answers

1. John the Baptist 2. The Sadducees
3. False. The people looked like trees walking around (Mark 8:24) 4. Nicodemus
5. Simon (Peter) 6. False. Peter ran away (Mark 14:50) 7. A.D. 26/27 8. True
9. "The time has come, the kingdom of God is near" 10. 35 miracles 11. 40 parables 12. Lazarus
13. Nazareth 14. 3 15. The Pharisees

Quiz #6
THE LIGHT OF THE WORLD

1. True or false? Jesus walked on the water of the Sea of Galilee.

2. Which Gospels state that Jesus taught with authority and not like the teachers of the law?

3. Who said to Jesus, "What do you want with us, Jesus of Nazareth? Have you come to destroy us?"?

4. True or false? When Jesus needed money to pay the temple tax, he told Peter to go fishing and to look in the mouth of the first fish he caught. There Peter found the money he needed.

5. Where was Jesus when he said, "I and the Father are one"?

6. Jesus told people not to focus on the speck of sawdust in their brother's eye when they had what in their own eye?

7. True or false? Jesus spent about ten years teaching and performing miracles with his disciples.

8. Where did Jesus make his base in Galilee?

9. In which of the Gospels is Jesus called "the Lamb of God"?

10. Who was the only person to call Jesus "the Lamb of God"?

11. There is one saying of Jesus which is not found in the four Gospels but comes in another book in the New Testament. Which New Testament book does the saying come in?

12. To which group who opposed him did Jesus say, "At the resurrection people will neither marry nor be given in marriage"?

13. True or false? Jesus said he was the good farmer.

14. Who did Jesus take in his arms and bless?

15. True or false? Jesus' first miracle took place at a wedding.

Quiz #7

THE LIGHT OF THE WORLD

1. True or false? Jesus spoke Aramaic.

2. When did Jesus make a whip of cords?

3. What did Jesus say it is hard for a rich man to do?

4. What was the name of the Pharisee who invited Jesus for a meal?

5. Which Gospel was written by a doctor?

6. Before Jesus started his ministry, what work did he do?

7. What were the first words of Jesus recorded by Matthew?

8. To whom did Jesus say, "Do not put the Lord your God to the test"?

9. In what town could Jesus perform very few miracles because of the people's lack of faith?

10. According to the Pharisees, Jesus broke the law when he healed on the Sabbath. What other Sabbath law did he break?

11. True or false? Jesus was so pure that he was never tempted.

12. Complete the first beatitude, "Blessed are the poor in spirit..."

13. True or false? Jesus' mother and brother wanted to take charge of him because they thought he was out of his mind.

14. What percentage of the 1,071 verses in Matthew's Gospel contain the spoken word of Jesus; to the nearest 10%?

15. Who asked Jesus, "How many times shall I forgive my brother when he sins against me? Up to seven times?"?

Answers

1. True (John 6:41) 2. When he threw the money-changers out of the temple
3. Enter the kingdom of heaven 4. Simon 5. Luke's Gospel 6. He was a carpenter
7. "Let it be so now; it is proper for us to do this to fulfil all righteousness" (Matthew 3:15) 8. The devil
9. Nazareth 10. He allowed the disciples to pluck and eat corn on the Sabbath
11. False. Jesus was often tempted, but never gave in to temptation. 12. "...for theirs is the kingdom of heaven."
13. True (Mark 3:20-21) 14. 60 per cent 15. Peter

Quiz #8

THE LIGHT OF THE WORLD

1. Who asked Jesus for a drink at a well?

2. True or false? When Jesus was a teenager, baseball was his favorite sport.

3. Complete the second beatitude, "Blessed are those who mourn..."

4. What did Jesus say about a city on a hill?

5. True or false? Jesus spoke more about heaven and hell than anyone else in the Bible.

6. To whom did Jesus say, "...with God all things are possible"?

7. True or false? In chapter 4 of John's Gospel Jesus is seen as the soul-winner as he speaks with Zacchaeus.

8. Fill in the missing word: "The people were amazed at his teaching, because he taught them as one who had ____."

9. Complete the third beatitude, "Blessed are the meek..."

10. Lazarus had two sisters: Martha was one sister. Who was the other?

11. What special request did James and John ask of Jesus?

12. What trick question did the disciples of the Pharisees and the Herodians ask Jesus?

13. What reply did Jesus give to the trick question posed by the disciples of the Pharisees and the Herodians?

14. In Jesus' parable about the man who was mugged, who were the two people who ignored him?

15. True or false? In chapter five of John's Gospel Jesus heals a man who had been ill for eight years.

Answers

1. A Samaritan woman **2.** False. The Gospels give no details about Jesus' teenage years **3.** "...for they will be comforted" **4.** It cannot be hidden **5.** True **6.** His disciples **7.** False. Jesus spoke to the woman of Samaria. **8.** Authority **9.** "...for they will inherit the earth" **10.** Mary **11.** To sit at his right and left hand when he comes in his glory **12.** "Is it right to pay tax to Caesar or not?" **13.** "Give to Caesar what is Caesar's, and to God what is God's" **14.** A priest and a Levite **15.** False. The man had been ill for 38 years (John 5:5)

Quiz #9
THE LIGHT OF THE WORLD

1. Complete the fourth beatitude, "Blessed are those who hunger and thirst for righteousness..."

2. True or false? In chapter 6 of John's Gospel Jesus is depicted as the water of life.

3. True or false? Jesus said that anyone who marries a divorced woman commits adultery.

4. What was the one exception that Jesus made when he said that anyone who divorces his wife makes her an adulteress?

5. In Jesus' Parable of the Ten Virgins, what did the five foolish girls neglect to do?

6. Who did Jesus say would be remembered wherever the gospel was preached throughout the world?

7. Complete the fifth beatitude, "Blessed are the merciful..."

8. Which Gospel was written by an ex tax-collector?

9. True or false? The Gospels describe one visit Jesus made to Malta.

10. Who gave to God all the money she had to live on?

11. What is the name given to Jesus' most famous prayer which begins, "Our Father in heaven"?

12. At what Feast did Jesus stand up and say, "If anyone is thirsty, let him come to me and drink"?

13. What are the final words of Jesus, as recorded in Acts?

14. Complete the sixth beatitude, "Blessed are the pure in heart..."

15. In whose house was Jesus when he said, "I have not come to call the righteous, but sinners"?

Quiz #10
THE LIGHT OF THE WORLD

1. Jesus said that the Queen of the South would condemn the people of his generation for their lack of faith. What group of people would also stand up in condemnation?

2. To whom did Jesus say, "Sell everything you have and give to the poor"?

3. Complete the seventh beatitude, "Blessed are the peacemakers..."

4. Why did Jesus say, "The Sabbath was made for man, not man for the Sabbath"?

5. Who said of Jesus, "He is possessed by Beelzebub!"?

6. What happened to the house built on sand?

7. How many times is Jesus called "Son of David" in Matthew's Gospel?

8. Which Gospel was written by a man who never mentions himself in it by name, but refers to himself as "the disciple whom Jesus loved"?

9. True or false? In chapter 9 of John's Gospel Jesus says he is the light of the world.

10. Fill in the missing word: Jesus said, "Heaven and earth will pass away, but my _____ will never pass away."

11. What sin was Jesus condemning in his parable about the Pharisee and the tax-collector?

12. What animals went rushing over a cliff into the sea?

13. When did Peter fall at Jesus' feet and say, "Go away from me, Lord, I am a sinful man"?

14. True or false? Jesus was sold into slavery by his brothers.

15. When healing a little girl Jesus said, "Talitha koum." What do these words mean?

Answers

1. The men of Nineveh 2. The rich young ruler 3. "...for they will be called the sons of God"
4. Because the Pharisees condemned him for allowing his disciples to eat corn on the Sabbath
5. The teachers of the law 6. It fell down 7. 10 times 8. John's Gospel
9. True (John 9:5) 10. Words 11. Pride 12. Pigs
13. After Jesus told Peter to drop his nets into the sea, and they caught a large number of fish
14. False. That was Joseph in the Old Testament. 15. "Little girl, I say to you, get up!"

Quiz # 11
THE LIGHT OF THE WORLD

1. True or false? Jesus told a story about a housewife who lost her ring.

2. Jesus only once gave someone a name in his parables. Who was it?

3. How many loaves of bread did Jesus use to feed the 4,000?

4. How many baskets full of leftovers were collected after the feeding of the 4,000?

5. How many baskets full of leftovers were collected after the feeding of the 5,000?

6. Complete the eighth beatitude: "Blessed are those who are persecuted because of righteousness…"

7. To whom did Jesus say, "Follow me, and let the dead bury their own dead"?

8. Fill in the missing word, from the healing of the two blind men: "According to your _____ will it be done to you."

9. In John's Gospel Jesus gave himself a name by saying "I am…" seven times. What was the first name?

10. In John's Gospel Jesus gave himself a name by saying "I am…" seven times. What was the second name?

11. In John's Gospel Jesus gave himself a name by saying "I am…" seven times. What was the third name?

12. In John's Gospel Jesus gave himself a name by saying "I am…" seven times. What was the fourth name?

13. In John's Gospel Jesus gave himself a name by saying "I am…" seven times. What was the fifth name?

14. In John's Gospel Jesus gave himself a name by saying "I am…" seven times. What was the sixth name?

15. In John's Gospel Jesus gave himself a name by saying "I am…" seven times. What was the seventh name?

Answers

1. False. It was a coin (Luke 15:8) 2. Lazarus the beggar 3. 7 loaves 4. 7 baskets
5. 12 baskets 6. "…for theirs is the kingdom of heaven"
7. The disciple who said to Jesus, "First let me go and bury my father." 8. Faith 9. The bread of life
10. The light of the world 11. The gate (door) 12. The good shepherd 13. The resurrection and the life
14. The way and the truth and the life 15. The true vine

Facts 1

THE LIGHT OF THE WORLD

We don't know the date of Jesus' birth. Jesus' birthday is celebrated on December 25 because that was the date of the Jewish Festival of Lights, called the Festival of Hanukkah, which fell on 25 to 30 Kislev (our November to December).

The present era was calculated to begin with the birth of Jesus Christ, that is A.D. 1. The initials A.D. stand for Anno Domini "in the year of our Lord."

In the sixth century Abbot Dionysius Exigutus fixed the present Christian era. He calculated that this occurred 754 years after the founding of the city of Rome. Today scholars say that it was 750 B.C., which places the birth of Jesus at 4 B.C.

The historian Josephus, in his *Antiquities of the Jews*, states that Herod's death took place in 4 B.C. Since we know from Matthew 2:1 and Luke 1:5 that Herod was still alive when Jesus was born, Jesus' birth was no later than 4 B.C.

The wise men depicted on Christmas cards as kings, are traditionally called Melchior, Caspar and Balthazar. Matthew says that these visitors were following a star, so it is likely that they were astrologers rather than kings. The Bible doesn't give their names.

When the baby Jesus was presented in the temple (Luke 2:24), Joseph gave the offering allowed for a poor man, which was a pair of doves, rather than a lamb.

When Jesus was born, Mary "wrapped him in cloths" (Luke 2:7). Jewish mothers believed that if they wrapped up their babies firmly in bandages, then the baby's limbs would grow straight.

Jesus was circumcised, as were all other Jewish male babies, on the eighth day after his birth. This Jewish custom dated back to Abraham's time: "You are to undergo circumcision, and it will be the sign of the covenant" (Genesis 17:11-12).

Since Jesus was sinless, why was he baptized? Jesus was "born under law" (Galatians 4:4) and so it was right for him to be baptized "to fulfil all righteousness" (Matthew 3:15). This included being consecrated for his work.

In the Old Testament, priests were consecrated to God when they first started their ministry. This included washing, clothing and anointing the priests as described in Exodus 29:4-7.

Facts 2

THE LIGHT OF THE WORLD

Jesus told his disciples that they should preach the gospel to all nations and baptize believers. In the early church, baptism became a sign of being a follower of Jesus (Acts 16:33).

In the Bible, names were highly significant and gave information about the person. The name "Jesus" was chosen by God (Matthew 1:21). It means "the Lord saves".

In the Old Testament, God the Father was never called by the name which Jesus used of him, "Abba". Originally "Abba" was the Aramaic word used by a small child, which is equivalent to "Dad" or "Daddy".

Matthew's genealogy of Jesus, Matthew 1:1-17, shows that the blessing brought by Jesus, the Son of David, was not restricted to one race. Four women, all Gentiles (non-Jews) are mentioned: Tamar, Rahab, Ruth and Bathsheba.

Early Christians saw the "magi from the east," who were Gentiles, as a fulfilment of the words of Isaiah 60:3, "Nations will come to your light, and kings to the brightness of your dawn."

The Bible does not say how many wise men came to see Jesus. The traditional number of three came about because three gifts are mentioned.

King Herod was infamous for his cruelty and paranoia. He had any potential rival murdered. His favorite wife, Mariamne, all her male relatives, and some of his own sons were executed on his instructions.

At his birth, Jesus was put to sleep "in a manger" (Luke 2:7). The second century Christian writer, Justin Martyr, who was born in Palestine, said that Joseph found a cave which was used as a stable.

Shepherds still tend their flocks of sheep around Bethlehem. It has been pointed out that shepherds do not spend the night in the fields during winter. This indicates that Jesus may have been born in spring or summer.

To show that Jesus really was the promised and long-awaited Messiah, Matthew emphasizes Jesus' credentials and qualifications. He does this with over a hundred quotations from and allusions to the Old Testament.

Facts 3

THE LIGHT OF THE WORLD

In his Gospel, Mark portrays Jesus as the active and obedient Servant of God. Jesus' constant obedience is seen in the 47 occurrences in Mark's Gospel of the Greek word euthus, which means "immediately", "at once".

At his baptism, Jesus was publicly declared as God's Messiah (John 1:31-34). He identified himself with our sin in his baptism. Jesus had no sin of his own and so could become the substitute for the sins of humankind (2 Corinthians 5:21).

The four symbols in Ezekiel 1:10 and Revelation 4:7 have been applied to the four Gospels in the following way: the lion has been linked with Matthew's Gospel, the ox with Mark's Gospel, the man with Luke's Gospel, and the eagle with John's Gospel.

John's Gospel includes no parables, but has many metaphors about ordinary things, such as water, harvest, bread, light, a shepherd and a grain of wheat. These are used to convey spiritual truth.

The woman in Jesus' parable who lost one coin (Luke 15:8-10), would have been greatly upset since it was probably part of her dowry. A set of coins with holes drilled through them were strung together and worn on the forehead.

No one knows the precise date of Jesus' return. He said that this date was not known by the angels or even by himself, but only by the Father (Matthew 24:36).

Jesus knew the Scriptures (our Old Testament) thoroughly. But then so did most Jews. All Jewish boys (but not girls) went to the village school, held in the synagogue.

The level of literacy among the Jews was among the highest in the Roman Empire.

The record of Jesus' temptations in the desert (Matthew 4:1-11) must have originated with Jesus himself, as no one else was present. From this we deduce that Jesus knew that Satan was no illusion.

Jesus experienced temptation in a more profound and deeper way than anybody else. He alone endured every temptation right through to its depths without giving in part way through (Hebrews 4:15).

Facts 4

THE LIGHT OF THE WORLD

The Gospels tell us that Passover fell on a Friday in the year of Jesus' death. This fits the astronomical data for either A.D. 30 or A.D. 33, but not for A.D. 31 or A.D. 32.

Jesus' healing miracles were usually performed with a word of command. He had the kind of authority over disease that an officer has over subordinates. Twice Jesus "gave the order" without even seeing the patient.

Jesus never touched a patient in exorcisms, as he did in other healings. Exorcisms were done by word alone. The conflict was between the demon and Jesus, with the patient the battleground.

Outside Jesus' many healing miracles, the Gospels record a total of only eight other miracles. Five of these supplied food or drink to meet a real shortage. According to the Old Testament prophecy, the future Messiah would feed the hungry.

When Jesus silenced the storm at sea, he was proclaiming his divinity. The Jews were afraid of the sea, regarding it as out of human control and only God could control it (Psalm 89:9).

To the Jews, wealth was a sign of God's blessing. Thus, the disciples were astounded by Jesus' statement that it is extremely difficult for a wealthy man to enter heaven.

In John's Gospel, the Greek word for sign, *semeion*, is used to describe a miracle. The miracles were signs that the Messiah had come (Isaiah 35:5).

The Gospels record that Jesus had "compassion" on people. The Greek word used *splagchnizesthai* refers to the entrails, which were thought to be the seat of the emotions. When Jesus saw a widow's grief or a leper's deformity he was churned up inside with love and pity.

The strict rabbis (teachers) did not allow a rabbi to speak to a woman in public. A rabbi could not greet his own wife or daughter in a public place.

Three Days that Changed the World

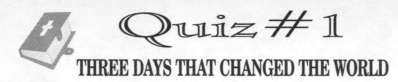

Quiz # 1

THREE DAYS THAT CHANGED THE WORLD

1. Which Old Testament book has a verse in it which is taken as a Messianic prophecy about Jesus being betrayed by a friend?

2. In Matthew's Gospel, which two women were the first people to see Jesus alive again?

3. When Jesus said, "Eloi, Eloi, lama sabachthani?" which psalm was he quoting from?

4. True or false? As Jesus was being arrested, a disciple seized his sword and cut off the high priest's servants thumb and Jesus healed it.

5. True or false? Jesus was crucified between two criminals.

6. Pilate had a notice fastened to the cross stating the charge against Jesus: JESUS OF NAZARETH, THE KING OF THE JEWS. In what three languages was it written?

7. Why did the Jewish leaders object to this notice?

8. Which Old Testament book has a verse in it which is taken as a Messianic prophecy about Jesus being betrayed for 30 pieces of silver?

9. When Jesus cried out from the cross, "Eloi, Eloi, lama sabachthani?" who did the people think he was calling to?

10. According to Mark's Gospel, after the Sanhedrin condemned Jesus for blasphemy, what did the guards do?

11. True or false? After Jesus died there was an earthquake in Jerusalem.

12. Who taunted Jesus by saying that if he was the Son of God he should come down from the cross?

13. Who mocked Jesus by saying that they would believe in him if he came down from the cross?

14. Fill in the missing word uttered by those taunting Jesus: "He saved others, but he can't _____ himself."

15. True or false? Pilate's wife referred to Jesus as an "innocent man."

Answers

1. The book of Psalms (41:9) 2. Mary Magdalene and the other Mary 3. Psalm 22:1
4. False. The disciple cut off his ear (Matthew 26:51-52) 5. True (Mark 15:27) 6. Latin, Greek, and Aramaic
7. They wanted the notice to say, "This man claimed to be King of the Jews" 8. Zechariah 9. Elijah
10. They beat him 11. True (Matthew 27:51) 12. Those who passed by
13. The chief priests, the teachers of the law, and the elders 14. Save 15. True (Matthew 27:19)

Quiz #2

THREE DAYS THAT CHANGED THE WORLD

1. During the first Lord's Supper, who said, "Take and eat; this is my body"?

2. In the Garden of Gethsemane, which of his three disciples did Jesus tell to watch with him in prayer?

3. Which Old Testament book has a verse in it which is taken as a Messianic prophecy about Jesus being accused by false witnesses?

4. When the soldiers mocked Jesus, what did they put on his head?

5. When Jesus died, what was torn in two from top to bottom?

6. According to Matthew's Gospel, who rolled a big stone in front of the tomb after Jesus had been laid inside?

7. On what day of the week was Jesus crucified?

8. Who does Matthew say watched Jesus die "from a distance"?

9. True or false? Whenever the New Testament speaks of the "blood" of Jesus, it is referring to his death.

10. Who washed his hands in front of a crowd to show that he was not responsible for Jesus' death?

11. When the soldiers mocked Jesus, what item of clothing did they put on him?

12. Where was Jesus when a large crowd came to arrest him, armed to the teeth with clubs and swords?

13. After Jesus died, who thrust a spear into Jesus' side?

14. As well as blood, what also came out of Jesus' side after it had been pierced with a spear?

15. Name three of the five friends of Jesus who were standing at the foot of the cross.

Answers

1. Jesus 2. Peter, James, and John 3. The book of Psalms
4. A crown of thorns 5. The inner curtain of the temple 6. Joseph of Arimathea 7. Friday
8. Many women who had followed Jesus from Galilee 9. True 10. Pilate 11. A (scarlet) robe
12. The Garden of Gethsemane 13. A soldier 14. Water
15. His mother, his mother's sister, Mary, the wife of Clopas; Mary Magdalene; the apostle John

Quiz #3

THREE DAYS THAT CHANGED THE WORLD

1. When Judas and the guards came to the Garden of Gethsemane, by what prearranged sign did Judas identify Jesus in the darkness?

2. Which Old Testament book has a verse in it which is taken as a Messianic prophecy about Jesus being beaten?

3. Why did Jesus' enemies not arrest him when he was preaching in the temple?

4. True or false? As Jesus was dying, three soldiers divided Jesus' clothes between them.

5. Why did the soldiers cast lots to decide who should have Jesus' tunic?

6. When Jesus was praying in the Garden of Gethsemane, what did his disciples do?

7. What is the Thursday before Jesus' death now called?

8. What is the Friday when Jesus died now called?

9. Who said, "What I have written, I have written"?

10. During the Last Supper, what did Jesus give to Judas Iscariot?

11. In Acts, who preached a sermon which said that Jesus was nailed to a cross?

12. True or false? Jesus warned his disciples that they would all fall away and lose faith in him.

13. To whom did Jesus say, "Do not weep for me; weep for yourselves and for your children"?

14. According to Paul's letter to the Corinthians, what do those who are perishing think of the message of the cross?

15. How many silver coins did Judas receive for betraying Jesus?

Answers

1. By a kiss **2.** Isaiah 53:4-5 **3.** Because they were afraid it would cause a riot **4.** False. It was four (John 19:23) **5.** Because they didn't want to tear it **6.** Sleep **7.** Maundy Thursday **8.** Good Friday **9.** Pontius Pilate **10.** A piece of bread dipped in the wine **11.** Peter **12.** True (Mark 14:27) **13.** The "daughters of Jerusalem" who were following him and crying as he walked through Jerusalem on the way to be crucified **14.** They think it is foolishness **15.** 30

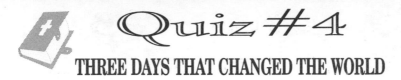

Quiz #4

THREE DAYS THAT CHANGED THE WORLD

1. Who said, "I have betrayed innocent blood"?

2. True or false? At Jesus' trial the false witnesses against Jesus could not agree with each other.

3. Who said that it was expedient that one man should die for the people?

4. Which Old Testament book has a verse in it which is taken as a prophecy about Jesus being offered vinegar for his thirst?

5. In which of his letters does Paul mention the "offence" of the cross?

6. Why did the Jews ask Pilate to give orders for the soldiers to break the legs of the men on the crosses?

7. Who was the first person to see Jesus alive?

8. Which group of people who did not believe in any resurrection did Jesus rebuke, saying that they were in error and did not know the Scriptures or God's power?

9. Which Old Testament book has a verse in it which is taken as a Messianic prophecy about Jesus having his side pierced?

10. In which of his letters does Paul say that he longs to know the power of Christ's resurrection?

11. According to Luke's Gospel, when Jesus was first brought before Pilate, he was accused of subverting the nation. Name one of the two specific crimes he was said to have committed.

12. After the Lord's Supper, before going into the Garden of Gethsemane, what did Jesus and his disciples do?

13. True or false? John says in his Gospel that when Judas went to betray Jesus "it was night."

14. To whom did Jesus say, "You will see the Son of Man sitting at the right hand of the Mighty One"?

15. Name one of the two sons of the man who was forced to carry Jesus' cross.

Answers

1. Judas Iscariot **2.** True (Mark 14:59) **3.** Caiaphas **4.** The book of Psalms 69:21 **5.** Galatians 5:21 **6.** To hasten their death, because they did not want the bodies to be on the crosses during the Sabbath, which began at six o'clock **7.** Mary Magdalene **8.** The Sadducees **9.** Zechariah (12:10) **10.** Letter to the Philippians 3:10 **11.** Opposing payment of taxes and proclaiming himself as King **12.** They sang a hymn **13.** True (John 13:30) **14.** To the high priest **15.** Alexander and Rufus

Quiz #5

THREE DAYS THAT CHANGED THE WORLD

1. When did Jesus say that his blood was poured out for the forgiveness of sins?

2. Fill in the missing words from Paul's first letter to the Corinthians: "If Christ has not been raised, your faith is _____ and you are still in your _____."

3. True or false? No event in ancient history is as well documented as Jesus' death and resurrection

4. Who said to Jesus, "Even if all fall away on account of you, I never will".

5. True or false? Jesus said to Peter, "Before the owl hoots, you will disown me three times".

6. Name one of the two friends who invited a stranger to a meal and found it was the risen Jesus.

7. Where did Judas fling the money he had been given to betray Jesus?

8. Who picked up the money Judas returned?

9. What name was given to the field bought with the money Judas returned?

10. Which Old Testament book has a verse in it which is taken as a Messianic prophecy about lots being cast for Jesus' clothes?

11. Which prisoner was released instead of Jesus at the Passover Festival?

12. True or false? Jesus' body was placed in a new tomb.

13. What did the crowd say when Pilate asked them what he should do with Jesus?

14. Why did Jesus' disciples meet in a locked room after his death?

15. What was the first thing that happened to Jesus after he was condemned to death?

---

14. They were afraid of the leaders of the Jews **15.** He was flogged

12. True (Matthew 27:59) **13.** They yelled, "Crucify him!"

8. The chief priests **9.** The Field of Blood **10.** The book of Psalms (22:18) **11.** Barabbas

5. False. Jesus said, "Before the rooster crows" (Matthew 26:34) **6.** Cleopas **7.** In the temple

1. At his institution of the Lord's Supper **2.** Futile, sins **3.** True **4.** Peter

Answers

Quiz # 6

THREE DAYS THAT CHANGED THE WORLD

1. When Pilate found that Jesus came from Galilee, what did he do, in an attempt to evade responsibility?

2. According to Mark's Gospel, what did Mary Magdalene, Mary the mother of James, and Salome bring to Jesus' tomb?

3. Who said, when he met the risen Jesus, "My Lord and my God"?

4. Why is Thomas often called "Doubting Thomas"?

5. When the soldiers mocked Jesus, what did they put in his hand?

6. What did the soldiers say to Jesus as they knelt in front of him and ridiculed him?

7. What had Jesus just been doing when he asked his disciples if they were still sleeping?

8. Which psalm has a verse in it which is taken as a Messianic prophecy about none of Jesus' bones being broken?

9. A man called Simon was forced to carry Jesus cross. Where did Simon come from?

10. Jesus was crucified at the third hour: what time was this?

11. For how many hours did Jesus hang on the cross?

12. What came over all the land from the sixth hour to the ninth hour?

13. When Jesus called out "My God, my God, why have you forsaken me?" what drink was he offered?

14. Where was Jesus when he told his disciples that the spirit was willing but the flesh was weak?

15. Why did Jesus' friends wait till Sunday before coming to anoint Jesus' body with spices?

Answers

1. Pilate sent Jesus to Herod Antipas, tetrarch (ruler) of Galilee 2. Spices to anoint Jesus' body 3. Thomas 4. Because he said he would not believe Jesus was alive until he had seen and touched him 5. A staff 6. "Hail, King of the Jews" 7. Praying 8. Psalm 22 9. Cyrene 10. Nine o'clock in the morning 11. 6 hours 12. Darkness 13. Vinegar/wine vinegar 14. In the Garden of Gethsemane 15. Because to anoint with spices was regarded as work, and all work was forbidden on the Saturday, because it was the Sabbath

Quiz #7

THREE DAYS THAT CHANGED THE WORLD

1. Who helped Joseph of Arimathea take Jesus' body from the cross?

2. On the afternoon Jesus rose from the dead, he joined two friends as they were walking from Jerusalem to what village?

3. True or false? This village was five miles from Jerusalem.

4. Who said that he was certain that Jesus was a righteous man?

5. When three women went to visit Jesus' tomb, what question did they discuss on the way?

6. Which Old Testament figure did Jesus mention in connection with the Son of man being in the heart of the earth for three days and nights?

7. At Jesus' trial before the Sanhedrin, what accusation did the witnesses make?

8. Which Old Testament book has a verse in it which is taken as a Messianic prophecy about Jesus being buried with the rich?

9. When Judas went up to Jesus in the Garden of Gethsemane, how did Jesus address him?

10. After Jesus was laid in the tomb, why did his enemies go to Pilate?

11. True or false? According to Mark's Gospel, the women went to the tomb just after sunrise?

12. Peter and John both ran to Jesus' tomb, who reached it first?

13. Who was the first disciple to enter the tomb?

14. Who was the first disciple to believe that Jesus was alive?

15. Which two enemies became friends as a result of the arrest and trial of Jesus?

Answers

1. Nicodemus 2. Emmaus 3. False. It was about 7 miles (Luke 24:13) 4. A centurion 5. Who would roll the stone away from the tomb for them 6. Jonah 7. That Jesus would destroy the Temple of God and rebuild it in 3 days 8. Isaiah 9. Friend 10. They wanted a guard put on the tomb in case the disciples stole the body 11. True (Mark 16:2) 12. John 13. Peter 14. John 15. Pilate and Herod Antipas

Quiz #8

THREE DAYS THAT CHANGED THE WORLD

1. Who were the two disciples who followed at a distance after Jesus was arrested?

2. Where was Peter when a maid said to him, "You also were with that Nazarene"?

3. What was Peter doing when the maid spoke to him?

4. True or false? Peter twice denied knowing Jesus.

5. True or false? Peter's northern accent gave him away.

6. When Mary of Magdalene first saw the risen Jesus who did she think he was?

7. Who wrote about Jesus dying on a "tree"?

8. When Mary of Magdalene recognized the risen Jesus, what single Aramaic word did she say to him?

9. Name one of the two ways in which the tomb was made secure against thieves.

10. Who rolled back the stone at the entrance to the tomb and sat on it?

11. Complete these words of Jesus: "Simon, Simon, Satan has asked to..."

12. To make the disciples understand that dangerous times were facing them, what did Jesus tell them to sell in order to buy a sword?

13. The prophecy of which Old Testament prophet was fulfilled when a field was bought with the money Judas returned?

14. What did Jesus say to Herod Antipas?

15. After Jesus was arrested, how did John gain entry into the high priest's house?

Answers

1. Peter and John **2.** In the courtyard of the high priest's house **3.** Warming himself by the fire **4.** False. It was 3 times (Mark 14:72) **5.** True (Luke 22:59) **6.** The gardener **7.** Peter **8.** Rabboni **9.** A seal was put on the rock and guards were posted at the entrance **10.** An angel **11.** Sift you as wheat **12.** Cloak **13.** Jeremiah **14.** Nothing **15.** John was allowed in because he knew the high priest

Quiz #9

THREE DAYS THAT CHANGED THE WORLD

1. What was the first saying of Jesus from the cross?

2. What was the second saying of Jesus from the cross?

3. What was the third saying of Jesus from the cross?

4. What was the fourth saying of Jesus from the cross?

5. What was the fifth saying of Jesus from the cross?

6. What was the sixth saying of Jesus from the cross?

7. What was the seventh saying of Jesus from the cross?

8. In which of his letters did Paul write that Christ was raised from the dead through the glory of the Father?

9. According to Luke, what did Jesus tell his disciples to pray for as they arrived at the Garden of Gethsemane?

10. Who strengthened Jesus as he prayed in the Garden of Gethsemane?

11. True of false? As Jesus prayed in the Garden of Gethsemane sweat like drops of blood fell from him.

12. Who wrote that Jesus was a lamb without blemish or defect?

13. After Peter disowned Jesus three times, who turned and looked straight at him?

14. What is the Sunday on which Jesus rose from the dead now called?

15. How many legions of angels did Jesus say he could call to his assistance?

9. Pray not to fall into temptation **10.** An angel **11.** True (Luke 22:44) **12.** Peter **13.** Jesus **14.** Easter Day **15.** 12
6. "It is finished" (John 19:30). **7.** "Father, into your hands I commit my spirit" (Luke 23:46). **8.** Romans
4. "My God, My God, why have you forsaken me?" (Mark 15:34). **5.** "I am thirsty." (John 19:28).
3. "Dear woman here is your son," and to the disciple, "Here is your mother!" (John 19:26).
2. "I tell you the truth. Today you will be with me in paradise" (Luke 23:43).
1. "Father, forgive them; for they do not know what they are doing" (Luke 23:34).

Answers

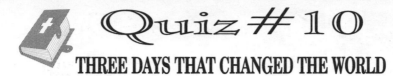

Quiz # 10

THREE DAYS THAT CHANGED THE WORLD

1. Which Old Testament book has a verse in it which is taken as a Messianic prophecy about Jesus being killed with sinners?

2. After Peter denied knowing Jesus, what did he do?

3. After Judas betrayed Jesus and returned the money, what did he do?

4. Which Old Testament book was Jesus quoting from when he spoke about a shepherd being struck and the sheep being scattered?

5. True or false? Luke records that Jesus was blindfolded when the soldiers mocked him.

6. Who declared that Jesus had done nothing to deserve death?

7. According to Luke, who told the women who visited Jesus' grave that he was not there but had risen?

8. When the women passed on the message, why did the disciples not believe them?

9. Who stood outside Jesus' tomb crying?

10. True or false? On the day he rose from the dead, Jesus appeared to Peter, and spoke to him privately.

11. Who did the risen Jesus tell to feed his lambs?

12. Which psalm has a verse in it which is taken as a Messianic prophecy about Jesus having his hands and feet pierced?

13. What did Jesus do to prove to his disciples that he was not a ghost?

14. Fill in the missing word from the angels' message to the women: "Why do you look for the living among the _____?"

15. True or false? The Roman soldiers reported to Pilate that an angel had petrified them.

Answers

1. Isaiah 53:12 **2.** Peter went out and cried bitterly **3.** Judas killed himself **4.** Zechariah 13:2 **5.** True (Luke 22:64)
6. 7.2 angels **8.** "Their words seemed like nonsense" **9.** Mary Magdalene
10. True (Luke 24:34) **11.** Peter **12.** Psalm 22 **13.** He ate a piece of cooked fish **14.** Dead
15. False. The Jewish leaders bribed them and they reported that the disciples had stolen the body (Matthew 28:13)

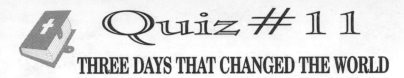

Quiz # 11

THREE DAYS THAT CHANGED THE WORLD

1. What did John note about the strips of linen that had been around Jesus' body and the burial cloth that had been around his head?

2. What were Jesus' first words when he greeted his disciples on the evening of the day he rose from the dead?

3. When did Mary realize that the man in the garden was Jesus?

4. When did the two disciples in Emmaus realize that the stranger was Jesus?

5. How long did Thomas have to wait before he saw Jesus for himself?

6. In his conversation with Thomas, who did Jesus say are the blessed people?

7. What were the disciples arguing about during the Last Supper?

8. According to Mark, why did the women say nothing about the angels' message?

9. Fill in the missing words from Jesus' conversation with the two friends on Sunday afternoon: "He explained to them what was said in all the _____ concerning himself."

10. According to Mark's Gospel, as Jesus was being nailed to the cross, what was he offered?

11. To whom did Jesus say, "Today you will be with me in Paradise"?

12. Who was the high priest who condemned Jesus?

13. The Sanhedrin found Jesus guilty of what crime?

14. According to Jewish law, what was the punishment for this crime?

15. What relation was Annas to Caiaphas?

Answers

1. The burial cloth was folded up by itself, separate from the strips of linen **2.** "Peace be with you" **3.** When Jesus said her name **4.** When he sat down for a meal with them, said grace, and broke the bread **5.** A week **6.** "Those who have not seen and yet have believed" **7.** Which of them was the greatest **8.** Because they were afraid **9.** Scriptures **10.** Wine mixed with myrrh **11.** To the thief who believed, "Remember me when you come into your kingdom" **12.** Caiaphas **13.** Blasphemy **14.** Death **15.** Father-in-law

Facts 1
THREE DAYS THAT CHANGED THE WORLD

Isaiah chapter 53 gives astonishing details about the death of Jesus. The servant is pierced and wounded, taken away by oppression and led as a lamb to the slaughter. His grave is "with the rich".

Gethsemane, which means "oil-press," was a garden, perhaps an enclosed olive orchard, on the slopes of the Mount of Olives. It was a favorite rendezvous for Jesus and his disciples.

In biblical times, the table at which people ate a meal was in a U shape, with the host in the middle of the U. The guests reclined on couches, leaning on their left elbow, with their right hand free.

At the Last Supper, John, reclining at Jesus' right hand, would have been very close to him, close enough to speak privately without anyone hearing (John 13:25).

If the host wanted to show special friendship to a guest, he gave a piece of food taken from the main dish. It has been suggested that in this way Jesus was making a last appeal to Judas (John 13:26).

When Jesus shouted out from the cross "It is finished," it was not a cry of loneliness or defeat, but a cry of achievement. He had accomplished what he had been born to do.

The Old Testament prefigures the cross of Jesus. God provided the Old Testament sacrifices (Leviticus 1–7) as a pointer to the way of salvation. The New Testament writers often refer to Jesus' death as a "sacrifice."

When Jesus told Peter and John to prepare for the Passover meal, they were to look out for a man carrying a jar of water. This was a prearranged secret sign. Carrying water was women's work, so men very rarely carried a jar of water.

Crucifixions were commonplace in Roman times. Because it was a dishonorable form of death Roman citizens were not crucified, except for treason.

Before being crucified, criminals were scourged (beaten) with a whip. The thongs of the whip were barbed with pieces of lead or bone. This punishment caused considerable bleeding and sometimes death.

Criminals facing crucifixion walked through the city carrying the cross-piece. A placard giving the reason for the conviction was hung around the neck, or carried on ahead, and then fastened to the cross.

Facts 2

THREE DAYS THAT CHANGED THE WORLD

One of the objections raised against the resurrection appearances of the risen Jesus is that they could have been hallucinations. Hallucinations, however, are not experienced by over 500 people at the same time (1 Corinthians 15:6).

Jerusalem was transformed during the time of the Passover. The population of Jerusalem may have been about 30,000, but there were six times as many people in Jerusalem during the Passover.

As a terrible warning to other would-be criminals, people were crucified outside the walls of cities, in public places. Hence the reference in Mark's Gospel to "those who passed by."

Sometimes a victim took days to die. This accounts for Pilate's surprise when Joseph asked for Jesus' body.

The Roman writer, Cicero, wrote, "Crucifixion is indeed one of the most abominable torments that the very inventive genius of torture has imagined."

To speak of the "trial" of Jesus is an oversimplification. The Gospels record five different examinations of Jesus.

Jesus first "trial" was held in the home of Annas, before a hastily gathered group of members of the Sanhedrin. The witnesses did not agree, so Annas asked Jesus directly if he was the Son of God. His reply was taken to be blasphemy.

Jesus' second hearing was held at dawn, before the full Sanhedrin, the supreme court of the Jews, presided over by Caiaphas. At this trial, Jesus was officially condemned to death.

Since Roman law did not allow the Jews to carry out the death sentence, Jesus was taken to Pilate for the third hearing. Blasphemy was not a crime under Roman law, so the Jews submitted the charge of revolutionary activity.

Faced with Jesus' obvious innocence, Pilate tried to avoid responsibility by sending Jesus to Herod Antipas, the tetrarch of Galilee, who was in Jerusalem for the Passover. This fourth hearing was a farce. No judicial proceedings are recorded.

Herod returned Jesus to Pilate. After further questioning, Pilate's verdict was that Jesus was innocent but when the Jews threatened to report Pilate to Caesar, he ordered Jesus' execution.

Facts 3

THREE DAYS THAT CHANGED THE WORLD

Jewish law required that there had to be a 24 hour delay between the passing of a verdict of guilty and the sentence of death. This law was broken by the Sanhedrin.

Jewish law did not allow the charge to be altered when a case was passed on to the Roman authorities. But the charge against Jesus was changed from blasphemy to insurrection.

It was also laid down that trials requiring the death penalty should not be held on a feast day or the day preceding a feast day.

Annas was the father-in-law of the high priest. He himself had been high priest until a Roman prefect had deposed him 15 years earlier. Many Jews still regarded him as high priest.

The "scarlet robe" of Matthew 27:28, a parody of the emperor's purple robe, would have been a soldier's red cape. The "staff" represented a royal scepter and the "crown of thorns" a royal crown.

In dreadful mockery, the soldiers knelt in front of Jesus. Their "Hail, king of the Jews!" (Matthew 27:29) parodied the formal greeting "Ave Caesar".

Most victims of crucifixion eventually fell into unconsciousness, but Jesus remained fully conscious until the end. He died suddenly with a prayer.

The wine mixed with myrrh which was offered to Jesus and which he declined (Mark 15:23) was a narcotic drink. According to the Babylonian Talmud, kind ladies from Jerusalem provided this drink to numb the senses of the victim.

Each new Jewish day begins, not at dawn, but at sunset. The Sabbath would therefore have started at six in the evening on the day Jesus was crucified, hence the haste.

Pilate had his headquarters at Caesarea. He was in Jerusalem for the Passover Festival, a time of potential unrest.

When in Jerusalem, Pilate stayed in the Praetorium, the official Jerusalem residence of the procurator, and the Roman military headquarters (Matthew 27:27).

Facts 4

THREE DAYS THAT CHANGED THE WORLD

It was not usual to bury the bodies of criminals. They were left for the dogs and vultures to eat.

The word "paradise" comes from a Persian word meaning "a walled garden." In Persia, it was a special honour to be invited to walk in the garden with the king.

A letter from the furst century by a non-Christian Syrian writer, Mara bar Serapion, a Syrian sage, refers to the folly of the Jews in "executing their wise king."

If the body of Jesus was really in the tomb all the time, the authorities would not have needed to say that the disciples had stolen the body. They could simply have produced it.

Jesus' resurrection was quite different from the coming back to life of Lazarus. Lazarus had to die again. Jesus' resurrection shows that he had passed through into another dimension of life.

When the risen Jesus met with his disciples, he told them to look at his feet as well as his hands, indicating that his feet had also been nailed to the cross.

In the time of Jesus, a dead body was laid on a stone shelf in a cave with a stone in front of the entrance. After about a year, when only the bones were left, they were collected and put into an ossuary (a stone box).

Jewish law did not allow women to act as witnesses in a law court. But the first witnesses to Jesus' resurrection, with instructions to pass on the message, were women. No Jew would have invented this.

Eye-witness accounts of an incident usually differ slightly as witnesses pick out different details. This is a mark of authenticity. In modern police investigations, detectives are suspicious of stories that are too similar. This applies to the accounts of the resurrection given in the Gospel.

The "curtain of the temple" separated the Holy Place from the Most Holy Place. Under Jewish law, only the high priest could go through, and then only once a year.

The tearing of the curtain symbolizes the destroying of the barrier between God and men.

100 Key Events

Quiz # 1
100 KEY EVENTS

1. **The Creation** On what day did God create man?

2. **The Creation** True or false? God made the fish, the birds and the animals on day five.

3. **The Creation** Fill in the missing word: "God said, 'Let us make man in our ____.' "

4. **The Fall** From which tree in the garden were Adam and Eve not allowed to eat?

5. **The Fall** Which creature tempted Eve?

6. **The Fall** Eve was persuaded to eat the fruit for three reasons: name two.

7. **Sin Is Passed On** Who hated his brother?

8. **Sin Is Passed On** What offering did Abel make?

9. **Sin Is Passed On** Fill in the missing word: God said, "Your brother's ____ cries out to me."

10. **The Flood** Who was described as "a righteous man, blameless among the people of his time, and he walked with God"?

11. **The Flood** Fill in one of the missing words: "Now the earth was ____ in God's sight and full of ____."

12. **The Flood** How many humans were kept safe in the ark?

13. **The Tower of Babel** Before the tower of Babel was built how many languages were there in the world?

14. **The Tower of Babel** What was the name of the plain in Babylonia where the tower of Babel was built?

15. **The Tower of Babel** Fill in the missing words: "They used ____ instead of stone, and ____ for mortar."

Answers

1. The sixth day **2.** False. God made the fish and birds on day 5, and animals on day 6 **3.** Image (Genesis 1:26) **4.** The tree that gives knowledge of what is good and bad (Genesis 2:17) **5.** A serpent **6.** The fruit of the tree was good for food; pleasing to the eye; desirable for gaining knowledge (Genesis 3:6) **7.** Cain **8.** A firstborn lamb **9.** Blood **10.** Noah **11.** Corrupt and violence **12.** 8 **13.** "The whole world had one language" **14.** Shinar **15.** Brick and bitumen

Quiz #2

100 KEY EVENTS

1. *Abraham's Call* Who was Abraham's father?

2. *Abraham's Call* Where was Abraham living when God told him to leave his country?

3. *Abraham's Call* True or false? Abraham took Lot, who was his cousin, with him when he left his country.

4. *The Covenant* Fill in one of the missing words: "Do not be afraid, Abram. I am your ____, your very great ____."

5. *The Covenant* The Lord told Abraham to count the stars. Why?

6. *The Covenant* What was the sign of God's covenant (agreement) with Abraham?

7. *Sacrifice of Isaac* Who said, "God himself will provide the lamb for the burnt offering"?

8. *Sacrifice of Isaac* When Abraham prepared to sacrifice Isaac, he bound Isaac and placed him on the altar. What was between Isaac and the altar?

9. *Sacrifice of Isaac* After Abraham sacrificed a ram in place of his son Isaac, what name did Abraham give to that place?

10. *Isaac and Rebekah* Who did Abraham entrust with the responsibility of finding a wife for his son Isaac?

11. *Isaac and Rebekah* Where did this person place his hand as Abraham made him swear that he would not let Isaac marry a daughter of the Canaanites?

12. *Isaac and Rebekah* What did Abraham's servant pray that the girl who met him and his camels would do if she was the one who was going to become Isaac's wife?

13. *Birth of Esau and Jacob* What did God say to Rebekah when she asked, "Why is this happening to me?" when the babies jostled within her?

14. *Birth of Esau and Jacob* Which of the twin boys was born first: Esau or Jacob?

15. *Birth of Esau and Jacob* Fill in the missing words: "Isaac, who had a taste for wild game, loved ____, but Rebekah loved ____."

---

13. "Two nations are in your womb" (Genesis 25:23) 14. Esau 15. Esau, Jacob
10. Abraham's servant 11. Under Abraham's thigh 12. She would offer to water his camels
7. Abraham, answering Isaac's question, "Where is the lamb for the burnt offering?" 8. Wood 9. The Lord Will Provide
4. Shield and reward 5. Because that would be the number of his offspring 6. Circumcision
1. Terah 2. Haran 3. False. Abraham did take Lot, but Lot was Abraham's nephew

Answers

Quiz #3
100 KEY EVENTS

1. *Jacob Gets The Blessing* What type of stew did Esau sell his birthright for?

2. *Jacob Gets The Blessing* True or false? Jacob tricked his father into giving him his blessing by allowing him to feel his smooth skin.

3. *Jacob Gets The Blessing* Fill in the missing words: "Esau ___ ___ ___ against Jacob because of the blessing his father had given him."

4. *Jacob's Sons* What did Jacob's sons became the founders of?

5. *Jacob's Sons* When Jacob thought that Laban had given him his daughter Rachel to marry, which of Laban's daughters had in fact been given to Jacob?

6. *Jacob's Sons* True or false? Reuben was Jacob's firstborn son.

7. *Joseph's Dreams* When Joseph told his brothers about his first dream, how did they react?

8. *Joseph's Dreams* In Joseph's second dream, what replaced the eleven sheaves of corn?

9. *Joseph's Dreams* In Joseph's second dream, what did the sun and the moon stand for?

10. *Joseph Into Egypt* Which of Joseph's brothers tried to stop Joseph from being sold?

11. *Joseph Into Egypt* For how many shekels of silver did Joseph's brothers sell him?

12. *Joseph Into Egypt* True or false? The Ishmaelites took Joseph to Israel.

13. *Joseph's Family Go To Egypt* Pharaoh dreamt of the same number of fat cows, thin cows, good ears of corn and thin ears of corn. How many were there each time?

14. *Joseph's Family Go To Egypt* Which of Jacob's sons did Joseph keep in Egypt when his remaining brothers returned to Jacob?

15. *Joseph's Family Go To Egypt* For how long did the Egyptians mourn Jacob?

Answers

1. Lentil stew 2. False. Jacob had the smooth parts of his skin covered with goatskin, so Isaac would think he was Esau 3. Held a grudge 4. The 12 tribes of Israel 5. Leah 6. True
7. They hated Joseph even more 8. 11 stars 9. His father and his mother
10. Reuben (Genesis 29:32) 11. 20 shekels of silver
12. False. The Ishmaelites took Joseph to Egypt (Genesis 37:28) 13. 7 14. Benjamin 15. 70 days

Quiz #4
100 KEY EVENTS

1. **Birth of Moses** Why was Moses hidden among the reeds along the bank of the River Nile?

2. **Birth of Moses** What was Moses' waterproof basket made out of?

3. **Birth of Moses** Who discovered the baby among the reeds?

4. **Moses Kills A Man** Why did Moses kill the Egyptian?

5. **Moses Kills A Man** On the following day who did Moses stop a fight between?

6. **Moses Kills A Man** True or false? Moses ran away from Pharaoh and fled to Jerusalem.

7. **The Burning Bush** Fill in the missing words: "I am the God of your father, the God of ___, the God of ___ and the God of ___."

8. **The Burning Bush** True or false? Moses saw that the bush was on fire but it did not burn up.

9. **The Burning Bush** When Moses heard the Lord speaking to him and saw the burning bush why did he hide his face?

10. **The Plagues and Passover** What relation of Moses did the Lord provide to speak for Moses to the Israelites?

11. **The Plagues and Passover** What was the first plague?

12. **The Plagues and Passover** As a result of the second plague, what would Pharaoh find in his ovens and kneading troughs?

13. **Crossing The Red Sea** Why did the Israelites eat unleavened bread (bread without yeast) on the eve of the Exodus?

14. **Crossing The Red Sea** A pillar of fire shed light for the Israelites by night, what guided them by day?

15. **Crossing The Red Sea** True or false? The Israelites crossed through the sea on dry ground, with a wall of water on both sides.

Quiz #5
100 KEY EVENTS

1. *Receiving The Law* What is the eighth commandment in the Ten Commandments?

2. *Receiving The Law* Where was Moses when he received the Ten Commandments?

3. *Receiving The Law* On how many stone tablets were the Ten Commandments written?

4. *The Tabernacle* True or false? The upright frames of the tabernacle were made from mahogany.

5. *The Tabernacle* Fill in the missing word: "Make the tabernacle with ten ___ of finely twisted linen and blue, purple and scarlet yarn."

6. *The Tabernacle* Why did the Israelites have to bring clear oil of pressed olives to the tabernacle?

7. *Food In The Wilderness* What meat did the Israelites eat in the desert?

8. *Food In The Wilderness* True or false? The Israelites were allowed to collect enough manna for two days on the sixth day, so they did not have to collect any on the Sabbath.

9. *Food In The Wilderness* Except for the manna collected on the sixth day, what happened to any manna that was not eaten on the day it was collected?

10. *Spies Enter and Return* Name two of the three kinds of fruit which the spies brought back from Canaan.

11. *Spies Enter and Return* Most of the spies who returned from Canaan said they felt like what, in their own eyes, and in the eyes of the Nephilim?

12. *Spies Enter and Return* Who were the only two spies to say to Moses that they should enter Canaan and attack the people?

13. *Joshua* Who did Joshua take over from as the commander-in-chief of the Israelites?

14. *Joshua* Fill in the missing words: "Do not let this ___ ___ ___ ___ depart from your mouth; meditate on it day and night, so that you may be careful to do everything written in it."

15. *Joshua* How many spies did Joshua secretly send in to Jericho to spy out the land?

Quiz #6
100 KEY EVENTS

1. **Jericho** When Joshua came near to Jericho, he found a man standing in front of him who was later identified as the commander of the Lord's army. What did he have in his hand?

2. **Jericho** Who were the only inhabitants of Jericho who were spared from being killed when Joshua took the city?

3. **Jericho** What part of the city of Jericho collapsed when the trumpets were blown on the seventh day?

4. **Conquest** Patched sandals, old clothes and moldy, stale bread were part of their disguise. Who dressed like this to deceive the Israelites?

5. **Conquest** When Joshua was fighting against the Amorites what most unusual event happened in the sky?

6. **Conquest** Fill in the missing words: "The Lord hurled large ____ down on them from the sky, and more of them died from the ____ than were killed by the swords of the Israelites."

7. **Gideon** In which unusual place was Gideon threshing wheat when God called him to save Israel?

8. **Gideon** Who was Israel's enemy in Gideon's time?

9. **Gideon** Gideon started with thirty-two thousand men in his army. How many did he go into battle with?

10. **Samson** The last judge was Samson. Who was Samson's father?

11. **Samson** With the jaw-bone of which animal did Samson boast that he had killed a thousand men?

12. **Samson** What was the answer to the riddle Samson set: Out of the eater, something to eat; out of the strong, something sweet?

13. **Ruth** Fill in the missing words: "Where you go I will go, and where you stay I will stay. Your ____ will be my ____ and your ____ will be my ____."

14. **Ruth** Who did Ruth marry?

15. **Ruth** Which king of Israel's grandfather was Ruth's son?

Answers

1. A drawn sword **2.** Rahab and her family **3.** The walls **4.** The Gibeonites **5.** The sun stood still **6.** Hailstones, hailstones **7.** A wine-press **8.** The Midianites **9.** 300 men **10.** Manoah **11.** A donkey's jaw-bone **12.** What is sweeter than honey? What is stronger than a lion? (Judges 14:18) **13.** People, people, God, God **14.** Boaz **15.** King David (Ruth's son Obed was David's grandfather.)

Quiz #7
100 KEY EVENTS

1. *Call of Samuel* Who mistook Hannah's fervent prayer for drunkenness?

2. *Call of Samuel* How many times did the Lord call the boy Samuel before Samuel knew who was speaking to him?

3. *Call of Samuel* Fill in the missing word: "I am about to do something in Israel that will make the ears of everyone who hears it ____."

4. *Anointing of Saul* Why could you spot Saul in a crowd?

5. *Anointing of Saul* What was Saul looking for when Samuel met him and realized that the Lord wanted him to anoint Saul?

6. *Anointing of Saul* Fill in the missing word: "As Saul turned to leave Samuel, God changed Saul's ____."

7. *Saul's Disobedience* The dancing women sang, "Saul has slain his thousands, and David his tens of thousands." How did Saul react to these words?

8. *Saul's Disobedience* Why did God say to Saul, "Because you have rejected the word of the Lord, he has rejected you as king"?

9. *Saul's Disobedience* Openly disobeying God, who did Saul consult at Endor?

10. *Choice of David* How many of Jesse's sons did Samuel reject?

11. *Choice of David* Where was David when Samuel was looking for the right member of Jesse's family to anoint?

12. *Choice of David* Fill in the missing words: "From that day on the ____ ____ ____ ____ came upon David in power."

13. *Goliath* Where did Goliath come from?

14. *Goliath* How many smooth stones did David select from a stream?

15. *Goliath* Where did David's bull's-eye shot hit the giant Goliath?

Answers

1. Eli **2.** 3 times **3.** Tingle **4.** He was a head taller than everyone else. (1 Samuel 9:2) **5.** Saul was searching for his father's lost donkeys. **6.** Heart **7.** This refrain galled Saul. He was very angry! **8.** Because Saul disobeyed God's command and did not totally destroy the people, sheep, and cattle of the Amalekites **9.** A witch **10.** Seven sons **11.** David was looking after the sheep **12.** Spirit of the Lord **13.** Gath **14.** 5 stones **15.** On his forehead

Quiz #8

100 KEY EVENTS

1. *David and Jonathan* True or false? The deep friendship and love David and Jonathan had for each other was said to surpass that of a man for a woman.

2. *David and Jonathan* Fill in the missing words: "And Jonathan made David reaffirm his oath out of ___ for him, because he ___ him as he ___ himself."

3. *David and Jonathan* True or false? David said to Jonathan, "Whatever you want me to do, I'll do for you."

4. *David as King* At which town was David anointed king over Judah?

5. *David as King* How old was David when he became king over Israel as well as Judah?

6. *David as King* For how many years did David reign in Jerusalem?

7. *Capture of Jerusalem* Who said to David about Jerusalem: "You will not get in here; even the blind and the lame can ward you off'"?

8. *Capture of Jerusalem* Fill in the missing words: "Anyone who conquers the Jebusites will have to use the ___ ___."

9. *Capture of Jerusalem* Who was the father of the following children, and where were they born? Shammua, Shabob, Nathan, Solmon, Ibhar, Elishua, Nepheg, Japhia, Elishama, Eliada and Eliphelet.

10. *The Ark Taken to Jerusalem* What happened to Uzzah after touching the ark of God?

11. *The Ark Taken to Jerusalem* When Michal, Saul's daughter, saw David leaping and dancing before the Lord as the ark of God entered Jerusalem, how did she react?

12. *The Ark Taken to Jerusalem* What did the ark symbolize?

13. *Bathsheba* True or false? David did not know the name of the beautiful woman who he watched bathing.

14. *Bathsheba* To whom was Bathsheba married?

15. *Bathsheba* What happened to Uriah in the next battle after David had ordered that he should be left alone in the front line?

Quiz #9
100 KEY EVENTS

1. *The Census* Who did David decide he would make a census of?

2. *The Census* Which army commander questioned the wisdom of making such a census?

3. *The Census* As a punishment for taking the census, the Lord said David could choose between three options: a famine, being chased in battle, or a plague. Which did David choose?

4. *Solomon Asks For Wisdom* Where was Solomon when he had the dream in which he asked for wisdom?

5. *Solomon Asks For Wisdom* Fill in the missing words: "Give your servant a ___ heart to govern your people and to distinguish between ___ and ___."

6. *Solomon Asks For Wisdom* In the first test of Solomon's wisdom after his dream, which three people were brought before him?

7. *Building of the Temple* Why was David not allowed to build the temple in his lifetime?

8. *Building of the Temple* From where did Solomon get cedar wood for the temple?

9. *Building of the Temple* Did Solomon conscript three hundred men, three thousand men or thirty thousand men to build the temple?

10. *Queen of Sheba* When the Queen of Sheba visited Solomon, which of the following did she not bring with her: camels, horses, spices, gold, or precious stones?

11. *Queen of Sheba* True or false? When the Queen of Sheba saw Solomon's wealth, she was unimpressed and said that all the reports she had heard about him were greatly exaggerated.

12. *Queen of Sheba* Fill in the missing words: "Because of the Lord's eternal love for Israel, he has made you king, to maintain ___ and ___."

13. *Division of the Kingdom* Starting with Jeroboam I and ending with Hoshea, did the northern kingdom have 18, 19, or 20 kings?

14. *Division of the Kingdom* Who was the first king of the southern kingdom of Judah?

15. *Division of the Kingdom* Which town was the capital of Judah?

---

13. Israel had 19 kings **14.** Rehoboam **15.** Jerusalem
10. Horses **11.** False. The Queen of Sheba said, "Not even half was told me" **12.** Justice and righteousness
7. Because David had been involved in so many wars **8.** From Lebanon **9.** 30,000
4. Solomon was at Gibeon **5.** Discerning, right, wrong **6.** 2 mothers and a baby
1. The fighting men of Israel and Judah **2.** Joab **3.** David chose a plague

Answers

Quiz # 10
100 KEY EVENTS

1. *Elijah on Mount Carmel* Who opposed Elijah on Mount Carmel?

2. *Elijah on Mount Carmel* The true God was the one who answered by what?

3. *Elijah on Mount Carmel* Fill in the missing words: "A cloud as small as a ___ ___ is rising from the seas."

4. *The Still Small Voice* On which mountain was Elijah when God said, "Go and stand on the mountain in the presence of the Lord"?

5. *The Still Small Voice* What was the first thing that Elijah heard on the mountain?

6. *The Still Small Voice* The second thing that Elijah observed on the mountain was an earthquake, what was the third thing?

7. *Elisha and Naaman* What was Elisha doing as Elijah threw his cloak over him?

8. *Elisha and Naaman* What was the matter with commander Naaman?

9. *Elisha and Naaman* Who said, "If only my master would see the prophet who is in Samaria! He would cure him"?

10. *Hezekiah* Who said, "The god of Hezekiah will not rescue his people from my hand"?

11. *Hezekiah* Which prophet advised Hezekiah to trust God?

12. *Hezekiah* What happened to Sennacherib when he returned home in disgrace?

13. *Isaiah's Vision of God* As a result of his vision of God, Isaiah became a prophet: Isaiah dates it by the death of which king?

14. *Isaiah's Vision of God* Fill in the missing words: "___, ___, ___ is the Lord Almighty; the whole earth is full of his glory."

15. *Isaiah's Vision of God* What touched Isaiah's lips in this vision?

---

15. A live coal from the altar

12. Some of his sons murdered him in the temple of his god **13.** King Uzziah **14.** Holy, holy, holy

10. An officer in King Sennacherib's army **11.** Isaiah

9. A young Israelite maidservant of Naaman's wife who had been captured from Israel

4. Mount Horeb (Sinai) **5.** A strong wind **6.** A fire **7.** Driving a yoke of oxen **8.** He had leprosy

1. The prophets of Baal **2.** The God who answered by fire **3.** man's hand

Answers

43

Quiz # 11
100 KEY EVENTS

1. *Josiah Finds the Law* How old was Josiah when the Book of the Law was found?

2. *Josiah Finds the Law* What was the name of the high priest who discovered the Book of the Law?

3. *Josiah Finds the Law* True or false? When Josiah heard the Book of the Law read he tore his robes.

4. *Amos Thrown Out of Bethel* Where was Amos living when God told him to prophecy in Israel?

5. *Amos Thrown Out of Bethel* Fill in the missing words: "I will turn your religious feasts into ___ and all your singing into ___."

6. *Amos Thrown Out of Bethel* To show the people how crooked they had become, Amos pictured God as a builder, holding what?

7. *Hosea and His Wife* What was the name of Hosea's wife?

8. *Hosea and His Wife* About whom did Hosea complain, "There is no faithfulness, no love, no acknowledgment of God in the land"?

9. *Hosea and His Wife* Fill in the missing words: "I will ___ their waywardness and ___ them freely."

10. *Samaria Destroyed* True or false? Samaria was the capital of the southern kingdom of Judah.

11. *Samaria Destroyed* What was the name of the King of Assyria who defeated Samaria in 722 B.C.?

12. *Samaria Destroyed* Fill in the missing words: "They sacrificed their ___ and ___ in the fire."

13. *Fall of Jerusalem* Which king captured Jerusalem in 587 B.C.?

14. *Fall of Jerusalem* To which land were the people of Judah deported?

15. *Fall of Jerusalem* Which exile from Jerusalem interpreted dreams for the king of Babylon?

---

13. King Nebuchadnezzar **14.** Babylon **15.** Daniel
10. False. Samaria was capital of the northern kingdom of Israel **11.** Sennacherib **12.** Sons, daughters
6. A plumb line **7.** Gomer **8.** The Israelites **9.** Heal, love
1. 26 years old **2.** Hilkiah **3.** True (2 Kings 22:11) **4.** Tekoa (in southern Judah) **5.** Mourning, weeping

Answers

Quiz # 12
100 KEY EVENTS

1. *Jeremiah's Letter* To whom did Jeremiah write a long letter?

2. *Jeremiah's Letter* Who later read the letter, and prayed for the release of the people?

3. *Jeremiah's Letter* True or false? Jeremiah told his readers to settle down and plant gardens.

4. *Ezekiel's Visions* Fill in the missing word: "The Lord set me in the middle of a valley; it was full of ____."

5. *Ezekiel's Visions* What question was Ezekiel asked about the valley of dry bones?

6. *Ezekiel's Visions* How did Ezekiel react to the initial vision recorded in his prophecy?

7. *Daniel and the Lions* True or false? Daniel survived in the lions' den because he killed all the lions.

8. *Daniel and the Lions* Fill in the missing word: "My God sent his ____, and he shut the mouths of the lions."

9. *Daniel and the Lions* What was the name of the king who was tricked into making Daniel spend a night with the lions?

10. *Esther* True or false? Esther married King Xerxes after coming first in a nation-wide beauty contest.

11. *Esther* Mordecai, an exiled Jew living in Susa, plays a prominent role in the book of Esther. How was he related to Esther?

12. *Esther* What is the name given to the feast that celebrates the deliverance of the Jews through Esther?

13. *First Return: Ezra Gives the Law* To which city did Cyrus, king of Persia, allow the Israelites to go back to?

14. *First Return: Ezra Gives the Law* True or false? 6,720 exiles, and 42,360 donkeys returned as the first group of exiles.

15. *First Return: Ezra Gives the Law* What did these exiles take back to Jerusalem that had been removed by King Nebuchadnezzar?

---

15. Articles belonging to the temple of the Lord
13. Jerusalem 14. False. There were 6,720 donkeys, and 42,360 exiles
8. Angel 9. King Darius 10. True (Esther 2:17) 11. Mordecia was Esther's cousin 12. Purim
6. Ezekiel fell face down 7. False. The lions were very much alive when Daniel left them (Daniel 6:24)
1. The exiles in Babylon 2. Daniel 3. True (Jeremiah 29:5) 4. Bones 5. "Can these bones live?"

Answers

Quiz # 13
100 KEY EVENTS

1. *Nehemiah Rebuilds the Walls* True or false? It took Nehemiah 520 days to rebuild the walls of Jerusalem.

2. *Nehemiah Rebuilds the Walls* Fill in the missing words: "We ____ to our God and posted a guard ____ and ____."

3. *Nehemiah Rebuilds the Walls* What was Nehemiah's occupation in Babylon?

4. *Second Temple* Fill in the missing word: "Is it a time for your yourselves to be living in paneled houses, while this ____ remains a ruin?"

5. *Second Temple* When the second temple was dedicated were 100 bulls or 1,000 bulls sacrificed?

6. *Second Temple* Two Old Testament prophets who have Bible books bearing their name encouraged the Israelites to complete the rebuilding of the temple. Zechariah was one, who was the other?

7. *Malachi's Vision* Malachi prophesies that the Lord will send the prophet Elijah. Who is identified as being this prophet in the New Testament?

8. *Malachi's Vision* Fill in the missing word: "I will send my ____, who will prepare the way before me."

9. *Malachi's Vision* Malachi said that the coming "day" of the Lord would burn like what?

10. *Birth of John the Baptist* Who were John the Baptist's parents?

11. *Birth of John the Baptist* True or false? Zechariah was a priest.

12. *Birth of John the Baptist* What unusual thing happened to Zechariah which lasted until his son John was given his name?

13. *The Genealogies of Jesus* Name one of the two Gospels that have genealogies of Jesus.

14. *The Genealogies of Jesus* Fill in the missing words: "____ was the father of Isaac, Isaac was the father of ____."

15. *The Genealogies of Jesus* What do the following people mentioned in Matthew's genealogy have in common? Tamar, Rahab, Ruth and Bethsheba.

---

15. They were all women and they were all Gentiles (non-Jews)
12. He was struck dumb **13.** Matthew and Luke **14.** Abraham, Jacob
7. John the Baptist **8.** Messenger **9.** A furnace **10.** Elizabeth and Zechariah **11.** True (Luke 1:5)
3. Nehemiah was the king's cupbearer **4.** House **5.** 100 bulls were sacrificed **6.** Haggai
1. False. It took Nehemiah 52 days to rebuild the walls (Nehemiah 6:15) **2.** Prayed, day, night

Answers

Quiz #14
100 KEY EVENTS

1. **Birth of Jesus** How many children had Mary had before she gave birth to Jesus?

2. **Birth of Jesus** Who said, to whom, "Today in the town of David a Savior has been born to you; he is Christ the Lord"?

3. **Birth of Jesus** Fill in the missing words: "So they hurried off and found ___ and ___, and the ___, who was lying in the manger."

4. **Visit of Wise Men** True or false? There were only three wise men.

5. **Visit of Wise Men** Where were the wise men when they asked, "Where is the one who has been born king of the Jews?"?

6. **Visit of Wise Men** What were the three gifts the wise men gave to Jesus?

7. **Death of Herod** How did Joseph know that Herod was set to kill Jesus?

8. **Death of Herod** Where did Joseph, Mary and Jesus flee to as refugees?

9. **Death of Herod** After Joseph heard that Herod was dead, where did he settle down with Mary and Jesus?

10. **Jesus at Twelve in the Temple** True or false? Jesus stayed behind in Jerusalem because he wanted to have a good look at Herod's magnificent temple.

11. **Jesus at Twelve in the Temple** To whom did Jesus say: "Didn't you know I had to be in my Father's house?"

12. **Jesus at Twelve in the Temple** Fill in the missing words: "And Jesus ___ in wisdom and stature, and in favor with ___ and ___." (Luke 2:52)

13. **John the Baptist** To whom did this fiery preacher say, "You brood of vipers!"?

14. **John the Baptist** Fill in the missing words: "He will baptize you with the ___ ___ and with ___." (Matthew 3:11)

15. **John the Baptist** True or false? John wore clothes made of sheepskin.

---

15. False. They were made of camel's hair (John 3:4)

11. Mary 12. Grew, God, men 13. The Pharisees and Sadducees (religious leaders) 14. Holy Spirit, fire

10. False. Jesus listened to and asked questions of the teachers in the temple courts (Luke 2:41-50)

6. Gold, frankincense (incense) and myrrh 7. The Lord warned him in a dream 8. Egypt 9. Nazareth

4. False. We are not told how many wise men there were 5. In Jerusalem

1. None. She was a virgin 2. The angel, to the shepherds 3. Mary, Joseph, baby

Answers

Quiz # 15

100 KEY EVENTS

1. *Jesus' Baptism* Did John the Baptist baptize Jesus, or did Jesus baptize John the Baptist?

2. *Jesus' Baptism* What did people see coming down on Jesus after he was baptized?

3. *Jesus' Baptism* Where did the voice come from which said, "This is my Son, whom I love; with him I am well pleased"?

4. *Jesus' Temptations* True or false? In Jesus' first temptation, the devil offered him some roast lamb to eat.

5. *Jesus' Temptations* Fill in the missing word which Jesus spoke to the devil: "Do not put the Lord your God to the ___."

6. *Jesus' Temptations* In the third temptation, did the devil take Jesus up a very high mountain or out in a boat on the Sea of Galilee?

7. *John The Baptist Arrested* True or false? After his temptation, Jesus stayed in the south; he only moved to Galilee when John was arrested.

8. *John The Baptist Arrested* Why was John arrested?

9. *John The Baptist Arrested* Why did King Herod keep John in prison instead of immediately killing him?

10. *Call of First Disciples* Which of Jesus' twelve disciples was `Peter's brother?

11. *Call of First Disciples* About whom did Jesus say: "Here is a true Israelite, in whom there is nothing false"?

12. *Call of First Disciples* Who is the only disciple whose martyrdom is recorded in the pages of the Bible?

13. *First Miracle* True or false? Mary was not present at the marriage feast in Cana.

14. *First Miracle* What instruction did Jesus give to the servants concerning the lack of wine?

15. *First Miracle* Fill in the missing words: "He thus revealed his ___, and his disciples put their ___ in him."

Answers

1. John the Baptist baptized Jesus **2.** The Holy Spirit in the form of a dove **3.** It was "a voice from heaven" **4.** False. Jesus was tempted to turn stones into bread **5.** Test **6.** A very high mountain **7.** True (Mark 1:14) **8.** Because John had told Herod Antipas that his marriage to his brother's wife was wrong **9.** Herod was afraid to kill him because he was a righteous man **10.** Andrew **11.** Nathanael (Bartholomew) **12.** James the brother of John; he was beheaded by Herod Agrippa I **13.** False. It was Mary who told Jesus that the hosts had run out of wine (John 2:1-3) **14.** "Fill the jars with water." **15.** Glory, faith

Quiz # 16
100 KEY EVENTS

1. *Jesus in Nazareth* True or false? When Jesus visited his home town of Nazareth during his public ministry he was driven out of the town.

2. *Jesus in Nazareth* Fill in the missing words: "He has anointed me to preach ____ ____ to the poor."

3. *Jesus in Nazareth* Where did Jesus go on the Sabbath "As his custom was"?

4. *Sermon on the Mount* Are there six, eight, or twelve beatitudes in the Sermon on the Mount?

5. *Sermon on the Mount* Fill in the missing words: "____ your enemies and ____ for those who persecute you."

6. *Sermon on the Mount* When Jesus told people not to worry, what did he tell people to look at?

7. *Jesus Heals on the Sabbath* Which group of people were furious with Jesus when he healed a man with a shriveled arm on the Sabbath?

8. *Jesus Heals on the Sabbath* Who said, "There are six days for work. So come and be healed on those days, not on the Sabbath"?

9. *Jesus Heals on the Sabbath* Fill in the missing word: "You ____! Doesn't each of you on the Sabbath untie his ox to give it water?"

10. *Feeding of 5,000* When Jesus fed 5,000 people, how many loaves of bread and how many fish did the disciples have to start with?

11. *Feeding of 5,000* Did the figure "five thousand" include women and children, or did it just refer to men?

12. *Feeding of 5,000* After everyone had eaten, how many baskets full of leftovers were there?

13. *Peter's Declaration* When Peter said to Jesus, "You are the Christ, the Son of the living God," what question had Jesus just asked his disciples?

14. *Peter's Declaration* Fill in the missing words spoken by Jesus to Peter: "I will give you the keys of the ____ of ____."

15. *Peter's Declaration* Just after Peter's declaration, to whom did Jesus say, "Get behind me, Satan!"?

---

14. Kingdom, heaven **15.** Peter

11. It just referred to men **12.** 12 baskets **13.** "Who do you say I am?"

7. The Pharisees **8.** The synagogue ruler **9.** Hypocrites **10.** 5 loaves of bread, 2 fish

1. True **2.** Good news **3.** To the synagogue **4.** 8 beatitudes **5.** Love, pray **6.** "Look at the birds of the air."

Answers

Quiz #17
100 KEY EVENTS

1. *Transfiguration* How many of Jesus' disciples witnessed his transfiguration?

2. *Transfiguration* Which two people from the Old Testament were seen at Jesus' transfiguration?

3. *Transfiguration* Fill in the missing word: "His face shone like the ___."

4. *Private Teaching* When the disciples argued about which of them was the greatest whom did Jesus stand beside him as he taught his disciples about true greatness?

5. *Private Teaching* Fill in the missing word: "For he who is ____ among you all—he is greatest."

6. *Private Teaching* True or false? When John told Jesus that they had tried to stop a man from driving out demons in his name because he was not one of them, Jesus replied, "Do not stop him."

7. *Raising of Lazarus* Fill in the missing words: "I am the resurrection and the ___. He who believes in me will ___, even though he dies."

8. *Raising of Lazarus* Was Lazarus the brother of Mary and Martha, or the brother of James and John?

9. *Raising of Lazarus* For how many days had Lazarus been dead when Jesus arrived at his tomb?

10. *Palm Sunday* On which animal did Jesus ride as he went into Jerusalem on the day we now call Palm Sunday?

11. *Palm Sunday* Which articles of clothing did some of the crowd throw on the ground in front of Jesus?

12. *Palm Sunday* Fill in the missing word: "Blessed is the ____ who comes in the name of the Lord!"

13. *Judas Goes to the Priests* True or false? Judas Isacariot, who betrayed Jesus, was one of his twelve disciples.

14. *Judas Goes to the Priests* Did Judas go to the chief priests and say he could betray Jesus, or did the chief priests ask Judas to do this?

15. *Judas Goes to the Priests* Finish the sentence: "[Judas] watched for an opportunity to betray Jesus ___ ___ ___ ___ ___."

Quiz #18
100 KEY EVENTS

1. **Last Supper** Which of Jesus' disciples protested when Jesus came to wash his feet?

2. **Last Supper** Which is the only Gospel to record the event of Jesus washing his disciples' feet?

3. **Last Supper** Fill in the missing word: "I have set you an ___ that you should do as I have done for you."

4. **Eating the Meal** What did Jesus say the bread he gave his disciples represented?

5. **Eating the Meal** What did Jesus say the wine he gave his disciples represented?

6. **Eating the Meal** Fill in the missing word: "Do this in ___ of me."

7. **Gethsemane** While Jesus prayed in Gethsemane, what did Peter, James and John keep on doing?

8. **Gethsemane** True or false? In Gethsemane Jesus prayed, "My Father, if it possible, may this cup be taken from me."

9. **Gethsemane** Fill in the missing words: "The ___ is willing, but the body is ___."

10. **Crucifixion** True or false? Jesus was crucified inside the boundary of the temple.

11. **Crucifixion** Who were the two people Jesus was speaking to when he said from the cross, "Dear woman, here is your son... Here is your mother"?

12. **Crucifixion** Who arranged for the wording of the notice on the cross to read: "JESUS OF NAZARETH, THE KING OF THE JEWS"?

13. **Resurrection** On which day of the week did Jesus' disciples discover that his tomb was empty?

14. **Resurrection** Which of the eleven disciples was not with the other disciples when the risen Jesus appeared to them on the evening of the day he rose?

15. **Resurrection** To whom did the risen Jesus say, "Take care of my sheep"?

---

12. Pilate **13.** Sunday **14.** Thomas **15.** Peter

7. They kept on falling asleep **8.** True (Matthew 26:39) **9.** Spirit, weak **10.** False. Jesus was crucified just outside Jerusalem (John 19:17-18) **11.** To his mother Mary and to "the disciple whom he loved," John

1. Peter **2.** John's Gospel **3.** Example **4.** His body **5.** His blood **6.** Remembrance

Answers

Quiz #19
100 KEY EVENTS

1. **Ascension** During Jesus' ascension what hid him from the sight of his disciples?

2. **Ascension** Fill in the missing word: "He lifted up his hands and ___ them."

3. **Ascension** How did Jesus' disciples react to his ascension? Were they angry, sad, or did they worship him?

4. **Pentecost** What did the disciples hear on the day of Pentecost?

5. **Pentecost** What did the disciples see on the day of Pentecost?

6. **Pentecost** True or false? Some people made fun of the disciples and accused them of being drunk.

7. **Stephen's Trial** Fill in the missing word: "[Stephen] did great wonders and ___ signs among the people."

8. **Stephen's Trial** True or false? The last thing Stephen did as he was being martyred was to ask God to forgive those who were killing him.

9. **Stephen's Trial** At the feet of which young man did those stoning Stephen lay their clothes?

10. **Saul's Conversion** What activity was Saul engaged in when he had his dramatic conversion experience?

11. **Saul's Conversion** Fill in the missing word: "I am ___, whom you are persecuting."

12. **Saul's Conversion** What was the name of the town that Saul was near when he fell to the ground as he saw a light from heaven flash around him?

13. **Barnabas Goes to Find Paul** Why was Barnabas at first the only person to befriend Paul in Jerusalem?

14. **Barnabas Goes to Find Paul** When Barnabas needed help teaching the new Christians in Antioch, he went to find Paul. Where was Paul?

15. **Barnabas Goes to Find Paul** Who first sent Paul and Barnabas out as missionaries?

Answers

1. A cloud 2. Blessed 3. Jesus' disciples worshiped him 4. A very strong wind 5. Tongues of fire 6. True (Acts 2:13) 7. Miraculous 8. True 9. Saul, (who became Paul) 10. Persecuting Christians 11. Jesus 12. Damascus 13. The Christians were afraid because they thought it was a trick 14. Tarsus 15. The Christians in Antioch, in response to a command from the Holy Spirit

Quiz #20

100 KEY EVENTS

1. **Peter's Vision** In `Peter's vision he was told to kill and eat food he considered to be unclean. How did Peter react in his vision? Did he agree to eat the food or did he refuse to eat the food?

2. **Peter's Vision** What was the name of the Roman centurion who Peter visited after his vision?

3. **Peter's Vision** Fill in the missing word: "God ___ men from every nation who fear him and do what is right."

4. **Council of Jerusalem** Christian leaders in Jerusalem met to solve what argument?

5. **Council of Jerusalem** At this meeting which leading Christian said, "We believe it is through the grace of our Lord Jesus that we are saved, just as they are"?

6. **Council of Jerusalem** Fill in the missing word: "We should not make it difficult for the ___ who are turning to God."

7. **Paul into Europe** What experience made Paul decide to cross over from Asia into Europe?

8. **Paul into Europe** Did Paul's first visit to Europe occur on his first, second or third missionary journey?

9. **Paul into Europe** At which port did Paul and his companions land in Europe?

10. **Paul Is Arrested** in Jerusalem. Fill in the missing word: "when the rioters saw the commander and his soldiers, they stopped ___ Paul."

11. **Paul Is Arrested** in Jerusalem In his speech to the crowds, Paul said he had been taught by what leading rabbi?

12. **Paul Is Arrested** in Jerusalem At first the Jerusalem crowd listened quietly to him. At what point were they furious?

13. **Paul Goes to Rome** Which Roman official said to Paul, "You have appealed to Caesar. To Caesar you will go!"

14. **Paul Goes to Rome** True or false? Paul was kept under house arrest in Rome for two years.

15. **Paul Goes to Rome** Which book of the Bible concludes with this verse? "Boldly and without hindrance he [Paul] preached the kingdom of God and taught about the Lord Jesus Christ."

Answers

1. Peter refused to eat the food 2. Cornelius 3. Accepts 4. Should Gentile converts be circumcised 5. Peter 6. Gentiles 7. In a vision, he saw a man from Macedonia who said, "Come over to Macedonia and help us." 8. His second missionary journey 9. Samothrace 10. beating 11. Gamaliel 12. When Paul said that God had sent him to preach to Gentiles 13. Festus 14. True (Acts 28:30) 15. The book of Acts

Facts 1

100 KEY EVENTS

The opening verse of the Bible states that, "In the beginning God created…" In the Old Testament the Hebrew word used for "create" is only used of God's actions and never of human actions.

Genesis 3:1 says that "the serpent was more crafty" than any of the other animals that God had made. He used his cunning to sell a lie to Eve and to entice her to rebel against God. The devil, or Satan, is referred to as "that ancient serpent" in Revelation 20:2.

The tower of Babel was probably modeled on Mespotamian temple-towers, which were known as ziggurats. Built on a square base, it had stepped, sloping sides which led to a small shrine at the top.

God told Noah to build an "ark" (Genesis 6:14). The only other time the word for "ark" is used in the Old Testament is for the basket which the baby Moses was placed on the bank of the River Nile. That "ark" was also made watertight by being coated with pitch.

When God called Abraham, he promised to bless him in seven ways (Genesis 12:2-3). The seventh promise, that "all peoples on earth would be blessed through you" (Genesis 12:3), is mentioned in the New Testament and referred to Abraham's physical descendants (Acts 3:25) and spiritual descendants (Galatians 3:8).

When Abraham was told to count the stars, God promised him "So shall your offspring be" (Genesis 15:5), Abraham must have realized that God was saying that he would have countless descendants. Eight thousand stars can be seen in the Near-Eastern night sky.

When, at the very last moment, a ram was sacrificed in place of Isaac, the idea that one life being given for another (substitutionary sacrifice) is mentioned for the first time in the Bible. In Mark 10:45, Jesus' life is said to be a ransom for (that is, "instead of") many.

The girl who met Abraham's servant as he was looking for a wife for Isaac, was the daughter of Bethuel, son of the wife of Abraham's brother (Genesis 24:15). So when Isaac married Rebekah he married his father's great-niece.

The Lord told Rebekah an unusual thing when he said of her unborn twin boys, "the older will serve the younger" (Genesis 25:23). For it was the accepted custom that the younger son was subservient to the older. The Lord was saying of God's people that they were specially chosen, or elected, by him.

Facts 2

100 KEY EVENTS

Out of his twelve sons, Jacob was especially fond of the two born to his wife Rachel, Joseph and Benjamin. When Rachel was barren, she exclaimed, "Give me children, or I'll die" (Genesis 30:1)! Rachel died giving birth to Benjamin.

In the Old Testament God often made his will known through dreams. Although his parents and brothers did not like Joseph's dreams, they had no problem understanding that they meant that Joseph would rule over them.

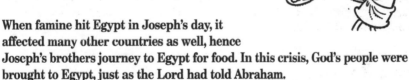

The Midianites sold Joseph to Potiphar. The slave trade among the various tribes of the Arabian Desert was well-known in those days.

When famine hit Egypt in Joseph's day, it affected many other countries as well, hence Joseph's brothers journey to Egypt for food. In this crisis, God's people were brought to Egypt, just as the Lord had told Abraham.

According to Exodus 2:2, Moses was "a fine child." He is called "no ordinary child" in Acts 7:20. His deliverance as a baby is a picture of the deliverance God would work through him for God's enslaved people in Egypt.

After Moses killed a cruel Egyptian for beating a Hebrew, Moses stopped two Hebrews fighting each other. One asked Moses, "Who made you a ruler and judge over us?" Little could he have known that 40 years later this is exactly what Moses became!

When Moses saw the burning bush, he was told to take off his sandals. God's presence, rather than the ground itself, made the ground holy. By taking off his sandals Moses acknowledged that he was standing in the holy presence of God.

Egyptian Pharaohs had a metal cobra on the front of their head-dress as a symbol of their power and authority. When Moses threw his staff on the ground and the Lord turned it into a snake, Moses was demonstrating that God's power was stronger than Pharaoh's.

Facts 3

100 KEY EVENTS

The exact crossing place of the Red Sea is specified as "directly opposite Baal Zephon" (Exodus 14:2). The Hebrew for "Red Sea" is the "Sea of Reeds." As reeds do not grow in salt water, the crossing is unlikely to have been in the north end of the Gulf of Suez. An Egyptian papyrus has placed Baal Zephon at the southern end of Lake Menzaleh.

We refer to the summary of God's law of Exodus 19:2-17 as the "Ten Commandments." Exodus 20:1 says, "God spake all these words." The Ten Commandments literally mean the "Ten Words." They are also known by the Greek term "Decalogue," which means "Ten Words."

For the Israelites, the tabernacle was God's royal tent. The Ten Commandments were placed inside the ark of the covenant. On top of the ark were two golden cherubim. Among the treasures found in King Tutankhaun's Egyptian tomb, are two winged guardians made to shield sacred places.

Rahab provided secret shelter for the spies who entered Jericho. Josephus says that Rahab was an innkeeper. Archeological evidence shows that houses were built into the walls of Jericho. Late Bronze Age fortifications at Jericho reveal casement (hollow) walls, which may have provided Rahab with her rooms.

When the Israelites attacked the city of Jericho, they were told to make a long blast on the trumpets. Such psychological warfare was meant to induce confusion, if not panic. In one of the Dead Sea Scrolls, "The War of the Sons of Light against the Sons of Darkness," the Levites were told to do this.

When Gideon was called by the Lord to lead the Israelites he was "threshing wheat in a winepress". Normally this would have been done in the open so the wind could blow the chaff away. But Gideon could stay hidden from the Midianites in a winepress.

Samson undertook the vows of a Nazirite (meaning "dedicated") and for him these lasted for his whole life. A Nazirite was never to cut his hair, so when Samson told Delilah the secret of his strength, he committed a great sin.

As seen in the book of Ruth, when a piece of land was sold, the seller took off his sandal as a way of showing, in public, that he renounced his rights to it.

When he anointed Saul, Samuel was following a custom that had applied to priests when they were appointed to serve God. But from this moment on in the Bible the phrase "the anointed of the Lord" usually referred to the king.

Facts 4

100 KEY EVENTS

When Saul visited the medium at Endor, God may have allowed her to see the spirit of Samuel, or she may have had contact with an evil spirit, or she might have read Saul's thoughts through telepathy.

David was anointed by Samuel in the presence of his brothers. But when David became king over Judah he was anointed again in a public ceremony by his own tribe. This was to underline the fact that he had been chosen by God to be king.

The ancient Greeks, to whom the Philistines were probably related, developed a practice in which a war was decided by two champions fighting each other. It was called, "trial by battle ordeal".

As a sign of the friendship between them, Jonathan made a covenant with David. When Jonathan gave David not only his robe, but his belt, sword and bow he was ratifying this covenant and probably acknowledging that David would be king in his place.

When David conquered Jerusalem, he had a capital city of great strength. It was only 11 acres in extent and had no more than 3,500 inhabitants, it was almost impenetrable as it was surrounded on three sides by steep valleys.

The great value of Jerusalem to David was that it had never been conquered by the Israelites, so could be claimed by no tribe. It really was "David's city."

The floor plan of Solomon's temple had three divisions: a portico, main hall and inner sanctuary. This type of plan was often used in Semitic buildings. Sites at Syrian Ebla and at Tell Tainat in the Orontes basin reveal this tripartite division.

The Queen of Sheba probably came from the region of southwest Arabia. It was ideally situated to trade in the lucrative luxury goods which came by sea from India and east Africa. These goods were transported on caravan routes throughout the Arabian Desert.

Naaman was probably the commander-in-chief of the forces of Ben-Hadad II, who was king of Aram. Naaman's greatest victory came when the Arameans defeated the Assyrians in the Battle of Qarqar in 853 B.C.

Isaiah had his famous vision in the year that King Uzziah died, 740 B.C. During Uzziah's reign, 792 to 740 B.C., Uzziah had ruled in a godly way. But he was punished with leprosy because he burned incense in the temple—something which only the priests were permitted to do.

Facts 5
100 KEY EVENTS

When Jehoiachin had only been ruler of Jerusalem for three months, the Babylonian army captured Jerusalem. The king was taken off to Babylon, along with 10,000 people.

When the Babylonians conquered Jerusalem, they offered Jeremiah a comfortable retirement in Babylon. But they did not make him their prisoner and he chose to remain with his people in Jerusalem.

It is thought that synagogues started in the Exile, when people, far away from the temple, met together to pray to God.

Jerusalem's broken down walls meant that the people were defenseless against any enemies. Thucydides describes Athens being in a similar state after it had been destroyed by the Persians in 480-479. Excavations in Jerusalem show that the eastern terraces collapsed for lack of a wall.

John the Baptist preached in an area known as the Desert of Judea (Matthew 3:1). This is probably the 20-mile plateau that stretches from Jerusalem down to the Dead Sea and the River Jordan. In such a desert area he would have needed to feed on desert food: locusts and wild honey.

In 2 Kings 1:8, Elijah is described as wearing a garment of hair with a leather belt. By dressing in the same way, John the Baptist was making a symbolic statement: a prophet had again risen in the land.

Nearly all Christmas cards depict Jesus being born in a stable. But the earliest Christian traditions say that he was born in a cave which may have been used as a stable. The only biblical indication that Jesus was born in a stable is that Mary placed Jesus in a manger, an animal's feeding trough.

Luke and Matthew record their own genealogies of Jesus (Luke 3:23-38; Matthew 1:1-16). While Matthew begins with Abraham, the father of the Jewish people, Luke traces Jesus' origin back to Adam.

The King Herod who was visited by the wise men was not a Jew, but an Idumean. He had been appointed king of Judea by the Roman Senate.

Herod built many magnificent buildings in Jerusalem, including pagan altars, monuments, amphitheaters, and most notably of all, the temple in Jerusalem.

Herod's temple was begun in 20 B.C. It was completed in A.D.64. It was as high as a fifteen storey building. The Most Holy Place and the Holy Place followed the dimensions of the previous temples. The Romans razed it to the ground in A.D.70.

Facts 6
100 KEY EVENTS

The only fact we know about Jesus' boyhood is that he went to the temple in Jerusalem when he was twelve years old. All Jewish adult males were supposed to go to three religious festivals every year: the Passover, Pentecost and the Feast of Tabernacles.

Luke records that John the Baptist began his preaching ministry in the fifteenth year of the reign of Tiberius Caesar, which was probably A.D. 25-26. Luke also notes that the Roman prefect of that time, who ruled Judea, Samaria and Idumea, was Pontius Pilate.

Herod the Great died in 4 B.C. His territory was then split up and ruled by his three sons: Archelaus, Herod Antipas and Herod Philip. Luke also notes (Luke 3:1) that Lysanias was tetrarch of Abilene, and a number of inscriptions bearing his name have been found.

Luke records that at Jesus' baptism, the Holy Spirit descended on him "in bodily form like a dove" (Luke 3:22). This was an important sign. John the Baptist had been told that the person on whom the Holy Spirit came would baptize people with the Holy Spirit (John 1:33).

John the Baptist was arrested and then beheaded because he publicly rebuked Herod the tetrarch for marrying his brother Philip's wife, while Philip was still alive! The woman was Herodias who was a granddaughter of Herod the Great.

Herodias married her uncle, Herod Philip. While Herod the tetrarch was their guest in Rome, Herodias left her uncle for the tetrarch.

There are four lists of Jesus' apostles: Matthew 10:2-4; Mark 3:16-19; Luke 6:14-16 and Acts 1:13. The order in which the names of the apostles are listed varies. But the list always starts with Peter, the leader of the Twelve, and always concludes with Judas Iscariot, who betrayed Jesus.

Nazareth is called Jesus' hometown, not because he was born there, but because he grew up there. When he revisited Nazareth, he infuriated the people by commending the faith of two non-Israelites, a widow in Zarephath and Naaman, a commander in the army of the king of Aram.

In Capernaum, Jesus healed a demon-possessed man. To pagans, a "demon" was a supernatural being which could be good or bad. To Jesus, demons were evil spirits.

Facts 7

100 KEY EVENTS

On one occasion, Jesus fed 5,000 people at one time. This number refers only to the men; the women and children may have brought the numbers to over 10,000 people. The size of this crowd is quite staggering, as the closest towns, Capernaum and Bethsaida, probably only had a population of five thousand between them.

When Jesus was transfigured only his inner circle of three close disciples were with him: Peter, James and John. Two figures from the Old Testament appeared with Jesus. It is thought that Moses represents the old covenant and its promise of salvation, and Elijah represents the prophets.

Caesarea Philippi, a particularly pagan area, had been built by one of Herod the Great's sons, Philip, who named the town after himself and Tiberius Caesar. It had originally been called Paneas, after the Greek god Pan.

Jesus said, "I tell you that you are Peter, and on this rock I will build my church" (Matthew 16:18). This is a play on words. In Greek, "Peter" is *petros*, and "rock" is *petra*. Jesus would build his church on Peter's inspired confession.

When Jesus arrived at the tomb of his friend Lazarus, Lazarus had been dead for four days. Jews thought that the soul remained in the body for three days after death, hoping that the body might come alive again. But after three days all hope was gone. John says that many Jews put their faith in Jesus when he raised Lazarus.

When Jews saw Jesus entering Jerusalem on a donkey, their minds would have gone back the time when Solomon, David's son, rode on a donkey on his way to be publicly acclaimed as king. Jesus, the Son of David, was now arriving to claim his kingship, just as the prophets had said (Zechariah 9:9).

When Jesus washed his disciples' feet at the Last Supper, he was performing a most menial act of service. Disciples did most things for rabbis, but one thing that was specifically excluded was to undo the thongs of their sandals. Jesus gave his disciples a lesson in humility.

During the Last Supper, when Jesus gave his disciples the bread, he said "Do this in remembrance of me." The first Passover was always meant to be remembered by the Jews as the time when God delivered them from Egypt. Jesus wanted his followers to remember he was their Passover lamb, who was about to take away their sin.

Facts 8

100 KEY EVENTS

After the Lord's Supper, Jesus went to pray in Gethsemane. The word means "oil press." It remains the site of an olive orchard to this day, and was probably used as a place where the oil was squeezed, or pressed, from the olives in Jesus' day.

The word "Calvary" (Luke 23:33) comes from a Latin translation of an Aramaic word—the "Golgotha" of Matthew 27:33, which means "skull." The Gospels say that this was sited outside Jerusalem, that it was fairly conspicuous and that a garden with a tomb in it was nearby.

The entrance tombs were usually sealed to prevent vandals from entering and to stop any animals from disturbing the bodies. Jesus' tomb was sealed by the authority of Rome, and guarded by the best soldiers in the world. These Roman soldiers would be executed themselves had they fallen asleep on duty.

Jesus' ascension, according to the most reliable historian, Dr. Luke, took place in the vicinity of Bethany. Bethany was a village, a mile or so to the south-east of Jerusalem, on the eastern slope of the Mount of Olives. It was the final stage on the road between Jericho and Jerusalem.

Today 'Pentecost' is known as the birthday of the Christian church. It also goes under the name of the Feast of Weeks and the Feast of Harvest. Luke's account of the Day of Pentecost in the Acts happened on the fiftieth day after the Sabbath of Passover week. The apostles were filled with the Holy Spirit.

During Stephen's speech, after which he was martyred, he mentions a fact not recorded in the Old Testament, that Moses was educated in all the wisdom of the Egyptians. This is hardly surprising since he grew up in Pharaoh's household. Josephus and Philo both say that Moses was noted for his great learning.

Peter had been brought up to believe that Gentiles were unclean in God's sight and should be avoided. Hence God gave him a vision in which he is specifically told to kill and eat some of the most unclean things imaginable, four-footed animals and reptiles.

When Christians met to sort our their differences at the Council of Jerusalem, they decided that they should not make it difficult for Gentiles who were turning to God. So they agreed that non-Jews did not have to be circumcised when they became Christians.

From First to Last

Quiz # 1

FROM FIRST TO LAST

1. True or false? The first three words of John's Gospel and the first three words of Genesis are the same.

2. Name the first event described in the book of Genesis?

3. Fill in the gap: God's first words in the book of Genesis were, "Let there be ___."

4. True or false? Adam's first recorded words were spoken to Eve.

5. True or false? Eve was the first to eat from the tree of the knowledge of good and evil.

6. What was the first thing Adam and Eve realized after they had eaten from the tree of the knowledge of good and evil?

7. What was the last possession that God gave Adam and Eve before they left the Garden of Eden?

8. Give the name of Adam and Eve's youngest son.

9. Who was the father of all who played the harp and flute?

10. Tubal-Cain was the father of what group of people?

11. According to Genesis, when the flood came, how long was it before the rain came to an end?

12. After the rain ceased, how long was it before the water stopped rising?

13. When did Noah know that the water had dried up?

14. True or false? Noah and his family were in the ark for 6 months.

15. True or false? The first bird Noah sent from the ark was a robin.

Answers

1. True. (Genesis 1:1 and John 1:1) 2. Creation 3. Light 4. False. They were spoken to God (Genesis 2:23) 5. True (Genesis 3:6) 6. They were naked 7. Clothes 8. Seth 9. Jubal 10. All who forge tools out of bronze or iron 11. 40 days 12. 110 days 13. When the dove brought back an olive leaf 14. False. It was 371 days 15. False. The bird was a raven (Genesis 8:7)

Quiz #2
FROM FIRST TO LAST

1. Where were the different languages first created?

2. Who is the oldest man in the Bible?

3. Give the name of the first man in the Bible who is recorded as going straight to heaven without dying.

4. To whom did God first promise to give the whole land of Canaan?

5. What was the last act of Lot's wife?

6. How many strangers did Abraham see when he was sitting by the great trees of Mamre?

7. Why did Sarah laugh when she first heard she was going to have a child?

8. At the very last minute, what stopped Abraham killing his son?

9. What was the very first piece of land that God's people owned in the Holy Land?

10. Which of Isaac's twin sons was born last?

11. True or false? Esau sold his birthright (his inheritance rights as the firstborn) for a plate of stew.

12. In order to marry Laban's daughter, Rachel, how many years did Jacob work without wages?

13. How many children did Jacob have?

14. Who was the youngest of Jacob's son?

15. True or false? In Joseph's first dream, the sun, moon and eleven stars were bowing down to him.

Answers

1. Babel **2.** Methuselah was 969 when he died **3.** Enoch **4.** Abraham **5.** She looked back at Sodom **6.** 3 **7.** Because she was 90 years old **8.** An angel called him to stop and showed him a ram **9.** A field with a cave in it which Abraham bought from the Hittites for a burial place for Sarah **10.** Jacob **11.** True (Genesis 25:29-34) **12.** 14 years (after 7 years he was tricked into marrying Leah) **13.** 13 **14.** Benjamin **15.** False, It was his second dream (Genesis 37:5-9)

Quiz #3

FROM FIRST TO LAST

1. In whose household did Joseph first live in Egypt?

2. In Pharaoh's dream what did the last seven cows do to the first seven cows?

3. True or false? Pharaoh made Joseph the highest executive in all Egypt, and put a rope around his neck.

4. When Joseph first saw his youngest brother Benjamin in Egypt, what did he do?

5. What is the final event in the book of Genesis?

6. True or false? With its 50 chapters, Genesis is the longest book in the Old Testament.

7. In what country are the Israelites when the book of Exodus begins?

8. True or false? Moses was the oldest child in his family.

9. When God spoke to Moses from the burning bush, what was the first thing he asked Moses to do?

10. What was Moses' first reaction when God asked him to lead the Israelites out of slavery?

11. Who was the first Israelite whom Moses encountered on his return journey to Egypt?

12. What was the first miracle God gave Moses, to show that God's power was with him?

13. Pharaoh's magicians were able to produce the first two plagues, but what was the first plague they could not reproduce?

14. What was the last plague upon the land of Egypt?

15. Fill in the gaps: on that first Passover night, the Lord said to Moses and Aaron: "This month is to be for you the ___ month, the ___ month of your year."

Quiz #4
FROM FIRST TO LAST

1. What group of Israelites was consecrated before the Lord on the first day the Israelites were led out of the land of Egypt?

2. Where did the Israelites last see their Egyptian oppressors?

3. Fill in the two missing words from God's first message given to Moses on Mount Sinai: "You yourselves have seen what I did to Egypt, and how I carried you on ____ ____ and brought you to myself."

4. What is the first of the Ten Commandments?

5. What is the first commandment with a promise?

6. Fill in the missing word from the last commandment: "You shall not ____."

7. Why did Moses break the first two tablets of stone containing the Ten Commandments?

8. What day of every week was to be a day of rest?

9. True or false? In the first verses of the book of Numbers, Moses is commanded to take a census of the people.

10. At the end of how many months did the Israelites leave Sinai and set out for the promised land?

11. Of the two spies in favor of entering the promised land, who was the first to speak to the people?

12. True or false? Moses had to wait until all of the adults who had left Egypt had died, with the exception only of the two brave spies. When the last man died, they set off again for the promised land.

13. Complete this verse, from Moses' final blessing upon the people: "The eternal God is your refuge, and underneath..."

14. True or false: Moses died without ever seeing the promised land.

15. In what country did Moses die?

Quiz #5

FROM FIRST TO LAST

1. Who was Moses' first choice as his successor to take over the leadership of the Israelites?

2. What was the first physical barrier to conquering the Promised Land?

3. Who walked in front of the people?

4. What were they carrying?

5. Name the first city encountered by the Israelites when they entered the Promised Land.

6. True or false? The Israelites marched round the city walls a total of seven times.

7. On the last time they marched round the city, what did all the people have to do?

8. Fill in the missing two words from Joshua's last words to the people: "Throw away the ____ ____ that are among you and yield your hearts to the Lord."

9. Where were Joseph's bones finally laid to rest?

10. Who was the first deliverer in the book of Judges?

11. When asked to deliver his people, who protested, "My clan is the weakest in Manasseh, and I am the least in my father's family"?

12. True or false? The first oppressors of the Israelite people in the book of Judges were the Philistines.

13. In the temple of what Philistine god did Samson slay his last Philistines?

14. The book of Judges closes with the exploits of which judge?

15. Who was the last judge of Israel?

Answers

1. Joshua **2.** The River Jordan — and there were no bridges or boats **3.** The priests **4.** The ark of the covenant **5.** Jericho **6.** False. It was 13 times (Joshua 6:12-15) **7.** Shout. **8.** foreign gods **9.** Shechem **10.** Othniel **11.** Gideon **12.** False. The first recorded oppressor was the king of Aram (Judges 3:10) **13.** The temple of Dagon **14.** Samson **15.** Samuel

Quiz #6

FROM FIRST TO LAST

1. According to Israelite law, the firstborn offspring of every womb belongs to whom?

2. Who was the first high priest of Israel?

3. Who is the first priest referred to in the Bible?

4. Who was the first king of Israel?

5. What is the name of a youngest son who was anointed king?

6. What was Saul's last act?

7. The last surviving member of Saul and Jonathan's family suffered from what disability?

8. Fill in the missing word, from David's last words to the people: "When one rules over men in righteousness, he is like the brightness after ____."

9. In David's last instructions to his son Solomon, to whom did he ask Solomon to show kindness?

10. After the division of the kingdom, why did Jeroboam, the first king of Israel, establish shrines with golden calves at Bethel and Dan?

11. Who was the last king of the northern kingdom of Israel?

12. In the last days of Jerusalem, who was beaten, and almost killed, on grounds of sedition?

13. Zedekiah, the last king of Judah, was captured by whom?

14. True or false? Daniel, a prince of Judah, was among the first group of men deported to Babylon.

15. In his letter to the deportees in Babylon, how many years did Jeremiah say they would spend in exile?

Answers

1. To God **2.** Aaron **3.** Melchizedek **4.** Saul **5.** David **6.** He killed himself
7. He was crippled in both feet **8.** rain **9.** The sons of Barzillai of Gilead
10. To stop the people going to Jerusalem to worship God **11.** Hoshea **12.** Jeremiah
13. King Nebuchadnezzar of Babylon **14.** True (Daniel 1:4-6) **15.** 70 years

Quiz #7
FROM FIRST TO LAST

1. According to Matthew's Gospel, rather than worrying about what one will eat or drink, Christ's followers should first seek what?

2. Before criticizing a brother, because of the speck of sawdust in his eye, what should a follower of Christ first do?

3. Add the missing word Jesus said about the end of time: "Many who are first will be ____."

4. What did Jesus say is the first and greatest commandment?

5. According to Mark chapter 13, before Jesus comes again, to whom must the gospel first be preached?

6. When the religious leaders brought a sinful woman to Jesus, he said that the one without sin should be the first to do what?

7. True or false? The disciples were first called Christians in Jerusalem.

8. In his letter to the Romans, Paul states that the gospel is to be given first to which group of people?

9. Fill in the missing word from Paul's letter to the Romans: "For in the gospel a righteousness of God is revealed, a righteousness that is by ____, from first to last."

10. In Paul's letter to the Corinthians, Paul writes that in the church, God has appointed second, prophets, and third, teachers. Which group comes first of all?

11. According to Paul, the first man, Adam, became a living being. What did the last Adam become?

12. In his condemnation of hypocrisy, what did Jesus tell the Pharisees to cleanse first?

13. At the last day, who, according to Paul, will rise first?

14. Complete these words from John's first letter: "We love because he [God]..."

15. Toward the end of his life, John wrote the book of Revelation. This contains letters to how many churches?

Answers

1. God's kingdom and his righteousness 2. Remove the plank from his own eye 3. last
4. "Love the Lord your God with all your heart and with all your soul and with all your mind"
5. All nations 6. Throw a stone at her 7. False. It was Antioch. (Acts 11:26) 8. Jews
9. Faith 10. Apostles 11. A life-giving Spirit 12. The inside of the cup and dish
13. The dead in Christ 14. "first loved us" 15. 7

Quiz #8

FROM FIRST TO LAST

1. In the book of Revelation, the risen Christ calls himself the first and the last, the "A to Z". What is the first letter of the Greek alphabet?

2. What is the last letter of the Greek alphabet?

3. Which is John's shortest letter?

4. Who was the first Christian martyr?

5. What event marked the beginning of the Christian church?

6. Who was healed in the first healing miracle recorded in Acts?

7. Where did the first healing miracle in Acts take place?

8. Who were the first two disciples to be thrown into prison?

9. True or false? The first apostle to preach the gospel in Samaria was Peter.

10. Where was Paul going when he saw the risen Christ?

11. Complete this sentence summarizing the content of Paul's first sermons: "At once he began to preach in the synagogues that..."

12. Who was the first Christian to come to see Paul in Damascus?

13. God taught Peter that he must preach to Gentiles (foreigners) as well as to Jews: in what city was the first Gentile home Peter entered?

14. Who were Peter's first Gentile converts?

15. According to the record in Acts, where was Paul when he first said that since the Jews were rejecting his message, he would preach to the Gentiles?

Quiz #9
FROM FIRST TO LAST

1. In what book of the Bible are King David's last words recorded?

2. What is the last book of the Old Testament?

3. True or false? David built the first temple in Jerusalem.

4. What is the first word of the last five psalms?

5. According to Mark's Gospel, what did Jesus do immediately before he died?

6. According to Paul, what is the last enemy that is to be destroyed?

7. According to Paul's letter to the Corinthians, what will happen when the last trumpet sounds?

8. What is the first word of each of the Beatitudes?

9. Who was the first person to speak with Job following all of his calamities?

10. Give the four missing words from this verse in Proverbs: "The path of the righteous is like the..."

11. Who, according to the first verse of the book of Proverbs is the author of the book of Proverbs?

12. True or false? The first word of the book of Psalms is identical to the first word of the Beatitudes.

13. Fill in the four blank spaces from the first two sentences spoken by the teacher who wrote the book of Ecclesiates. The same word appears each time:
"___! ___!" says the Teacher. "Utterly ___! Everything is ___!"

14. According to the writer of Ecclesiastes, what is the destiny of everyone?

15. What is the shortest book in the Old Testament?

Quiz # 10

FROM FIRST TO LAST

1. What is the shortest prayer in the Bible?

2. True or false? God told Jeremiah that he knew him before he was born.

3. Lamentations is a funeral lament at the destruction and final days of what city?

4. The first singers and musicians were women: who led the dancing after the crossing over the Red Sea?

5. In the new beginning after the Exile, who led the music?

6. True or false? Although most songs and hymns were based on traditional folk tunes, occasionally a singer created a new tune.

7. Daniel's first confrontation with the King of Babylon was over his refusal to eat what?

8. The last place on earth Jonah wanted to go was where?

9. Complete Daniel's interpretation of the meaning of the first word which was written on the wall at Belshazzar's feast, " MENE: God has numbered the days of your reign and..."

10. In what book of the Bible is the town of Bethlehem first mentioned?

11. In what book of the Bible is it first recorded that the Messiah would be born in Bethlehem?

12. Complete this verse from Proverbs: "The first to present his case seems right, till..."

13. The phrase, "The just shall live by faith" comes four times in the Bible. In what book does it first appear?

14. What is the name of the first Gospel?

15. The prophet Habakkuk took issue with God: what was his first complaint?

Quiz # 11
FROM FIRST TO LAST

1. Which prophet prophesies that when the Lord is ready to come to his people, he will first be preceded by a messenger?

2. What is the first letter in the New Testament canon?

3. Where did Mary and Joseph first make their home after leaving Bethlehem with Jesus?

4. Who was sent by God as a forerunner, to prepare the way for Jesus?

5. According to the first Beatitude, which people are blessed?

6. According to the last Beatitudes, who are also blessed?

7. What was the first thing that happened to Jesus after he was baptized?

8. What were God's first words at Jesus' baptism?

9. When did Andrew first meet Jesus?

10. True or false? Jesus first saw Nicodemus when Nicodemus was sitting under a fig tree.

11. Who is the first person to be healed in the Gospel of Matthew?

12. What was the first reaction of the disciples when they saw Jesus walking on the lake?

13. Who was the first disciple to affirm that Jesus was the Son of God?

14. Who was the first person Jesus brought back to life?

15. What was the last miracle to be performed by Jesus before his death?

Quiz # 12
FROM FIRST TO LAST

1. Fill in the missing word: Jesus said, "Whoever humbles himself like this ___ is the greatest in the kingdom of heaven."

2. True or false? Jesus was the first person ever to have ridden the colt on which he rode into Jerusalem.

3. In the Parable of the Tenants and the Vineyard, who was the last person sent by the owner of the vineyard to collect the fruit?

4. What is the last book in the Bible?

5. In the Parable of the Talents, who ended up with no talents at all?

6. According to John's Gospel, what finally drove the Pharisees and scribes to call an emergency meeting of the Sanhedrin and arrange for Jesus to be silenced?

7. What was the last straw that led Judas to betray Jesus?

8. True or false? The last verse of the Gospel of John indicates that all of Jesus' works were recorded in the Gospel.

9. Which Gospel has the most chapters?

10. According to Matthew, what were the last words of Jesus?

11. True or false? According to Luke, the last words of Jesus were given in the upper room in Jerusalem.

12. Who were the first two missionaries sent out from the church at Antioch?

13. What was the first island at which Paul stopped on his first missionary journey?

14. According to Jesus, if someone wants to rob a strong man, what must he do first?

15. What did Jesus tell the 72 disciples to do when they first entered a house?

---

14. Tie up the strong man **15.** "Peace to this house"
Olives, near Bethany (Luke 24:50-51; Acts 1:8) **12.** Paul and Barnabas **13.** Cyprus
10. "Surely I am with you always, to the very end of the age." **11.** False. His last words were spoken on the Mount of
8. False (John 21:25) **9.** Matthew with 28 chapters
6. The raising of Lazarus **7.** When the woman anointed Jesus with perfume and Judas' protest was overruled by Jesus
1. child **2.** True (Mark 11:2) **3.** His son **4.** Revelation. **5.** The last servant

Answers

75

Quiz # 13
FROM FIRST TO LAST

1. On which of Paul's missionary journeys did he first enter Europe?

2. When was Paul first told that he would suffer for his apostolic calling?

3. According to the book of Acts, who was the first person to be healed by Paul?

4. Where did Paul's first healing take place?

5. Where, according to Acts, was Paul first thrown into prison?

6. To the nearest five, how many chapters in the New Testament were written by Paul?

7. When Paul left the Christians in Ephesus, what had he said to make many of them cry?

8. According to Acts, at what city was Paul first flogged?

9. At what city did Paul first meet his beloved friend Timothy?

10. What was the last city at which Paul stopped on his third and last missionary journey?

11. At the end of how many years did Paul the prisoner decide to appeal to Caesar for justice?

12. When Paul was speaking at his last trial in Caesarea, at what point did Festus cry out, "Your great learning is driving you insane!"?

13. In the last verses of the book of Acts what is Paul doing?

14. True or false? The last chapters of Acts tell of Paul's second visit to Rome.

15. When Acts ends, for how many years has Paul been a house prisoner in his own rented house?

Quiz # 14
FROM FIRST TO LAST

1. What is the first church of the seven churches listed in Revelation?

2. What is the last church of the seven churches listed in Revelation?

3. What emotion does John first feel after he sees his vision in Revelation 1?

4. What is the last word at the end of the book of Revelation?

5. True or false? In the first and the last chapters of the book of Revelation, Jesus is mentioned as being the Alpha and the Omega.

6. True or false? The first verse of the book of Hebrews names the author of the book.

7. Add the two missing words from the first sentence of the letter to the Hebrews, "In these ___ ___ he [God] has spoken to us by his Son."

8. Give the missing word from verse 1 of 1 Peter, "To God's elect, ___ in the world."

9. True or false? All three epistles by the apostle John open with his name somewhere in the first two verses.

10. In the last chapter of the epistle to the Ephesians, the author writes, "Finally, be strong..." What does he then tell his readers to do?

11. In which of his letters does Paul say that his ambition is to preach the gospel where nobody has yet heard it.

12. In the letter to the Colossians, Paul reminds the church of his circumstances. What is noteworthy about the circumstances from which he is writing?

13. At the end of Galatians, Paul writes, "Finally, let no-one cause me trouble..." What reason does Paul give?

14. At the end of 2 Corinthians, Paul's "finally" gives four brief commands. Name one of the four.

15. What epistle begins first by telling Christians to "Consider it pure joy, my brothers, whenever you face trials of many kinds"?

Quiz #15

FROM FIRST TO LAST

1. According to Paul's letter to the Romans, who was then living in Rome, but had been the first convert to Christ in the whole of Asia?

2. What epistle begins its first chapter by praising God for the comfort that he gives Christians in trouble so that they can comfort others who are in need?

3. In what Pauline epistle does the first chapter include a criticism of his readers' divided church?

4. Supply the missing word from the beginning of John's Gospel: "In the beginning was the ___"

5. About whom was Jesus speaking when he said, "If I want him to remain alive until I return, what is that to you?"?

6. True or false? When someone asked Jesus if he could wait until his father had died before becoming a follower, Jesus agreed.

7. Who does Matthew place first in his list of the twelve apostles?

8. True or false? In the Parable of the Vineyard, the workers who came first and worked all day received the same wages as the workers who came at the eleventh hour.

9. When, in Matthew's Gospel, the Pharisees said, "This last deception will be worse than the first," to what were they referring?

10. The census referred to by Luke, was the first census to take place during whose governorship of Syria?

11. What should a farmer first consider before building a watchtower?

12. During the wedding at Cana, why was the master of the banquet surprised?

13. When writing to the Corinthian Christians about the Lord's Supper, Paul said that their meetings did more harm than good. What was his first specific criticism?

14. What was the name of the first person in Timothy's family to have a sincere faith?

15. In his instructions about the Lord's Supper in 1 Corinthians, what does Paul say Christians must do first, before eating the bread and drinking the wine?

Answers

1. Epenetus 2. 2 Corinthians 3. 1 Corinthians 4. Word 5. John, the disciple whom Jesus loved 6. False. Jesus said, "Follow me, and let the dead bury their own dead" 7. Simon (Peter) 8. True (Matthew 20:9-10) 9. They said the disciples might steal Jesus' body and tell people he was alive 10. Quirinius 11. The cost 12. Because the best wine had been served last instead of first 13. When they met together, there were divisions among them 14. His grandmother Lois 15. Examine themselves to make sure they are not taking part in an unworthy manner

Quiz # 16

FROM FIRST TO LAST

1. At the beginning of the book of Judges, which tribe was chosen by God to be the first to fight the Canaanites?

2. In the prophet Elijah's first recorded words, what does he prophecy?

3. True or false? At the Transfiguration, Elijah and Moses spoke to Jesus about his death.

4. Name two of the three things that Nehemiah did when he first heard about Jerusalem's broken-down walls.

5. Of Job's three friends, who was the first to jump in and counsel him?

6. How long did the three friends sit with Job in silence, before they tried talking to him?

7. True or false? In the last chapter of the book of Job, Job is blessed more than before his calamities.

8. True or false? In his opening sentence, the prophet Nahum states that he is writing about Jerusalem.

9. The last verse of the book of Leviticus indicates where Moses received all of the commands within Leviticus: what was that place?

10. The last verse of Exodus states that in all their travels, God's presence was with the people, indicated by a cloud during the day, and by what at night?

11. The last verse of Ruth tells us that she was the great grandmother of which king?

12. According to the traditional understanding of Paul's authorship, and in the order they are given in the Bible, what is the last of Paul's epistles?

13. 2 Timothy may have been the last letter Paul wrote before his execution. Supply two of the three missing words from his summary of his Christian ministry: "I have fought the good ____, I have finished the ____, I have kept the ____."

14. In the Gospel accounts of the Last Supper, name the only Gospel that does not record Jesus' words about his body and blood?

15. What is the name given to the last meal that the people of Israel ate before they left the land of Egypt?

---

14. The Gospel of John **15.** The Passover meal

9. Mount Sinai **10.** Fire **11.** David **12.** Philemon **13.** fight, race, faith

5. Eliphaz **6.** 7 days and 7 nights **7.** True (Job 42:12) **8.** False. It was Nineveh. (Nahum 1:1)

1. Judah **2.** A drought **3.** True (Luke 9:30) **4.** Mourned (wept), fasted and prayed

Answers

Quiz #17
FROM FIRST TO LAST

1. True or false? The book of Job is in the Wisdom Literature section of the Old Testament.

2. In the last words of his first letter, what does John tell people to keep themselves from?

3. Supply the missing word from Jesus' words to his disciples in Matthew's Gospel, "He who stands firm to the ___ will be saved."

4. According to the Preacher who wrote Ecclesiastes, what do you have to do in the days of your youth?

5. In the Preacher's description of old age, name one of the two sounds that grow faint, marking the onset of deafness?

6. In Isaiah's commission to be a prophet, when he had a vision of God in glory, what were God's first words to him?

7. What was Isaiah's response to God's first words in the vision?

8. Complete this promise from Isaiah: "The grass withers and the flowers fade but the word of our God..."

9. In Paul's letter to the Galatians, what does he say led to his first preaching the gospel to them?

10. True or false? The writer to the Hebrews says that the first covenant has been made obsolete by the coming of Christ.

11. In his third letter, who does John condemn on the grounds that he loves to be first?

12. What are the last words of Jesus in the Bible?

13. True or false? In Matthew's Gospel, the first person Jesus speaks to is a soldier.

14. What are the first words of Jesus in John's Gospel?

15. After Andrew met Jesus, what was the first thing he did?

Facts 1
FROM FIRST TO LAST

The first five books of the Bible are known as the Pentateuch, a Greek term meaning "five volumes or books."

The Jews call the first five books "the Book of the Law," or "the Torah." Torah is a Hebrew word meaning *"law"*, but one which conveys the idea of life-giving instructions rather than restrictive legislation.

Moses has traditionally been regarded as the author of the Pentateuch. His education as a prince of Egypt would have made him well fitted for this task (Exodus 24:4; Number 33:1-2; Deuteronomy 31:9).

The longest chapter in the Bible is Psalm 119, with 176 verses.

The shortest verse in the Bible is merely two words in length. "Jesus wept." (KJV)

The longest verse in the Bible is Esther 8:9, which has 90 words in the King James Version.

The Bible was originally written in three languages. The Old Testament was written in Hebrew and Aramaic, the New Testament in Greek.

Old Testament passages which were written in Aramaic include Ezra 4:8-6:18; 7:12-26; Jeremiah 10:11; Daniel 2:4-7:28.

Aramaic was the language in which trade was conducted in the Ancient East, and during the Assyrian era it was the language of diplomacy. Before the exile, only Jewish officials knew Aramaic (2 Kings 18:26-28).

After the exile, the Jews who returned to Jerusalem spoke Aramaic. When the Levites read out the Scriptures, they had to translate them into Aramaic (Nehemiah 8:8).

The word "Bible" is the equivalent of the Greek word *biblia* which means books.

Facts 2

FROM FIRST TO LAST

At the end of the fourth century, and the very beginning of the fifth century, the Roman scholar, Jerome, translated the Bible into Latin. This was the Church's official Bible in the Middle Ages.

After the Reformation, there was a desire to translate the Bible into the ordinary language of the people. Translators also wished to go back to the original languages rather than rely on Jerome's Latin translation.

One reason for the fresh interest in ancient Greek came after the Turkish conquest of Constantinople in 1453 which caused many fine Greek scholars to flee the city and travel to the west.

One of the first English translations of parts of the Bible was by the Venerable Bede who, in the seventh century, translated John's Gospel into Anglo Saxon.

The first person to translate the Bible from Latin into English was John Wycliffe (1330-1384). Wycliffe was Master of Balliol College, Oxford, and he produced his translation with the help of some of his pupils.

William Tyndale (1494-1536) was the first person to translate the New Testament into English from its original languages. In 1534 he also produced the first printed New Testament in English.

In the time of Tyndale, English law forbade the translation of the Bible into English. While in hiding on the continent, Tyndale was captured and executed.

It is said that Tyndale's last words were: "Lord, open the King of England's eyes."

The first Bible to be circulated in England with official approval, was Coverdale's Bible, published in 1535. This was the first complete, printed English Bible.

Coverdale was not himself a scholar, but was a friend of Tyndale. His New Testament and Pentateuch translations were based on those of Tyndale.

The first Bible to be produced by a committee was the Authorized Bible, published in 1611. Estimates state nine-tenths of the New Testament reproduces Tyndale's translation.

Facts 3

FROM FIRST TO LAST

The first Roman Catholic New Testament was published in 1582, and the Old Testament in 1609 and 1610.

The first Roman Catholic Bible is called the Douai Bible, because it was prepared by Roman Catholic scholars in exile in Douai and Rheims.

The main work of translation for the Douai Bible was done by an Oxford theologian, Gregory Martin. From 1749, and 1772, this Bible was carefully revised by Bishop Richard Challoner.

Seven is a significant number for beginnings. The creation occurs in seven days (including the day of rest). Seven lambs confirm an oath (Genesis 21:29-30). Seven days elapse before a newborn male is circumcised.

The oldest known fragment of an actual gospel, rather than a quote from a Gospel, that has been discovered is a portion of John's Gospel (18:21-33, 37-38). It dates from the first half of the second century.

The first letter that Paul wrote is generally believed to be his letter to the Galatians, though some scholars think that 1 Thessalonians came first. These letters probably predate the Gospels.

The first psalm of the book of Psalms is a wisdom psalm. As a wisdom psalm, it teaches the right and wrong way in which a child of God should go.

The last psalm of the book of Psalms is one of many psalms of praise. It presents attributes of God that ought to be praised and then elicits a response from listeners.

In ancient literary practice it was customary for the first few verses of a letter to include the author's name. This style is followed by the letters in the New Testament, with the exception of the letter to the Hebrews.

The first divine act of the Bible, the Creation, is placed first in many Christian creeds. The Apostles' Creed begins: "I believe in God the Father Almighty, Maker of heaven and earth."

It is commonly recognized that Jesus spoke Aramaic. Now and then an Aramaic phrase is recorded in the New Testament. Jesus' words in Mark 5:41, "Talitha koum," are Aramaic and mean, "Little girl, get up."

Facts 4

FROM FIRST TO LAST

The two books of Chronicles portray a panorama of biblical history until the exile. The book begins with Adam and ends with the proclamation of King Cyrus of Persia.

Chronicles covers much of the same ground as Samuel and Kings, but from a different perspective. The Chronicler's purpose was to encourage the tiny group of exiles in Babylon by recounting God's work and purpose for them.

In Hebrew Bibles the books of 1 and 2 Chronicles are one book. The division was made when the Old Testament was translated into Greek in the second-century B.C.

Ezra-Nehemiah (originally one book) continues the record of Chronicles, covering the next hundred years.

It is generally believed that Chronicles and Ezra-Nehemiah was written by, or edited by, Ezra, and finished by about 440 B.C.

The longest prophetic book in the Old Testament is the book of Jeremiah. It has fewer chapters but more verses than Isaiah.

There are 929 chapters in the Old Testament.

There are 260 chapters in the New Testament.

Luke contributed the greatest amount of writing in the New Testament. He wrote the gospel of Luke and the Acts of the Apostles.

The apostle Paul wrote the largest number of books in the New Testament.

Traditionally, Paul is regarded as the writer of the letters; Romans, 1 and 2 Corinthians, Galatians, Ephesians, Philippians, Colossians, 1 and 2 Thessalonians, 1 and 2 Timothy, Titus and Philemon.

Facts 5
FROM FIRST TO LAST

The book of Job may have been written in its present form during the time of Solomon, or during the Exile. The events it describes, however, predate Abraham.

"Babel" is an early name for Babylon. It is likely that Babylon was the oldest city in the world. Isaiah's prophecy about the fall of Babylon came true (Isaiah 13:19-20).

Jewish scholars living in Alexandria, Egypt, in the second century B.C. translated the Hebrew Old Testament into Greek. This version is called the Septuagint (literally "70"), after the seventy scholars who reputedly did this work.

The "Septuagint" is often abbreviated to "LXX", which is the form which appears in the footnotes of contemporary Bibles.

When a New Testament writer quoted an Old Testament verse, he sometimes used the "Septuagint" translation. This explains the difference in wording from that of the Hebrew Old Testament, upon which modern translations are based.

The word "Apocrypha" is applied by Protestants to the 14 books that were in the Septuagint but were not in the Hebrew Bible. The books are given the name "deuterocanonical" by Roman Catholics.

The apocryphal books were written between the Old Testament and New Testament eras. They include: Sirach, Baruch, the book of Wisdom, first, second, third and fourth Maccabees.

There are a total of 66 books in the Bible: 27 in the New Testament and 39 in the Old Testament.

Only one book of the Bible, the book of Acts, is written as an historical account of the life of the early church following Jesus' resurrection.

The first three Gospels are called the Synoptic Gospels. "Synoptic" is from the Greek word "synopsis" (*syn*: with, and *opsis*: a view). This title has been given because these three Gospels have much material in common.

Facts 6

FROM FIRST TO LAST

Many explanations have been given for the repetition of material in the Synoptic Gospels. One is that there was a written or spoken collection of the sayings of Jesus which the Gospel writers used.

By looking at the material which is unique to each Gospel, it is possible to get an idea of the personal aims of the Gospel writers.

The Gospel of John is different from the other three gospels in that it is less of a narrative, but gives more emphasis to the identity of Jesus and his teachings.

Paul's letters, 1 and 2 Timothy, and Titus are called the Pastoral Epistles. This name, first given in the eighteenth century, is an apt description because the letters are concerned with helping and training two young Christian leaders.

The writers of the final three books of the Old Testament, Haggai, Zechariah, and Malachi, are known as the post-exilic prophets. They wrote after the Israelites returned from captivity in Babylon.

The division of the Bible into chapters occurred in the thirteenth century A.D. Some ascribe this division to Cardinal Hugo de St Caro. Others credit Stephen Langton, archbishop of Canterbury.

When the first eyewitnesses began to die, Christians felt the need for written accounts of Jesus' words and works (Luke 1:1).

The Roman Christian, Papias, wrote in 140 A.D. that about thirty years after the death of Christ, Mark began to record the words and sermons of Peter. Papias calls Mark "the interpreter of Peter."

Copies of Paul's letters were circulated among the churches and towards the end of the first century some churches began to form a collection of his letters.

By studying the writings of early Christians, it is possible to work out which New Testament books they knew. For example, in 95 A.D., Clement, writing from Rome, quoted from 1 Corinthians.

By the end of the first century some churches had already collected together ten of Paul's letters. The church at Rome also had a copy of the letter to the Hebrews.

Facts 7

FROM FIRST TO LAST

There is strong evidence that by the early years of the second century the four Gospels had been grouped together and were well known as one corpus.

In the British Museum there are some papyrus fragments dating from the first half of the second century. These fragments appear to be from a Christian manual, the writer of which is very familiar with all four Gospels.

By the middle of the second century heretical teachings and pseudo-Christian writings forced the leaders of the church to draw up a list of authentic "books of the New Covenant."

The word "canon" comes from the Greek *kanon*, and means a builder's rule or level. It came to be applied to writings regarded as holy Scripture.

Some writings were at once accepted as part of the canon. About some there was debate. The most important criteria was that the book was genuinely by an apostle, or by a close associate of an apostle?

In 1740 an Italian scholar, L. A. Muratori, published a Latin list of New Testament books which he had found in Rome. This list is often referred to as "The Muratorian Fragment or Canon" which dates from 190 A.D.

The Muratorian Fragment probably represents the Roman canon at the end of the second century: four Gospels, Acts, 13 Pauline epistles, 2 epistles of John and Revelation.

Books about which there was some doubt were: James, Jude, 2 Peter, 2 and 3 John, Revelation and Hebrews. It was after a great deal of prayer and deliberation that the Canon was finally established.

The first official church-wide statements of a canon was made in the eastern church in 367 (in the pastoral letter of Athanasius) and in the west at the Council of Carthage in 397. These edicts confirmed the existing practice of all the churches.

Travel Itineraries

Quiz # 1
TRAVEL ITINERARIES

1. Who planned to travel to Tarshish?

2. When Cain left Eden, where did he go?

3. Who was taken as a prisoner to the island of Patmos?

4. Who traveled to Dothan in search of his brothers?

5. True or false? Jesus was once caught in a storm on the Red Sea.

6. How many years did it take the Israelites to travel from Kadesh Barnea to the Zered Valley?

7. True or false? Moses crossed the Jordan into Canaan.

8. Following Paul's conversion, did he go to Jerusalem or Arabia first?

9. Fill in the gap from the testimony of Ezekiel: "The Spirit lifted me up between earth and heaven and in visions of God he took me to ___."

10. True or false? God promised that the Israelites would travel to a land rich in gold and jewels.

11. Which city did Joshua and the people travel around once for six days and seven times on the seventh day?

12. When Demas deserted Paul, where did he go?

13. Whose army marched to Jerusalem in the reign of King Jehoiachin?

14. Who went with Naomi from Moab to Bethlehem?

15. In which town did Samson fall in love with a young Philistine woman?

Answers

1. Jonah 2. To the land of Nod 3. John 4. Joseph 5. False. It was the Sea of Galilee (Mark 4:35-41) 6. 38 years 7. False. It was Joshua (Joshua 3:1) 8. Arabia 9. Jerusalem 10. False. They were to go to a land flowing with milk and honey! (Exodus 3:8) 11. Jericho 12. Thessalonica 13. Nebuchadnezzar 14. Ruth 15. At Timnah

Quiz #2

TRAVEL ITINERARIES

1. Which town, less than two miles from Jerusalem, did Jesus travel to in order to visit the bereaved sisters Mary and Martha?

2. Put the following towns in the order in which Paul visited them during the course of his travels: Rome, Berea, Athens.

3. Name two of the people who traveled to the great tree of Moreh before pitching their tents on the hills east of Bethel.

4. In what book of the Bible is King Solomon described as "coming up from the desert like a column of smoke"?

5. According to Proverbs, whose "house leads down to death and her paths to the spirits of the dead"?

6. In John's vision of the woman and the dragon, where did the woman flee for 1,260 days—the mountains, the city or the desert?

7. From where did David set out when he was told by his father to visit his brothers?

8. According to Isaiah, whose fugitives "flee as far as Zoar, as far as Eglath Shelishiyah"?

9. Where was Moses told to go so he could view the land of Canaan?

10. Outside which town did Jesus bring back to life the only son of a widow?

11. To whom did Paul write, "I will go to Spain and visit you on the way"?

12. Fill in the missing word in this verse from Jeremiah: "Go up and down the streets of ____, look around and consider, search through her squares."

13. According to the book of Samuel, who went up every year from Ramathaim to Shiloh to worship God? (1 Samuel 1:1-3)

14. Where did the Babylonian army take Zedekiah after capturing him on the plains of Jericho?

15. When did David move to Hebron?

Answers

1. Bethany 2. Berea, Athens, Rome 3. Abram, Sarai, Lot and their servants 4. Song of Songs 5. The adulteress 6. The desert 7. Bethlehem 8. The fugitives of Moab 9. To Mount Nebo 10. Nain 11. The church at Rome 12. Jerusalem 13. Elkanah and his family 14. To Riblah, the Babylonian headquarters in Syro-Palestine 15. After the death of Saul

Quiz #3

TRAVEL ITINERARIES

1. From which direction did the wise men come?

2. Who welcomed three visitors when his tents were pitched near the great trees of Mamre?

3. How long did Paul stay in Corinth when he founded the church there?

4. True or false? In Jesus' parable about a mugging, the man was traveling up from Jericho to Jerusalem.

5. After Jesus walked on the water, where did the boat come ashore?

6. In what direction did Mary and Joseph go when they fled from Herod with the child Jesus?

7. When the Hebrew slaves left Egypt, what shorter route did God forbid them to take because it was more dangerous?

8. Who did the writer of Ephesians promise to send to Ephesus?

9. Name three places in mainland Italy that we know Paul visited.

10. When Paul set out from Macedonia, which was the only church to support him by sending aid?

11. Who, according to Isaiah, will travel on the Way of Holiness?

12. To which city did David eventually take Goliath's head?

13. According to Chronicles, people as far away as Issachar, Zebulun and Naphtali brought food to the celebrations at Hebron. Name two of the four beasts of burden mentioned.

14. What did Solomon's men bring him when they sailed back from Ophir?

15. Where were Joshua and the tribes when Joshua sent out two spies to Jericho?

Answers

1. The East 2. Abraham 3. 18 months
4. False. He was traveling down from Jerusalem to Jericho (Luke 10:30) 5. Gennesaret 6. South-west
7. The road through Philistine country 8. Tychicus 9. Rhegium, Puteoli, Rome, Forum of Appius, Three Taverns
10. The church at Philippi 11. The redeemed 12. Jerusalem 13. Donkeys, camels, mules and oxen
14. 420 talents of gold 15. Shittim, the last camp site before crossing over the Jordan into Canaan

Quiz #4
TRAVEL ITINERARIES

1. In his first letter to the Corinthians, Paul wrote that he intended to stay in what city until Pentecost?

2. Who accompanied Jesus on his final journey to Golgotha, carrying Jesus' cross?

3. After David took a census, plague swept through the land, but God stopped it when it reached what town?

4. At which port on the island of Sicily did the ship on which Paul was sailing put in for three days?

5. From where to where did Mary and Joseph have to travel to record their names in the census?

6. True or false? Philip was among Paul's companions when Paul traveled to Cyprus.

7. The judge Gideon led a surprise attack against Midianite raiders who came from what direction against the Israelites?

8. In what sea was Paul shipwrecked?

9. True or false? Jesus went by boat to the region of Dalmanutha.

10. Who was brought from the house of Makir in Lo Debar to live with David at Jerusalem?

11. Who traveled from Rome with Tychicus to Colosse?

12. According to the book of Ruth, which two brothers left their homes in Bethlehem for Moab but never returned?

13. Why did these two brothers go with their parents to Moab?

14. Where did Absalom flee after killing Amnon, David's son?

15. When Paul was transferred to Caesarea from Jerusalem how many armed men protected him?

Answers

1. Ephesus 2. Simon of Cyrene 3. Jerusalem 4. Syracuse 5. From Nazareth to Bethlehem
6. False. Philip never made a journey with Paul 7. The East 8. The Mediterranean Sea
9. True (Mark 8:10) 10. Mephibosheth, the crippled son of Jonathan 11. Onesimus
12. Mahlon and Kilion, sons of Elimelech and Naomi 13. Because of a famine 14. To Geshur
15. 470 (200 soldiers, 70 horsemen, 200 spearmen)

Quiz #5

TRAVEL ITINERARIES

1. Who were instructed by David to stay in Jericho until their beards had grown back before returning to Jerusalem?

2. After Lazarus died, who went out to meet Jesus as he came to Bethany?

3. Paul's ship sailed with difficulty in the more sheltered waters off the eastern and southern coasts of Crete, before docking at what anchorage near Lasae?

4. The Roman centurion rejected Paul's advice that they should winter near Lasae, and determined to sail on toward what port further along the coast?

5. "After I go through Macedonia, I will come to you." Did Paul write this to Christians at Rome, Thessalonica, or Corinth?

6. Where did the Philistines take Samson when they captured him?

7. How many traveling companions did Paul have aboard the ship that was shipwrecked?

8. After the shipwreck, how many people, besides Paul, survived?

9. True or false? The Lord told Ezekiel that the leaders of Israel would face judgment because they were like shepherds and his people were like sheep wandering around without direction.

10. Which city were Jesus and the disciples leaving when they met Bartimaeus?

11. When Ezra and his company set out on the hazardous journey back from Babylon to Jerusalem, why, according to Ezra, did he not ask the king to provide soldiers and horsemen to protect them?

12. In which direction did Jonah choose to go when he was told by God to go north-east to Nineveh?

13. Who took her young son to Shiloh but returned without him?

14. Who, according to Ecclesiastes, only has to walk along a road to show everyone how stupid he is?

15. For how many years did the Israelites wander in the desert after the exodus from Egypt?

Answers

1. David's men who each had half his beard and half his clothes cut off by the Ammonites
2. Martha 3. Fair Havens 4. Phoenix 5. Corinth 6. To Gaza 7. 275 8. 275: none were lost
9. True (Ezekiel 34:7-10) 10. Jericho 11. Because Ezra had told the king that God protects everyone who trusts him
12. He sailed east to Tarshish 13. Hannah 14. A fool 15. 40 years

Quiz #6
TRAVEL ITINERARIES

1. To which city did Peter come only to find himself in open conflict with Paul?

2. Who fled to Seirah after he killed Eglon, King of Moab, with a double-edged sword?

3. On his third missionary journey, in what order did Paul visit Rhodes, Patara and Cos?

4. "Have you journeyed to the springs of the sea or walked in the recesses of the deep?" Who put this question to Job?

5. Who told the prophet Amos, "Go back to the land of Judah... Don't prophesy any more at Bethel"?

6. Which young man was sent by Paul to Thessalonica to encourage the church?

7. Why did Moses flee from Egypt to Midian?

8. Where did Ezra assemble the family heads and camp for three days before returning to Jerusalem?

9. Off which island was Paul shipwrecked?

10. Where was Jacob going when he had the dream about the ladder reaching up to heaven?

11. Did Paul tell Timothy that Crescens or Luke had left him to go to Galatia?

12. Fill in the missing word from Isaiah's prophecy about the restoration of Egypt: "In that day there will be a ____ from Egypt to Assyria."

13. Who escaped from Gath and hid in the cave of Adullam?

14. Who was on the road to Damascus when he was converted?

15. Mary, Joseph and baby Jesus traveled to which city, where they met the devout and holy man Simeon?

---

13. David **14.** Saul **15.** Jerusalem

9. The island of Malta (Melita) **10.** On his way to Haran **11.** Crescens **12.** highway

6. Timothy **7.** Because news that he had killed an Egyptian began to spread **8.** Ahava Canal

1. Antioch **2.** Ehud **3.** Cos, Rhodes, Patara **4.** God **5.** Amaziah, the priest of Bethel

Answers

Quiz #7

TRAVEL ITINERARIES

1. From which port in Mysia did Paul sail to Macedonia?

2. Why did Joseph's brothers first travel down to Egypt?

3. Did Joab send for a wise woman from Tekoa or from Baal Hazor and ask her to take a message to David?

4. Where did God send the disobedient people after Babel?

5. "They will enter Zion with singing; everlasting joy will crown their heads." Who will enter Zion?

6. Which disciple traveled from Azotus to Caesarea preaching in all the towns?

7. Who did David send out with his army to besiege Rabbah while he stayed in Jerusalem?

8. Who left Philippi to care for Paul but was sent back there after he himself had been very ill?

9. About how far was Emmaus from Jerusalem?

10. True or false? Feeling tired from the journey, Jesus sat down by a well outside the town of Sychar.

11. Sychar was in what district in central Palestine?

12. From which port did Jonah sail when he boarded a ship to flee from the Lord?

13. What did the Philistines take from Ebenezer to Dagon's temple in Ashdod?

14. When Joseph sent his brothers back to Canaan to fetch Jacob, what instruction did he give them?

15. Who sent the Magi to Bethlehem?

Quiz #8
TRAVEL ITINERARIES

1. Where was Paul when John Mark left him to return to Jerusalem?

2. True or false? Paul's intended destination was Corinth when he was shipwrecked.

3. To whom did God say, "Leave here, turn eastward and hide in the Kerith Ravine, east of the Jordan"?

4. True or false? Jesus visited Cana in Galilee to attend a wedding reception.

5. When Paul was surrounded by difficulties in Macedonia, who came to him with good news from Corinth?

6. When Jesus met Zacchaeus, he was passing through which town on his way to Jerusalem?

7. Who was instructed to go to Perath and hide his linen belt in the rocks there?

8. Which two men were sent with Paul and Barnabas to Antioch by the Council of Jerusalem?

9. Philip was on the road to which town when he met the Ethiopian eunuch?

10. In which town were Paul and Barnabas when they met the Jewish sorcerer, Elymas?

11. Where did Moses meet Zipporah who became his wife?

12. Which two towns on Cyprus does Luke say Paul visited?

13. Fill in the missing words: "You will receive power when the Holy Spirit comes on you; and you will be my witnesses in ___, and in all ___ and ___, and to the ends of the earth."

14. Where did Samuel take the people to confirm Saul as king?

15. Name two of the areas from where, according to Matthew, those baptized by John the Baptist came.

Quiz #9

TRAVEL ITINERARIES

1. What sea did Barnabas and Mark cross in order to reach Cyprus?

2. After leaving Nob, when he was fleeing from Saul, in what order did David visit Mizpah, the Cave of Adullam and Gath?

3. True or false? Jesus performed healings in the region of the Decapolis.

4. Did Boaz accompany Ruth on frequent journeys to Jerusalem?

5. According to Ezra, did the Jews who left Babylon to return to Jerusalem number fewer or more than 42,000?

6. True or false? Paul was taken under guard to Caesarea by night.

7. A detachment of how many soldiers and spearmen protected Paul on the 30-mile journey to Antipatris?

8. Seventy horsemen took Paul on the final stage of the journey from Antipatris to where?

9. On his second missionary journey, where did Paul go when he left Thessalonica?

10. Who did the Lord tell to meet Ahaz at the end of the aqueduct of the Upper Pool, on the road to the Washerman's Field?

11. Who was the prophet Isaiah told to take with him to meet Ahaz?

12. Complete this message which the prophet Isaiah was told to give Ahaz: "Be careful, keep calm and..."

13. Where did Noah's Ark finish its journey?

14. From which port did Paul (and Barnabas) set sail when they started the first missionary journey?

15. What journey had David just finished when Michal saw him leaping and dancing?

Answers

1. The Mediterranean Sea **2.** Gath, the Cave of Adullam, Mizpah **3.** True (Mark 7:31-37)
4. No, there are no records of any such journeys **5.** More: there were 42,360 **6.** True (Acts 23:23)
7. 400: 200 soldiers and 200 horsemen **8.** Caesarea **9.** To Berea and then to Athens **10.** Isaiah
11. His son, Shear-Jashub **12.** don't be afraid **13.** On the mountains of Ararat **14.** Seleucia
15. He was accompanying the Ark of God from the house of Obed Edom to Jerusalem

Quiz # 10
TRAVEL ITINERARIES

1. When Abraham and his family left Ur, what city did they travel to?

2. Was it Haman himself or the king's couriers who went to all the provinces to distribute the edict concerning the annihilation of the Jews?

3. Which animal in Daniel's vision charged towards the west and the north and the south?

4. Were Paul and Barnabas in Lystra, Iconium, or Antioch when they were called Hermes and Zeus?

5. How many men did Moses send out from the Desert of Paran to explore the land of Canaan?

6. Why did Saul go to the Crags of the Wild Goats in the Desert of En Gedi?

7. What was by the sheep pens in the Desert of En Gedi?

8. Which king of Persia allowed God's people to leave Babylon and go up to Jerusalem to rebuild the temple?

9. From where was Jesus traveling when he saw the fruitless fig tree?

10. Where was Jesus going when he saw the fruitless fig tree?

11. After passing through Amphipolis and Apollonia Paul came to a town in which he established a Christian church. Which town?

12. From what country did King Ahab's wife Jezebel come?

13. Name two of the three women who, according to Mark, followed Jesus from Galilee to care for him.

14. Did Jesus' mother make a three-month visit to Elizabeth in a town near the Sea of Galilee or a town in the hill country of Judea?

15. Where, according to Matthew, did Jesus tell his eleven disciples to meet him after the resurrection?

Answers

1. Haran 2. The king's couriers 3. The ram 4. Lystra 5. 12 men 6. To look for David
7. A cave 8. Cyrus 9. Bethany 10. Jerusalem 11. Thessalonica 12. Sidon
13. Mary Magdelene, Mary the mother of James and Joses, and Salome
14. A town in the hill country of Judea 15. Galilee

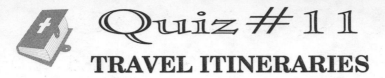

Quiz # 11

TRAVEL ITINERARIES

1. Why did the people of Jabesh Gilead journey through the night to Beth Shan?

2. Fill in the missing word: "David continued up the Mount of ____ weeping as he went; his head was covered and he was barefoot."

3. Which people refused the Israelites entry into their territory when they were at Kadesh?

4. According to Nehemiah 12, who left the villages around Jerusalem to come to the city for the dedication of its new walls: the women and children, the singers, the carpenters or the old men?

5. In the Sermon on the Mount, what road was described as broad with a wide gate?

6. True or false? Ezekiel was told to go to the Valley of Ben Hinnom with the elders and priests.

7. Why did Jesus go up to Jerusalem on the occasion when he healed the man at the pool of Bethesda?

8. True or false? John the Baptist went to the River Jordan to baptize people.

9. Where did Amaziah flee when a conspiracy against him emerged in Jerusalem?

10. When the crowd stoned Paul and Barnabas at Lystra, what did they do with the two bodies?

11. Where did Jesus send the man who was born blind?

12. When Joseph set out in his chariot to meet his father coming up from Canaan, in what region did the meeting take place?

13. On Paul's first missionary journey, which island did he visit?

14. To which city had Peter traveled when he met Tabitha (Dorcas)?

15. When did David travel to Horesh?

---

1. To take down the bodies of Saul and his sons from the wall at Beth Shan **2.** Olives **3.** The Edomites **4.** The singers (from the villages of the Netophathites, Beth Gilgal, Geba and Azmaveth) **5.** The road that leads to destruction **6.** False. Jeremiah received this instruction from the Lord (Jeremiah 19:1-12) **7.** For a Jewish feast **8.** True (Matthew 3:6) **9.** To Lachish **10.** They dragged their bodies outside the city and left them **11.** To the Pool of Siloam **12.** In the region of Goshen **13.** Cyprus **14.** Joppa **15.** When he was hiding from Saul

Answers

Quiz # 12

TRAVEL ITINERARIES

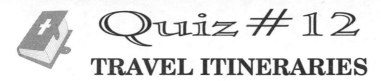

1. The prophet Elijah came from which city in Gilead?

2. On Paul's last missionary journey, why did he decide to sail past Ephesus?

3. Was the town which Elisha often visited Seir, Shunem or Sychar?

4. What animal accompanied Balaam on his early morning journey with the princes of Moab?

5. When Joshua was in Jericho, to what town did he send spies?

6. To which city did Elisha travel to see a sick king?

7. True or false? Nehemiah went to meet Sanballat and Geshem in the villages on the plain of Ono.

8. According to Luke, as Jesus approached Jerusalem for the last time, he came to two villages, at the Mount of Olives, and there he sent his disciples for the colt. One village was Bethany, what was the other village?

9. What town was Elijah's base, when he wasn't doing his circuit as a judge?

10. Who climbed to the top of Mount Gerizim to deliver a message to the citizens of Shechem about an olive tree, a fig tree, a vine and a thorn-bush?

11. True or false? As Paul was throwing wood on to a fire on the island of Malta, a tarantula fastened itself onto his hand.

12. Why did the islanders think Paul must be a god?

13. Which prophet wrote: "See, the Lord rides on a swift cloud and is coming to Egypt"?

14. When David was on the run from Saul, he moved down to the Desert of Maon, and from there he sent messengers to which very wealthy man who was shearing sheep?

15. Where was Jesus when Nicodemus came to see him secretly at night?

Quiz #13

TRAVEL ITINERARIES

1. Who came to visit Joshua at the camp in Gilgal falsely claiming that they had traveled a long way?

2. On Paul's third journey, when he was at Ephesus, he sent Erastus on ahead of him to Macedonia. Which of Paul's friends went with Erastus?

3. Which mighty warrior was driven away from his home in Gilead by his half-brothers because they would not share their inheritance with him?

4. When the Hebrew slaves left Egypt, what Egyptian town did they set out from?

5. Which mother-in-law arrived in Bethlehem with her daughter-in-law at harvest time?

6. Where were Joshua and his army when the Gibeonites sent messengers asking him to protect them from the armies of the five kings?

7. True or false? When Joshua received the message from the men of Gibeon, he said, "You fight your own battles, and we will fight the Lord's battles."

8. Who went out at night through the Valley Gate towards the Jackal Well and Dung Gate to examine the walls of Jerusalem?

9. True or false? Jesus always traveled on foot.

10. On which two of his missionary journeys did Paul visit Corinth?

11. According to the book of Revelation, where will Satan go after the thousand-year reign of Christ on earth?

12. Which country, condemned by Isaiah, "sends envoys by sea in papyrus boats over the water"?

13. Fill the gap: "Jesus was led by the Spirit into the ____ to be tempted by devil."

14. Who was told to, "Mark out two roads for the sword of the King of Babylon to take, both starting from the same country"?

15. Whose route was guided by a star?

---

11. To the 4 corners of the earth **12.** Cush (Ethiopia) **13.** Desert **14.** Ezekiel **15.** The Magi!
9. False. He also traveled by boat and donkey **10.** Second and third
7. False. He set out at once, marching through the night (Joshua 10:9) **8.** Nehemiah
1. The people of Gibeon **2.** Timothy **3.** Jephthah **4.** Rameses **5.** Naomi **6.** At Gilgal

Answers

Quiz # 14

TRAVEL ITINERARIES

1. Who said to the Lord that he had been "roaming through the earth and going to and fro in it"?

2. Was Jeremiah instructed by the Lord to go down to a house of a carpenter, a potter or a tent-maker?

3. Did the Lord send Samuel on a journey to Socoh or Bethlehem to find Jesse and his sons?

4. According to Mark's Gospel, when Peter said, "You are the Christ," Jesus and the disciples were in the vicinity of which town?

5. In Jesus' Parable of the Good Samaritan, how many people traveled along the road?

6. After Jonathan shot his three warning arrows into the field where David was hiding, where did David go?

7. Following the first persecution of the church, the apostle Philip traveled to which city?

8. Which island was John exiled to when he wrote the book of Revelation?

9. In Paul's vision, was he invited to make a journey to Macedonia or Thessalonica?

10. From where, according to Isaiah, will people come to Zion, "Bearing gold and incense and proclaiming the praise of the Lord"?

11. When Saul searched the hill country of Ephraim and the districts of Shaalim and Zuph, what was he looking for?

12. Who traveled to Judah armed with letters for the governors of the Trans-Euphrates region asking them to ensure his safe journey?

13. Who would benefit from fleeing to a city of refuge?

14. Which Hittite did David summon to Jerusalem before sending him out to battle with Joab?

15. When Naomi went back to Bethlehem, which of her daughters-in-law stayed in Moab?

---

13. Someone who had accidentally killed a person **14.** Uriah, the husband of Bathsheba **15.** Orpah
10. From Sheba **11.** His father's lost donkeys **12.** Nehemiah
6. To Nob, to see Ahimelech, the priest **7.** Samaria **8.** Patmos **9.** Macedonia
5. 4: the priest, the Levite, the Good Samaritan and the traveler who was robbed
1. Satan **2.** To the house of a potter **3.** Bethlehem **4.** Caesarea Philippi

Answers

Quiz #15

TRAVEL ITINERARIES

1. Philip was on the road to which town when he met the Ethiopian eunuch?

2. Where did Saul go to find a medium?

3. According to Jeremiah, when Zedekiah and his soldiers fled from Jerusalem to escape from Nebuchadnezzar armies, which direction did they head?

4. As Zedekiah tried to escape, where was he caught?

5. To which city did Peter travel to meet the Roman centurion Cornelius?

6. True or false? Jesse sent David to the Valley of Elah with grain and bread for his brothers.

7. Who came down from Judah to visit Nehemiah in the citadel of Susa?

8. True or false? A queen came from Samaria to talk to Solomon.

9. Who moved from Canaan to live in Sodom?

10. Fill in the missing word from Isaiah's prophecy: "Who is this coming from ____, from Bozrah with his garments stained crimson?"

11. Where was Joseph taken by the Ishmaelite traders?

12. Fill in the missing words: "These things I remember as I pour out my soul: how I used to go with the multitude, leading the procession to ____ ____ ____ ____."

13. What journey did Moses ask Pharaoh to allow the Israelites to make?

14. Did Paul visit Cyprus on his first or second missionary journey?

15. To which city did Paul return, taking Barnabas with him, after fourteen years' absence?

Answers

1. Gaza **2.** To Endor (6 miles north-west of Shunem) **3.** Towards the Arabah **4.** In the plains of Jericho **5.** Caesarea **6.** True (1 Samuel 17:17-19) **7.** His brother, Hanani (Nehemiah 1:2) **8.** False. The queen came from Sheba (1 Kings 10:1) **9.** Lot and his family **10.** Edom **11.** To Egypt **12.** The house of God **13.** A 3 day journey into the desert to offer sacrifices **14.** Paul visited Cyprus on his first missionary journey **15.** Jerusalem.

Quiz #16
TRAVEL ITINERARIES

1. What did Ezra and the people do on first arriving in Jerusalem: feast, fast, rest or worship?

2. In the book of Esther, who travelled through the streets of Susa on a king's horse?

3. What town did Jesus enter when a centurion came asking for help?

4. True or false? The people in the region of Gadara begged Jesus to stay there and teach them.

5. Fill in the missing word from the psalms: "He led them by a straight way to a ___ where they could settle."

6. To which city had Paul traveled when he preached in the Areopagus?

7. While Apollos was at Corinth, Paul took the road through the interior, and arrived at a town whose goddess was Diana: where was this?

8. At what coastal town did Jesus heal a woman's little daughter?

9. True or false? Jesus traveled only in Palestine and Samaria.

10. Why did some Pharisees tell Jesus to leave Galilee?

11. Supply the missing word: "He leads me beside ___ waters."

12. When God told Joshua that his territory would extend to the Great Sea on the west, which sea is meant?

13. True or false? God said to Joshua: "Your territory will extend from the Great River, the Mississippi..."

14. True or false? Abram and Sarah traveled to Egypt to escape a famine, but were thrown out because they lied (something the Egyptians detested).

15. Supply the missing word: "If I settle on the far side of the sea even there your hand will ___ me."

Answers

1. Rest for 3 days **2.** Mordecai **3.** Capernaum **4.** False. They begged him to leave (Matthew 9:34)
5. city **6.** Athens **7.** Ephesus **8.** Tyre **9.** False. He went to Tyre and Sidon, and to the Decapolis region
10. Because Herod Antipas, tetrarch of Galilee, wanted to kill him **11.** quiet (still) **12.** The Mediterranean
13. False. The great Euphrates (Joshua 1:4) **14.** True (Genesis 12:19-20) **15.** guide

Facts 1

TRAVEL ITINERARIES

Nearly all the events covered by the Bible took place in a part of the world known today as "the Near East."

Luke 9:51 tells us that "Jesus resolutely set out for Jerusalem". Luke's words emphasize that Jesus was determined to see his mission through to its end, that is, to his death in Jerusalem.

The Holy Land is given a number of names in the Bible. In the time of Abraham and the exodus it was known as Canaan, and the original inhabitants were known as the Canaanites.

Canaan became known as the Promised Land, because it was the land promised to Abraham and his descendants; and also Israel, because the descendants of Israel (another name for Jacob) settled there.

When the kingdom of Israel divided into two, the northern kingdom kept the name Israel, while the southern kingdom was called Judah. David was descended from the tribe of Judah, which had chosen him as their king from the beginning.

The kingdom of Israel and its capital city Samaria were conquered by the Assyrians who resettled the population in other parts of the empire. The northern kingdom was then repopulated by foreigners, who eventually became known as Samaritans.

Judah was all that was left of the original Israel. After the conquest by Babylon, the people of Judah were deported to Babylon, but were later allowed to return to Jerusalem. Judea was the name of this small district within the Persian Empire.

In 135 A.D., the Romans renamed the country Palestine, taking the name from the Philistines, who lived along the coast, and with whom the Romans were familiar. To them, the whole country was Philistine country!

When the Israelites first came to Canaan it was a cosmopolitan center of international trade, with strong fortified cities. The hill country, however, was relatively unpopulated.

The land of Moab, Ruth's home, was a strip of arable land in the Transjordan, lying between the Dead Sea and the desert, with the Arnon River to the north and the Zered River to the south.

Following successive conquests by many empires, from the Babylonian Empire to the Roman Empire, many Jews were "dispersed" to other lands. These Jews, known as Diasapora Jews, attempted to maintain their heritage in these foreign lands.

Facts 2

TRAVEL ITINERARIES

The Mount of Olives is a limestone ridge a little over a mile in length, running approximately north to south, just east of Jerusalem. It provides a beautiful panoramic view of the city.

Paul was largely responsible for the spread of Christianity to non-Jews. He came from Tarsus, a cosmopolitan center of trade. He was justly proud of being a Roman citizen.

Most of the events mentioned in the Old Testament are located between Dan in the north, and Beersheba in the south, and between the coast of the Mediterranean Sea in the west and the high plateau beyond the Jordan in the east.

Midway along the western shore of the Dead Sea and 35 miles south-east of Jerusalem are the hot water springs of En Gedi, ensuring rich vegetation all year round. En Gedi means "spring" or "fountain".

The word "Bethlehem" comes from the Hebrew words *beth* meaning "house", and *lehem*, meaning "bread."

Bethlehem is about six miles southwest of Jerusalem, on the edge of the desert of Judah. It is on a rocky spur of the mountains, just off the road to Hebron and Egypt.

The traditional site of Jesus' baptism is in the wide river valley of the lower Jordan River, about five miles to the east of Jericho.

A Sabbath day's journey (Acts 1:12) was about three quarters of a mile (2,000 paces). Jews who kept the Old Testament regulations carefully would not travel further than this on the Sabbath.

Some Jews, wanting to get round the Sabbath travel regulations, would send a servant the day before with possessions to be left along the route, perhaps at a friends' house. The possessions marking a "home" from which the Sabbath day's journey could start again.

The sea port of Caesarea became a focal point for the spread of the gospel. Here God led Peter to preach to the Roman centurion Cornelius and his family. Paul landed at Caesarea after both his second and third missionary journeys (Acts 18:22 ; 21:8).

Caesarea, 23 miles south of Mount Carmel, had been built by Herod the Great over a period of 12 years. During New Testament times, it was the seat of Roman power and Pontius Pilate had his headquarters there.

Facts 3

TRAVEL ITINERARIES

Caesarea Philippi was in northern Palestine, on the southern slopes of Mount Hermon. It was outside Galilee, and was the capital of the province ruled over by Herod Philip.

Nineveh was on the east bank of the Tigris River, more than 500 miles away from Israel. King Sennacherib made it the capital of Assyria in about 700 B.C.

When commanded to go to Nineveh, Jonah headed for Tarshish, in the opposite direction. Tarshish was located in the south of Spain, two thousand miles away from Palestine.

Roman milestones were placed along the fine roads built by the Romans. A Roman soldier was permitted by law to force a civilian to carry his pack from one milestone to another.

At the time of Christ, large Jewish populations could be found in cities such as Rome, Alexandria, Antioch and Ephesus. Paul was a "diaspora" Jew from the city of Tarsus in Cilicia.

Romans chapter 16 bears witness to the extent to which people traveled about the Roman empire, very often for commercial reasons.

Archaeological excavations at Ur, the city from which Abraham came, show that 500 years before the time of Abraham Ur was a wealthy and important city. Intricate works of art in gold and other precious metals reveal a standard of workmanship rarely surpassed in later ages.

The citizens of Ur worshiped the moon, as did the people of Haran, 560 miles further north, where Abraham and his family settled.

After the death of Abraham's father, Abraham and his wife and nephew traveled to southern Canaan, about a further 450 miles.

The city of Philippi was located in Macedonia, in the mountains. It was named after Philip of Macedon, the father of Alexander the Great. The city was a district capital and took on the air of a Roman imperial outpost.

Facts 4
TRAVEL ITINERARIES

In the time of Jesus, the land of Palestine was only 120 miles from north to south. Galilee lay in the extreme north, and Judea was in the south. In the middle lay Samaria.

The quickest route from Judea to Galilee lay through Samaria: a three-day journey. Such was the hatred felt by Jews for Samaritans, that most Jews preferred to cross the Jordan, travel up the east of the river, and recross north of Samaria, even though this took twice as long.

In ancient times most carrying of baggage and people was done by animals: mules, horses, camels and donkeys. Horses were used by soldiers for fighting wars, and pulling war chariots, but not for everyday purposes.

In the Old Testament, kings, judges, high priests and powerful leaders rode on donkeys, which were often very fine and beautiful animals, selling for high prices.

When traveling by donkey, the man rode the donkey and the woman walked. The woman of Shunem, who saddled a donkey, was doing something very unusual: it is a mark of her status that she rode the donkey (2 Kings 4:24).

In the Old Testament there is reference to wagons and carts (Genesis 46:5, Numbers 7:6-8). There were four-wheeled covered wagons, and two-wheeled carts, both pulled by oxen.

Wheels were small, heavy discs of wood, sometimes solid, and sometimes with spokes. On the rocky roads full of potholes, riding in a cart could not have been a pleasure.

Most people walked, unless they had luggage with them. In the Gospels Jesus is usually described as walking.

In the hills the roads were rocky tracks. Often the path would be faint and hard to make out. Even the great trade routes were full of potholes, though they had splendid names like "The King's Highway."

In 1200 B.C. an Egyptian wrote that roads in Canaan were "filled with boulders and pebbles... overgrown with reeds, thorns and brambles."

When a great leader was expected, road repairers would often go ahead to repair the road. This is an image used by Isaiah (Isaiah 40:3; 62:10).

Facts 5

TRAVEL ITINERARIES

The Persians were the first to develop an international road system to maintain. Their roads were fairly level tracks, and at intervals there were staging posts with fresh horses for government messengers.

Persian roads were little better than tracks. It took three months to travel the 1,600 miles from Sardis to Susa.

It was the Romans who turned road-making into a great technological achievement. The Romans built fifty thousand miles of roads throughout their empire and road maps could be bought in Rome.

As a result of the network of straight and level Roman roads, messengers and armies could travel quickly throughout the empire.

Roman roads were made of four layers: first sand, then pieces of stone and rock in concrete, then crushed stone in concrete, and finally a top layer of paving stones.

In New Testament times, wealthy people traveled by four-wheeled, horse-drawn chariots, or the very rich could hire two-wheeled chariots and drive themselves.

In Old Testament times, the Philistine people, often called the Sea People, dominated travel along the Mediterranean coast. Contemporary illustrations show them with a distinctive feathered headdress.

Goshen was in the eastern Nile Delta. It was a fertile land, very suitable for grazing. The Egyptians, who despised shepherds, were very happy to have Jacob's family settle in this remote area.

In Old Testament times there were primitive resting places along the major caravan routes. Often these would be caves.

As time passed, travelers could stay in the occasional khan: a series of stalls opening off a common courtyard. The innkeeper provided only a fire and fodder for the animals.

It was a sin to refuse hospitality to a stranger entering a town, or passing by one's tents in the desert. Anyone so welcomed came under the protection of the owner of the house or tent and was completely safe (Psalm 23:5; Genesis 19:8).

Facts 6

TRAVEL ITINERARIES

In Roman times, inns were built that were more like the inns known today. They had stables, kitchen, dining-room and bedrooms, even a smithy and workshop for repairs.

It is likely that some families offered accommodation to visitors, in the way people offer bed and breakfast today.

The Greek word used to describe the inn at which Mary and Joseph could find no room, was not the word for *khan* or for a private house, but *kataluma*, which means a temporary shelter. This was a sort of marquee, providing only shelter from the weather.

Inns were unsavory places. When Jesus sent his disciples on a preaching tour, he told them to stay in private houses. In the early church Christians were reminded of the importance of offering hospitality (Romans 12:13; Hebrews 13:1).

The seven churches in Revelation were along the route that would have been followed by a Roman "postman" delivering imperial messages.

Nazareth was a hillside town in Galilee 15 miles west of the Sea of Galilee and twenty miles east of the Mediterranean. Nazareth was 80 miles from Bethlehem.

The great "Way of the Sea" from Damascus to the Mediterranean coast and Egypt passed not far from Nazareth. It was a busy road, with caravans of merchants, and detachments of Romans soldiers traveling along it.

Jerusalem is 2,300 feet above sea-level, and the Dead Sea, near which Jericho stands, is 1,300 feet below sea level. The 15-mile long road from Jerusalem to Jericho drops very steeply.

The Jerusalem to Jericho road was a narrow mountain road, twisting sharply between high cliffs. The caves in these cliffs were hideouts for robbers, outlaws and guerrilla fighters.

In the fifth century, the Roman writer Jerome says that the road from Jerusalem to Jericho was called "The Red (or Bloody) Way."

Facts 7

TRAVEL ITINERARIES

The wise men who came to see Jesus saw the star "at its rising." They seem to have deduced that they should therefore go to Jerusalem. They saw the star again when they left Jerusalem.

Throughout the history of the Jews, during peril, famine or tyranny, God's people fled to Egypt. The Bible writers are sympathetic towards Egypt. Though often condemned, a final restoration is promised.

To travel from Philippi to Thessalonica involved a hard trek of rather more than 100 miles.

The city of Thessalonica, was the main city on the Egnatian Way, the great Roman road from the Adriatic Sea to the Middle East. It was therefore in a key position for the spread of the gospel.

In Paul's day, Athens was an intellectual and tourist center. Its heyday, however, had long passed, and Athens was less important than Corinth.

Corinth was known as the "bridge of Greece" because all north and south traffic had to pass through this city. It has been called "the market place of Greece". The Isthmian Games, second only in importance to the Olympic Games, were held in Corinth.

The wealthy city of Corinth was notorious for its vice. In Greek theater, if a man from Corinth appeared on the stage, he appeared as a drunkard. The Greeks had a verb, "to play the Corinthian," which meant to lead a dissolute and depraved life.

Corinth had many religious groups. It was known as a center for the healing cult of Asklepios. Also prominent was the Egyptian Isis cult.

Standing at the mouth of the Cayster River, Ephesus, the Roman capital of the province of Asia, was known as the market of Asia and the treasure house of Asia. The temple of Diana in Ephesus had the right of asylum, so Ephesus became a base for the criminals of the ancient world.

People from all over the world came to Ephesus to admire the temple of the goddess Diana, which was one of the seven wonders of the world.

People also came to Ephesus to buy the charms and spells for which Ephesus was famous. Called "Ephesian Letters" these were supposed to give safety in travel and success in enterprises.

River Deep Mountain High

Quiz #1

RIVER DEEP MOUNTAIN HIGH

1. Where were Adam and Eve first placed by God following their creation?

2. True or false? The garden where Adam and Eve lived was in Egypt.

3. How many rivers flowed through the Garden of Eden?

4. On which mountains did Noah's ark come to rest following the flood?

5. Give the names of two of the rivers in the Garden of Eden.

6. From what city on the River Euphrates did Abraham's family originate?

7. When Hagar left home for the first time, what was she next to when the angel found her in the desert?

8. Fill in the missing words: "He leads me beside quiet waters, he ___ ___ ___."

9. In Revelation 22, what flows from the throne of God?

10. What mountain-top citadel did David capture?

11. By what river did an Egyptian princess find a baby in a basket-boat?

12. On what day of creation did God separate the water and the dry land?

13. Supply the missing word from the Song of Moses: "In a ___ land he [God] found him, in a barren and howling waste."

14. When Joshua led the Israelites to the edge of the Jordan River, what miraculous event occurred?

15. True or false? The Gospels do not give the name of the mountain where Jesus was transfigured.

---

13. desert 14. The waters dried up and the people crossed over 15. True (Mark 9:2)

8. restores my soul 9. The river of life 10. Jerusalem 11. The Nile 12. Day 3

4. The mountains of Ararat 5. Pishon, Gihon, Tigris, Euphrates 6. Ur 7. A spring

1. The Garden of Eden 2. False. It was to the east, in Eden (Genesis 2:8) 3. 4

Answers

Quiz #2
RIVER DEEP MOUNTAIN HIGH

1. In Genesis 15, God promised to give Abraham and his descendants the land from the river of Egypt to the great river. What is the name of the great river?

2. Which large body of water did the Israelites cross after leaving Egypt on the exodus?

3. At the foot of which mountain did the Israelites sin by worshiping a golden calf?

4. How did Moses make the bitter water of Marah sweet?

5. What did Moses see for the first time from Mount Nebo?

6. What kind of people did Moses send into the Promised Land, from the wilderness at Kadesh?

7. True or false? Moses was buried in Jerusalem.

8. Which tribes of Israel did not settle in the Promised Land west of the Jordan River?

9. On what plains did Moses deliver his final speech to the Israelites before his death?

10. Supply the missing word from the Song of Miriam: "The horse and its rider he has hurled into the ____."

11. To whom were these words spoken: "Who cuts a channel for the torrents of rain... to water... a desert with no-one in it"?

12. Who said that in the day of the Lord's judgment, "The whole land will rise like the Nile; it will be stirred up and then sink"?

13. In Luke's Gospel, who did people try to hurl down a cliff?

14. In what valley did Goliath and David meet while the armies faced each other from opposite hills?

15. On the last night before his arrest, what valley did Jesus and the disciples cross over?

Quiz #3
RIVER DEEP MOUNTAIN HIGH

1. On which mountain did Joshua renew the covenant with the people of Israel following the defeat at Ai?

2. During the time of the judges, who uttered taunting parables from Mount Gerizim?

3. In which Old Testament book is the mount of assembly referred to?

4. In 2 Kings 23, what name is given to the hill where Solomon built shrines to false gods?

5. True or false? King David fled from his son Absalom to the Mount of Olives.

6. According to the prophet Zechariah, during the last days, upon which mountain will the feet of the Lord stand?

7. Which Old Testament book speaks about "a river whose streams make glad the city of God"?

8. True or false? Cities along the Euphrates River include Babylon, Ur, and Jerusalem.

9. Which river is mentioned the most in the Bible?

10. The judge Ehud fought the Moabites near what river?

11. In the book of Genesis, who took his son up a mountain?

12. Who told priests to take stones from a dry river bed?

13. Supply the missing word from John's vision in the book of Revelation: "The angel showed me the river of the water of life as clear as ___."

14. Where was Paul when Luke wrote, "On the Sabbath we went outside the city gate to the river, where we expected to find a place of prayer"?

15. Fill in the missing three words from Hosea's prophecy: "I will make the Valley of Achor a ___ ___ ___."

11. Abraham 12. Joshua 13. crystal 14. Philippi 15. door of hope
9. The Jordan River which is mentioned in 211 verses 10. The Jordan
7. Psalms 8. False. Jerusalem is nowhere near the Euphrates
1. Mount Ebal 2. Jotham 3. Isaiah 4. Hill of Corruption 5. True 6. The Mount of Olives

Answers

Quiz #4

RIVER DEEP MOUNTAIN HIGH

1. On what mountain was King Saul killed at the battle between his forces and the Philistines?

2. Who, according to the Psalmist, is like a tree planted by streams of water?

3. In the desert of Ziph, David spared King Saul's life and to prove it he took a jug of water, and what else that was by Saul's head?

4. In the desert of En Gedi, David spared King Saul's life and did what instead of killing Saul?

5. In Moses' instructions to the people recorded in Deuteronomy 11, on what mountain were the people to proclaim God's blessings?

6. In Moses' instructions to the people recorded in Deuteronomy 11, on what mountain were the people to proclaim the curses?

7. When David was fleeing from King Saul, he fled to what coastal country and became a vassal there?

8. After Elijah announced a drought, where did God tell him to go for water?

9. In the book of Genesis, who chose to live in a fertile place, instead of in the desert or the mountains?

10. Supply the missing three words from Jesus' prophecy about the destruction of Jerusalem which he spoke to the weeping women of Jerusalem: "Then [in that day] they will say to the mountains ___ ___ ___."

11. What desert did the Queen of Sheba cross when she visited Solomon?

12. True or false? In the book of Revelation, John wrote that in the new Jerusalem there would no longer be any sea.

13. The Psalmist wrote that the Lord surrounds his people just as what surrounds Jerusalem?

14. In Exodus, who led his sheep to the far side of the desert and then came to Horeb?

15. True or false? Jesus and his disciples baptized people in the River Jordan.

Answers

1. Mount Gilboa **2.** A man whose delight is in the law of the Lord **3.** A spear **4.** He cut a piece of material from Saul's robe **5.** Mount Gerizim **6.** Mount Ebal **7.** Philistia (the land of the Philistines) **8.** The Kerith Ravine where there was a brook **9.** Lot **10.** fall on us **11.** Arabian Desert **12.** True (Revelation 21:1) **13.** Mountains **14.** Moses **15.** False. Only Jesus' disciples and John the Baptist baptized people in the Jordan

Quiz #5

RIVER DEEP MOUNTAIN HIGH

1. On what mountain did the prophet Elijah confront the prophets of Baal, challenging their god to send fire from heaven?

2. Where did the prophet Elijah flee to where he heard the still small voice of God?

3. Fill in the missing two words from the sufferings endured by men of faith described in Hebrews 11: "They wandered in ___ and ___, and in caves and holes in the ground."

4. Ezekiel had a vision in which he saw a valley full of what?

5. True or false? Amos said to the people that they should let justice roll on "like the sea."

6. Where did Jesus tell people to flee to when they saw the abomination standing where it did not belong?

7. In Paul's catalogue of his sufferings, how long had he spent on the open sea?

8. In Paul's sufferings described in 2 Corinthians 11, fill in the missing word: "I have been in danger from ___, in danger from bandits, in danger from my own countrymen."

9. True or false? The Psalmist said, "I lift up my eyes to the cedars of Lebanon."

10. When the spies explored the land for Joshua, from which desert did they set out?

11. According to John's Gospel, in what pool did Jesus tell the blind man to wash?

12. What was the first indication, after Noah's ark grounded on Mount Ararat, that the flood was going down?

13. What, according to Isaiah, would have been like a river if the people had listened to God?

14. In Isaiah's prophecy about obedience, what would have been like the waves of the sea?

15. On what mountain was Elijah when his servant saw a cloud as small as a man's hand?

---

14. Their righteousness 15. Mount Carmel]

11. The pool of Siloam 12. The tops of the mountains were seen 13. Peace

8. rivers 9. False. He lifts his eyes to the hill (Psalm 121:1) 10. The Desert of Zin

5. False. He said, "like a river" (Amos 5:24) 6. To the mountains 7. A night and a day

1. Mount Carmel 2. Mount Horeb 3. deserts, mountains 4. Dry bones

Answers

118

Quiz #6

RIVER DEEP MOUNTAIN HIGH

1. Where did Elisha direct Naaman to wash in order to rid himself of leprosy?

2. By the rivers of which city did the Psalmist say that he wept and remembered Zion?

3. According to the prophet Isaiah, what mountain will be established as chief among the mountains?

4. In what valley was Naboth's vineyard?

5. What is the name of the mountainous land to which Moses escaped after he had killed the Egyptian?

6. Fill in the name of the river from Deborah's victory song in Judges: "The river ____ swept them away, the age-old river, the river ____."

7. According to Matthew, Jesus left Nazareth and went to what lakeside town?

8. During the storm at sea described in Acts, the sailors thought the ship was going to break up against the rocks. How did the soldiers stop the sailors escaping?

9. Fill in the missing words from Jesus' words about faith: "If you have faith as small as a mustard seed, you can say to this ____, 'Move from here to there' and it will move."

10. True or false? In Genesis, when the four kings fought against the five kings, to the south of the Dead Sea, the Valley of Siddim was a swamp.

11. Balak took Balaam to the top of what hill for his second oracle?

12. Balak took Balaam to the top of what hill for his third oracle?

13. In Acts, the angel told Philip to go south to what road?

14. In Psalm 44, what does the deer pant for?

15. Supply the missing two words from this verse in Proverbs: "The fountain of wisdom is a ____ ____."

Answers

1. The Jordan 2. By the rivers of Babylon 3. The mountain of the Lord 4. The Valley of Jezreel 5. Midian 6. Kishon 7. Capernaum 8. The soldiers cut the lifeboat's ropes and it fell away into the sea 9. mountain 10. False. It was full of tar pits (Genesis 14:10) 11. Pisgah 12. Peor 13. The desert road 14. Streams of water 15. bubbling brook

Quiz #7
RIVER DEEP MOUNTAIN HIGH

1. In the book of Obadiah, the prophet issues a judgment to those who are on a mountain named after Jacob's brother. What is that mountain's name?

2. The prophet Amos pronounced a woe on those who live on which mountain in the northern kingdom of Israel?

3. In the book of Joel, the prophet mentions a mountain that is holy. What is the name of that mountain?

4. Supply the missing name from Zechariah's prophecy: "What are you, O mighty mountain? Before ____ you will become level ground."

5. According to Isaiah, who has "measured the waters in the hollow of his hand... or weighed the mountains on the scales and the hills in a balance"?

6. In which desert did John the Baptist preach?

7. In which river did John the Baptist and his disciples baptize the repentant Jews?

8. After leaving Marah, where did the Israelites find twelve springs and seventy palm trees?

9. Fill in the missing word from Exodus: "The Lord descended to the top of Mount ____ and called Moses to the top of the mountain."

10. After leaving Elim, and before they came to Sinai, the Israelites traveled through which desert?

11. As the people of Israel wandered through the wilderness, they had two major problems. One was getting enough food. What was the other problem?

12. True or false? Abraham went to Mount Gerizim to sacrifice Isaac.

13. According to the Psalmist, who may ascend the hill of the Lord?

14. When God wanted to reduce the numbers in Gideon's army, he told Gideon to take his men to the water to drink. Which men did God not choose?

15. True or false? Jesus was tempted by the devil three times on the Sea of Galilee.

---

15. False. He was tempted in the desert (Luke 4:2)
13. "He who has clean hands and a pure heart" 14. The men who got down on their knees to drink
10. The Desert of Sin 11. Getting water 12. False. He went to Mount Moriah (Genesis 22:2)
6. The desert of Judea 7. The Jordan 8. Elim 9. Sinai
1. Mount Esau 2. Mount Samaria 3. Mount Zion 4. Zerubbabel 5. The Sovereign Lord

Answers

Quiz #8

RIVER DEEP MOUNTAIN HIGH

1. For how many days did the Israelites wander in the desert without finding water, after they had crossed the Red Sea?

2. Where were Jesus and the disciples when Jesus told Simon to let down his nets into the water?

3. True or false? Before Jesus chose his twelve disciples, he prayed all night in the Garden of Gethsemane.

4. At what place did Peter suggest that he, James, and John should build booths for Elijah, Moses and Jesus?

5. True or false? Jesus did many healings at Gennesaret, near the Sea of Galilee.

6. True or false? Jesus walked on the surface of the Dead Sea.

7. According to the Psalmist, what is "as if the dew of Hermon were falling on Mount Zion"?

8. Who blew a trumpet in the hills, and with the tribal army that rallied to him, captured the fords of the Jordan?

9. On the Day of Atonement, where was the scapegoat sent?

10. Supply the missing word from the verse in the Song of Songs: "Many waters cannot quench ____; rivers cannot wash it away."

11. What food did John the Baptist eat in the desert?

12. True or false? Jesus was tempted by the devil in the land of the Philistines.

13. Jesus calmed a storm on which sea?

14. Jesus healed a lame man next to the pool of Bethesda. In which city was this pool found?

15. On which mountain did Jesus speak of the future of the temple and the last days?

Answers

1. 3 days **2.** Sea of Galilee (Lake) **3.** False. He went out to a mountainside (Luke 6:12) **4.** The Mount of Transfiguration **5.** True (Mark 6:53-56) **6.** False. It was the Sea of Galilee (Matthew 14:22-23) **7.** When brothers live together in unity **8.** Ehud **9.** Into the wilderness **10.** love **11.** Locusts and honey **12.** False. He was probably tempted in the wilderness of Judea, southeast of Jerusalem **13.** The Sea of Galilee **14.** Jerusalem **15.** The Mount of Olives

Quiz #9

RIVER DEEP MOUNTAIN HIGH

1. Supply the missing four words from Jeremiah's prophecy: "If you stumble in safe country, how will you manage in the ___ ___ ___ ___?"

2. The writer to the Hebrews says that Christians have not come to a mountain burning with fire. What have they come to? Give one of the three descriptions in Hebrews 12.

3. What did Elijah use instead of a stick to make the water in the Jordan move back?

4. Who proclaimed these words to the people left in Jerusalem: "The mountains of Israel will become desolate so that no-one will cross them"?

5. To whom did Jesus say: "The water I give him will become in him a spring of water welling up to eternal life"?

6. Supply the missing word from Isaiah's prophecy of the future restoration: "The desert and the parched land will be glad; the ___ will rejoice and blossom."

7. Who said to the people, "The land you are crossing the Jordan to take possession of is a land of mountains and valleys that drinks rain from heaven"?

8. Who, at the command of Deborah, gathered his forces on Mount Tabor?

9. To what river did Deborah lure the king of Canaan?

10. Why did the people say to Jesus, "Our forefathers ate the manna in the desert"?

11. In what desert were the people when they said to Moses, "Why did you bring us out of Egypt to die in this terrible place?"?

12. Ezekiel was by which river when he saw visions of God?

13. What mountain was David speaking to when he said in his lament: "How the mighty have fallen in battle! Jonathan lies slain on your heights."

14. Supply the missing word from the Psalmist's song of praise: "He lifted me out of the slimy pit, out of the mud and mire; he set my feet on a ___."

15. When Jesus said, "What did you go out into the desert to see?", what was the answer?

---

1. thickets of the Jordan 2. Mount Zion, the heavenly Jerusalem, the city of the living God
3. His rolled up cloak 4. Ezekiel 5. The Samaritan woman at the well 6. "wilderness" 7. Moses
8. Barak 9. River Kishon 10. They wanted Jesus to perform a miraculous sign to enable them to believe in him
11. Desert of Zin 12. Kebar River 13. Mount Gilboa 14. rock 15. A prophet (John the Baptist)

Answers

122

Facts 1

RIVER DEEP MOUNTAIN HIGH

The land of Palestine is divided into five main geographical areas running roughly north to south parallel to the Mediterranean coast. There is also an area of desert in the south.

Moving from west to east the traveler passes through: the coastal plains; the low-lying hill country (called the Shephelah); the central highlands; the Jordan Valley; the high Trans-Jordan plateau.

The Negev (meaning "south") is the barren wilderness stretching south from Beersheba and the Dead Sea to the Gulf of Aqabah. The Desert of Zin is in the Negev.

In biblical times, the northern mountains of Carmel, Upper Galilee and northern Samaria were covered with dense woodland.

Mount Ebal is just north of Shechem and opposite Mount Gerizim, overlooking the Nablus Valley, the main east-west route into the central hill country. Mount Ebal rises 3077 feet above sea level.

A large altar, recently discovered on Mount Ebal, may be the altar built by Joshua (Joshua 8:30-35).

Mount Gerizim is 2,849 feet above sea level. Here, the Samaritans built a temple to rival the temple at Jerusalem. Though this was destroyed in 128 B.C., the Samaritans continued to worship on Mount Gerizim (John 4:20).

The Mount of Olives, a ridge of hills just east of Jerusalem across the Kidron Valley, was once covered with olive groves. It rises to a height of 2,660 feet.

One of the summits on the Mount of Olives is traditionally identified as the site of Christ's ascension.

The Mount of Olives is as important to Jews and Muslims as it is to Christians. In addition to the Old Testament references to the Mount, there is a vast Jewish burial ground there.

The Euphrates River, "the Great River," flows in a southeasterly direction for 1,780 miles. It is the longest river in western Asia. Cities of biblical importance along this river include Babylon and Ur.

Facts 2

RIVER DEEP MOUNTAIN HIGH

The Tigris River originates in the melting snows of the Taurus Mountains in Turkey and flows southeast for 1,150 miles, joining the Euphrates 40 miles north of the Persian Gulf.

Nineveh, Asshur and Baghdad are on the banks of the Tigris.

The fortress of Masada became the last refuge of the Jewish people in their revolt against Rome in 70 AD. The fortress is near the Dead Sea and is situated on a rock surrounded by ravines.

Dew was a very important characteristic of the Palestinian climate. An abundance of dew was seen as a blessing from the Lord (Deuteronomy 33:28), and its absence was seen as a curse (Haggai 1:10).

Hail is uncommon. When it occurred in the land it was seen as a punishment from the Lord (Ezekiel 13:11, 13). On one occasion it was seen as intervention for God's people during a battle (Joshua 10:11).

The patriarchs wandered in the central hill country of Palestine. They are portrayed as a pastoral people who avoided the urban life of Canaan.

A number of sites have been proposed for Mount Sinai (Mount Horeb). Deuteronomy 1:2 states that the journey from Horeb by way of Mount Seir to Kadesh-barnea takes eleven days. This points to a location in the south of the Sinai peninsula.

The route that the Israelites took from Egypt to the Promised Land is under debate. The best biblical description for the journey is found in Numbers 33.

The exact location of the Sermon on the Mount is in doubt. One possibility is near the town of Chorazin in Galilee, just north of the Sea of Galilee.

Snow-capped Mount Hermon marked the extreme north of the territory occupied by Joshua in the conquest. It is a range of mountains, covering about 18 miles, the highest peak rising to 9,232 feet above sea level.

Because Mount Hermon is close to Caesarea Philippi, it has been suggested as the probable site of the transfiguration.

Facts 3

RIVER DEEP MOUNTAIN HIGH

It is thought that the Dead Sea Scrolls formed the library of a Jewish sect called the Essenes. The scrolls are more than 1,000 years older than any other known biblical manuscript.

"Dead Sea" is a name coined in the second century A.D. for the large salt lake at the southern end of the River Jordan. In the Bible it is called the Salt Sea and the Sea of Arabah.

The Dead Sea is the lowest point on the earth's surface, about 1,294 feet below sea level. At its deepest point it is more than 1,300 feet lower than sea level.

The water of the Dead Sea is 25 to 30 per cent salt. It is the most saline natural body of water in the earth, and nothing can live in it. Earthquakes are frequent in this area.

The Jordan River, beginning at Lake Huleh in the north, is the lowest river in the world. From Lake Galilee the Jordan twists down for some 65 miles to the Dead Sea in the south.

The Jordan River is from 90 to 100 feet wide and is rapid and muddy: General Naaman scorned the unappealing Jordan (2 Kings 5:12).

From early spring to late autumn, the Jordan Valley is hot. The heat and luxuriant vegetation turn the valley into a jungle. In ancient times, lions and other wild beasts roamed "the thickets of the Jordan."

In Old Testament times, the Jordan formed a boundary and military frontier. Many battles were fought in the fords of the Jordan.

Jericho is in the southern part of the Jordan Valley, nearly ten miles north-west of the Dead Sea. Old Testament Jericho was at an oasis fed by a perennial spring, and was sometimes called "The City of Palms."

The Jericho of the Old Testament was one of the oldest cities in the world. It was, however, a ruin in New Testament times. New Testament Jericho was a little to the south of the original site having been built by King Herod as a winter residence.

The Mediterranean Sea is frequently called "the Sea" in the Old Testament. It is also called "The Great Sea." In some Bibles it is sometimes called "the sea behind," "the western sea" or "the uttermost sea."

Facts 4
RIVER DEEP MOUNTAIN HIGH

In New Testament times, Galilee stretched west from the Jordan River almost to the coastal plain. It covered an area of about 44 miles long and 25 miles wide.

Galilee was ruled over by Herod Antipas from 4 B.C. to his deposition in A.D. 39. His new capital, Tiberias, does not appear to have been visited by Jesus.

Upper Galilee is mountainous, rising to almost 4,000 feet above sea level. Lower Galilee has low wooded hills and fertile plains.

Nazareth was an insignificant town in Lower Galilee. It was on the hills overlooking the Plain of Esdraelon.

The Sea of Galilee was called the Sea of Kinnereth in the Old Testament, taking its name from the name of an ancient Canaanite town (Joshua 11:2; 19:35). The lake formed a boundary to the Promised Land.

In the New Testament the Sea of Galilee is also called the Lake of Gennesaret, and the Sea of Tiberias.

The Sea of Galilee is pear-shaped, about 13 miles long from north to south and nearly 8 miles wide at its greatest width. It is the lowest fresh-water lake in the world.

Much of Jesus' ministry took place around the Sea of Galilee, largely along the northwestern side, which is open, with the hills about two miles distant and green slopes stretching down to the sea.

On the eastern shore of the Sea of Galilee was the land of the Gerasenes where Jesus met a man possessed by many demons. The eastern side of the lake is steep, with a wall of sharply rising hills.

The Sea of Galilee abounds in fish, and around the western shores of the lake there were prosperous trading and fishing towns, including Tiberias, Capernaum and Bethsaida.

Rich Man, Poor Man

Quiz # 1

RICH MAN, POOR MAN

1. Who was the first son of Adam and Eve?

2. Name one of Noah's three sons.

3. Who lived for the longest according to the Bible?

4. In the book of Genesis what was the name of the man who never died?

5. Which ruler's house in Egypt did the Lord punish because Abraham's wife told the people that she was Abraham's sister?

6. What was the name of Abraham's rich relative who lived in Sodom?

7. What was the name of Sarah's Egyptian maid?

8. What was the name of Hagar's son?

9. Who was Rachel's father?

10. Who became Jacob's first wife?

11. How were Jacob's two wives related to each other?

12. Who was the mother of Reuben?

13. Who was the mother of Judah?

14. Who was the mother of Joseph?

15. Who was the mother of Benjamin?

Quiz #2

RICH MAN, POOR MAN

1. What was the name of the Egyptian officer who bought Joseph from the Ishmaelites?

2. Which of Jacob's twelve sons was the father of Er and Onan?

3. Who was Manasseh and Ephraim's father?

4. Who drew Moses out of the River Nile when he was in a basket?

5. What was the name of Moses' father-in-law?

6. What was the name of Moses' wife?

7. How were Moses and Aaron related?

8. Who was the son of Nun who succeeded Moses as the leader of Israel?

9. What was the name of the man who owned a talking donkey?

10. What was the name of the left-handed judge who fought the Moabites?

11. Who was the female judge who led the Israelites against the Canaanites?

12. Which Israelite judge laid a fleece out over night to see if the Lord wanted him to lead Israel against the Midianites?

13. Which Israelite judge confronted the Philistines and slew many of them with a jawbone of a donkey?

14. Luke wrote his Gospel and the Acts of the Apostles for a person whose name is found in the first few verses of both books. Who is he?

15. What was Matthew's occupation before he was called to be Jesus' disciple?

Answers

1. Potiphar 2. Judah 3. Joseph 4. Pharaoh's daughter 5. Jethro 6. Zipporah 7. They were brothers 8. Joshua 9. Balaam 10. Ehud 11. Deborah 12. Gideon 13. Samson 14. Theophilus 15. Tax collector

Quiz #3

RICH MAN, POOR MAN

1. What did Jesus say must be done to a strong man before anyone can enter his house and carry off his possessions?

2. Who said this to a Syro-Phonecian woman: "First let the children eat all they want, for it is not right to take the children's bread and toss it to their dogs"?

3. What righteous man, who was born before Jesus, acknowledged that Jesus surpassed him because he was "before" him?

4. What type of person did Jesus allow to cast the first stone at the woman caught in adultery?

5. Who was the eldest son of Gideon?

6. As a result of the death of which king did David compose a famous lament?

7. In the first chapter of 1 Kings, which of David's sons was trying to take possession of the throne of Israel?

8. Which king's decree is recorded in the first chapter of Ezra?

9. Which captured Jewish king received a regular allowance from the king of Babylon?

10. Which Jewish prophet who lived in the time of Ahab is mentioned in the last chapter of the book of Malachi?

11. According to the last verse of the book of Deuteronomy, who did the most powerful and awesome deeds in the sight of all Israel?

12. Who was the righteous and most famous king of Israel descended from Ruth?

13. Which rich and powerful man did Ruth marry?

14. How was Ruth related to Naomi?

15. From which people was Ruth descended?

Answers

1. He must be tied up 2. Jesus 3. John the Baptist 4. The one without sin
5. Jether 6. King Saul 7. Adonijah 8. King Cyrus' decree 9. King Jehoiachin
10. Elijah 11. Moses 12. King David 13. Boaz
14. She was her daughter-in-law 15. The Moabites

Quiz #4

RICH MAN, POOR MAN

1. Who was Israel's first king?

2. Who was Saul's son who befriended David?

3. Who defeated Goliath?

4. Who was king over Israel when the confrontation with Goliath occurred?

5. What was the name of Saul's daughter whom he gave to David as a wife?

6. Ahimilech the priest, Samuel the judge, Jonathan the son of Saul, and Achish the king of Gath, protected which future king of Israel?

7. Which king of Israel slaughtered priests while chasing after David?

8. Which of David's wives had once been married to Nabal?

9. Which Philistine king did David serve under?

10. Who did the medium at Endor say she saw after she had "brought him up"?

11. Who was the commander of David's army?

12. How old was David when he became king over all of Israel?

13. True or false? Mephibosheth was related to David.

14. What was the name of the prophet who confronted David after his adulterous affair?

15. Absalom led a revolt against his father who was king of Israel. Who was Absalom's father?

Answers

1. Saul 2. Jonathan 3. David 4. Saul 5. Michal 6. David 7. Saul 8. Abigail
9. Achish 10. Samuel 11. Joab 12. 30 years old 13. False. He was related to Saul (2 Samuel 9:1-13)
14. Nathan 15. David

Quiz #5

RICH MAN, POOR MAN

1. Who succeeded David?

2. Who was Solomon's mother?

3. Which king of Israel asked the Lord if he could build a temple for the Lord?

4. During the reign of which king of Israel was the temple built?

5. True or false? King David was known as the wisest man in all of Israel.

6. True or false? King Solomon was known for his skills in constructing Psalms.

7. Which royal dignitary came to King Solomon with spices, precious stones, and 120 talents of gold?

8. Which group of people were responsible for King Solomon's spiritual decline?

9. Which prophet tore a new cloak into twelve pieces in front of Jeroboam as he told him that the nation of Israel would be divided into two kingdoms?

10. Who was the first king of the southern kingdom of Judah?

11. Who was the first king of the northern kingdom of Israel?

12. True or false? King Jeroboam gave special respect to the Levites, assuring them that they alone would be priests in his kingdom.

13. Which king, who came from Egypt, attacked Jerusalem and carried off the treasures of the temple during King Rehoboam's reign?

14. True or false? King Abijah was King Rehoboam's son.

15. Who was the son of King Jeroboam who succeeded him in Israel?

Quiz #6

RICH MAN, POOR MAN

1. What was the name of the last king of the northern kingdom of Israel?

2. True or false? King Hezekiah was known as being one of Judah's worst kings.

3. Who was the king of Assyria who conquered the northern kingdom of Israel when Hoshea was king?

4. Who was King Hezekiah's son who became a wicked king in Judah?

5. Who was the king of Judah who rediscovered the law?

6. Who was the Babylonian king who conquered the southern kingdom of Judah?

7. Who was the first king from Judah who was taken prisoner to Babylon?

8. Which king of Judah was blinded immediately after seeing his sons put to death and was then deported to Babylon?

9. What was the name of the king of Persia who decreed that the temple should be rebuilt in Jerusalem?

10. Who led the people of Israel from Babylon back to Jerusalem during the reign of King Artaxerxes?

11. Who was a cupbearer to King Artaxerxes who petitioned this king so that he could return to Jerusalem to rebuild the city's walls?

12. Which Israelite renewed the covenant with the Lord following the rebuilding of the temple and the rebuilding of the walls of Jerusalem?

13. Who did King Xerxes divorce before he married Esther?

14. Who influenced King Xerxes to decree that all of the Jews throughout his entire kingdom should be killed?

15. Who persuaded King Xerxes to permit all of the Jews within his kingdom to defend themselves against their enemies?

---

12. Ezra 13. Vashti 14. Haman 15. Esther
7. King Jehoiachin 8. King Zedekiah 9. King Cyrus 10. Ezra 11. Nehemiah
3. Shalmaneser 4. Manasseh 5. King Josiah 6. King Nebuchadnezzar
1. Hoshea 2. False. King Hezekiah was known as one of Israel's best kings (2 Kings 18:1-12)

Answers

Quiz #7
RICH MAN, POOR MAN

1. Who was known to be a righteous and blameless man but lost seven sons and three daughters and was afflicted with terrible sores?

2. True or false? Satan appears before the Lord at the beginning of the book of Job.

3. Who appeared to Job out of a storm leaving Job speechless?

4. Who wrote the book of Proverbs according to its first verse?

5. Who was the author of the book of Ecclesiastes according to its first verse?

6. Who saw the Lord in his temple in the year that King Uzziah died and as a result was commissioned to prophesy?

7. What name did the Babylonians give to Daniel?

8. Who interpreted King Nebuchadnezzar's dream about a statue which had many different metals?

9. Who set up a gold statue on the plain of Dura and commanded his subjects to bow down to it?

10. Who were the three Israelites King Nebuchadnezzar threw into the fiery furnace?

11. Which king of Babylon ate grass like the wild animals?

12. Which king of Babylon saw handwriting appear on the wall?

13. What Israelite was thrown into the lions' den?

14. Who was the king at the time that Daniel was thrown in the lions' den?

15. Who was the king who overthrew Babylon on the night that the Babylonian king saw the handwriting on the wall?

---

12. King Belshazzar 13. Daniel 14. King Darius 15. King Darius
10. Shadrach, Meshach, and Abednego 11. King Nebuchadnezzar
6. Isaiah 7. Belteshazzar 8. Daniel 9. King Nebuchadnezzar
1. Job 2. True (Job 1:6-11; 2:1-6) 3. The Lord 4. Solomon 5. Solomon

Answers

Quiz #8

RICH MAN, POOR MAN

1. Who was Mary's husband?

2. Who met Jesus in the wilderness where Jesus had fasted for 40 days and 40 nights?

3. Who baptized Jesus?

4. Who were the first two disciples that Jesus called who were fishing in the Sea of Galilee at the time?

5. Who were the sons of Zebedee, called "sons of Thunder," whom Jesus called to follow him?

6. Who was the first disciple who confessed that Jesus was the Son of God?

7. Which disciple's mother-in-law did Jesus heal?

8. Who criticized the disciples when they were picking grain on the Sabbath?

9. Jesus called two disciples named James to follow him. One was the son of Zebedee, the other was the son of whom?

10. What was the other name of the woman called Magdalene?

11. What was the name of the demon-possessed man who lived in the land of the Gerasenes?

12. What was the name of the synagogue official who came to Jesus to ask for his daughter to be healed?

13. What did the woman with a hemorrhage do to be healed by Jesus when she was in a large crowd with him?

14. In one of Jesus' parables, who came to the aid of the man who was attacked on the road to Jericho from Jerusalem?

15. What was the name of the woman whom Jesus said was worried and bothered by so many things that she was too busy to simply be with Jesus?

Answers

1. Joseph **2.** The devil **3.** John the Baptist **4.** Simon who was called Peter and Andrew **5.** James and John **6.** Peter **7.** Peter's **8.** The Pharisees **9.** Alphaeus **10.** Mary **11.** Legion **12.** Jairus **13.** She touched the edge of Jesus' cloak **14.** The Good Samaritan **15.** Martha

Quiz #9

RICH MAN, POOR MAN

1. To whom did Jesus teach the prayer we now know as the Lord's Prayer?

2. Who did Jesus say were like whitewashed tombs, who appear beautiful on the outside but inside are filled with dead men's bones?

3. Who said he was the "good shepherd" who lays down his life for the sheep?

4. What was the nationality of the healed leper who returned to give thanks to Jesus?

5. What was Zacchaeus' occupation?

6. Why did Zacchaeus climb a sycamore tree in order to see Jesus?

7. What was the name of the blind man whom Jesus healed as he traveled to Jerusalem?

8. Whose image was on the coin that the Pharisees showed to Jesus when they asked him a trick question about paying taxes?

9. Who was the brother of Mary and Martha who Jesus raised from the dead?

10. True or false? The Pharisees brought Jesus a donkey so that he could ride into Jerusalem.

11. Which two disciples asked Jesus if he would grant them the favor of sitting on his right and left hand when he came into his glory?

12. Which of Jesus' disciples did Satan enter?

13. Which disciple denied Jesus three times on the night that Jesus was betrayed?

14. Whose ear was cut off on the night that Jesus was betrayed?

15. To whose house did Jesus' captors first take him on the night he was betrayed?

Answers

1. The disciples **2.** The Pharisees **3.** Jesus **4.** He was a Samaritan
5. He was a tax collector **6.** Because he was short **7.** Bartimaeus **8.** Caesar's image **9.** Lazarus
10. False. Two of Jesus' disciples brought the donkey to Jesus (Luke 19:28-35)
11. James and John the sons of Zebedee **12.** Judas **13.** Peter **14.** Malchus, the high priest's slave
15. The high priest's house

Quiz # 10
RICH MAN, POOR MAN

1. To whom did Pilate send Jesus?

2. Who was the Roman ruler who handed Jesus over to be crucified?

3. Who did the crowd demand to be freed from prison when Jesus was on trial?

4. Who carried Jesus' cross?

5. What type of people were crucified on the crosses to the right and left of Jesus?

6. Who asked Pilate for Jesus' body?

7. True or false? John was the first person to come to the tomb on the day that Jesus rose from the dead.

8. True or false? A man named Cleopas was one of the people walking with Jesus on the road to a village named Emmaus.

9. When the wine ran out at the wedding in Cana of Galilee, who told Jesus?

10. What was the nationality of the woman who Jesus met at a well?

11. Which disciple said that eight months' wages would not be enough to feed 5,000 people?

12. What group of Jewish people are described as those "who say there is no resurrection"?

13. Who was the high priest when Jesus was crucified?

14. Who was the father-in-law of the high priest when Jesus was crucified?

15. What was the name of Simon Peter's father?

Answers

1. Herod Antipas 2. Pontius Pilate 3. Barabbas 4. Simon of Cyrene
5. They were criminals 6. Joseph of Arimathea
7. False. Mary Magdalene, Joanna, and Mary the mother of James went to Jesus' tomb first (Luke 24:10)
8. True (Luke 24:13-18) 9. Mary, Jesus' mother 10. She was a Samaritan 11. Philip 12. The Sadducees
13. Caiaphas 14. Annas 15. John

Quiz #11

RICH MAN, POOR MAN

1. True or false? Joseph of Barsabbas is mentioned as one of the people present at Jesus' crucifixion.

2. Who preached the sermon on the Day of Pentecost?

3. Which apostle was with Peter when he healed a lame man at the temple gate called Beautiful?

4. Who, according to Peter, was the stone which was rejected by the builders?

5. What were the names of the two people who lied to the Holy Spirit and then dropped dead?

6. Who was the Pharisee who defended Peter after the Jewish leaders had told him not to preach in the name of Jesus?

7. Who was the first Christian martyr?

8. Who was the first Christian to preach in Samaria?

9. Who helped to restore Saul's sight?

10. Philip preached to an Ethiopian eunuch on the road to Gaza. What was this Ethiopian's employment?

11. What was Saul of Tarsus' other name?

12. What was the name of the centurion to whom Peter preached?

13. What is the name of the person whom Peter raised from the dead in Joppa whose name is translated as Dorcas?

14. Who was the leader of the church in Jerusalem?

15. Who killed James?

Facts 1

RICH MAN, POOR MAN

When King Herod died his three sons ruled over his divided kingdom. From 4 BC-AD 37 Herod Antipas ruled as tetrarch of Galilee and Peraea. The region of Gaulanitus, Ituraea, and Trachonitis was ruled by Herod Philip from 4 BC to AD 34. Archelaus ruled Judea, Samaria and Idumea until from 4 BC-AD 6.

The person who lived the longest in the Bible is Methuselah. He lived 969 years. Other people in Genesis 5 also lived long lives. For example, Mahalalel lived 895 years.

Noah is the son of Lamech. About his son Noah, Lamech says, "He will comfort us in the labor and painful toil of our hands caused by the ground the Lord has cursed" (Genesis 5:29). He comforts humankind by building the ark and so became the means of rescuing humankind.

Although the book of Lamentations does not name its author, the consensus of Jewish tradition attributes it to Jeremiah. A superscription to the Vulgate, the Latin Bible, reads "Jeremiah sat weeping and lamented with this lamentation over Jerusalem."

The prophet Jeremiah is described in a variety of ways. He has been called "the weeping prophet" (Jeremiah 9:1; 13:17), the "prophet of loneliness" (Jeremiah 16:2), and the "reluctant prophet" (Jeremiah 1:6).

The prophet Isaiah was born into an influential, upper-class family. He lived most of his life in Jerusalem. Tradition has it that he was martyred during the reign of Manasseh (696-642 BC) by being sawn in two inside a large hollow log.

Timothy was the son of a Greek father and a Jewish mother named Eunice. Paul referred to him as his "true son in the faith." Timothy received two letters from Paul now known as 1 Timothy and 2 Timothy.

Titus was a convert from Paul's ministry and was later an emissary to the church at Corinth. When Paul writes to him, in the letter we now call "Paul's letter to Titus," Titus has been left in Crete to lead the work there.

The name Beelzebul mean "lord of flies." It is the Greek form of the Hebrew word *"Baal-Zebul"* who was a deity of the Ekronites (2 Kings 1:2). It is used in the Gospels as a name for Satan.

Moses was timid about speaking. The Lord provided Aaron, his brother, to be his mouthpiece (Exodus 4:10-17).

Facts 2

RICH MAN, POOR MAN

Job's friends who spoke to him in the midst of his calamity-Eliphaz, Bildad, Zophar and Elihu-gave poor comfort to Job since they tried to find some reason in Job's life for his acute suffering.

Many significant women of the Bible were infertile or "barren" at some point in their lives. Such women include Sarah, Rebekah, Rachel, Samson's mother, and Hannah, Samuel's mother.

The name James is the English equivalent of the Hebrew name Jacob.

Of the 41 times James appears in the Bible, it refers 19 times to James the son of Zebedee and brother of John, 4 times to James the son of Alphaeus and 3 times to a son of Mary.

In the New Testament a "pillar of the church," was a recognised leader of the church, like James, Peter, and John (Galatians 2:9).

Jesus is not only mentioned in the New Testament. The Jewish historian Josephus mentions Jesus in his writings known as *The Antiquities of the Jews.*

Jesus is called by many different names. For example, he is called "Immanuel" (which means "God with us"); "Root of David"; "The Lion of the tribe of Judah"; "The Bright and Morning Star" and "the shoot from the stump of Jesse."

John the Baptist was known as "the Baptist" since his ministry involved preaching repentance and performing baptisms in the Jordan River.

The name Moses is derived from the verb, "to draw out". It was a suitable name for a man who was drawn out of the River Nile .

Jacob's name came from the fact that he grasped the heel of his twin brother Esau during their birth.

Facts 3

RICH MAN, POOR MAN

Titus, a fellow worker of Paul, was left in Crete to oversee the work there (Titus 1:5). The Jewish Christians in Jerusalem wanted Titus, a Gentile, to be circumcised. Paul, however, did not circumcise him (Galatians 2:3).

Joseph, the husband of Mary, appears only in the narratives of Jesus' infancy and boyhood. This has led many to speculate that he had died before Jesus' public ministry began.

The man who stepped forward to bury Jesus was Joseph of Arimathea. He was a rich man and a member of the Sanhedrin.

The name Isaac is related to the verb "to laugh". Isaac was the promised son of Abraham who was born to Sarah when Abraham was 100 years old.

Isaiah's name means "Yahweh is salvation." His name is similar in meaning to the names Joshua, Elisha and Jesus.

Matthew's Gospel has an extensive genealogy of Jesus (Matthew 1:1-17). One of its unusual features is that it includes four non-Jewish women: Tamar and Rahab, (both prostitutes), Bathsheba, (an adulteress) and Ruth (a Moabitess).

Ancient Near Eastern genealogies sometimes omit people from the lines of descent for a variety of reasons. Genealogies were used to authenticate hereditary succession, and inheritance rights, to confirm biological descent, and to establish geographical and ethnological relationships.

Old Testament genealogies appear in many places in Genesis. For example, in Genesis 4 Cain's lineage is given. In Genesis 5:1-32, Adam's lineage is traced through Noah. In Genesis 10 Noah's descendants are listed.

The most comprehensive genealogical list in the Bible is found in 1 Chronicles chapters 1-9. It covers people from Adam to Saul.

Paul had a number of traveling partners with him on his missionary journeys. Such companions included Barnabas, Silas, Luke, Titus and Timothy.

Facts 4

RICH MAN, POOR MAN

The angel Gabriel is mentioned twice in the New Testament. He appears to Zechariah the priest announcing the birth of his son (Luke 1:11-20) and announces the impending conception and birth of Jesus to Mary (Luke 1: 26-38).

The angel Gabriel appears twice in the Old Testament. In Daniel 8:16 he is the one "who looked like a man." In Daniel 9:21 he appears to Daniel when he is praying at the time of the evening sacrifice.

The very short New Testament letter, 3 John, is written to a man named Gaius. This man was beloved by John and is commended for the truth of his life and his hospitality.

The name Gideon means "cutter down," "feller" or "hewer." He and his followers cut down many Midianite oppressors in the time of the judges (Judges 7-8).

Gamaliel, the Jewish rabbi who taught Paul, was a member of the Sanhedrin and a teacher of Paul. He was the first of seven successive leaders of the school of Hillel to be honored with the title Rabban ("Our Rabbi/Master").

The great Old Testament prophet Jeremiah dictated his prophecies to his scribe Baruch who in turn read them to the people (Jeremiah 36).

In the days of Jesus, tax collectors were viewed with contempt because they collected money for the Romans who occupied the Jewish land. They were often corrupt. Two prominent tax collectors became followers of Jesus: Matthew and Zacchaeus.

Famous slaves in the Old Testament include Hagar, Joseph, and the nation of Israel during their time in Egypt.

Famous slaves in the New Testament include Onesimus who belonged to Philemon, and Malchus who had his ear cut off on the night of Jesus' betrayal. Malchus was the slave of the high priest.

Famous rich people in the Old Testament include Abraham, Pharaoh, Boaz, King David, King Solomon and King Nebuchadnezzar.

Names and Nicknames

Quiz # 1
NAMES AND NICKNAMES

1. According to Genesis who gave names to the animals?

2. In the Old Testament who named her son Ben-Oni as she lay dying?

3. How many Old Testament books bear the names of men?

4. According to Genesis who was given a name which meant that he would provide comfort for his father?

5. Which son of the patriarch Jacob bears the name meaning "good fortune"?

6. Which Old Testament character named his first born Manasseh to help him forget his family and his troubles?

7. What does the name Ebenezer, which Samuel gave to a stone, mean?

8. According to Psalm 49, who had land named after themselves?

9. In the account of creation what does God call the light?

10. According to Isaiah 60, what name will be given to the gates of the city of Zion?

11. What does the name Abram mean?

12. In Genesis a heap of stones left by Laban and Jacob was called Mizpah. What does it mean?

13. According to Numbers 32, what did Nobah rename Keneth?

14. In Malachi what will be called the "Wicked Land"?

15. At Lystra what name did the enthusiastic citizens give the apostle Paul?

Quiz #2
NAMES AND NICKNAMES

1. What is the meaning of the name Salome?

2. When was Adam's wife first called "Eve"?

3. Who renamed his son Benjamin after the death of the boy's mother?

4. What is the appropriate meaning of the Old Testament name Nabal?

5. Which Old Testament character's name means "hairy"?

6. One of Jacob's sons had a name which sounds like the Hebrew for "reward." Which one was it?

7. What name meaning "twice fruitful" did Joseph give to his second child?

8. According to 2 Samuel what does the name Baal Perazim mean?

9. According to Ecclesiastes what has already been named?

10. In the account of the creation what does God call the darkness?

11. According to Isaiah 62 what names will no longer be used to describe Zion?

12. What is the meaning of the name Abraham?

13. In the Old Testament why did Jacob name a place Peniel?

14. According to Deuteronomy what name did the Ammonites give to the Rephaites?

15. Of whom was it said "He will be called a Nazarene"?

Answers

1. Peace 2. After the Fall 3. Jacob 4. Fool 5. Esau 6. Issachar 7. Ephraim 8. The lord who breaks out 9. Everything that exists 10. Night 11. Deserted and Desolate 12. Father of many 13. He saw God's face and survived there 14. Zamzummites 15. Jesus

Quiz #3
NAMES AND NICKNAMES

1. By what name is the Mediterranean island, once named Alashiya, known today?

2. True or false? The name Saul means "answered".

3. What is the most confusing name in the Bible?

4. What Aramaic name did Jesus give to Peter?

5. Which New Testament place name means "skull"?

6. According to Genesis which patriarch's name means deceiver?

7. True or false? The name Zebulun given to a son of Jacob means "brave".

8. Who named his first son saying, "I have become an alien in a foreign land"?

9. According to 2 Samuel what was Solomon's other name?

10. What is the ironic meaning of the name of the runaway slave Onesimus?

11. According to Genesis what did God call the expanse that separated the waters?

12. In chapter 62 of Isaiah which name meaning "my delight is in her" will be given to Zion?

13. In Genesis, what name did Abraham give to the place where he swore an oath with Abimelech?

14. Which wicked man was buried at a place named the Valley of Achor?

15. What name was given to the place where Joshua had the Israelites circumcised?

---

12. Hephzibah 13. Beersheba 14. Achan 15. Gilgal
8. Moses 9. Jedidiah 10. Useful 11. Sky
6. Jacob 7. False. It probably means "honor" (Genesis 30:20)
1. Cyprus 2. False. It means "asked" 3. Babel 4. Cephas 5. Golgotha

Answers

Quiz #4
NAMES AND NICKNAMES

1. What does the Old Testament name Hannah mean?

2. What name is given to the first five books of the Old Testament?

3. In the Old Testament what was the name given to the places where a person who had accidentally killed another could flee?

4. According to Genesis 10 why was Peleg, the son of Eber, so named?

5. Which of Jesus' disciples was called the Zealot?

6. Which Old Testament name means "God is my judge"?

7. Who named a well Esek because his herdsmen quarreled with those of Gerar?

8. True or false? The name of the patriarch Joseph means "may he add".

9. What name, meaning "my God is helper," did Moses give to his second son?

10. In the Old Testament which prophet told King David to give his son Solomon the name Jedidiah?

11. According to Ezekiel 48 what will be named after the tribes of Israel?

12. As recorded in Genesis, what did God call the ground at creation?

13. According to Isaiah 62 which new name, meaning "married," will be given to Zion?

14. What name did Abraham give to the place where he nearly sacrificed Isaac?

15. According to Genesis why is Succoth so named?

---

1. Grace **2.** Pentateuch **3.** Cities of Refuge **4.** The earth was divided and his name means division **5.** Simon **6.** Daniel **7.** Isaac **8.** True **9.** Eliezer **10.** Nathan **11.** The gates of the city of God **12.** Land **13.** Beulah **14.** The Lord will provide **15.** Because Jacob built shelters there

Answers

Quiz #5

NAMES AND NICKNAMES

1. What Aramaic name does John use for the Sheep Gate in Jerusalem?

2. What name was given to non-Greeks who nevertheless spoke Greek themselves?

3. How many letters in the New Testament are named after their author?

4. By what name does the writer of Ecclesiastes refer to himself?

5. Why was Isaac given his name?

6. What does the nickname Boanerges mean?

7. The name Deborah is derived from the name of an insect. Which one?

8. As recorded in Joshua by what name was Hebron formerly known?

9. On his way to meet Esau, Jacob saw two angels and exclaimed "This is the camp of God." What name did he give to the place?

10. According to Numbers 11, what name was given to the place where the Israelites buried people who had craved other food?

11. What does Jedidiah, the name God gave to Solomon, mean?

12. Who in the Old Testament named his daughters Jemimah, Keziah and Keren Happuch?

13. What did God call the waters during the week of creation?

14. According to Jeremiah 3, what will Jerusalem be called in the future?

15. In the Old Testament by what name was Esau also known?

Answers

1. Bethesda **2.** Hellenists **3.** 7. **7.** Those of James, Peter (2), John (3) and Jude **4.** Qoheleth **5.** Isaac means "he laughs" Sarah laughed when she heard that she was to have a son in her old age **6.** Sons of Thunder **7.** Bee **8.** Kiriath Arba **9.** Mahanaim **10.** Kibroth Hattaavah **11.** Loved by the Lord **12.** Job **13.** Seas **14.** The Throne of the Lord **15.** Edom

Quiz #6

NAMES AND NICKNAMES

1. According to the book of Joshua by what new name was Kiriath Sepher known?

2. Which disciple of Jesus, also called Barsabbas and Justus, failed to be selected to replace Judas Iscariot?

3. What does the Hebrew name "Hermon" mean?

4. How many New Testament letters bear the names of people?

5. What is the uncomplimentary meaning of the name Leah?

6. In the Old Testament why did Hannah name her son Samuel?

7. When did God first reveal his name as Yahweh?

8. According to Genesis, Jacob named an altar El Elohe Israel within sight of which city?

9. According to Genesis 26, how many wells did Isaac name?

10. In the Old Testament what name was given to the place where Rebekah's nurse, Deborah, died?

11. According to Numbers 21 what name did Israel give to the region belonging to the King of Arad after they had destroyed it?

12. In the Old Testament who named a pillar after himself because he had no son?

13. What is the meaning of the name Edom?

14. Who in Old Testament wanted to be called Mara instead of her real name?

15. As recorded in Jeremiah 7 what new name will be given to Topheth?

Answers

1. Debir **2.** Joseph **3.** Sanctuary

4. 11. 1 Timothy, 2 Timothy, Titus, Philemon, James, 1 Peter, 2 Peter, 1 John, 2 John, 3 John, Jude

5. Weak eyes or wild cow **6.** Samuel sounds like the Hebrew for "heard of God". He was an answer to Hannah's prayer

7. To Moses at the burning bush **8.** Shechem **9.** Three **10.** Allon Bacuth **11.** Hormah **12.** Absalom

13. Red **14.** Naomi **15.** Valley of Slaughter

Quiz #7

NAMES AND NICKNAMES

1. According to Exodus 15 why did the Israelites call a place Marah?

2. In the book of Judges why did the Israelites rename Gilgal, Bokim?

3. In the New Testament what was the name of the temple gate where Peter and John healed a beggar?

4. According to Numbers by what name was Joshua originally known?

5. As recorded in 1 Samuel 23 what name was given to the place where Saul stopped pursuing David?

6. According to Acts 13 what was the name of the false prophet who met Paul and Barnabas?

7. What does the name Moses mean?

8. In the book of Daniel who was renamed Abednego?

9. What is the meaning of the common Old Testament name Eliab?

10. In the Old Testament who named her child Reuben thinking that her husband would now love her?

11. Who gave the patriarch Jacob the name Israel?

12. According to Deuteronomy, what name was given to Bashan in honor of its owner Jair?

13. Where did Absalom erect the pillar he named after himself?

14. What is the meaning of the name Tabitha?

15. According to the book of Ruth why did Naomi wish to be called Mara?

___

Answers

1. Because of the bitter water. **2.** Because they met an angel there who made them weep **3.** Beautiful **4.** Hosea **5.** Sela Hammahlekoth **6.** Bar-Jesus **7.** Drew out **8.** Azariah **9.** God is father **10.** Leah **11.** God **12.** Havvoth Jair **13.** The King's Valley **14.** Gazelle **15.** It means bitter and she felt the Lord had made her life bitter

Quiz #8

NAMES AND NICKNAMES

1. According to Jeremiah, why will Topheth be named the Valley of Slaughter?

2. In the Old Testament by what name was Bethel formerly known?

3. What name did the Israelites give to the bread from heaven?

4. What name did the judge Gideon give to the altar where he met an angel of the Lord?

5. According to Acts what was Mark's other name?

6. What does the name "Israel" mean?

7. True or false? The Old Testament name Rachel means "calf."

8. What does the name Ichabod mean?

9. According to Acts who bought a field named Akeldama?

10. What does Akeldama mean?

11. According to Genesis 4:26 what did men begin to do for the first time?

12. Which child of Leah has a name meaning "attached"?

13. Where was Jacob given the name Israel?

14. By what name is Yam Suph better known?

15. In the Old Testament who named the temple pillars Jakin and Boaz?

Answers

1. Because the dead will be buried there until there is no more room **2.** Luz **3.** Manna **4.** The Lord is Peace **5.** John **6.** God strives **7.** False, Rachel means ewe **8.** "The glory has departed" **9.** Judas Iscariot **10.** Field of Blood **11.** Call on the name of the Lord **12.** Levi **13.** Bethel **14.** Sea of Reeds **15.** Huram

Quiz #9

NAMES AND NICKNAMES

1. According to Jesus who loved to have men call them "Rabbi"?

2. Which patriarch renamed Luz, calling it Bethel?

3. According to Exodus why did Moses build an altar called the Lord is My Banner?

4. Which Old Testament hero was known as Jerub-Baal?

5. According to the book of Acts, where were the disciples first called Christians?

6. In the New Testament what title was given to the son of Zechariah and Elizabeth in later life?

7. Which of Jesus' disciples was known as Didymus?

8. In the Old Testament who did not drink alcohol, shave or approach dead bodies?

9. What does the name of the Old Testament patriarch Jacob mean?

10. According to the book of Revelation what does the names Alpha and Omega mean?

11. Why did Adam call his wife Eve?

12. True or false? Bilhah, the slave of Rachel, named her child Dan.

13. According to Genesis 35 what name did Jacob give to the place where God spoke with him?

14. As recorded in Joshua what name did the Danites give to the captured city of Leshem?

15. True or false? The name Jabez sounds like the Hebrew for "pleasure".

Quiz #10

NAMES AND NICKNAMES

1. What was the name of the companion of Cleopas who met Jesus on the road to Emmaus?

2. According to Isaiah what name will the virgin give to her son?

3. Why did the disciples of Jesus call him "Teacher" and "Lord"?

4. In the Old Testament Laban called it Jegar Sahadutha. What did Jacob call it?

5. According to Numbers 11 what place was given its name because fire from the Lord burned among the Israelites?

6. As recorded by the prophet Zechariah, who took two staffs calling one "Favor" and the other "Union?"

7. By what name was Simon, one of the leaders of the Antioch Church also known?

8. What does the name of the Old Testament prophet Jonah mean?

9. True or false? Rhoda, the name of the servant girl who opened the door to Peter after his escape from prison, means "orchid."

10. What was Abraham called before God changed his name?

11. What does the name of the prophetess Anna mean?

12. What name did Cain give to the city he built in Genesis 4?

13. Why did Cain name the city he built in Genesis 4, Enoch?

14. Which name, meaning "my struggle" did Rachel give to one of her servants children?

15. In the Old Testament who named one of her children Zerah because he was born with a scarlet thread on his wrist?

Answers

1. His name is not recorded 2. Immanuel 3. Because he was their Teacher and Lord
4. Galeed 5. Taberah 6. God 7. Niger 8. Dove 9. False. It means rose 10. Abram 11. Grace
12. Enoch 13. It was the name of his son 14. Naphtali 15. Tamar.

Quiz # 11
NAMES AND NICKNAMES

1. But for the intervention of his mother what name would have been given to John the Baptist?

2. According to Isaiah 60 what name is to be given to the walls of the city of Zion?

3. In Genesis, why was the town Lot fled to named Zoar?

4. Which location in the Promised Land was so named because the spies found clusters of grapes there?

5. At Lystra what name did the citizens give Barnabas?

6. How many of Jesus' disciples names are replicated?

7. According to Zechariah 8, Jerusalem will be called the city of what?

8. How many Old Testament books bear the names of women?

9. In 1 Corinthians 1, Paul mockingly asks if his readers were baptized into whose name?

10. According to Genesis, by what name was Jegar Sahadutha, or Galeed also known?

11. What was Sarah called before her name was changed by God?

12. In the New Testament whose name means "Son of Encouragement"?

13. What name did Adam give to the son who replaced the murdered Abel?

14. Which name, meaning "happy" did Leah give to the child of her servant Zilpah?

15. What name was given to the twin of Zerah who "broke out" of the womb before his brother?

Answers

1. Zechariah 2. Salvation 3. Because it was a small town
4. Valley of Eschol 5. Zeus 6. 2, Simon and James 7. Truth
8. Two, Ruth and Esther 9. Paul's 10. Mizpah 11. Sarai
12. Barnabas 13. Seth 14. Asher 15. Perez

154

Facts 1

NAMES AND NICKNAMES

Eve is the first person in the Bible to have two names: Eve and woman.

The word "abba" meaning "father" occurs only three times in the New Testament.

Jonah was the first Hebrew prophet to be sent into a pagan country. Jonah hated the idea that he should tell the wicked people of Nineveh to repent. Through Jonah, the Jewish people learned that God cared for all the nations.

The place name Bethlehem means "house of bread."

The name "David" is mentioned 58 times in the New Testament. Despite some spectacular failures, David was "a man after God's own heart," and he became a model for Israel's future Messiah.

El, a basic name used for God or gods, occurs widely in Semitic literature and can also mean an image revered as a god.

Jerusalem is called by its shortened form "Salem" in Genesis 14:18. "Salem" is related to the Hebrew word for "peace" (Hebrews 7:2).

The name "Teacher" given to Jesus (Mark 4:38) was often conferred upon people who passed on teaching to a group of disciples.

In the Gospels, Jesus' often referred to himself as "Son of Man."

The name Lucifer means "light bearer" in Latin.

Ruah, the Hebrew name for the Spirit of God, occurs 378 times in the Old Testament and eleven times in its Aramaic form in Daniel.

When the Lord called people to fulfil his Divine purposes. For this new role he often gave them new names. Such people were Abraham (Abram), Sarah (Sarai), Israel (Jacob) and Peter (Simon) to name just a few.

Facts 2

NAMES AND NICKNAMES

The tetragrammaton, YHWH, was considered too sacred to be pronounced so the Hebrew "adonai" (my Lord) was substituted when it was read out loud.

In the Bible children are named 28 times by their mothers.

The name "Adam" means "mankind" and is used over 500 times in that sense in the Bible.

"Baal," the name commonly used of foreign gods, means "master," "possessor," "Lord" or "husband."

The Hebrew word "beth" means simply "house" or "building" and is often used as the first part of a place name, for example: Bethlehem; Bethesda and Beth-Gilgal.

The Greek name Eutychus, belonging to the young man Paul raised from the dead, appropriately means "lucky" (Acts 20:7-12).

"Pneuma," the Greek word used for the Holy Spirit, occurs 379 times in the New Testament.

The name Jesus means "The Lord saves."

The title "Rabbi" means "my great one" or "my master" or "my teacher." It was a commonplace term of respect.

Two people in the Bible were called Jonah: the Old Testament prophet and the father of Simon Peter (Matthew 16:17).

Four people in the New Testament are named Philip: two sons of Herod the Great, the apostle, and one of the seven chosen in Acts to serve the Church.

The naming of "woman" by Adam is an example of the conferring of a name conveying status.

Facts 3

NAMES AND NICKNAMES

"Mary" is the Greek form of the Hebrew name "Miriam".

The name Zechariah or Zacharias is given to 28 men in the Bible.

The name prefix "Bar" which occurs frequently in the Bible means "son of".

"Shaddai" translated Almighty is used 48 times in the Old Testament for God.

The title "Lamb of God" appears only twice in the New Testament, both in John's Gospel (John 1:29, 36).

Two towns are named Bethlehem in the Old Testament, Bethlehem in Judah where Jesus was born, and Bethlehem in the territory of Zebulun (Joshua 19:15).

Jacob's children born to his wives' maidservants were named by Jacob's wives rather than by their biological mothers.

Nicodemus, the name of the man who came to see Jesus at night, means "conqueror of the people."

Jesus was a fairly common name in the first half of the first century A.D.

Peter's confession of Jesus as Messiah appears only in the Synoptic gospels.

The New Testament name Simon is a later form of the Old Testament name Simeon.

The name "The Holy One of Israel" occurs 29 times in the book of Isaiah.

Paul uses the expression "Son of God" 15 times in the New Testament.

Children are named 18 times in the Bible by their fathers.

Facts 4

NAMES AND NICKNAMES

"Shaddai", meaning "Almighty" occurs 31 times alone in the book of Job.

"Benjamin," the literal meaning of which is "son of my right hand," means "lucky".

The name "Calvary" occurs only once in the Authorized Version in Luke 23:33.

Five people carry the name Herod in the Bible.

The city of Jerusalem was called Jebus by the Jebusites.

By the end of the first century the name Jesus had all but disappeared from usage because Jews despised it and Christians revered it.

According to John the disciple Andrew is the first person to call Jesus "Messiah" (John 1:41).

Who Said That?

Quiz # 1
WHO SAID THAT ?

1. Who lied when she said, "I did not laugh"?

2. Who asked an angel, "How can I be sure of this? I am an old man and my wife is well on in years"?

3. Who called to Adam, "Where are you?"?

4. True or false? Jesus said to Judas, "Friend, do what you came for"?

5. Who named her son Ichabod saying, "The glory has departed from Israel"?

6. Which Roman official stated categorically, "What I have written, I have written"?

7. Who asked Isaiah, "What will be the sign that the Lord will heal me and that I will go up to the temple of the Lord on the third day from now?"?

8. Who made this excuse, "They gave me the gold, and I threw it into the fire, and out came this calf"?

9. Who asked, "Am I my brother's keeper?"?

10. Which king said, "Has your God, whom you serve continually, been able to rescue you from the lions?"?

11. Who asked David, "Am I a dog, that you come at me with sticks?"?

12. "Go! This man is my chosen instrument." Who said this to Ananias?

13. Did Deborah or Esther say to Barak, "I will go with you"?

14. Which disciple responded to Jesus, "Yes Lord, you know that I love you"?

15. Who called out from a cave, "I have been very zealous for the Lord God Almighty"?

Answers

1. Sarah, **2.** Zechariah **3.** God **4.** True (Matthew 26:50)
5. The wife of Phinehas **6.** Pilate **7.** Hezekiah **8.** Aaron **9.** Cain **10.** Darius
11. Goliath **12.** The Lord, about Paul **13.** Deborah **14.** Peter **15.** Elijah

Quiz #2

WHO SAID THAT ?

1. Which Old Testament prophet responded to the Lord's call with the words, "Here am I. Send me"?

2. Who instructed some servants, "Fill the jars with water"?

3. "O man of God, there is death in the pot!" Who said this to Elisha?

4. Who was afraid and said, "What I did must have become known"?

5. "Rabbi, we know you are a teacher who has come from God." Who said this?

6. Who promised, "I will come back and take you to be with me"?

7. True or false? Adam said to Eve, "You will not surely die."

8. Which group of people declared, "Saul has slain his thousands, and David his tens of thousands"?

9. Who said to Elijah, "let me kiss my father and mother goodbye"?

10. Which disciple said, "Unless I see the nail marks in his hands... I will not believe it"?

11. Who said, "Please test your servants for ten days. Give us nothing but vegetables to eat and water to drink"?

12. "It would not be right for us to neglect the ministry of the word of God in order to wait on tables." Who said this?

13. Which three men agreed, "If we are thrown into the blazing furnace, the God we serve is able to save us from it"?

14. Who explained to the crowd at Pentecost, "These men are not drunk, as you suppose"?

15. "The donkeys are for the king's household to ride on, the bread and fruit are for the men to eat, and the wine is to refresh those who become exhausted in the desert." Who said this to king David?

Answers

1. Isaiah 2. Jesus 3. The company of the prophets in Gilgal 4. Moses 5. Nicodemus 6. Jesus 7. False, the serpent said this (Genesis 3:4) 8. The women of the towns of Israel 9. Elisha 10. Thomas 11. Daniel 12. The Twelve 13. Shadrach, Meshach and Abednego 14. Peter 15. Ziba, Mephibosheth's steward

Quiz #3

WHO SAID THAT ?

1. Did Solomon, Job, or David say "In you, O Lord, I have taken refuge; let me never be put to shame"?

2. Who requested, "Lord teach us to pray"?

3. Who presented the Israelites with a choice when he said, "Choose for yourselves this day whom you will serve"?

4. Who said, "You are the God who sees me"?

5. Who swore, "I don't know the man"?

6. Whose address on Mars Hill began, "Men of Athens! I see that in every way you are very religious"?

7. Who said, "I am the good shepherd"?

8. Which Old Testament prophet cried out, "Ah, sovereign Lord! Are you going to destroy the entire remnant of Israel in this outpouring of your wrath on Jerusalem?"?

9. Was it Joseph, Isaac or Abraham who said, "The voice is the voice of Jacob, but the hands are the hands of Esau"?

10. "Do whatever he tells you." Who gave this instruction to servants at a wedding?

11. Which mother cried, "I cannot watch the boy die"?

12. Who offered these words of comfort, "Do not be afraid, Mary, you have found favor with God"?

13. Who called out, "Treason! Treason!"?

14. Which king said, "As I was lying in my bed, the images and visions that passed through my mind terrified me"?

15. Did Saul, David or Jonathan ask "Do you think it is a small matter to become the king's son-in-law?"?

Quiz #4

WHO SAID THAT ?

1. Who made this claim, "All the prophets testify about him that everyone who believes in him receives forgiveness of sins through his name"?

2. Which disciple responded to the risen Christ with the words, "My Lord and my God"?

3. Which young boy said to a frightened king, "Let no-one lose heart on account of this Philistine; your servant will go and fight him"?

4. Who spoke these words, "Let the little children come to me, and do not hinder them"?

5. "The boy has not awakened." Who said this to Elisha?

6. True or false? Jesus said, "I lay down my life for the sheep."

7. Which priest said to the men of Judah and Benjamin, "You have been unfaithful; you have married foreign women, adding to Israel's guilt. Now make consecration to the Lord, the God of your fathers"?

8. Who prayed and restored life to a young girl with the instruction, "Tabitha arise"?

9. Which mighty warrior said, "If the Lord is with us, why has all this happened to us?"?

10. Was it Mary or Martha who said, "The teacher is here and is asking for you"?

11. Who said to Elisha, "When I bow down in the temple of Rimmon, may the Lord forgive your servant for this"?

12. "The battle is the Lord's, and he will give all of you into our hands." Who believed this?

13. True or false? It was the high priest who said to Peter, "Didn't I see you with him in the olive grove?"

14. Did Elijah or Elisha say to a widow, "How can I help you? Tell me, what do you have in your house?"?

15. Who gave the excuse, "I have just got married, so I can't come"?

Answers

1. Peter 2. Thomas 3. David 4. Jesus 5. Gehazi 6. True (John 10:15)
7. Ezra 8. Peter 9. Gideon 10. Martha
11. Naaman 12. David 13. False, the high priest's servant (John 18:26)
14. Elisha 15. An invited guest in the Parable of the Great Banquet

Quiz #5

WHO SAID THAT ?

1. Who spoke these words recorded in the last book of the Old Testament, "Surely the day is coming; it will burn like a furnace. All the arrogant and every evildoer will be stubble"?

2. Whose servants carried the news, "The fever left him yesterday at the seventh hour"?

3. "Curse God and die!" Whose advice was this?

4. Who said to Peter, "Get behind me, Satan"?

5. Which preacher gave this advice, "Remember your creator in the days of your youth"?

6. Which son asked his father, "Where is the lamb for the burnt offering?"?

7. Who asked Jesus, "Good teacher, what must I do to inherit eternal life?"?

8. "Is that you, you troubler of Israel?" Did King Ahab, Obadiah or Jezebel say this to Elijah?

9. Who decided on this course of action, "I will set out and go back to my father and say to him: Father, I have sinned against heaven and against you"?

10. Which queen exclaimed, "I came and saw with my own eyes. Indeed, not even half was told me"?

11. Which king made this excuse, "I was afraid of the people and so I gave in to them"?

12. Who said, "Show me a denarius. Whose portrait and inscription are on it?"

13. "All right, say Shibboleth." Who devised this test for the survivors of Ephraim?

14. Which disciple urged Jesus, "not just my feet but my hands and my head as well"?

15. Which man said to his friends, "Doubtless you are the people, and wisdom will die with you"?

Quiz # 6

WHO SAID THAT ?

1. Which patriarch said concerning Bethel, "This is none other than the house of God; this is the gate of heaven"?

2. Two men agreed, "The land we passed through and explored is exceedingly good." Who were they?

3. Which disciple said to Jesus, "We have left everything to follow you"?

4. Who asked shepherds at a well, "Do you know Laban, Nahor's grandson?"?

5. "Grant that one of these two sons of mine may sit at your right and the other at your left in your kingdom." Who asked this of Jesus?

6. Who asked his workers, "Whose young woman is that?"?

7. Who admitted, "I have acted like a fool and have erred greatly"?

8. Who questioned Jesus, "But, Lord, why do you intend to show yourself to us and not to the world?"?

9. Which wife advised, "Have a gallows built, seventy-four feet high, and ask the king in the morning to have Mordecai hanged on it"?

10. "Here is a true Israelite, in whom there is nothing false." To whom did Jesus say this?

11. Who told Peter, "Put your sword away"?

12. True or false? Moses said about Benjamin, "Let the beloved of the Lord rest secure in him."

13. Did Stephen, Paul, Philip, or Peter ask the Ethiopian eunuch, "Do you understand what you are reading?"

14. Who told a parable which began, "There were two men in a certain town, one rich and the other poor"?

15. Which royal person said, "There is a man in your kingdom who has the spirit of the holy gods in him"?

Quiz #7

WHO SAID THAT ?

1. Who said, "With a donkey's jaw-bone I have killed a thousand men"?

2. Which blind man called out, "Jesus, Son of David, have mercy on me"?

3. Who cried out to the Lord, "What am I to do with these people? They are almost ready to stone me"?

4. Which great friend of David said, "My father Saul is looking for a chance to kill you"?

5. Which man used this line in his preaching, "Cast your bread upon the waters, for after many days you will find it again"?

6. "I am a woman who is deeply troubled. I have not been drinking wine or beer; I was pouring out my soul to the Lord." Who protested her innocence to Eli with these words?

7. Who spoke these words of praise around the throne in heaven: "You are worthy, our Lord and God, to receive glory and honor and power, for you created all things"?

8. "Is it nothing to you, all you who pass by? Look around and see. Is any suffering like my suffering?" Which weeping prophet said this?

9. Which man in authority said to Paul, "You have permission to speak for yourself"?

10. Who, described as a devout believer in the Lord, asked, "Is it really you, my lord Elijah?"?

11. True or false? Martha said to Jesus, "Lord, if you had been here, my brother would not have died."

12. Which lady sang these words, "Sing to the Lord, for he is highly exalted. The horse and its rider he has hurled into the sea"?

13. Was it Naomi, Martha or Esther who said to her daughters-in-law, "Go back each of you to your mother's home"?

14. Who asked his friends, "Why are you so afraid? Do you still have no faith?"?

15. Who said to Job, "Are you the first man ever born? Were you bought forth before the hills?"?

Quiz #8

WHO SAID THAT ?

1. Who sat at the city gate and said to each other, "Why stay here until we die?... so let's go over to the camp of the Arameans and surrender"?

2. Which group of people said to Pilate, "We have a law, and according to that law he must die"?

3. True or false? Mordecai asked, "What is it, Queen Esther? What is your request?"

4. "You study the Scriptures because you think that by them you possess eternal life." Who said this to the Jews who questioned him?

5. Who said to David, "What is your servant that you should notice a dead dog like me?"?

6. "Master, master, we're going to drown!" Who said this to Jesus in Luke's gospel?

7. Who instructed his servants, "Stay here with the donkey while I and the boy go over there. We will worship and then we will come back to you"?

8. "My daughter, should I not try to find a home for you, where you will be well provided for?" Who said this?

9. Who asked the chief priests, "What are you willing to give me if I hand him over to you?"?

10. Which two family members asked Rebekah, "Will you go with this man?"?

11. Who asked Jacob, "How old are you?"?

12. Which Old Testament prophet delivered the word of the Lord that included the statement, "You have wearied the Lord with your words"?

13. Which impetuous disciple said to Jesus, "Tell me to come to you on the water"?

14. Was it Bildad or Eliphaz who advised Job, "Can a man be of benefit to God?"?

15. Who said, "Just as Moses lifted the snake in the desert, so the Son of Man must be lifted up"?

---

12. Malachi 13. Peter 14. Eliphaz 15. Jesus
10. Rebekah's mother and brother 11. Pharaoh
5. Mephibosheth 6. The disciples 7. Abraham 8. Naomi 9. Judas Iscariot
1. 4 lepers 2. The Jews 3. False, King Xerxes (Esther 5:3) 4. Jesus

Answers

Quiz #9

WHO SAID THAT ?

1. Did men from Gilgal, Beth Shemesh or Ashdod say, "Who can stand in the presence of the Lord, this holy God? To whom will the ark go up from here?"?

2. Which Old Testament prophet instructed his servant, "Get some flour"?

3. Who said to Jesus, "but even the dogs eat the crumbs that fall from the masters' table"?

4. Which Old Testament prophet advised his travelling companions, "Pick me up and throw me into the sea"?

5. Who advised Isaiah, "Go out, you and your son Shear-Jashub to meet Ahaz at the end of the aqueduct of the Upper Pool"?

6. Did Solomon, Hezekiah or Ahab say, "I intend, therefore, to build a temple for the Name of the Lord my God"?

7. "Come, be our commander, so we can fight the Ammonites." Who made this request of Jephthah?

8. Who said, "Draw your sword and run me through"?

9. "Talitha Koum!" Who gave this instruction?

10. Who said, "My silver has been returned. Here it is in my sack"?

11. Which old man on an island said, "On the Lord's day I was in the Spirit, and I heard behind me a loud voice like a trumpet"?

12. Who asked his wife, "Don't I mean more to you than ten sons?"?

13. Who made the request of Philip, "Sir, we would like to see Jesus"?

14. Who flattered Solomon, "How happy your men must be! How happy your officials who continually stand before you and hear your wisdom"?

15. Who said to God, "Stretch out your hand and strike his flesh and bones, and he will surely curse you to his face"?

---

14. Queen of Sheba **15.** Satan (concerning Job)

13. Some Greeks who arrived in Jerusalem for the feast

10. Joseph's brothers **11.** John **12.** Elkanah

6. Solomon **7.** The elders of Gilead **8.** Saul **9.** Jesus

1. Beth Shemesh **2.** Elisha **3.** The Syro-phoenician woman **4.** Jonah **5.** The Lord

Answers

Quiz #10
WHO SAID THAT ?

1. Which major prophet said, "I was among the exiles by the Kebar River"?

2. Who said to Peter and John, "Go and make preparations for us to eat the Passover"?

3. Was it Micaiah or Micah who prophesied against Ahab, "I saw all Israel scattered on the hills like sheep without a shepherd"?

4. Whose final words of blessing included the words, "May the angel who has delivered me from all harm bless these boys"?

5. "Are you only a visitor to Jerusalem and do you not know the things that have happened there in these days?" Who asked this question of a travelling companion?

6. Who warned Asahal, "Stop chasing me! Why should I strike you down? How could I look your brother Joab in the face?"?

7. True or false? Peter protested, "Although I have done nothing against our people or against the customs of our ancestors, I was arrested in Jerusalem and handed over to the Romans."

8. Who instructed Joseph, "Get up, take the child and his mother and escape to Egypt"?

9. Which queen said, "How can I bear to see disaster fall on my people? How can I bear to see the destruction of my family?"?

10. Who prayed, "Father, forgive them, for they do not know what they are doing"?

11. "I'm convinced! My son Joseph is still alive. I will go and see him before I die." Who said this before setting out for Egypt?

12. Who asked Rebekah, "Please give me a little water from your jar"?

13. In Jesus' parable, who said, "Give us some of your oil; our lamps are going out"?

14. "If you are the Son of God, throw yourself down." Who tempted Jesus in this way?

15. Did Joab, Joram, or Joash send this message to Jehoshaphat, "Will you go with me to fight against Moab?"?

Answers

1. Ezekiel 2. Jesus 3. Micaiah 4. Jacob 5. Cleopas 6. Abner, the commander of Saul's army 7. False, Paul (Acts 28:17) 8. An angel of the Lord 9. Esther 10. Jesus 11. Israel/Jacob 12. Isaac's servant who met her at a well outside Nahor 13. The foolish five virgins 14. The devil 15. Joram

Quiz # 11

WHO SAID THAT ?

1. Who told Jeroboam, king of Israel, "Amos is raising a conspiracy against you in the very heart of Israel. The land cannot bear all his words"?

2. Who prayed, "Lord, do not let this sin be held against them"?

3. Which prophet said to a king, "Prepare a poultice of figs"?

4. Who said to David, "May my lord pay no attention to that wicked man Nabal. He is just like his name—his name is Fool and folly goes with him"?

5. Was it the Pharisee or the tax collector in Jesus' parable who prayed, "I thank you that I am not like other men—robbers, evildoers, adulterers"?

6. Who asked the Lord, "How can I save Israel? My clan is the weakest in Manasseh, and I am the least in my family"?

7. "Where is the one who has been born king of the Jews? We saw his star in the east and have come to worship him." Who said this?

8. Who said to Jonah, "How can you sleep? Get up and call on your god! Maybe he will take notice of us, and we will not perish"?

9. True or false? The men of Athens said to the apostles, "We want to hear you again on this subject."

10. Who said to Eli, "Here I am; you called me"?

11. "The Lord's name for you is not Pashhur, but Magor-Missabib." Which prophet said this after being released from stocks?

12. Whose parents said, "Ask him. He is of age; he will speak for himself"?

13. Who lamented, "Utterly meaningless! Everything is meaningless"?

14. Who challenged the Pharisees, "What do you think about the Christ?"?

15. Which prophetic figure claimed, "After me will come one more powerful than I, whose sandals I am not fit to carry"?

Quiz # 12

WHO SAID THAT ?

1. Who tempted Jesus by saying, "If you are the Son of God, tell this stone to become bread"?

2. Which wife cynically commented, "How the king of Israel has distinguished himself today, disrobing in the sight of the slave girls of his servants as any vulgar fellow would"?

3. Who protested against God's call with the words, "Who am I that I should go to Pharaoh and bring the Israelites out of Egypt?"?

4. Which New Testament writer claimed, "I have fought the good fight, I have finished the race, I have kept the faith"?

5. Was it Peter, Andrew or Matthew who said, "Here is a boy with five small barley loaves and two small fish, but how far will they go among so many?"?

6. True or false? John the Baptist said, "You brood of vipers. Who warned you to flee from the coming wrath?"?

7. "The God of heaven will give us success. We his servants will start rebuilding, but as for you, you have no share in Jerusalem or any claim or historic right to it." Who said this to Sanballat, Tobiah and Geshem?

8. Who announced Jesus to the crowds with the words, "Here is the man"?

9. "Didn't I tell you not to sin against the boy? But you wouldn't listen! Now we must give an accounting for his blood." Which of Joseph's brothers said this?

10. Who said to Jesus, "Here and now I give half of my possessions to the poor, and if I have cheated anybody out of anything, I will pay back four times the amount"?

11. Which king said to Paul, "Do you think that in such a short time you can persuade me to be a Christian?"?

12. Who posed this question to Jesus, "Are you the one who was to come or shall we expect someone else?"?

13. Which teacher explained, "It is not the healthy who need a doctor, but the sick"?

14. Who said to Elisha about an ax, "O my Lord, it was borrowed"?

15. Which Moabite woman said to Naomi, "Let me go to the fields and pick up the leftover grain"?

Quiz #13

WHO SAID THAT ?

1. Who said, "I appeal to you for my son Onesimus"?

2. Which king gave the order, "Go and make a careful search for the child"?

3. This servant of God said, "As for me and my house, we will serve the Lord." Who was he?

4. Was it Solomon, Saul or Samuel who gave the order, "Muster the forces and see who has left us"?

5. Who said to his parents, "I have seen a Philistine woman in Timnah; now get her for me as my wife"?

6. Who muttered against Jesus, "This man welcomes sinners, and eats with them"?

7. Which left-handed man came with tribute to Eglon king of Moab saying, "I have a secret message for you, O king"?

8. "Quick, let me have some of that red stew! I'm famished!" Who said this to his brother?

9. Who confessed, "The Lord has given and the Lord has taken away. Praise the name of the Lord"?

10. True or false? Saul said to Mephibosheth, "I will surely show you kindness for the sake of your father Jonathan."

11. Did Peter, Paul, Jesus, or James say "Take off the grave clothes and let him go"?

12. Who advised Rehoboam to tell the complaining people, "My little finger is thicker than my father's waist. My father laid on you a heavy burden; I will make it even heavier"?

13. Who asked, "O Sovereign Lord, what can you give me since I remain childless and the one who will inherit my estate is Eliezer of Damascus?"?

14. Was it Agrippa, Felix, or Festus who said to Paul, "Your great learning is making you insane"?

15. Did Rebekah, Naomi, or Hannah say, "I prayed for this child, so now I give him to the Lord"?

---

12. The young men who had grown up with him **13.** Abraham **14.** Festus **15.** Hannah

10. False, David said this (2 Samuel 9:7) **11.** Jesus

7. Ehud **8.** Esau **9.** Job

6. The Pharisees and teachers of the law

1. Paul **2.** Herod **3.** Joshua **4.** Saul **5.** Samson

Answers

Quiz # 14

WHO SAID THAT ?

1. Did Balaam or Barak say, "Build me seven altars here, and prepare seven bulls and seven rams"?

2. Which brother saw his sister inflicted with leprosy and pleaded with Moses, "Please, my lord, do not hold against us the sin we have so foolishly committed"?

3. Was it Moses, Manasseh or Manoah who said to his wife, "We are doomed to die! We have seen God"?

4. Who protested, "Should a man like me run away? Or should one like me go to the temple to save his life? I will not go"?

5. Did Jesus say to his disciples, "Come and have breakfast"?

6. Who said to Zedekiah the king "They (the Babylonians) will not hand you over"?

7. "Here I am today, eighty-five years old. I am still as strong today as the day Moses sent me out." Who said this to Joshua at Gilgal?

8. Which son said to Jacob, "If you will send our brother along with us, we will go down and buy food for you"?

9. Which king protested about the Lord's instruction to him by saying, "But what about the hundred talents I paid for these Israelite troops?'"?

10. Which disciple declared to Jesus, "You are the Christ, the son of the living God"?

11. Who spoke up on behalf of the poor saying to nobles and officials, "You are exacting usury from your own countrymen"?

12. Was it a poor man, a rich man, a Jewish man or a Samaritan who asked Jesus, "Teacher, what good thing must I do to get eternal life?"?

13. Which king instructed his messengers, "Go and consult Baal-Zebub, the god of Ekron, to see if I will recover from this injury"?

14. Who expressed his generosity with the words "Come over here. Have some bread and dip it in wine vinegar"? Was it Boaz or Hosea?

15. Who said to Jesus, "Lord, if you are willing you can make me clean"?

Answers

1. Balaam said this to Barak 2. Aaron, regarding Miriam 3. Manoah
4. Nehemiah 5. Yes, after his resurrection 6. Jeremiah 7. Caleb 8. Judah
9. Amaziah 10. Peter 11. Nehemiah 12. A rich man
13. Ahaziah 14. Boaz 15. A man with leprosy

Quiz # 15

WHO SAID THAT ?

1. Who made the excuse, "The serpent deceived me, and I ate"?

2. Who reassured some women, "Do not be afraid, for I know that you are looking for Jesus, who was crucified. He is not here; he has risen"?

3. Who said to Isaac, "This is from the Lord. We can say nothing to you one way or the other. Here is Rebekah; take her and go"?

4. True or false? Martha said about Lazarus' tomb, "By this time there is a bad odor, for he has been there four days."

5. This Old Testament prophet said, "Ah, Sovereign Lord, I do not know how to speak; I am only a child."

6. Who identified Jesus with the words, "Behold the lamb of God"?

7. Was it Jews or Jesus' disciples who responded to Jesus' teaching saying, "This is a hard teaching. Who can accept it?"?

8. Who promised Solomon, "I will give you what you have not asked for—both riches and honor—so that in your lifetime you will have no equal among kings"?

9. "This is my body, which is for you; do this in remembrance of me." Who said this on the night he was betrayed?

10. What was the surprising source of this comment, "What have I done to you to make you beat me these three times?"?

11. Who told David, "Your servant Uriah the Hittite is dead"?

12. True or false? Jesus said to his disciples, "Not one stone here will be left on another."

13. Who said to a horseman, "What do you have to do with peace?"?

14. Was it Joseph's brothers or Nebuchadnezzar's advisers that said, "Here comes that dreamer! Come now, let's kill him"?

15. Who said, "Now I know without a doubt that the Lord sent his angel and rescued me from Herod's clutches"?

13. Jehu **14.** Joseph's brothers **15.** Peter
10. Balaam's donkey **11.** One of Joab's messengers **12.** True (Matthew 24:2)
5. Jeremiah **6.** John the Baptist **7.** Jesus' disciples **8.** The Lord **9.** The Lord Jesus
1. Eve **2.** The angel at the tomb **3.** Laban and Bethuel **4.** True (John 11:39)

Answers

Quiz # 16
WHO SAID THAT ?

1. Who said, "My father has made trouble for the country. See how my eyes brightened when I tasted a little of this honey?"?

2. Whose daughter demanded, "I want you to give me right now the head of John the Baptist on a platter"?

3. "Is the Lord's arm too short? You will now see whether or not what I say will come true for you." Who said this to Moses reassuring him about the promise of quail?

4. Was it the chief priests or the disciples who asked Jesus "Who is the greatest in the kingdom of heaven?"?

5. "I am the most ignorant of men; I do not have a man's understanding." Who made this confession?

6. Who declared, "Even if all fall away on account of you, I never will"?

7. Was it Adam or Eve who said to God, "I heard you in the garden, and I was afraid because I was naked, so I hid"?

8. True or false? Jesus said, "Saul, Saul, why do you persecute me?"?

9. Which concerned mother said, "If Jacob takes a wife from among the women of this land, from Hittite women like these, my life will not be worth living"?

10. Who said to Araunah when he was buying a threshing-floor, "I insist on paying the full price. I will not take for the Lord what is yours, or sacrifice a burnt offering that costs me nothing"?

11. Who asked the crowd, "Which one do you want me to release to you: Barabbas, or Jesus who is called Christ?"?

12. Which patriarch said to God, "If only Ishmael might live under your blessing"?

13. Who lied when she claimed, "Yes, the men came to me but I did not know where they had come from. At dusk...the men left. I don't know which way they went"?

14. True or false? Jesus' family said about him, "He is out of his mind."

15. Who said to Joseph, "I too had a dream: on my head were three baskets of bread"?

Answers

1. Jonathan **2.** Herodias' daughter **3.** The Lord **4.** The disciples
5. Agur, son of Jakeh (Proverbs 30:2) **6.** Peter **7.** Adam **8.** True (Acts 9:4)
9. Rebekah **10.** King David **11.** Pilate **12.** Abraham **13.** Rahab
14. True (Mark 3:21) **15.** The chief baker

Quiz #17

WHO SAID THAT ?

1. Which prophet cried out, "Woe to me! I am ruined! For I am a man of unclean lips and I live among a people of unclean lips"?

2. Who asked Philip, "Why shouldn't I be baptized?"?

3. Who said to his brothers, "I am about to die. But God will surely come to your aid and take you up out of this land"?

4. "Go make the tomb as secure as you know how." Who gave this instruction?

5. Who told the Israelites, "I am now a hundred and twenty years old and I am no longer able to lead you"?

6. Who said to Jesus, "I have no one to help me into the pool when the water is stirred"?

7. Which prophet answered the Lord, "I see a boiling pot, tilting away from the north"?

8. Who said while being stoned, "Look, I see heaven open and the Son of Man standing at the right hand of God"?

9. Which king of Moab said, "A people has come out of Egypt, they cover the face of the land and have settled next to me"?

10. Which disciple asked Jesus, "Lord, how many times shall I forgive my brother when he sins against me? Up to seven times?"?

11. Who said to Paul, "The magistrates have ordered that you and Silas be released. Now you can leave"?

12. Was it Job, Joel or Joseph who declared, "I know that my redeemer lives"?

13. True or false? The Pharisees said about Jesus, "See this is getting us nowhere. Look how the whole world has gone after him."

14. Who was the speaker in Revelation who stood in the sun and cried out with a loud voice, "Come, gather together for the great supper of God"?

15. Who said to his traveling companions, "Now I urge you to take some food. You need it to survive. Not one of you will lose a single hair from your head"?

Answers

1. Isaiah 2. The Ethiopian eunuch 3. Joseph 4. Pilate 5. Moses
6. The invalid at the pool of Bethesda
7. Jeremiah 8. Stephen 9. Balak 10. Peter 11. The jailer 12. Job
13. True (John 12:19) 14. An angel 15. Paul

Quiz # 18

WHO SAID THAT ?

1. Who said, "Arise, Balak, and listen; hear me son of Zippor. God is not man, that he should lie"?

2. Who asked Pharaoh's daughter, "Shall I go and get one of the Hebrew women to nurse the baby for you?"?

3. "I cannot redeem it because I might endanger my own estate." Who said this to Boaz?

4. Who asked Paul and Silas, "What must I do to be saved?"?

5. True or false? David said to Saul, "I cut off the corner of your robe but did not kill you."

6. Who advised Jesus, "Send the crowd away so they can go to the surrounding villages and countryside and find food and lodging"?

7. Did David or Delilah say, "The Philistines are upon you"?

8. Who encouraged Hobab the Midianite, "Come with us and we will treat you well, for the Lord has promised good things to Israel"?

9. Which disciple said to Jesus, "Show us the father"?

10. Who said, "I am a Jew born in Tarsus of Cilicia"?

11. Which woman said, "If I just touch his clothes, I will be healed"?

12. "If only my master would see the prophet who is in Samaria! He would cure him of his leprosy." Who gave this advice concerning Naaman?

13. Who pleaded with Ishmael, son of Nethaniah, "Don't kill us! We have wheat and barley, oil and honey, hidden in a field"?

14. True or false? Caiaphas said, "I am innocent of this man's blood. It is your responsibility."

15. "Go into the prostitute's house and bring her out and all who belong to her." Who gave this instruction to his two spies?

13. 10 of 80 bearded men thrown in a cistern 14. False, Pilate said this (Matthew 27:24) 15. Joshua
11. The woman who had bled for twelve years 12. The young Israelite servant girl who served Naaman's wife
6. The Twelve 7. Delilah 8. Moses 9. Philip 10. Paul
4. The Philippian jailer 5. True (1 Samuel 24:11)
1. Balaam 2. Miriam 3. The kinsman redeemer

Answers

Quiz # 19

WHO SAID THAT ?

1. Who gave this verdict on Jesus, "Surely this was a righteous man"?

2. Which king said about Ahimaaz, "He's a good man. He comes with good news"?

3. Was it two men dressed in white or three strangers who asked the apostles, "Men of Galilee, why do you stand here looking into the sky?"?

4. Who turned down favors from a king with the words, "You may keep your gifts for yourself and give your rewards to someone else"?

5. "I do believe; help me overcome my unbelief." Were these the words of a father whose son was healed or a Pharisee who asked Jesus about the kingdom of heaven?

6. Was it Crispus, Gallio, or Felix who said, "Since it involves questions about words and names and your own law—settle the matter yourselves"?

7. "Every boy that is born you must throw into the Nile." Who gave this instruction?

8. Which prophet gave this instruction concerning Joshua the high priest: "Put a clean turban on his head"?

9. Who told Simon Peter, "They have taken the Lord out of the tomb, and we do not know where they have put him"?

10. "The virgin will be with child and will give birth to a son, and will call him Immanuel." Which prophet gave these details about a sign from God for Ahaz?

11. Which king gave the order, "Cut the living child in two and give half to one and half to the other"?

12. "Let us put up three shelters—one for you, one for Moses and one for Elijah." Which disciple who witnessed the transfiguration made this suggestion?

13. Who offered the apostles money saying, "Give me also this ability so that everyone on whom I lay my hands may receive the Holy Spirit"?

14. Who tested her husband with the words, "How can you say I love you, when you won't confide in me?"?

15. True or false? Felix said to Paul, "I will hear your case when your accusers get here."

Quiz #20
WHO SAID THAT ?

1. Who complained, "All these years I've been slaving for you and never disobeyed your orders. Yet you never gave me even a young goat so I could celebrate with my friends"?

2. Which king prayed, "May the Lord, who is good, pardon everyone who sets his heart on seeking God"?

3. When Isaiah was commissioned did cherubim, seraphim, archangels or messengers from God call to one another saying, "Holy, holy, holy is the Lord Almighty"?

4. Which disciple asked, "How can a man be born when he is old?"?

5. True or false? Nehemiah admitted, "I was ashamed to ask the king for soldiers and horsemen to protect us from enemies on the road."

6. Which king inspired by his love for Absalom asked, "Is the young man Absalom safe?"?

7. Was it 3,000 men from Judah or 5,000 foot soldiers from Bethel who said to Samson, "We've come to tie you up and hand you over to the Philistines"?

8. Who asked the first Christian martyr, "Are these charges true?"?

9. Was it Zebulan, Zophar or Zechariah who said to his friend, "Oh how I wish that God would speak, that he would open his lips against you"?

10. "Bless me—me too my father!" Who pleaded with his father in this way?

11. Who argued against Peter saying, "You are a Jew, yet you live like a Gentile and not like a Jew"?

12. Who questioned himself with the words, "Why are you downcast, O my soul? Why so disturbed within me?"

13. Which son of Jehiel said to Ezra, "Rise up; this matter is in your hands. We will support you so take courage and do it"?

14. Who, according to Revelation, will stand far off and cry, "Woe, woe, O great city, O Babylon, city of power! In one hour your doom has come"?

15. "Why does your face look so sad when you are not ill? This can be nothing but sadness of heart?" Who said this to Nehemiah?

Quiz #21
WHO SAID THAT ?

1. Who said to David, "Why are you alone? Why is no one with you?"?

2. Who moaned, "If only we had died in Egypt! Or in the desert!"?

3. Which prophet included these words in his prayer, "The engulfing waters threatened me, the deep surrounded me, seaweed was wrapped around my head"?

4. Which three people agreed about Paul, "This man is not doing anything that deserves death or imprisonment"?

5. Who asked, "Son, why have you treated us like this?"?

6. "I will not ask; I will not put the Lord to the test." Who said this?

7. Did Jonah, Joel or Job say, "God does not restrain his anger; even the cohorts of Rahab cowered at his feet"?

8. Who asked the crowds at Jairus' house, "Why all this commotion and wailing?"

9. Which son of Zechariah addressed all those living in Judah and Jerusalem, saying, "The battle is not yours, but God's"?

10. "I am not ashamed of the gospel, because it is the power of God for the salvation of everyone who believes." Who said this?

11. Which woman asked Jesus, "Where can you get this living water?"?

12. Who told the Israelites in his farewell speech, "I will call upon the Lord to send thunder and rain. And you will realize what an evil thing you did in the eyes of the Lord when you asked for a king"?

13. "I have found the Book of the Law in the temple of the Lord." Who said this to the secretary Shaphan?

14. Was it the disciples, the Pharisees or Roman officials who asked Jesus, "How did the fig tree wither so quickly?"?

15. Who heard Isaiah's message and concluded, "There will be peace and security in my lifetime"?

---

13. Hilkiah, the priest 14. The disciples 15. Hezekiah
9. Jahaziel 10. Paul 11. The Samaritan woman at the well 12. Samuel
4. King Agrippa, Felix, Bernice 5. Mary, mother of Jesus 6. Ahaz 7. Job 8. Jesus
1. Ahimelech the priest 2. The wandering Israelites 3. Jonah

Answers

Facts 1

WHO SAID THAT ?

A key aspect of the nature of God in the Old Testament is that he speaks directly to his people. The importance of this is that he reveals himself as a God who desires meaningful relationships and is superior to other gods who cannot speak (see Jeremiah 10:5).

The first question in the Bible is God's question to Adam, "Where are you?" (Genesis 3:9).

Peter's confession at Caesarea Philippi that Jesus is the Christ is recorded in three of the Gospels (Matthew 16:13-16; Mark 8:27-29; Luke 9:18-21). In all accounts Jesus tells the disciples not to tell anyone else that he is the Christ.

Old Testament prophets are moral teachers who are closely associated with organized worship. They are often outspoken about empty formality in religious life (see Isaiah 1:10-17; Amos 5:21-24; Hosea 6:6; Micah 6:6-8).

In John 6:60 the disciples respond to Jesus' teaching with the statement, "This is a hard saying, who can listen to it?" This suggests that they understood that Jesus' teaching was both hard to understand and hard to accept.

Philip's conversation with the Ethiopian eunuch (Acts 8:26-40) suggests the eunuch was reading aloud from Isaiah. This was (and to some extent still is) the norm. Oriental people often read aloud even when there is no intention of being heard by others.

The book of Proverbs is full of wise sayings giving practical instructions about how to live. The Hebrew word translated "proverb" is a broad term used of short phrases and longer discourses of instruction. Elsewhere in the Old Testament it is simply translated "parable".

Stephen was stoned after making a speech to the Jewish council and he became the first Christian martyr (see Acts 7). His speech is one of the earliest examples of Christian preaching, surveying as it does Israelite history.

One of the most surprising statements about Jesus' teaching is, "he taught them as one who had authority, not as the teachers of the law" (Mark 1:22). It is remarkable that people who increasingly relied on the teachers of the law in order to understand Scripture could contrast such teachers with Jesus who didn't merely repeat traditions but brought a new authority.

Luke 10:39 informs us that Mary sat at the feet of Jesus. It was common practice for teachers to sit with their disciples around their feet although the specifics of such customs seemed to vary at different times. It symbolized submission and respect.

The Book of Daniel is difficult to date but its first part concerns a Jewish man in exile who consistently expresses his confidence in God and refused to compromise in matters of faith and religious life.

Facts 2

WHO SAID THAT ?

The Hebrew title for the book of Deuteronomy is simply "these are the words". This reflects its main content: God's words to his people.

The first question in the New Testament is that of the wise men, "Where is the one who has been born king of the Jews?" (Matthew 2:2).

The Ten Commandments are collectively known as the Decalogue, meaning literally "the ten words". Throughout the centuries Jewish people have understood these ten words as the basis of all Jewish law, and the benchmark of all religious life and conduct.

Jesus himself shows us that quoting from the Bible is a useful thing to do. This is how he deals with the devil before the start of his public ministry when he was tempted in the desert (Luke 4:1-13).

The most famous example of Jesus' teaching is to be found in the Sermon on the Mount (Matthew 5-7). This may be a summary of what Jesus taught on one occasion or a compilation of various sermons.

The Bible can be read aloud in about 70 hours.

The book of Psalms contains many examples of the psalmist talking and reasoning with himself. Perhaps the best example is Psalm 42-43 (originally one psalm) with the refrain "Why are you downcast, O my soul? Why so disturbed within me?"

John 14-16 contain Jesus' words of comfort and instruction to his disciples. Unique to John's Gospel these chapters have become known as "the farewell discourses."

Deborah is the only woman in the Bible identified as a judge. Her instructions to Barak were that he should lead the Israelite army against Sisera. She gave thanks to God for the ensuing victory in a great poem (Judges 4-5).

Jesus is frequently addressed as "Rabbi". This is simply a title of distinction given to those who teach and its nearest equivalent is "master" or "sir."

Facts 3

WHO SAID THAT ?

Moses undertakes a very special role as mediator between God and man. He has direct access to God and is portrayed as an obedient servant who mediates the covenant to the people. The writer to the Hebrews understands Moses as one who foreshadows the ministry of Jesus, the mediator of the new covenant.

The first recorded words of Jesus' public ministry are, "Repent, for the kingdom of heaven is near" (Matthew 4:17).

Peter's ministry becomes very significant after the resurrection. He is the first to address the crowds on the Day of Pentecost.

Angels perform a special role as God's messengers making known his word to human beings. Their messages frequently bring the opportunity of salvation (see Acts 11:13-14).

The phrase "I am coming soon" punctuates the text of the final chapter of the Bible occurring three times (Revelation 22:7, 12, 20).

Moses and Aaron suffered a great deal because the people of Israel "grumbled" at them (see Exodus 15:24; Numbers 14:1, 29).

The first speech recorded in the New Testament belongs to the angel of the Lord who appeared to Joseph in a dream predicting Jesus' birth (see Matthew 1:20-21).

The New Testament word "parable" is a broad term, which can be used of practical sayings and stories, and can be used of quite short metaphorical phrases and similes. Literature throughout the centuries has made use of parabolic phrases and stories.

Isaiah 13-23 contain a series of prophetic oracles of judgment against 13 nations who stand in opposition to God and his people. Ezekiel 25-32 contains a similar series of oracles against seven nations.

James 3:1-12 discusses the evil power of the tongue. The tongue is described as "a restless evil, full of deadly poison" (verse 8), which "corrupts the whole person" (verse 6).

The first words God spoke to man and woman were words of blessing (see Genesis 1:27-30).

Facts 4

WHO SAID THAT ?

Jesus' first recorded words are, "Why were you searching for me? Didn't you know I had to be in my father's house?" (Luke 2:49).

The judges were responsible for making impartial judgments but also became important political and military figures. Othniel was the first judge of Israel; Deborah was the first woman judge.

When Jesus is asked, "Which is the greatest command in the Law?" he responds with two quotations from the Old Testament taken from Deuteronomy 6:5 and Leviticus 19:18.

Zechariah was struck with temporary dumbness because he didn't believe Gabriel's message (see Luke 1:11-22).

The address "son of man" is used over one hundred times in the book of Ezekiel.

Some of the Psalms are best described as conversations with God. Many of these contain the vocative address "O God" or "O Lord". They are honest and often urgent pleas to God. Psalm 38 is a good example.

Hagar was found by the angel of the Lord by a fountain (Genesis 16:7). This is the first angel visitation recorded in the Bible.

Jesus emphasizes the importance of keeping oaths in Matthew 5:33-37. His point is that his followers should have a scrupulous regard for the truth and be known as people of their word.

In the entire book of Esther, God is not mentioned once. But his guidance and presence is assumed throughout.

The word "disciple" simply means "learner". Being a disciple includes listening to the words of your teacher.

There are many poems and songs in the book of Psalms that express praise to God for his work, his goodness and his love. Of particular importance is the "hallelujah" collection (Psalms 146-150).

Facts 5

WHO SAID THAT ?

Prophets existed in Old Testament times from the time of Moses. Moses is described as a prophet of special status because God spoke to him face to face and he was able to perform miracles (Deuteronomy 34:10-12).

Conversation and debate is key to the content of the book of Job. Job, his three friends, and God, speak together in this gripping story that is told through speeches, replies and monologues.

In every day conversations we use phrases from the Bible all the time. Here are a few: weighed and found wanting, the root of all evil, a word in season, casting pearls before swine, an eye for an eye.

Binding agreements in the Bible are called covenants. There are 7 covenants in the Bible between God and his people.

Rachel died in childbirth and her final words were to name her son Ben-Oni (son of my trouble). Jacob renamed him Benjamin (son of my right hand).

Jesus' use of parables is quite surprising. He chose to speak to the crowds almost exclusively in parables.

Psalm 119, the longest chapter in the Bible, is a celebration of God's word emphasizing its eternal worth and value (verses 89, 105).

Every chapter of the Book of Hebrews either contains a quotation from the Old Testament or mentions an Old Testament character by name.

The Gospels give us over one hundred examples of Jesus using parabolic language.

It has been suggested that 1 Peter is largely made up of a sermon that was delivered to first century baptismal candidates. This would explain the dominant imperatives (commands and exhortations) throughout its chapters.

In Luke 4:31-37 Jesus drives out an evil spirit from a man who was shouting out and taunting him. Jesus' command "Be quiet" achieves its desired effect and underlines his amazing authority.

Facts 6

WHO SAID THAT ?

Psalm 118:8 is the middle verse of the entire Bible. Its message is particularly relevant to us as we consider conversation and lifestyle: "It is better to take refuge in the Lord than to trust in man."

The most quoted verse from Job occurs in chapter 19:25 "I know that my redeemer lives". This verse has almost become inseparable from the inspiring music to which it was set by the composer Handel.

Perjury has been considered a serious offence in law codes governing communities throughout the centuries. In Jeremiah 7:9 it is listed alongside stealing, murdering, committing adultery and idolatry.

The Bible denounces false prophets because they lead people astray and may be motivated by financial reward or deceit (see Nehemiah 6:12-13; Jeremiah 6:13-15).

Occasionally the gospel writers record the exact Aramaic phrases Jesus uses. Two examples are Mark 5:41 "Talitha koum" and Mark 15:34 "Eloi, Eloi, lama sabachthani?"

Eat, Drink and Be Merry

Quiz # 1

EAT, DRINK AND BE MERRY

1. What tasted "like something made with olive oil" when it was ground and baked? It also tasted like wafers made with honey.

2. What does the word "manna" mean?

3. In which Old Testament book do your find the words, "A man can do nothing better than to eat and drink and find satisfaction in his work"?

4. In which New Testament letter is it written, "It is better not to eat meat or drink wine or do anything else that will cause your brother to fall"?

5. Who were critical of Jesus eating with tax collectors and "sinners"?

6. Jesus enjoyed receiving hospitality more than once in the home of two sisters and a brother. What were their names?

7. Who in the New Testament was blind for three days during which time he did not eat or drink anything?

8. What advice does the book of Proverbs give to its readers about, "those who drink too much wine or gorge themselves on meat"?

9. Which group of Christians did Paul accuse of misbehaving at the Lord's Supper, because some people remained hungry while others got drunk?

10. What did God forbid concerning an animal that had died by itself?

11. When Jesus' disciples urged him, "Rabbi, eat something," how did Jesus reply?

12. Olive oil had many purposes in Bible times. What did James' letter say oil should be used for?

13. Who plotted to get Lot drunk?

14. What was a favorite food for Isaac?

15. Which queen agreed that she and her maids should fast for three days and nights?

Answers

1. Manna

2. "What?" Or, "What is it?" **3.** Ecclesiastes 2:24 **4.** Romans

5. The Pharisees **6.** Mary, Martha and Lazarus **7.** Saul, who became Paul

8. Do not join them **9.** The Corinthians **10.** You were not allowed to eat it

11. "I have food to eat that you know nothing about" **12.** Anointing a sick person **13.** His two daughters

14. Wild game **15.** Queen Esther

Quiz #2

EAT, DRINK AND BE MERRY

1. According to Paul what must the man who eats everything not do in connection with the person who only eats vegetables?

2. Which two Old Testament books record a governor giving this order: "Do not eat any of the most sacred food until there is a priest ministering with Urim and Thummin"?

3. How many people were in the crowd when Jesus said, "They have already been with me three days and have nothing to eat"?

4. Who wrote, "We give you this rule: 'If a man will not work, he shall not eat'. "?

5. What food and drink did Melchizedek bring when he blessed Abram?

6. When Abraham invited his three visitors to stay for a meal, what did he give them to eat?

7. Who gave a boy a drink of water from a well?

8. True of false? Breakfast is never mentioned in the Old Testament.

9. What was the nationality of the man brought to David who was given to eat "part of a cake of pressed figs and two cakes of raisins"?

10. Who wrote, "No priest is to drink wine when he enters the inner court"?

11. In the Bible, what is God's second recorded question?

12. Who was commanded to eat bread while he lay for 390 days on his side?

13. As the Israelites prepared to leave Egypt what were they told must be eaten inside the house?

14. Which Bible book asks, "Is tasteless food eaten without salt?"?

15. What does the book of Proverbs tell us not to do with a stingy man's food?

Quiz #3

EAT, DRINK AND BE MERRY

1. Which Old Testament prophet had a vision of two baskets of figs?

2. True or false? Babies were not given special food in the Old Testament as they were breast-fed until they were two or three years old.

3. Which book of the Bible records ten banquets?

4. Who described Israel's misery in the following way? "I am like one who gathers summer fruit at the gleaning of the vineyard; there is no cluster of grapes to eat, none of the early figs I crave."

5. About which type of tree did Jesus say, "May no one ever eat fruit from you again"?

6. One of the most famous Bible verses has the words, "I will come in and eat with him." Which verse?

7. Which prophet recorded this warning from God, "I will make this people eat bitter food and drink poisoned water"?

8. Who became a bride because she said, "I'll draw water for your camels too"?

9. Who did Absalom order his men to kill when he "is in high spirits from drinking wine"?

10. According to Jesus, John the Baptist "came neither eating nor drinking", but what was John accused of?

11. Jesus said, "The Son of Man came eating and drinking." What was Jesus accused of being?

12. What fruit woven in blue, purple and scarlet yarn decorated the edge of the priests' robes in the book of Exodus?

13. What accusation did Isaiah bring against "those who are heroes at drinking wine and champions at mixing drinks"?

14. Which Old Testament prophet accused the Israelites of unfaithfulness by asking, "Now why go to Egypt to drink water from the Shihor?"?

15. What fruit-bearing plant did Jesus liken himself to?

Answers

1. Jeremiah 2. True 3. Esther 4. Micah 5. A fig tree 6. Revelation 3:20
7. Jeremiah 8. Rebekah 9. Amnon 10. John was accused of having a demon
11. Jesus was accused of being a drunkard and a glutton 12. Pomegranates
13. They acquitted the guilty for a bribe and denied justice to the innocent 14. Jeremiah 15. The vine

Quiz #4

EAT, DRINK AND BE MERRY

1. To whom was the following request made, "Sell us food to eat and water to drink for their price in silver"?

2. Jesus reminded the Pharisees of the following incident from the Old Testament. "He entered the house of God and ate the consecrated bread, which is lawful only for priests to eat." About whom was Jesus speaking?

3. True or false? When God told Noah to build the ark, he told him to take animals on board, and also lots of food.

4. What does a person have to do to have the right to eat from the tree of life?

5. When were the Egyptians not able to drink water from the river Nile?

6. Who was told to, "Eat this scroll; then go and speak to the house of Israel"?

7. Three men risked their lives to fetch water for David from the well near the gate of Bethlehem. What did David do with the water?

8. Who said, "Stay in that house, eating and drinking whatever they give you, for the worker deserves his wages"?

9. According to the apostle Paul, what are the fruits of the Spirit?

10. Who, in the New Testament, said, "Do not worry about your life, what you will eat or drink"?

11. In which book of the Bible are we told that honey is good for us and that we should eat it?

12. Which Old Testament prophet said that God's people would "eat but not have enough" because they had deserted the Lord?

13. Which Old Testament prophet said that God's people would "have plenty to eat" until they were full?

14. What was the answer to Samson's riddle "Out of the eater, something to eat; out of the strong, something sweet"?

15. The men who explored Canaan returned with a single cluster of what hanging on a pole carried by two men?

Quiz #5

EAT, DRINK AND BE MERRY

1. Who gave the following order, "Collect all the food of these good years that are coming and store up the grain under the authority of Pharaoh"?

2. In what unusual place did Samson find a beehive?

3. Who is in no danger of eating "the bread of idleness"?

4. Who said to Jesus, "even the dogs eat the crumbs that fall from their masters' table"?

5. Who asked the following question, "Do people pick grapes from thorn-bushes, or figs from thistles?"?

6. Who in the Old Testament told a king, "Even if you were to give me half your possessions, I would not go with you, nor would I eat bread or drink water here"?

7. Which judge regained his strength when he drank water from the hollow place in Lehi?

8. True or false? Every year at the Passover meal the Israelites ate roast beef with bitter herbs.

9. Which prophet prophesied that the Edomites would have a trap set for them by those who ate their bread?

10. Why did Jesus and his disciples not even have time to eat?

11. In which of Jesus' parables does a farmer say to himself, "Take life easy; eat, drink and be merry"?

12. What did David prepare for Abner when he came to David at Hebron?

13. Who in the Old Testament allowed each guest to drink whatever they liked?

14. After Solomon had asked the Lord for wisdom he sacrificed some offerings in front of the ark of the Lord's covenant. What did he do next?

15. When Hagar was sent away who gave her some food and a skin of water before she left?

Quiz # 6

EAT, DRINK AND BE MERRY

1. With what food did Jonathan refresh himself when he was in a wood during a battle?

2. Which book of the Bible states, "They eat the bread of wickedness and drink the wine of violence"?

3. Who quoted this famous proverb, "The fathers eat sour grapes, and the children's teeth are set on edge"?

4. True or false? Fasting had become an act of hypocrisy for some religious leaders in New Testament times.

5. True or false? There is no record that Jesus ever fasted.

6. In which of Jesus' parables do the following words appear, "For I was hungry and you gave me nothing to eat, I was thirsty and you gave me nothing to drink"?

7. Where were the Israelites when they complained to Moses, "Why did you bring us out of Egypt to this terrible place? It has no grain or figs, grapevines or pomegranates. And there is no water to drink"?

8. Who gave "clothes and sandals, food and drink, and healing balm" to whom?

9. Who said, "I give you every seed-bearing plant on the face of the whole earth and every tree that has fruit with seed in it. They will be yours for food"?

10. Who vowed, "If God will be with me and will watch over me on this journey I am taking and will give me food to eat and clothes to wear so that I return safely to my father's house, then the Lord will be my God"?

11. Who ordered his children, "Go back and buy us a little more food"?

12. What did Joseph say he would take in exchange for food from the Egyptians when they first came to him during the famine?

13. Who "seized all the goods of Sodom and Gomorrah and all their food"?

14. Who was given this instruction, "Fill the men's sacks with as much food as they can carry, and put each man's silver in the mouth of his sack"?

15. When the king of Israel saw that Elisha had trapped the blinded Arameans he asked the prophet, "Shall I kill them, my father? Shall I kill them?" How did Elisha reply?

---

15. Elisha ordered that a great feast should be prepared for the prisoners

9. God 10. Jacob 11. Israel/Jacob 12. Their livestock 13. The four kings 14. The steward of Joseph's house

6. The Parable of the Sheep and Goats 7. Kadesh, in the Desert of Zin 8. Soldiers to prisoners

5. False. Jesus fasted for forty days and forty nights in the desert (Matthew 4:2)

1. Honey 2. Proverbs 3. Ezekiel 4. True (Matthew 6:16-18)

Answers

Quiz #7

EAT, DRINK AND BE MERRY

1. Who was the Psalmist referring to when he declared, "Let me not eat of their delicacies"?

2. True or false? In the desert, Jesus was tempted to turn stones into biscuits.

3. What tasted as sweet as honey in Ezekiel's mouth?

4. "You will plant vineyards and cultivate them but you will not drink the wine or gather the grapes." What happened to these grapes?

5. Who told the Israelites not to listen to Hezekiah and made the following false promise: "Then every one of you will eat from his own vine and fig-tree and drink water from his own cistern"?

6. "After Gaal son of Ebed and his brothers had gone out into the fields and gathered grapes and trodden them they held a festival in the temple of their god." While they were eating and drinking who did they curse?

7. Which Old Testament book states, "you have eaten the fruit of deception"?

8. What kind of heart, according to Proverbs, has a continual feast?

9. Who said to Joseph, "Give us food. Why should we die before your eyes? Our money is used up"?

10. What were the Israelites told to do so that God's blessing would be on their food and water?

11. Who was meant to benefit from fields left unploughed and unused every seven years, and from vineyards and olive groves left untended every seven years?

12. To whom were the Israelites not allowed to lend money at interest or sell food at a profit?

13. What kind of first fruits from their soil did God say the Israelites should bring to the house of the Lord at the Feast of Ingathering?

14. Who was promised that his food would be rich and that he would "provide delicacies fit for a king"?

15. According to the opening chapter of Acts what command did the risen Jesus give to his disciples while he was eating with them?

Quiz #8

EAT, DRINK AND BE MERRY

1. To whom did David say, "You will always eat at my table"?

2. Where in the Bible does wisdom say, "Come, eat my food and drink the wine I have mixed"?

3. Which Old Testament prophet prophesied that a siege would become so severe that people would "eat the flesh of their sons and daughters... [and] eat one another's flesh"?

4. In which of Jesus' parables does a servant beat the menservants and maidservants and eat and drink and get drunk?

5. According to Proverbs 25:21 what should you do if your enemy is hungry?

6. If a priest bought a slave or if a slave was born in his house what might the slave expect to receive?

7. Who "grew fat and wicked; filled with food, he became heavy and sleek. He abandoned the God who made him"?

8. Which beauty queen was provided with beauty treatments and special food?

9. Where was the food mentioned in the following verse to be stored, "You are to take every kind of food that is to be eaten and store it away as food for you and for them"?

10. As 150 Jews and officials ate at his table, who had prepared for him each day one ox, six choice sheep and some poultry?

11. What instruction did God give the Israelites about eating a young goat?

12. If you sit down to eat with a ruler, why should you not "crave his delicacies"?

13. In reply to Joseph's question, "Where do you come from?", who said, "From the land of Canaan . . . to buy food"?

14. Which army officer had such a good steward that he did not have to concern himself with anything except the food he ate?

15. What, according to one of Jeremiah's visions, was so bad that they could not be eaten?

Quiz #9

EAT, DRINK AND BE MERRY

1. Who is the first person in the Bible who is recorded as becoming drunk?

2. True or false? In the desert John the Baptist used to eat wild honey and locusts.

3. Who appeased David's anger with 200 loaves of bread, two skins of wine, five dressed sheep, five seahs of roasted grain, 100 cakes of raisins and 200 cakes of pressed figs?

4. In which Old Testament book does someone long to give the one she loves spiced wine to drink?

5. Food was set before this visitor, but he said, "I will not eat until I have told you what I have to say." Who was the visitor?

6. When Joseph's brothers went back to Egypt they took some nuts with them, which are only mentioned once in the Bible. What sort of nuts were they?

7. What no longer appeared the day after the Israelites ate food for the first time from the land in Canaan?

8. Who told the widow of Zarephath, "The jar of flour will not be used up and the jug of oil will not run dry until the day the Lord gives rain on the land"?

9. In a time of acute famine who prophesied, "About this time tomorrow, a seah of flour will sell for a shekel and two seahs of barley for a shekel at the gate of Samaria"?

10. Who did Paul remind were once greedy, drunkards, slanderers and swindlers?

11. Who was told, "By the sweat of your brow you will eat your food"?

12. Who had seven sons who took turns holding feasts in their homes, and invited their three sisters to eat and drink with them?

13. To whom did Paul write, "All food is clean"?

14. Who used the following ruse, "The men put worn and patched sandals on their feet and wore old clothes. All the bread of their food supply was dry and moldy"?

15. In which Old Testament book is it said, "Food gained by fraud tastes sweet to a man, but he ends up with a mouth full of gravel"?

Answers

1. Noah **2.** True (Matthew 3:4) **3.** Abigail **4.** Song of Songs **5.** Abraham's servant **6.** Pistachio **7.** The manna stopped coming **8.** Elijah **9.** Elisha **10.** The Corinthians **11.** Adam **12.** Job **13.** The Romans **14.** The people of Gibeon **15.** Proverbs

Quiz # 10

EAT, DRINK AND BE MERRY

1. What is compared in the book of Proverbs to "apples of gold in pictures of silver".?

2. Who were told that they would never hunger again?

3. About which group of people did Paul write that they should "not be given to drunkenness"?

4. In which book of the Bible is it stated that "evildoers are those who devour my people as men eat bread"?

5. How many Jews formed a conspiracy and bound themselves with an oath not to eat or drink until they had killed Paul?

6. Which Old Testament prophet records these words about Israel's faithless watchmen, "'Come,' each one cries, 'let us get wine! Let us drink our fill of beer!' "?

7. Which Old Testament book states that, "Stolen water is sweet; food eaten in secret is delicious"?

8. Who spent three days with David, eating and drinking, as their families had supplied provisions for them?

9. True or false? Jesus fed 5,000 people with five bread rolls and two small fish.

10. Identify two sorts of people mentioned in the Old Testament who were forbidden to consume alcohol.

11. Who wrote, "Do not let anyone judge you by what you eat or drink"?

12. Who said, "When you enter a town and are welcomed, eat what is set before you"?

13. What is Nathan describing to David here: "It shared his food, drank from his cup and even slept in his arms"?

14. True or false? 200 ornamental pomegranates decorated each of the two free standing pillars in Solomon's temple.

15. Joseph was joined in prison by two people who knew a great deal about food and wine. Who were they?

Quiz #11

EAT, DRINK AND BE MERRY

1. After Jesus rose from the dead, he ate some food to prove he was not a ghost. What did he eat?

2. Who was using goblets brought from the temple when the inscription, MENE, MENE, TEKEL, PARSIN suddenly appeared on the wall?

3. In what town was David given, wheat and barley, flour and roasted grain, beans and lentils, honey and curds, sheep, and cheese from cows' milk?

4. Who, according to the book of Proverbs, "become poor and find that drowsiness clothes them in rags"?

5. Who prophesied of God's people that they would drink the milk of nations and be nursed at royal breasts?

6. Which Bible book says "A generous man will himself be blessed, for he shares his food with the poor"?

7. About whom did a priest of Midian say "Invite him to have something to eat"?

8. Which prophet said that he ate God's words in the following way: "When your words came, I ate them; they were my joy and my heart's delight"?

9. Where in the Bible are Christians told, "Do not get drunk on wine, which leads to debauchery"?

10. Who wrote that "He [God] makes... wine that gladdens the heart of man"?

11. What food did an angel tell Elijah to eat after he had slept under a broom tree after fleeing from Jezebel?

12. Who wrote, "those who get drunk, get drunk at night"?

13. Who was concerned that, "The food in our sacks is gone. We have no gift to take to the man of God"?

14. Which Old Testament prophet wrote: "On this mountain the Lord Almighty will prepare a feast of rich food for all peoples, a banquet of aged wine, the best of meats and the finest of wines"?

15. In the book of Revelation what does the tree of life produce?

Facts 1

EAT, DRINK AND BE MERRY

In New Testament times two women worked together using a hand mill to grind grain. One poured the grain into the mill, while the other turned the wheel of the top millstone. This sheds light on Jesus' saying in Matthew 24:41.

In times of famine bread could be made with not only grain, but could have "beans and lentils, millet and spelt" (Ezekiel 4:9) mixed with it.

Showbread (KJV), "Bread of Presence", means bread set before the presence, or, face of God. It consisted of a dozen loaves of unleavened bread arranged in two rows of six. It was set out on a low table in the tabernacle.

During the seven days following Passover the Israelites ate unleavened bread to remind them of their hasty departure from Egypt in the days of the Exodus.

In the days of Jesus a blessing or short prayer was offered before eating. Jesus did this when he blessed the bread before feeding the 5,000 in Matthew 14:19. The traditional Jewish blessing is, "Blessed art Thou, Jehovah our God, King of the world, who causes to come forth bread from the earth."

In Bible times quantities of food were measured more by volume than by weight. So a "homer", the largest measure for cereals, was equivalent to an "ass-load."

In Corinth, archaeologists have dug up two temples which contain rooms apparently used by pagans for their feasts in which meat that had been offered to idols was eaten. Hence Paul wrote his warning in 1 Corinthians 8:10.

In the Old Testament, blood shed for sacrifices was considered to be sacred. It stood for the life of the sacrificed animal. As life was sacred, so blood become sacred and had to be treated with respect. So the Israelites were told not to drink blood (Leviticus 17:11; 7:26-27).

The *tilapa*, also known as "St. Peter's fish," is a type of fish which carries its eggs and young fish within its mouth. When the mother fish wants to keep the young fish out of her mouth she picks up an object, preferably a bright one. This is the likely background to the unusual account in Matthew 17:24-27 where Peter finds a 4 drachma coin in the mouth of a fish.

One helpful way to study the book of Esther is to note how its numerous banquets set the scene for important developments in the plot (Esther 1:3-4; 5-8; 9; 2:18; 3:15; 5:1-8; 7:1-10; 8:17; 9:17; 9:18-32).

Facts 2

EAT, DRINK AND BE MERRY

In New Testament times washing one's hands before a meal was the common practice and was observed as a religious duty, especially by the Pharisees (Mark 7:3).

Gnosticism, a dangerous heresy, taught that the spirit was good and the body was evil. So the body had to be treated harshly and this led to asceticism. This is the apparent background for Paul's words in 1 Timothy 4:3, "They [the Gnostics]... order them to abstain from certain foods."

The food which Nebuchadnezzar ate would have had its first portion offered to idols and some of his wine would have been poured out on a pagan altar. This explains why Daniel "resolved not to defile himself with the royal food and wine" (Daniel 1:8).

Cannibalism, due to severe sieges, is recorded in the Old Testament more than once (2 Kings 6:28-29; Ezekiel 5:10). Josephus records in his Jewish War, 6.3.4 that this also happened when Jerusalem was besieged in AD 70, "A woman... who... had fled to Jerusalem... killed her son, roasted him, and ate one half, concealing and saving the rest."

The Israelites were promised by the Lord that they would enter "a land flowing with milk and honey" (Joshua 5:6 KJV). This indicated abundant prosperity.

Israelites love pomegranates. The juice of pomegranates was highly prized (Song of Solomon 8:2). In the Promised Land, pomegranates were one of the fruits which were grown.

Double invitations were issued for formal meals in the New Testament. The first invitation was refused. "I cannot come. I am not worthy." But the guests were then sent a second invitation urging them to come and accept the invitation (Luke 14:16, 23).

In New Testament times, the nearer a guest sat to the host the more highly he was honored. In Jesus' parable, the beggar, Lazarus, sat at "Abraham's side" (Luke 16:22).

In the Bible, eating with someone was a sign of participation. So when Paul ordered that Christians in Corinth should "not even eat" (1 Corinthians 5:11) with an immoral Christian he was ordering complete isolation from such a sinning brother.

Israelites were used to eating insects. Skewered locusts were considered a delicacy. Grasshoppers were mixed with honey to take away their bitterness and were then cooked and eaten.

The importance of hospitality is often mentioned in the Bible and nomadic peoples welcomed strangers. But they had a tradition that the stranger was only welcome for 3 days and 4 hours, the length of time they thought their food sustained their guest.

Facts 3

EAT, DRINK AND BE MERRY

The Egyptians cultivated barley to feed their cattle. But bread made from barley was used by poor Jews. John notes that the five small loaves which Jesus used to feed 5,000 were barley loaves (John 6:9).

In the New Testament, the morning meal was a light one and usually consisted of bread, fruits, and cheese.

Grain makes bread and bread sustains nations. Millstones were so important to the Jews that their Law stated that no one could take the millstone as a pledge, as that would be like taking a man's life as a pledge (Deuteronomy 24:6).

Jesus used many everyday words in a figurative sense. Leaven, a ferment used in baking to make the bread rise, was likened to God's kingdom because it has power to change the whole (Matthew 13:33).

Jewish people loved feasts. They would often have music and dancing, as in the case when Herodias' daughter danced for Herod and his guests (Mark 6:32).

Feasts were very much part of the following Jewish religious festivals: The Sabbath, the Feast of the New Moons, the Year of Jubilee, Passover, Pentecost, the Feast of the Tabernacles and the Feast of Purim.

At the Passover meal Jesus shared with his disciples, everyone reclined on couches, around a table. The traditional way to recline was to lean on the table with one elbow and eat food with the other hand.

In Bible times the Jews did not eat with cutlery. They took a sop, a piece of bread, and dipped it into the soup or dip that was in the center of the table. The host of a feast might show his favor to a guest by offering a dipped sop to that guest (John 13:26-27).

In the Bible the word "bread" often stands for food in general. This is so in the Lord's Prayer and when Jesus said of himself, "I am the bread of life" (John 6:48).

Fish were often dried or salted and so preserved. This industry centered on Magdala, on the Sea of Galilee. Dried fish and bread were often eaten together, as in the case of Jesus feeding the 5,000.

The Dead Sea gives an endless supply of salt. But the outer layer of its rock salt was often hard and impure. It was used to spread on the temple courtyards in wet weather.

Facts 4

EAT, DRINK AND BE MERRY

Paul stated that deacons should "not indulge in much wine" (1 Timothy 3:8).

Paul urged Timothy to drink a little wine because of his frequent illnesses. It seems that Timothy suffered from some kind of stomach ailment (1 Timothy 5:23).

Sheep were bred by the Jews for their meat and milk. The fat in a sheep's tail was also prized.

The Jews did not usually cut bread with a knife. They broke or tore a piece of bread from the loaf. Acts 20:7 describes the Lord's Supper as a time when they came "together to break bread."

In the Old Testament meat was a luxury food. King Solomon's wealth was described in terms of how much meat was provided daily, "Solomon's daily provision were... ten head of stall-fed cattle, twenty of pasture-fed cattle and a hundred sheep and goats, as well as deer, gazelles, roebucks and choice fowl" (1 Kings 4:23).

It is not surprising that John the Baptist found enough honey for his daily diet of locusts and honey in the desert since swarms of bees settled not only in hollow trees (1 Samuel 14:25-27), but also in holes in rocks (Psalm 81:16; Deuteronomy 32:13).

To the Jews, the calf was considered a delicacy reserved for their special festivals. Hence the detail in Jesus' Parable of the Prodigal Son in which the father had the "fatted calf" killed (Luke 15:23 KJV).

Wine was stored in goatskins, but they had to be new ones, because wine gives off gas as it ferments and only a new skin was supple and strong enough to expand. Jesus referred to this in his saying recorded in Matthew 9:17.

The Hebrews usually ate only twice a day. The light morning meal, between 9 a.m. and noon, and the main meal of the day in the evening, in the cool of the day.

The Psalmist says that the sweetness of milk and honey is surpassed by that of the words of the Law (Psalm 19:10).

There are four accounts of the Lord's Supper in the New Testament (Matthew 26:26-28; Mark 14:22-24; Luke 22:19-22; 1 Corinthians 11:23-25). Each account includes the words "This is my body", emphasizing that the bread represents the body of Jesus which was given for his followers.

Facts 5

EAT, DRINK AND BE MERRY

When Jesus said, "Blessed is the man who will eat at the feast in the kingdom of God" (Luke 14:15), he was referring to the coming great Messianic banquet. The Bible often pictures the future kingdom as a feast (Isaiah 25:6; Matthew 8:11; 25:1-10; 26:29; Luke 13:29; Revelation 19:9).

The day Jesus instituted the Lord's Supper is a matter of great debate. From Scripture we know that it took place on the first day of the Feast of Unleavened Bread, or the day of preparation for the Passover, which was the 14th of Nisan. After sunset on the 14th of Nisan the Passover meal was eaten. As the Jewish day ended at sunset, this day was, technically, the 15th of Nisan, hence the debate.

In Bible times food was bartered for and paid for in markets. The traders sometimes had two sets of scales: one set they used for buying things and another set they used for selling things. (See Deuteronomy 25:13).

The six stone water jars mentioned in John 2:6 each held "twenty to thirty gallons" according to the translation. If each jar held fifteen gallons, and were each filled to the brim, Jesus' miracle produced up to 3,000 glasses of wine!

The Israelites were forbidden to eat animals classified as "unclean" such as camels, rabbits and pigs (Leviticus 11). This sheds light of Peter's problem about being told to eat "all kinds of four-footed animals" (Acts 10:12) which he saw in his vision.

After water, which was often impure, wine was the most common drink in Bible times. But it was used for more than just drinking. When mixed with olive oil it was used to clean and heal wounds, as the Good Samaritan knew (Luke 10:34).

Some women of Jerusalem were reputed to provide some local wine, laced with myrrh for condemned criminals as an anaesthetic. When Jesus was offered such a drink he refused it (Mark 15:23).

In New Testament days the most wealthy homes had wine cellars. They imported bottled wine from many Mediterranean countries. These bottles had pointed ends so they could be easily pushed into the ground and kept cool.

Fish was a common food in Jerusalem. One of its gates is called the "Fish Gate" and it is probable that this was the site of an ancient open-air fish market.

Medicines were made from fruit in the Old Testament. Isaiah told King Hezekiah to make a paste from figs and to apply it as a poultice to his painful boil (Isaiah 38:21).

Family Ties

Quiz # 1

FAMILY TIES

1. Which Bible characters had no mother?

2. Ishvi, Malki-Shua, and Jonathan were sons of which Israelite king?

3. Which Old Testament prophet was the son of Iddo?

4. True or false? Noah had four sons.

5. What family occasion does the book the Song of Solomon celebrate?

6. Who replaced Queen Vashti when she displeased her husband Xerxes?

7. Name the prophet Hosea's wife.

8. What was the name of Isaac's grandfather?

9. In Acts, which greedy couple tried to deceive the apostles?

10. What was the name of King David's third son?

11. Whose father was struck dumb by an angel before his son's birth?

12. How many daughters did Lot have?

13. What was the name of King Ahab's wicked wife?

14. Who captured the children of the unfortunate Old Testament character Job?

15. In Genesis, who hid her child under a bush expecting him to die?

---

10. Adonijah 11. John the Baptist's 12. 2 13. Jezebel 14. The Sabeans 15. Hagar
5. Marriage 6. Esther 7. Gomer 8. Terah 9. Ananias and Sapphira
1. Adam and Eve 2. Saul 3. Zechariah 4. False, he had 3 (Genesis 7:13)

Answers

Quiz #2

FAMILY TIES

1. What was the name of Saul's daughter who married King David?

2. How many wives did the patriarch Jacob have?

3. What was the name of Moses' mother?

4. How many women are named in Matthew's genealogy of Jesus?

5. Which Old Testament prophet was the son of Beeri?

6. What was the name of the apostle Peter's brother?

7. How many daughters-in-law went on to the ark?

8. What was the name of the synagogue leader whose daughter Jesus healed?

9. Who was King Saul's lame grandson?

10. Who was Adam and Eve's third son?

11. In Genesis, Lamech was the son of which long-lived character?

12. Alphaeus was the father of which apostle?

13. Whose wife was turned into a pillar of salt when Sodom was destroyed?

14. How many more sons did Job have after his time of testing had finished?

15. In which chapter of Proverbs is there a description of a noble wife?

12. James **13.** Lot's wife **14.** 7 **15.** Chapter 31
6. Andrew **7.** 3 **8.** Jairus **9.** Mephibosheth **10.** Seth **11.** Methuselah
1. Michal **2.** 4 **3.** Amram **4.** 4 **5.** Hosea

Answers

Quiz #3
FAMILY TIES

1. How many of David's brothers are named at their meeting with Saul?

2. Name Naomi's two daughters-in-law.

3. How old was Adam when his son Seth was born?

4. In Matthew 1:1 Jesus is referred to as the son of which two Old Testament characters?

5. Which Old Testament prophet was the son of Pethuel?

6. In Genesis which couple pretended to be brother and sister rather than husband and wife?

7. Which of Noah's sons was older, Shem or Japheth?

8. Who was the youngest of Jacob's sons?

9. Which Old Testament figure buried his wife in the field of Machpelah near Mamre?

10. In the New Testament, Elizabeth was the wife of which priest?

11. Jesus healed the mother-in-law of which apostle?

12. True or false? Abel killed Cain.

13. Whose son was told by God to build an ark?

14. Hosea called one of his children Lo-Ruhamah. What does this name mean?

15. How many sisters did King David have?

---

11. Peter **12.** False. Cain killed Abel (Genesis 4:8) **13.** Lamech's son **14.** Not loved **15.** 2
5. Joel **6.** Abraham and Sarah **7.** Japheth **8.** Benjamin **9.** Abraham **10.** Zechariah
1. 3 **2.** Ruth and Orpah **3.** 130 years old **4.** David and Abraham

Answers

208

Quiz #4

FAMILY TIES

1. Who was born first, Esau or Jacob?

2. Who was the sister of Jesus' friends Lazarus and Mary?

3. True or false? Reuben was the son of Leah and Jacob.

4. In the Old Testament what was the name of the widow who married Boaz?

5. Who was King Saul's father-in-law?

6. What was unusual about Jacob's wedding day?

7. In the Old Testament, who was the son of Haran?

8. Whose husband left Israel because of famine and then died in Moab?

9. What was the occupation of Moses' father-in-law?

10. Who was the mother of King Solomon?

11. According to Matthew's genealogy, who was the grandfather of Joseph, the husband of Mary?

12. Who rebuked King David when he killed Uriah in order to take his wife?

13. Which Old Testament builder was the son of Hacaliah?

14. Which patriarch gave his brother lentil stew?

15. Whose baby "leapt in the womb" when her cousin Mary came to visit her?

Quiz #5
FAMILY TIES

1. Who was the patriarch Isaac's favorite son?

2. Jemimah, Keziah and Keren-Happuch were daughters of which Old Testament character?

3. Which son of David killed his half-brother Amnon?

4. True or false? The prophet Isaiah was the son of Hilkiah.

5. Whose mother asked Jesus to place her sons next to him in heaven?

6. Whose son-in-law was the first king of Israel?

7. In Matthew's genealogy of Jesus how many generations are there from Abraham to David?

8. Name Hosea the prophet's unloved daughter.

9. How long did King David and Bathsheba's first child live?

10. How did King Solomon propose to resolve the case of two mothers claiming the same baby?

11. In the Old Testament who was the mother of Jacob's son Joseph?

12. In the book of Ruth what was the name of Naomi's daughter-in-law who remained in Moab?

13. Which Old Testament character was both father and grandfather to his children?

14. Whose brother died only to be brought back to life by Jesus several days later?

15. Who was the elder, Aaron or Moses?

Quiz #6

FAMILY TIES

1. Who is the father of all mankind?

2. In Genesis, what was the name of Isaac's brother-in-law?

3. What was Obed's famous grandson's first occupation?

4. Who was the favorite child of Isaac's wife, Rebekah?

5. In the Old Testament which royal prince got his head caught in the branches of a tree?

6. What was the name of Jacob's only daughter?

7. What prize did Caleb the spy offer to the person who captured Kiriath Sepher?

8. How many son's did Zilpah, the wife of Jacob have?

9. What was the name of Abraham's first-born son?

10. What was the name of the first child ever born?

11. How old was Jesus when his parents left him behind in Jerusalem?

12. Which Old Testament prophet was the son of Amittai?

13. What was the name of Queen Esther's cousin who raised her from childhood?

14. What family arrangements of King Solomon angered God?

15. Who was Jacob the patriarch's second son?

Answers

1. Adam 2. Laban 3. Shepherd 4. Jacob 5. Absalom
6. Dinah 7. His daughter, Acsah 8. 2
9. Ishmael 10. Cain 11. 12 12. Jonah 13. Mordecai
14. His many foreign wives 15. Simeon

Quiz #7
FAMILY TIES

1. How did Zechariah the priest inform the crowd of his son's name?

2. Which son of King David wished to marry his father's nurse Abishag?

3. True or false? The prophet Hosea's first child was called Jezreel.

4. Which of Jacob's sons was born immediately before Joseph?

5. In the Old Testament how many brothers did David's father Jesse have?

6. How many years did Jacob have to work for his bride, Rachel?

7. True or false? Methuselah was the father of Enoch.

8. Which relative watched the baby Moses as he was set adrift on the Nile?

9. What was the name of Jesus' mother?

10. Which brother of Joseph tried to rescue him from his other brothers?

11. King David's wife Abigail was the widow of which foolish man?

12. In the Old Testament who was the father of Gershom and Eliezer?

13. When they questioned Jesus about marriage at the resurrection, the Sadducees challenged him with a story about how many brothers?

14. According to Luke, who was the father of Mary's husband Joseph?

15. After his fortunes were restored, how many daughters did the Old Testament character Job have?

Answers

1. He wrote it down 2. Adonijah 3. True (Hosea 1:4) 4. Zebulun
5. 6 6. 14 7. False, Enoch was the father of Methuselah (Genesis 5:21)
8. His sister 9. Mary 10. Reuben 11. Nabal
12. Moses 13. 7 14. Heli 15. 3

Quiz #8

FAMILY TIES

1. Whose husband sold a field and pretended to give all the proceeds to the apostles?

2. Who was the mother of Abraham's son Ishmael?

3. How many sons did Bilhah bear to her husband Jacob?

4. True or false? Moses married Miriam.

5. How many months pregnant was Elizabeth when the angel Gabriel visited Mary?

6. Who asked, "Am I my brother's keeper?"?

7. Which Old Testament couple both changed their names?

8. What was the name of Jeremiah the prophet's father?

9. Who was the mother of Jacob's last child Benjamin?

10. Amnon and Absalom were sons of which famous king?

11. Which Old Testament woman is mentioned but not named in Matthew's genealogy of Jesus?

12. What had Peter's mother-in-law been suffering from when Jesus healed her?

13. Rehoboam was the son of which Old Testament king?

14. Which woman had no mother or father?

15. At the wedding at Cana who told Jesus the wine had run out?

Quiz #9

FAMILY TIES

1. When Jesus met her, how many husbands had the woman of Samaria had?

2. Gad and Asher were Jacob's sons by which wife?

3. True or false? Eliab was the first of Jesse's sons.

4. George Eliot's Mill on the Floss concludes with the words "In their death they were not divided." Of which two Old Testament characters was this originally said?

5. Which Old Testament priest fell off his chair and died when he heard his sons had been killed in battle?

6. In the Old Testament what was the name of Isaac's wife?

7. In Genesis who was the father of the twins Perez and Zerah?

8. According to Matthew's genealogy of Jesus, how many generations were there from Abraham to the exile?

9. Who fled from the attentions of Potiphar's wife?

10. What Hebrew word, used by Jesus, means "Father"?

11. In the New Testament , what was the name of Timothy's grandmother?

12. Which relative of Moses suffered from leprosy when she grumbled against God in the desert?

13. Which prophet was the son of Amoz?

14. Who was the patriarch Jacob's third son?

15. In Genesis, who was the husband of Keturah?

Answers

1. 5 2. Zilpah 3. True (1 Samuel 17:13) 4. Saul and Jonathan
5. Eli 6. Rebekah 7. Judah 8. 28 9. Joseph 10. Abba 11. Eunice
12. Miriam 13. Isaiah 14. Levi 15. Abram

Quiz # 10

FAMILY TIES

1. True or false? Esau and Jacob were twins.

2. According to Luke 8, who were Jesus' true brothers and sisters?

3. In the Old Testament who ate some honey not knowing it had been forbidden by his father?

4. What were the names of Aaron's sons who were killed by the Lord for offering unauthorized fire?

5. Who was the firstborn child of the Old Testament hero Joseph?

6. What was the relationship between King Saul and Abner, the commander of his army?

7. What nationality was Boaz's wife, Ruth?

8. In the Old Testament, who was the father of Enoch?

9. In the book of Numbers, whose daughters claimed property from Moses?

10. According to Judges, who found bees in the carcass of a lion while going to his wedding?

11. In Genesis, which brother guaranteed the safety of Benjamin as they traveled to Egypt for food?

12. Which Hebrew child was adopted by a daughter of Pharaoh?

13. What was the name of Samuel's father?

14. Name the son of Herod who was reigning in Judea when Jesus, Mary and Joseph returned to Nazareth.

15. Which king of Judah was the son of Josiah?

Quiz #11

FAMILY TIES

1. What was the name of Abraham's nephew and traveling companion?

2. What was the profession of the apostles Andrew and Peter?

3. Who was King Saul's son and a great friend of David?

4. What name, meaning "Not my people", did God tell Hosea to give to his child?

5. Who was the grandfather of the first king of Israel?

6. True or false? Jephunneh was the father of Caleb, one of the spies who entered Canaan.

7. In the Old Testament, who took her son to serve in the temple alongside the priest Eli?

8. Manasseh was the first-born of which Old Testament character?

9. Whose wife warned him to have nothing to do with Jesus?

10. What is the name of the inhabitant of Jericho whose family Joshua spared when he captured the city?

11. What was the name of the woman from Moab who is mentioned in Matthew's record of Jesus' family tree?

12. Whose husband danced naked before the ark of the Lord?

13. In Judges, who sacrificed his daughter in return for victory over the Ammonites?

14. Cushi was the father of which Old Testament prophet?

15. According to Matthew, who was the father of Mary's husband Joseph?

Quiz # 12
FAMILY TIES

1. What was the name of King Saul's wife?

2. True or false? Dan was the last son of Jacob's wife, Leah.

3. How old was Amon's son Josiah when he became king of Judah?

4. What was the name of Mordecai's cousin who married King Xerxes?

5. Who is the first woman mentioned in Matthew's genealogy of Jesus?

6. In the book of Judges, what was the name of the prophetess wife of Lappidoth?

7. In the Old Testament, what was the name of Nun's son?

8. Which son of Alphaeus became one of Jesus' apostles?

9. What was the name of Shealtiel's son who helped rebuild the walls of Jerusalem with Nehemiah?

10. What was the name of Moses' sister?

11. Iddo was the grandfather of which Old Testament prophet?

12. According to the book of 1 Samuel, which wife did Elkanah especially love?

13. To which of his sons did Jacob give a multi-colored coat?

14. In which Old Testament book do we read of the death of two brothers, Mahlon and Kilion?

15. Who named her son Ichabod when she heard of the death of her husband and father-in-law?

Answers

1. Ahinoam 2. False, he was Bilhah's first child (Genesis 30:6)
3. & 4. Esther 5. Tamar 6. Deborah 7. Joshua 8. James
9. Zerubbabel 10. Miriam 11. Zechariah 12. Hannah
13. Joseph 14. Ruth 15. The wife of Phineas, son of Eli

Quiz # 13

FAMILY TIES

1. True or false? According to Luke, Elizabeth was a descendant of Aaron.

2. Who warned her husband not to act offensively towards King David?

3. What was the name of the child born to Gideon by a Shechemite concubine?

4. Whose name means "the father of many nations"?

5. In the Old Testament, what is the collective name given to the sons of Shem?

6. Which of Noah's sons discovered his father lying drunk?

7. Who did the apostle Paul think of as his son?

8. Which Old Testament prophet married an Ethiopian and a Cushite?

9. Where did Noah and his family come to rest in the ark?

10. What was the name of the father-in-law of Ruth the Moabitess?

11. Which survivor of Jericho married Salmon the ancestor of King David?

12. True or false? Abraham had a son called Medan.

13. Jesus gave the name Boanerges to which brothers?

14. Which Old Testament character defiled Jacob's daughter Dinah?

15. Which king of Israel was the youngest of eight brothers?

Answers

1. True (Luke 1:5) 2. Abigail 3. Abimelech 4. Abraham
5. Arameans 6. Ham 7. Timothy 8. Moses 9. Mount Ararat
10. Salmon 11. Rahab 12. True (Genesis 25:2)
13. James and John 14. Shechem 15. David

Quiz # 14

FAMILY TIES

1. As recorded in Genesis, how old was Abraham when his father died?

2. In the New Testament, what was the name of the tent maker, Aquila's wife?

3. Who was the mother of Timothy?

4. How many sons did Ishmael, the son of Abraham, have?

5. Abigail and Zaruiah were sisters of which king of Israel?

6. Who was King Saul's eldest son?

7. What are the names of Laban's two daughters?

8. Who was the father of the apostle Matthew?

9. Buzi was the father of which Old Testament prophet?

10. Which of Noah's sons had children named Elam, Asshur, Arphaxad, Lud and Aram?

11. Who is referred to as "Great David's greater son"?

12. What was the name of Judas Iscariot's father?

13. Who was the servant of Jacob's wife, Rebekah?

14. In the Old Testament, who cooked a meal for her son so he could pretend to be his brother?

15. True or false? Timothy's mother Eunice was Greek.

Answers

1. 75 years old 2. Priscilla 3. Lois 4. 12 5. David
6. Jonathan 7. Leah and Rachel 8. Alphaeus 9. Ezekiel
10. Shem 11. Jesus 12. Simon 13. Deborah
14. Rebekah 15. False, she was a Jew (2 Timothy 1:5)

Quiz # 15

FAMILY TIES

1. Which nephew of David was killed by Joab at the stone of Gibeon?

2. In Genesis, Nahor was the brother of which patriarch?

3. In the Old Testament what was the name of Judah's son, the twin of Perez?

4. What did Abraham's wife do when she heard she was to have a son in her old age?

5. Which daughter of an Egyptian priest married Joseph?

6. Whose wife organized the murder of Naboth so her husband could claim his vineyard?

7. Who did the patriarch Abraham commission to find a wife for his son Isaac?

8. Whose mother sang a song known as the Magnificat?

9. In the New Testament who was the "Son of Man"?

10. Which two sons covered up Noah's nakedness after he became drunk?

11. In the Old Testament, which son of Judah refused to marry his brother's widow?

12. What was the name of the second of King David's brothers?

13. Which daughter of Jacob was raped by Shechem?

14. Which Persian ruler married Esther the Jewess?

15. In which chapter of his Gospel does Luke recount the Parable of the Prodigal Son?

Answers

1. Amasa 2. Abraham 3. Zarah 4. She laughed 5. Asenath 6. Ahab's 7. His servant 8. Jesus' mother 9. Jesus 10. Shem and Japheth 11. Onan 12. Abinadab 13. Dinah 14. Ahasuerus (King Xerxes) 15. Chapter 15

Quiz # 16
FAMILY TIES

1. What was the name of Jacob's only daughter?

2. Which brother and sister sang a duet in Exodus 15?

3. Did the apostle Peter have a wife?

4. What was the name of Shallum's wife, consulted by Hilkiah, following the discovery of the book of the law in the temple?

5. What was the name of Jacob's eighth son by his wife Zilpah?

6. In Exodus, which of his relations advised Moses to delegate some of his decisions to others?

7. Which son of Solomon was the last king of a united Israel?

8. Which of Lazarus' two sisters was busy preparing a meal while the other listened to Jesus?

9. Who is the first mother mentioned in the New Testament?

10. According to 2 Samuel which relative of King Saul cursed David, accusing him of being a man of blood?

11. Ahaziah, Jehoram and Athaliah were children of which evil King of Israel?

12. Dinah was Jacob's daughter by which wife?

13. The brothers Eschol, Mamre and Aner joined forces with whom in order to rescue Lot?

14. Which grandson of Zabdi sinned by taking some of the devoted spoil at Jericho?

15. What was the occupation of the man whose family Paul baptized at Philippi after an earthquake?

Quiz # 17
FAMILY TIES

1. What were the names of Lot's grandchildren?

2. As recorded in Proverbs 31 who instructed King Lemuel?

3. Whose mother wanted the head of John the Baptist?

4. Who was the father of Hoshea, the last king of Israel?

5. Which member of the family did the last plague of Egypt kill?

6. Which son of Nebat was the first king of the separated state of Israel after Solomon?

7. Which of Jacob's sons slept with his concubine Bilhah?

8. Who was the elder of Joseph's sons, Manasseh or Ephraim?

9. Which sons of Zeus and Leda were carved as figureheads on a ship in which Paul sailed?

10. True or false? Jesus had a half-brother named Simon.

11. Jezebel, the wicked wife of Ahab, was the daughter of which king?

12. In the Old Testament, which grandson of Shem became father of Peleg?

13. Who wore the skin of a goat in order to trick his blind father?

14. Which son of Ahitub was David's most famous priest?

15. How many genealogies of Jesus are recorded in the New Testament?

---

12. Eber 13. Jacob 14. Zadok 15. 2
9. Castor and Pollux 10. True (Mark 6:3) 11. Ethbaal, King of Sidon
4. Elah 5. The firstborn son 6. Jeroboam 7. Reuben 8. Manasseh
1. Moab and Benammi 2. His mother 3. Salome's

Answers

Quiz #18

FAMILY TIES

1. Who was the mother of Absalom, King David's son?

2. According to 2 Samuel, which son of Zadok was renowned for his running?

3. Which New Testament deacon had four daughters who were prophetesses?

4. Which good king of Judah was the son of Ahaz?

5. Who was the father of John the Baptist?

6. True or false? Jesus had four half-brothers.

7. After his escape from prison the apostle Peter went to the house of whose mother?

8. Who was the daughter of Lois mentioned by Paul in his letter to Timothy?

9. In the Old Testament who was the father of the hunter Nimrod?

10. Which son of King David was named Jeddiah by the prophet Nathan?

11. In Genesis, which son of Cush was a famous warrior?

12. In the Old Testament which son of Gera was renowned for being left-handed?

13. According to Romans which twin was loved by God whilst the other one was hated?

14. Who was the father of the apostles James and John, and the husband of Salome?

15. Which son of Jacob's name means "Good Fortune"?

Answers

1. Maacah 2. Ahimaaz 3. Philip 4. Hezekiah
5. Zechariah 6. True (Mark 6:3) 7. Mark's 8. Eunice 9. Cush
10. Solomon 11. Nimrod 12. Ehud
13. Jacob 14. Zebedee 15. Gad

Quiz #19

FAMILY TIES

1. Which chapter of Genesis highlights the first disagreement between a husband and wife?

2. What name means "My brother is king"?

3. Who was the father of Isaac's wife, Rachel?

4. In the Old Testament what was the name of Lot's father?

5. What disgrace was suffered by Sarah and Rachel in the Old Testament and Elizabeth in the New Testament?

6. What was the name of the wife of Heber, who, according to the book of Judges, killed Sisera with a tent peg?

7. How many sons did King Saul have?

8. Whose wife was a "helper fit for him"?

9. True or false? King David had a son called Daniel.

10. Moses' father-in-law, Jethro, had another name. What was it?

11. Who was the father of Abram; Nahor and Haran?

12. According to Genesis, Nebaioth was the eldest son of which character?

13. Eleazer was the son of which Old Testament priest?

14. Who was the father of the patriarch Joseph's wife, Asenath?

15. In Acts, which relative of the apostle Paul informed him of a plot to take his life?

---

13. Aaron 14. Potiphera 15. Nephew
10. Reuel 11. Terah 12. Ishmael
5. They were barren 6. Jael 7. 5 8. Eve 9. True (1 Chronicles 3:1)
1. Chapter 3 2. Ahimelech 3. Bethuel 4. Haran

Answers

Quiz #20

FAMILY TIES

1. Adonijah was King David's son by which wife?

2. What was the name of Ahab's son who clashed with the prophet Elijah?

3. How many children did the patriarch Jacob have?

4. How many children did Hannah, wife of Elkanah, have?

5. In Genesis, what did Joseph order to be hidden in his brother Benjamin's sack?

6. According to the Old Testament, who was born clutching his brother's heel?

7. According to Jesus, which son of Barachiah was murdered in the temple of God?

8. Which son of the patriarch Jacob gave his name to the family of priests?

9. According to Daniel, who was the father of Xerxes?

10. Who was King Saul's elder daughter?

11. Which close friend of the apostle Paul had a Jewish mother and a Greek father?

12. What was the name of Jacob's second son by Bilhah?

13. Before the birth of his natural sons who was due to receive the inheritance of Abraham?

14. True or false? Elizabeth, the wife of Zechariah the priest, was herself from a priestly family.

15. According to Genesis, who was the son of Seth and the father of Kenan?

---

11. Timothy **12.** Naphtali **13.** Eliezer the Damascene **14.** True (Luke 1:5) **15.** Enosh
9. Darius the Mede **10.** Merab
5. A silver cup **6.** Jacob **7.** Zechariah **8.** Levi
1. Haggith **2.** Ahaziah **3.** 13 **4.** 6

Answers

Quiz #21

FAMILY TIES

1. Whose son was Ahab, seventh king of Israel?

2. According to the writer of James, which woman was justified by her works?

3. Which child did his father Jacob rename when his mother died in childbirth?

4. What was the name of Jacob the patriarch's ninth child?

5. True or false? Seth was the third son of Adam and Eve.

6. According to Genesis which of Jacob's sons was a dreamer?

7. In the Old Testament, Abiram and his brother Dathan rebelled against which character?

8. Which woman did Jesus inform that her brother would rise again?

9. Whose husband was ordered to be killed by King David to cover up his adultery?

10. Which of Jesus' apostles was a twin?

11. In the Old Testament which son of Jared "walked with God"?

12. What was the name of the servant of Jonathan's son Mephibosheth?

13. In Genesis, who did Leah give to her husband Jacob as a concubine?

14. True or false? The apostle Paul testified before King Agrippa.

15. In the New Testament, what was the name of the mother of John Mark?

Answers

1. Omri 2. Rahab 3. Benjamin 4. Issachar
5. True (Genesis 4:25) 6. Joseph 7. Moses
8. Martha 9. Bathsheba's 10. Thomas 11. Enoch
12. Ziba 13. Zilpah 14. True (Acts 25:13) 15. Mary

Facts 1

FAMILY TIES

The Old Testament has no word that corresponds exactly to the English word "family."

In the Old Testament, cursing one's father or mother carried the death penalty (Exodus 21:15).

The nation of Israel was regarded as God's adopted son (Jeremiah 3:19).

Abel and Cain are the first recorded brothers in the Bible.

Five of the ten commandments mention family relationships, either implicitly or explicitly.

In the Bible it was usual for the man's parents to choose a wife for him.

When Boaz bought land that had once belonged to Elimelech he also acquired a wife called Ruth.

The patriarch Jacob had four wives, twelve sons and one daughter.

Paul devotes a whole chapter of 1 Corinthians to marriage-related issues (1 Corinthians 7).

Luke's genealogy of Jesus traces his ancestors directly back to God whilst Matthew's goes back to Abraham.

When she was told that God was going to fulfil his promise of giving Abraham and herself a child, Sarah laughed. Later she called the boy Isaac which means "he laughs."

Facts 2

FAMILY TIES

Paul tells fathers not to embitter their children or they will become discouraged.

In Bible times betrothal to be married was as binding as marriage itself.

Naomi is the first person to be called a mother-in-law in the Bible (Ruth 1:14).

Naamah is the first sister mentioned in the Bible (Genesis 4:22).

Adam, Eve and Jesus are the only people in the Bible who did not have human fathers.

In the Old Testament, wives would sometimes allow their husbands to have children by their servants in order to carry on the family line.

If a husband died, his brother was obliged to marry his widow in order to continue the family line.

A genealogy is a list of names linking ancestors or descendants of particular individuals.

Jesus had four half-brothers and an unknown number of half-sisters (Mark 6:3).

Jesus was born in Bethlehem because Joseph had returned to his family home for a census (Luke 2:1-3).

Great Love Stories

Quiz #1

GREAT LOVE STORIES

1. What was Bathsheba doing when David first saw her?

2. In 2 Samuel, why did David contrive to have Uriah the Hittite killed?

3. How many children did David and Bathsheba have, and what were their names?

4. How did God punish David for his adultery with Bathsheba?

5. Which Old Testament prophet admonished David for taking Bathsheba as his wife?

6. In the account of the creation of the world, on which day were Adam and Eve made?

7. In Genesis 2, what reasons did God give for creating woman?

8. What did Adam and Eve do right after eating the fruit of the tree of knowledge of good and evil?

9. In Genesis 4, what are the names of Adam and Eve's children?

10. What do the names Adam and Eve mean?

11. In the book of Ruth, whose fields did Ruth glean barley from?

12. Ruth and Boaz were the great grandparents of which Old Testament king?

13. In the book of Ruth, how was Naomi related to Boaz?

14. In the Old Testament, God said, "Be fruitful and increase in number; fill the earth" first to Adam and Eve and then again to whom?

15. In Judges, who fell in love with a woman from the Valley of Sorek?

Answers

1. Bathing **2.** Because David wanted Uriah's wife for himself **3.** They had 5 children in all: Shammua (or Shimea), Shobab, Nathan, Solomon (Jedidiah), and the first child **4.** David and Bathsheba's first child became ill and died; and God also said that the sword would never depart from his house **5.** Nathan **6.** The sixth day **7.** It was not good for man to be alone, and he needed a helper suitable for him **8.** They sewed fig leaves together and made coverings for themselves **9.** Cain, Abel, and Seth **10.** Adam means "man," and Eve means "living" **11.** Boaz **12.** King David **13.** Boaz was a relative of Naomi's dead husband, Elimelech **14.** To Noah and his family **15.** Samson

Quiz #2

GREAT LOVE STORIES

1. When Samson's first wife was given away to another man, what revenge did Samson take on the Philistines?

2. According to the book of Judges, where did Samson meet his first wife?

3. In Judges, who did Samson send to Timnah to get a Philistine woman as his wife?

4. What payment did the rulers of the Philistines promise Delilah in return for help in capturing Samson?

5. Which animal did Samson encounter on his way to meet his first wife?

6. To whom did Samson give the riddle, "Out of the eater, something to eat; out of the strong, something sweet"?

7. Which New Testament couple traveled with Paul and were mentioned by him in some of his letters?

8. Who disagreed with Samson over his choice of a bride?

9. Can you name the three different methods that Delilah used unsuccessfully when trying to subdue Samson?

10. Who went searching for a wife for Isaac?

11. In Genesis, what lie did Isaac tell to the men of Gerar?

12. Whose sister did Abraham's son Isaac marry?

13. In the book of Genesis, who was "a source of grief to Isaac and Rebekah"?

14. How did King Abimelech find out that Rebekah was Isaac's wife?

15. True or false? Peter took his wife with him when he went on his preaching missions.

Answers

1. He tied torches to the tails of foxes and set them loose among the corn belonging to the Philistines **2.** Timnah **3.** His father and mother **4.** Each ruler promised to give her 1100 shekels of silver **5.** A lion **6.** His wedding companions at his marriage to his first wife **7.** Priscilla and Aquila **8.** His parents **9.** She tied him with fresh thongs (bowstrings); new ropes and wove his hair into the fabric on the loom **10.** The chief servant of Abraham's household **11.** He said that Rebekah was his sister, not his wife **12.** Laban **13.** Esau and his wives, Oliibamah (Judith), and Adah (Basemath) **14.** He saw Isaac caressing Rebekah **15.** True (1 Corinthians 9:5)

231

Quiz #3

GREAT LOVE STORIES

1. What was the name of Abraham's second wife?

2. Who was the mother of Ishmael, Abraham's oldest son?

3. Why did Sarah laugh when a stranger promised her a son?

4. In Genesis, what happened to Lot's wife when she looked back at Sodom?

5. Where were Abraham and Sarah buried?

6. Who does the Lord describe in the Old Testament as "the mother of nations"?

7. When Abraham sent his servant to find a wife for Isaac, what did he give to Rebekah at the well?

8. Where did Rebekah first set eyes on Isaac?

9. Name Isaac and Rebekah's children in the order that they were born.

10. When Abraham's servant arrived at Haran to find a wife for Isaac, what prayer did he make at the well, that was subsequently answered?

11. True or false? Jacob loved Leah more than Rachel.

12. When Jacob married Leah, how many years had he worked for Laban?

13. How did Laban trick Jacob on his wedding night?

14. What were the names of Jacob and Rachel's children?

15. In the Old Testament, who was married to a prophetess and had a son called Maher Shalal-Hash-Baz?

Answers

1. Keturah **2.** Hagar **3.** She thought that she was too old to have a child **4.** She turned into a pillar of salt **5.** In the cave of Machpelah near Mamre, in a field Abraham bought from Ephron the Hittite **6.** Sarah **7.** He gave her a gold nose ring and two gold bracelets **8.** In the fields near his home as she was traveling there by camel **9.** Esau and Jacob **10.** "When I say to a girl, 'Please let down your jar that I may have a drink,' and she says, 'Drink, and I'll water your camels too,' let her be the one you have chosen." **11.** False. He loved Rachel more (Genesis 29:16-28) **12.** 7 years **13.** He gave Jacob Leah instead of Rachel **14.** Joseph and Benjamin **15.** Isaiah

232

Quiz #4

GREAT LOVE STORIES

1. How many children did Jacob and Leah have?

2. In the book of Genesis, what was Rachel's response to the problem of being barren?

3. Name the four women who had children with Jacob.

4. True or false? When Hagar was pregnant, she despised Sarah who mistreated her till she ran away.

5. How did Jacob's wife Rachel die?

6. When Joseph was a servant in Egypt, who fell in love with him?

7. Why was Joseph thrown into prison?

8. True or false? David married Abigail, wife of Nabal.

9. Which of the Ten Commandments refers to sexual relationships?

10. Who is reputed to be the author of the Old Testament book Song of Songs?

11. In 1 Samuel, which of Saul's daughters fell in love with David?

12. Which of Saul's daughters was offered first to David in marriage?

13. Who helped David to escape from Saul's men through a window?

14. How does an idol with goats' hair feature in 1 Samuel 19?

15. Complete these words spoken by the Beloved in the Song of Songs: "He has taken me to the banquet hall, and his banner ___ ___ ___ ___."

Answers

1. They had 7 children; 6 boys and 1 girl. **2.** She gave her maidservant Bilhah to Jacob so that Bilhah could bear children for her. **3.** Leah, Rachel, Bilhah, and Zilpah. **4.** True (Genesis 16:1-6) **5.** She died giving birth to Benjamin. **6.** The wife of his master, Potiphar. **7.** He refused the advances of Potiphar's wife who then him of trying to rape her. **8.** True. He married her after Nabal died (1 Samuel 25:39-40) **9.** The seventh commandment **10.** Solomon. **11.** Michal **12.** His eldest daughter Merab **13.** Michal **14.** Michal put it in David's bed to deceive Saul's men **15.** over me is love

Quiz #5

GREAT LOVE STORIES

1. Who wept when David requested that Michal be returned to him?

2. How many children did Michal and David have?

3. In 1 Kings, who did Solomon build a palace for?

4. Which town was given to Solomon's wife by her father as a wedding gift?

5. How many wives did King Solomon reportedly have?

6. In what way did Solomon do "evil in the eyes of the Lord"?

7. Which Egyptian rescued seven sisters and their flock of sheep from a group of shepherds?

8. Who arranged to have Naboth stoned to death so that she could give his vineyard to her husband?

9. True or false? Moses' wife was the prophetess, Deborah.

10. What were the names of Moses' two sons?

11. Who came to Moses in the desert and gave him good advice?

12. According to the book of Esther, who did Esther marry?

13. How did Esther save her husband's life?

14. By what other name was Esther known?

15. What is the name of the Jewish feast that celebrates the day when King Xerxes stopped the massacre of the Jews because of his love for Esther?

---

1. Paltiel, her second husband 2. None 3. His wife, Pharaoh's daughter 4. The town of Gezer, which Pharaoh had ransacked 5. 700 6. He did not obey the Lord completely but loved foreign wives who turned his heart to their gods 7. Moses 8. Jezebel 9. False. His wife was Zipporah, daughter of a priest of Midian (Exodus 2:16, 21) 10. Gershom and Eliezer 11. His father-in-law, Jethro (Reuel) 12. King Xerxes (King Ahasuerus) 13. She warned him of a plot by some of his officials to kill him 14. Hadassah 15. The Feast of Purim

Answers

Quiz #6

GREAT LOVE STORIES

1. In the first chapter of Hosea, what does the Lord command Hosea to do?

2. What is the name of Hosea's wife?

3. Who is referred to in this passage from Hosea, "She decked herself with rings... and went after her lovers, but me she forgot." ?

4. From which Old Testament book is the following passage taken: "How beautiful you are, my darling! Oh, how beautiful! Your eyes are doves"?

5. In the New Testament, how did the couple Ananias and Sapphira displease God?

6. What was Ananias and Sapphira's fate?

7. Who told Joseph not to divorce Mary?

8. True or false? Joseph chose the name Jesus for his son.

9. Which New Testament Gospel talks of Joseph and Mary's trip to Bethlehem?

10. Joseph was the descendant of which Old Testament king?

11. Why did Joseph and Mary go to Jerusalem each year?

12. Where did Joseph take his wife and child when he was told of Herod's plan to kill Jesus?

13. What were the names of John the Baptist's parents?

14. Which Old Testament couple were told that their descendants would be as many as the stars in the sky?

15. True or false? An angel told Zechariah that his son was to be called John.

Answers

1. To take an adulterous wife **2.** Gomer **3.** Israel **4.** Song of Songs **5.** They lied about the amount of money they had made from the sale of their property **6.** They both dropped down dead **7.** An angel appeared to Joseph in a dream **8.** False. The angel Gabriel told Joseph and Mary to name their son Jesus (Matthew 1:21) **9.** Luke's Gospel **10.** King David **11.** To celebrate the Feast of the Passover **12.** To Egypt **13.** Elizabeth and Zechariah **14.** Sarah and Abraham **15.** True (Luke 1:13)

Quiz #7

GREAT LOVE STORIES

1. What was God's first command to Adam and Eve?

2. In which of Paul's letters does he write about marriage and being single?

3. From which part of Adam's body was Eve made?

4. Supply the four missing words from this statement made by Adam in the Garden of Eden: "She shall be called 'woman' for she was ___ ___ ___ ___."

5. After the Fall, in what way did God say that woman's relationship with man would change?

6. In which Gospel does Jesus meet the Samaritan woman who has had many husbands?

7. In the account of Jesus and the Samaritan woman at the well, how many husbands had she been married to?

8. Whose wife was Asenath, daughter of Potiphera, priest of On?

9. What were the names of Joseph's two sons?

10. From which Old Testament book does Paul quote when writing to the Ephesians, "For this reason a man will leave his father and mother and be united to his wife"?

11. In which book is the following passage found: "The sons of God saw that the daughters of men were beautiful, and they married any of them they chose"?

12. True or false? Immediately before setting out to go to Canaan, Abraham and Sarah were living in Ur.

13. Why did Lot's sons-in-law not leave Sodom with him and his daughters?

14. Name one of the two Old Testament kings who took Sarah from Abraham, thinking she was his sister.

15. In Egypt, why did Abraham pretend that Sarah was not his wife?

---

14. Pharaoh, and Abimelech, king of Gerar **15.** He thought that he would be killed because she was so beautiful

13. Because they thought Lot was joking when he said that the city was about to be destroyed

12. False. They were living in Haran (Genesis 12:5)

6. John's Gospel **7.** 5 **8.** Joseph's **9.** Manasseh and Ephraim **10.** Genesis **11.** Genesis

5. God said that woman's desire would be for her husband and that her husband would rule over her

1. To be fruitful and increase in number **2.** 1 Corinthians **3.** A rib **4.** taken out of man.

Answers

Quiz #8

GREAT LOVE STORIES

1. Where did Jacob first meet Rachel?

2. How did Jacob greet Rachel at their first meeting?

3. Which Old Testament couple saved their nephew, King Ahaziah's son Joash, from being murdered by Athalia, and then kept him hidden for six years?

4. What god did Jezebel persuade her husband to worship?

5. In the New Testament, who publicly condemned Herodias' marriage to Herod Antipas?

6. To whom was Joanna, one of Jesus' followers, married?

7. In the New Testament, Paul spoke to which governor and his wife about righteousness, self-control, and judgment?

8. Who was accused by Saul's son, Ish-Bosheth, of sleeping with Rizpah, one of Saul's concubines?

9. How did Jacob mark the site where Rachel was buried?

10. What was the occupation of Priscilla and Aquila?

11. What were Abraham and Sarah's names before God changed them?

12. How old was Abraham when Sarah gave birth to Isaac?

13. How old was Isaac when Rebekah agreed to marry him?

14. Which of David's sons visited Bathsheba and requested Abishag as his wife?

15. In which New Testament Gospel is there an account of the Parable of the Ten Virgins?

Answers

1. At a well, where she had come to water her sheep 2. With a kiss
3. Jehoiada and his wife Jehosheba (King Ahaziah's sister and King Jehoram's daughter) 4. Baal 5. John the Baptist
6. Chuza, manager of Herod's household 7. Felix, governor of Judea and his wife Drusilla, a Jewess 8. Abner
9. With a stone pillar 10. They were tent makers 11. Abram and Sarai 12. 100 years old 13. 40 years old
14. Adonijah 15. Matthew's Gospel

Quiz #9

GREAT LOVE STORIES

1. In the Parable of the Ten Virgins, how many virgins went into the wedding banquet with the bridegroom?

2. In 1 Timothy, whose wives must be "women worthy of respect, not malicious talkers but temperate and trustworthy in everything"?

3. In his letter to Timothy, what are the four things that the apostle Paul counsels young widows to do?

4. Which New Testament writer wrote, "But those who marry will face many troubles in this life"?

5. In the book of Ruth, who were witnesses to Boaz's statement that he intended to marry Ruth?

6. True or false? In the book of Ruth, Boaz was entitled to marry Ruth as he was her husband's nearest kin.

7. According to the book of 1 Samuel, how did Hannah's husband Elkanah express his love for her?

8. Why did Elkanah's other wife, Peninnah, continually provoke Hannah?

9. In the New Testament, who had no union with his wife until she gave birth to their child?

10. According to Matthew's Gospel, to whom was Jesus talking when he said, "What God has joined together, let man not separate"?

11. Supply the missing word from the teaching Jesus gave to the Sadducees: "At the ____ people will neither marry nor be given in marriage."

12. In the Parable of the Wedding Banquet, who accepted the invitation to come to the feast?

13. Jesus taught that anyone who looked at a woman lustfully had already committed what with her in his heart?

14. Who is the author of Revelation referring to when he writes of the bride, the wife of the Lamb?

15. In the Old Testament, who said to his wife, "Don't I mean more to you than ten sons?"?

Answers

1. 5 **2.** Deacons **3.** To marry, have children, manage their homes and give the enemy no opportunity for slander **4.** Paul **5.** The elders and all the people at the gate **6.** False. There was a closer relative, who was entitled to first refusal (Ruth 3:12) **7.** Whenever the day came for Elkanah to sacrifice to the Lord, he would give Hannah a double portion of the meat **8.** Because Hannah was barren **9.** Joseph **10.** Some Pharisees **11.** resurrection **12.** The people who were invited in off the streets **13.** Adultery **14.** The Church **15.** Hannah's husband, Elkanah

Quiz # 10

GREAT LOVE STORIES

1. In which New Testament epistle is it written, "Husbands ought to love their wives as their own bodies"?

2. True or false? Paul said, "So guard yourself in your spirit and do not break faith with the wife of your youth."

3. Who does Paul encourage to, "Put to death, therefore, whatever belongs to your earthly nature: sexual immorality, impurity, lust, evil desires, and greed"?

4. Which Old Testament book contains the passage, "A wife of noble character who can find? She is worth far more than rubies. Her husband has full confidence in her"?

5. Who in the New Testament tells husbands to "be considerate as you live with your wives, and treat them with respect as the weaker partner"?

6. In Deuteronomy, what was the fate of a newly married wife who could not give evidence of her virginity?

7. Who was willing to travel hundreds of miles with a servant to marry a man she had never seen?

8. Which Old Testament wife cursed her husband for continuing to believe in God after his family and livestock had been killed and he had been inflicted with illness?

9. In the account of the wedding at Cana, who was surprised by the high quality of the wine served during the banquet?

10. Who in the Old Testament said, "I have made a covenant with my eyes not to look lustfully at a girl"?

11. In which New Testament letter are the faithful exhorted to keep the marriage bed pure, for God will judge adulterers and the sexually immoral?

12. True or false? In Old Testament times, men were encouraged to take foreign wives.

13. In the book of Isaiah, who is compared to a bridegroom rejoicing over his bride?

14. Who sought a suitable husband for her widowed daughter-in-law?

15. In Judges 1, who promised his daughter's hand in marriage to the man who attacked and captured the town of Debir, also called Kiriath Sepher?

Answers

1. Paul's letter to the Ephesians 2. False. It was the Old Testament prophet Malachi (Malachi 2:14-15)
3. The church of Colosse 4. The book of Proverbs 5. Peter 6. She would be stoned to death
7. Rebekah 8. Job's 9. The master of the banquet 10. Job 11. Hebrews
12. False. They were told to marry from among their own people (1 Kings 11:2)
13. God 14. Naomi 15. Caleb

Quiz # 11
GREAT LOVE STORIES

1. In the book of Judges, what did Caleb give his daughter Acsah as a dowry?

2. What was the name of King David's virgin companion who looked after him in his old age?

3. To which church is Paul writing when he suggests, "If they cannot control themselves, they should marry, for it is better to marry than to burn with passion"?

4. In 1 Timothy, who "should be the husband of but one wife"?

5. According to Deuteronomy, if a man refuses to marry his brother's widow, the widow is entitled to remove what from him in the presence of the elders?

6. In Paul's letter to Titus, who does he recommend to train young women to love their husbands and children?

7. In Paul's letter to Titus, what teaches people "to say "No" to ungodliness and worldly passions"?

8. What reason did Laban give to Jacob for tricking him into marrying Leah?

9. What did Laban give to his daughters when they got married?

10. Which unloved wife hoped that her husband would love her once she had given birth to a son?

11. Which couple is referred to in the following passage: "So she became his wife and he loved her"?

12. Apart from marriage, how were Leah and Rachel related to Jacob?

13. In the book of Esther, how did Queen Vashti anger the king?

14. In Deuteronomy, what person "must not take many wives, or his heart will be led astray"?

15. In Genesis, who pushed her son into deceiving her husband?

---

13. She refused to exhibit her beauty before his guests 14. The king of the Israelites 15. Rebekah
9. He gave each of them a servant girl 10. Leah 11. Isaac and Rebekah 12. They were cousins
8. It was not the custom to give the younger daughter in marriage before the older daughter
4. An overseer 5. One of his sandals 6. Older women 7. The grace of God that brings salvation
1. Land in the Negev and also the upper and lower springs of water 2. Abishag 3. To the church in Corinth

Answers

Facts 1

GREAT LOVE STORIES

The Hanging Gardens of Babylon, one of the seven wonders of the world, is reported to have been built by King Nebuchadnezzar II for one of his wives, to remind her of her homeland.

People in Biblical times rarely married for love, although it was generally accepted that love would result from being married, hence Leah's prayer that Jacob would love her once she had borne him a son (Genesis 29:32).

Israelite marriage was a business affair. The bridegroom's family paid a bride-price, a *mohar*, to the bride's father. This was compensation for loss of the woman as a worker and also for the loss of her offspring.

As soon as the mohar, the bride-price, had been paid, the girl was legally married (betrothed). A betrothal could only be broken by divorce or death, hence Joseph's desire to divorce Mary quietly before they were married (Matthew 1:19). The marriage was not consummated until the wedding.

A betrothal was seen as a binding contract and the couple were commonly called husband and wife, even though they were not yet married. This is why Joseph is called Mary's husband in Matthew 1:19.

The bride-price could not be spent by the bride's father, but he could use interest that was earned on it. When the daughter's parents or husband died, the bride-price had to be given to her. In Genesis 31:15, Leah and Rachel are angry with their father Laban because he had spent theirs.

In Deuteronomy, 50 shekels of silver was the usual minimum bride-price. This could be paid in kind. Jacob paid it by working for his father-in-law. Pharaoh gave Solomon a city when he married his daughter (1 Kings 9:16).

In the Song of Songs, the bride is referred to as "sister." This affectionate term occurs frequently in Near Eastern love poetry, indicating how close a husband is to his wife.

Ruth's request to Boaz to "spread the corner of your garment over me" (Ruth 3:9) symbolized a request for protection through marriage. It alludes to a Hebrew wedding custom whereby a new wife is covered with the corner of a prayer shawl.

Facts 2

GREAT LOVE STORIES

More than a hundred thousand inscribed clay tablets have been found dating from the Middle Bronze Age. These throw considerable light on the customs and laws of the ancient Near East in the time of Abraham.

It was customary for a childless couple to adopt a son to care for them during their lifetime and attend to their burial. The adopted son lost his rights if the couple subsequently had a son (Genesis 15:2).

An ancient law code, the Code of Hammurabi (c. 1750 B.C.), permitted a man to have a secondary wife (a concubine). The concubine, who was usually a slave, had well-defined rights.

One marriage contract, found at Nuzi, states, "If Gilimninu [the bride] does not bear children, she shall take a Lullu woman as a wife for Shennima [the bridegroom]…Gilimninu shall not send the handmaid's offspring away."

The Israelites were told not to marry foreigners, to avoid being tempted to worship foreign gods. As Numbers 36:6-9 explains, this prohibition also prevented the promised land being divided up by inheritance claims.

Matthew 25:1-10 illustrates the kind of festivities that accompanied a wedding. In the evening music was played whilst the groom, crowned with flowers or a diadem, set out with his friends in a procession to the bride's home.

The groom greeted his bride, who was given a blessing by her family. This was the only religious activity in the wedding. The bride was accompanied by bridesmaids who had helped her dress.

Descriptions of the bride's wedding dress in Jeremiah, Ezekiel and Revelation show that they were made from the finest linen and were richly embroidered. The bride was also adorned with many jewels and a thick veil, which explains why Jacob did not recognize Leah.

Facts 3

GREAT LOVE STORIES

The bride and groom walked in a torchlight procession, amid dancing and singing, back to the groom's house or to their new home, where the bridegroom's family held a feast.

Celebrations lasted a week, or even a fortnight (Genesis 29:27). During this time there was considerable drinking and eating, and also games and contests. The bride and groom were seated on a dais, and were treated as king and queen.

Throughout the wedding, a friend of the bridegroom acted as master of ceremonies.

If a man seduced or raped an unmarried woman, he was obliged by law to pay the woman's father a bridal price and to take the woman as his wife. This is what Shechem tried to do with Dinah, Jacob's daughter.

To be married, but remain childless, was considered shameful and was thought to be a mark of God's displeasure. If a wife was barren, it meant that there would be no descendants to continue the family line.

According to the law of Moses, if a widow was childless, her husband's eldest brother had to marry her and produce a son. This was called a Levirate marriage and is the law referred to in Matthew 22.

When a brother married his brother's widow, the eldest son of that marriage belonged to the first husband and carried his name. Onan, Judah's second son, was killed by God because he did not want to produce offspring with his brother's widow.

If there was no brother-in-law for a widow to marry, then this duty could be passed to the next-of-kin, the "kinsman-redeemer," as recorded in Ruth chapters 3 to 4.

Since Naomi had no more sons for Ruth to marry, it was a sacrifice for Ruth to accompany her mother-in-law Naomi back to her homeland. Ruth was willing to put Naomi's interests above her own.

Facts 4
GREAT LOVE STORIES

The Old Testament book Song of Songs, tells of deep human love. It looks at marriage sensitively from a woman's point of view and describes the purity and nobility of true love.

The Song of Songs is often interpreted as a devotional allegory in praise of the love of God and his people. Alternatively, it may be seen as a parable which, by celebrating human love, points beyond itself to the love of God.

The Parable of the Lost Coin in Luke 15 probably refers to a coin lost from a wedding headdress. Headdresses were made from coins strung together and were part of the bride's dowry.

A married man was absolved from military service for a period of one year after his marriage. This was to give him time to enjoy being with his wife, and probably also to give him time to produce an heir.

Israelites who strayed away from God and worshiped foreign gods were often described as committing adultery. This was often literally the case as worship of Canaanite deities sometimes involved sleeping with temple prostitutes.

Women were often given in marriage to seal treaties with foreign nations, hence the marriage of Solomon to Pharaoh's daughter.

In Old Testament times, if a man took a king's concubine, it indicated that he desired to become a ruler, hence Ish-Bosheth's concern for his inheritance when Abner slept with his father Saul's concubine (2 Samuel 3:7).

Hosea uses the courtship, marriage, and adultery of a husband and wife to describe God's relationship with his people.

When Abraham asked his servant to find a wife for Isaac, the servant had to place his hand under Abraham's thigh. This Babylonian custom emphasized the solemnity of the oath and the importance of continuing the family line. The thigh was often used to symbolize the "loins," the source of procreative power.

Facts 5

GREAT LOVE STORIES

There is no word for a "bachelor" in Hebrew, suggesting that marriage was the norm in Biblical times.

In New Testament times, the legal age for marriage was set at thirteen for boys and twelve for girls. This was probably one reason why parents played a major part in choosing a bride for their son.

Deuteronomy 24:1 allowed divorce if a man found something "indecent" (some uncleanness) in his wife. In that case the man merely had to issue a certificate stating that he was divorcing his wife.

In Old Testament times a woman could not divorce her husband. This was because, in the eyes of the law, she was a chattel with no legal rights.

In the time of Jesus, the teachers of the law were divided about what was meant by "uncleanness" in Deuteronomy 24. Some had a strict approach, saying that the only grounds for divorce were adultery or unchastity.

One school of rabbinical teaching interpreted "uncleanness" as meaning anything that might offend the husband. A woman could therefore be divorced for spoiling the evening meal.

When Jesus spoke out strongly against a lax approach to marriage and divorce, he was addressing a lively, strongly-debated issue.

The common Hebrew word for husband is 'ba'al', which means owner, possessor or master. Hence Boaz's question to his foreman, "Whose young woman is that?" (Ruth 2:5).

Crime and Punishment

Quiz # 1

CRIME AND PUNISHMENT

1. What is the first crime recorded in the Bible?

2. Under what pretext was Paul the apostle thrown into prison while in Philippi?

3. How did God protect Cain from being killed during his years as a wanderer?

4. In Genesis, what three punishments did God give the serpent for deceiving Eve?

5. In which Old Testament book is the following quotation found, "For dust you are and to dust you will return"?

6. How did God ensure that Adam and Eve could never return to Eden?

7. What two punishments did God give the woman for disobeying him in the Garden of Eden?

8. As recorded in Genesis, why did God want to flood the Earth?

9. Why did Noah curse Ham, his son, saying, "The lowest of slaves will he be to his brothers"?

10. What is the eighth commandment?

11. At the end of Abraham's pleading with God about Sodom and Gomorrah, God was prepared to save the cities if there were how many righteous men living there?

12. What deceit did Rebekah and Jacob commit against Isaac and Esau?

13. In which book of the Old Testament does the passage, "eye for eye, tooth for tooth" first appear?

14. In Genesis, what did Rachel steal from her father Laban?

15. When Joseph's brothers came to Egypt to buy food, which brother did Joseph imprison, while letting the others return to their homeland?

---

1. Cain's murder of his brother Abel **2.** It was claimed Paul was advocating customs that were unlawful for Romans to practice **3.** God put a mark on Cain **4.** The serpent had to crawl on its belly, eat dust and have humankind as its enemy **5.** Genesis **6.** God placed cherubim on the east side and a flaming sword that flashed in every direction **7.** Pains in childbirth and her husband would rule over her **8.** Because the Earth and the people in it were corrupt and full of violence **9.** Because Ham saw his father naked and told his brothers **10.** You shall not steal **11.** 10 **12.** Rebekah helped Jacob disguise himself as Esau in order to trick Isaac into blessing him **13.** Exodus **14.** Laban's household gods **15.** Simeon

Answers

Quiz #2

CRIME AND PUNISHMENT

1. During the Israelites' flight from Egypt, how did the Lord punish them for worshiping a golden calf?

2. How old was Joseph when his brothers threw him into a pit?

3. Which Old Testament judge had Agag, king of the Amalekites, executed?

4. In the book of Revelation, where did the angel throw Satan?

5. What were the occupations of the two men that Pharaoh had thrown into prison with Joseph?

6. According to the book of Deuteronomy, how many witnesses to a crime were needed before a man could be put to death?

7. Which New Testament writer called himself "an ambassador in chains"?

8. In the Old Testament, to whom did God say, "Whoever sheds the blood of man, by man shall his blood be shed"?

9. When Moses was still a young man, why did he suddenly leave Egypt?

10. Which two towns in the Old Testament were considered so corrupt that God completely destroyed them?

11. What is the sixth commandment?

12. According to the laws that God gave to Moses, what was the penalty for premeditated murder?

13. According to the laws that God gave to Moses, what was the penalty for accidental murder?

14. Where did Rebekah send Jacob when she found out Esau was planning to kill him?

15. On which mountain did God give the Law to Moses?

Quiz #3

CRIME AND PUNISHMENT

1. When Joseph lived in Egypt, for what alleged crime was he thrown into prison?

2. In Matthew's Gospel, which commandment did Jesus quote when he said that anger and insults were also forbidden?

3. How did God punish Moses for not trusting in him "enough to honor me as holy in the sight of the Israelites"?

4. What wrongdoing was God referring to in Deuteronomy when he said it, "blinds the eyes of the wise and twists the words of the righteous"?

5. Out of the two men that Joseph met in prison, who was hanged and who was saved?

6. According to Deuteronomy, who did the Israelites have to consult if they could not solve a case in their courts?

7. True or false? It says in Deuteronomy that a person can be put to death for someone else's sin.

8. After Abner had made his peace with David, why did Joab, leader of David's army, lure him back to Hebron and kill him?

9. In the book of Daniel, who was King Nebuchadnezzar referring to when he said that they would be cut up into pieces and their houses turned into heaps of rubble?

10. How was Saul's son Ish-Bosheth murdered?

11. What was the punishment recorded in Leviticus when a man married both a daughter and her mother?

12. Why did Joab, David's army commander, find it easy to kill Absalom?

13. Which of David's sons did King Solomon execute?

14. What was the crime brought before King Solomon by two prostitutes?

15. When David sinned against God by carrying out a census of fighting men, what three punishments did God present to David to choose between?

Quiz #4
CRIME AND PUNISHMENT

1. In which of his letters in the New Testament does Paul state that Christ is "the end of the law"?

2. In 1 Kings, what was the trumped-up charge that led Naboth the vineyard owner to be killed?

3. Name the crime of the woman who Jesus saved from being stoned.

4. What method of execution did King Xerxes use for Haman in the book of Esther?

5. In the book of Joshua, what crime did Achan commit after the fall of Jericho?

6. Who requested that Herod behead John the Baptist?

7. Which one of the disciples was the keeper of the money bag?

8. According to the book of Acts, who "dragged off men and women and put them in prison" in an attempt to destroy the church at Jerusalem?

9. In Romans, Paul quotes, "For it is written: 'It is mine to avenge; I will repay,' says the Lord." From which book in the Old Testament does this quotation originate?

10. In the book of Daniel, name the three Jews who King Nebuchadnezzar threw into the furnace.

11. On whose orders was Joab, commander of David's army, killed?

12. Which king had Daniel thrown to the lions for praying to God?

13. What crime was Hosea's wife guilty of?

14. True or false? According to the Law in Exodus, a man may legally kill a thief breaking into his home before sunrise, but after sunrise he cannot kill him.

15. Why did Herod arrest John the Baptist?

Quiz #5

CRIME AND PUNISHMENT

1. What were the professions of Samuel's sons, Joel and Abijah?

2. Which prophet condemned shopkeepers for using dishonest scales?

3. True or false? Paul told his friend Onesimus to pay back any money he had stolen.

4. In 2 Chronicles, why did King Joash's officials conspire to bring about his death?

5. What were the names of the husband and wife who died suddenly after lying to the apostles about the money they had given to the church in Jerusalem?

6. Which famous New Testament figure was present at the stoning of Stephen?

7. In which of his letters does Paul preach, "He who rebels against the authority is rebelling against what God has instituted"?

8. True or false? The Jews wanted to stone Jesus several times.

9. Who was Jesus speaking about when he said, "He is a liar and the father of lies"?

10. What was the name of the island to which the apostle John was exiled as a punishment for preaching?

11. In 1 Kings, which group of people was sentenced to death and executed by order of Elijah?

12. In which book of the Old Testament is the verse, "My son, if sinners entice you, do not give in to them"?

13. Name the two crimes Barabbas had committed, as recorded in Mark and Luke.

14. At which feast was it the custom for Pilate to release a prisoner chosen by the people?

15. Who was killed on the orders of Joshua and buried under a heap of rocks in a place thereafter known as the Valley of Achor?

Answers

1. They were judges **2.** Amos **3.** False. Paul offered to pay it back (Philemon 18) **4.** Because the king had murdered Zechariah (son of Jehoiada the priest) **5.** Ananias and Sapphira **6.** Saul, later known as Paul **7.** Letter to the Romans **8.** True **9.** The devil **10.** Patmos **11.** The prophets of Baal **12.** Book of Proverbs **13.** Murder and taking part in an insurrection in Jerusalem **14.** Feast of the Passover **15.** Achan

Quiz #6

CRIME AND PUNISHMENT

1. In 1 Kings, who was responsible for the death of Naboth the vineyard owner?

2. How did Samuel's sons, Joel and Abijah, upset the elders of Israel?

3. In 1 Kings, which king did Zimri, a chariot official, kill in order to become king himself?

4. In 2 Kings, which treacherous queen was killed during the coronation of her seven year-old nephew, Joash?

5. True or false? Manasseh, king of Judah, was famed for his love of God and his God-fearing rule.

6. What fate befell the youths who jeered at Elisha as he was on the road to Bethel?

7. On how many occasions did Paul the apostle receive 39 lashes from the Jews?

8. Who was imprisoned with Paul the apostle while they were in Philippi, Macedonia?

9. Who was converted while Paul the apostle was in prison in Macedonia?

10. While Paul and Silas were preaching in Thessalonica, why was their friend Jason dragged before the city officials?

11. According to Deuteronomy, what was the maximum number of lashes a guilty man could receive?

12. As he left Miletus to go to Jerusalem, who warned Paul the apostle that prison and hardships were facing him?

13. As recorded in the Gospels, if you look at a woman lustfully, what sin are you committing?

14. In the book of Revelation, to whom does John write, "I tell you, the devil will put some of you in prison to test you, and you will suffer persecution for ten days"?

15. Under which two Roman governors was Paul imprisoned in Caesarea?

---

12. The Holy Spirit 13. Adultery 14. The church in Smyrna 15. Governor Felix and Governor Festus

9. The jailer in charge of the prison 10. Because Jason had welcomed Paul and Silas into his house 11. 40

3. Elah 4. Athaliah 5. False (2 Chronicles 33:6) 6. They were mauled by 2 bears 7. 5 times 8. Silas

1. Jezebel, King Ahab's wife 2. As judges, they perverted the course of justice and accepted bribes

Answers

Quiz #7

CRIME AND PUNISHMENT

1. Who claimed he had been whipped, beaten, and stoned for being a servant of Christ?

2. Who was God punishing in the Old Testament when he said, "When you work the ground, it will no longer yield its crops for you"?

3. Why did the Pharisees condemn Jesus for healing a man with a shriveled hand?

4. True or false? According to the Law of Moses, it was a crime to consult a medium.

5. Two criminals were crucified with Jesus. What was their crime?

6. During the Israelites' time in the desert, a man was found breaking the Sabbath law and was stoned to death. What was he doing?

7. What was the name of the supreme law court of the Jews?

8. What was Jesus' answer to Peter's question, "How many times shall I forgive my brother when he sins against me? Up to seven times?"?

9. Who tried to persuade Pilate not to harm Jesus after he had been arrested?

10. Why did Judas Iscariot kiss Jesus when he found him in Gethsemane?

11. According to Jesus, what is the most important commandment?

12. In the account of Jesus being tried by the Sanhedrin, what crime had Jesus committed, according to two witnesses?

13. Why was Jeremiah arrested when he tried to leave the besieged city of Jerusalem to go to his property in the land of Benjamin?

14. Which Old Testament prophet described a plague of locusts, and said it was a foretaste of God's coming judgment on the Israelites?

15. When Paul and Silas were in prison in Philippi, what caused the prison doors to open and their chains to become loose?

Answers

1. The apostle Paul 2. Cain 3. Because it was the Sabbath day, and it was against the law to heal on the Sabbath 4. True (Leviticus 19:31) 5. Robbery 6. Collecting wood 7. The Sanhedrin 8. "I tell you, not seven times, but seventy-seven times." 9. Pilate's wife 10. He had prearranged for the guards to arrest the man that he kissed 11. "Love the Lord your God with all your heart and with all your soul and with all your mind and with all your strength." 12. Jesus had said he was able to destroy the temple of God and rebuild it in 3 days 13. It was thought that Jeremiah was deserting to the Babylonians 14. Joel 15. An earthquake

Quiz #8

CRIME AND PUNISHMENT

1. During the siege of Jerusalem, officials complained to the king that Jeremiah was discouraging the people and soldiers. How did they try to stop him?

2. What did Jesus tell people to do if they had their tunic taken away from them?

3. What eventually happened with the thirty pieces of silver that Judas had received for betraying Jesus?

4. True or false? Paul said, "Money is a root of all kinds of evil."

5. Who persuaded the Sanhedrin to release the apostles, saying, "If their purpose or activity is of human origin, it will fail. But if it is from God, you will not be able to stop these men"?

6. Which of the twelve disciples did King Herod have put to death by the sword?

7. Why did King Herod arrest Peter?

8. How did Peter escape from prison and enter the city after King Herod had ordered four squads of soldiers to guard him?

9. True or false? Paul wrote his letter to the church of Colosse while he was in prison.

10. Which parable does Jesus tell the disciples to teach them that they must always forgive one another?

11. Who said, "We must obey God rather than men"?

12. Why did the magistrates who threw Paul and Silas into prison in Macedonia then come forward to appease them and escort them from the prison?

13. True or false? The chief priests approached Judas Iscariot to ask him to betray Jesus.

14. Why did Caiaphas and the chief priests and elders decide against arresting Jesus during the Passover?

15. The words of which prophet were fulfilled by the actions of Judas Iscariot?

---

citizen **13.** False. Judas approached them **14.** Because they wanted to avoid a riot **15.** Jeremiah
Roman a was he because Paul told them and the apostles **12.** Because Paul told them he was a Roman
10. The Parable of the Unmerciful Servant **11.** Peter and the apostles **12.** Because Paul told them he was a Roman
8. An angel caused his chains to fall off and led him out of the prison and into the city **9.** True (Colossians 4:18)
5. Gamaliel, a Pharisee **6.** James, the brother of John **7.** King Herod wanted to please the Jews
field as a burial place for foreigners **4.** False. Paul said that it was "the love of money", not money itself (1 Timothy 6:10)
1. They imprisoned him in a dry water cistern **2.** To give their cloak too **3.** The priests and elders used them to buy a

Answers

Quiz #9

CRIME AND PUNISHMENT

1. What is the royal law that James refers to in his letter in the New Testament?

2. Complete this quotation from the letter to the Hebrews: "God is a consuming ____."

3. What did God say would happen if Adam and Eve ate of the tree of the knowledge of good and evil?

4. In the Parable of the Sheep and the Goats, why were the goats sent into eternal punishment?

5. When harvesting grapes and olives, why was it a crime to double-check that all the fruit had been picked?

6. How many brothers did Abimelech murder as recorded in the book of Judges?

7. How did the Lord destroy Sodom and Gomorrah?

8. What punishment befell Aaron's sons Nadab and Abihu when they offered unauthorized fire in their censers before the Lord?

9. To whom did John the Baptist say: "Don't accuse people falsely and be content with your pay"?

10. Complete Jesus' teaching from Matthew 7: "____ is the gate and ____ is the road that leads to destruction, and many enter through it."

11. Before he sent out his disciples to preach his message, what advice did Jesus give them about being arrested?

12. In Matthew 11, which three cities are denounced by Jesus because of their lack of repentance, despite miracles having been performed there?

13. In the Parable of the Talents, what happened to the man who hid his one talent in the ground?

14. When Paul despaired of getting justice in Palestine, he exercised his right as a Roman citizen and asked for his case to go to appeal. Who did he appeal to?

15. What happened to Lot's wife when she disobeyed God's command not to turn round and look back at Sodom?

---

13. The man had his talent taken from him. **14.** Caesar **15.** Lot's wife became a pillar of salt. **8.** They were burned to death. **9.** Soldiers **10.** "Wide" and "broad" **11.** The disciples were not to worry about what to say or how to say it for the Spirit of God would speak through them **12.** Korazin, Bethsaida, Capernaum **5.** Some had to be left for people who were destitute **6.** 70 **7.** By raining down burning sulfur from the heavens **1.** Love your neighbor as yourself **2.** Fire **3.** He said that they would die **4.** Because they did not help people in need

Answers

Quiz # 10

CRIME AND PUNISHMENT

1. According to the book of Revelation, for how many years was Satan to be locked away?

2. According to Paul, who masquerades as an angel of light?

3. How did God punish the Israelites who were afraid to enter the Promised Land?

4. Which of Joseph's brothers tried to rescue Joseph after he had been thrown into a pit?

5. In 2 Samuel, to whom does Nathan compare David because of his adultery with Bathsheba and the killing of Uriah?

6. In which book of the Old Testament is it written, "An evil man is snared by his own sin, but a righteous one can sing and be glad"?

7. What punishment did Paul command to be given to the sexually immoral man in the church in Corinth?

8. In the Parable of the Good Samaritan, who were the two people who passed by the robbers' victim without helping him?

9. In his letter, what does James describe as, "a fire, a world of evil among the parts of the body"?

10. Why did Pilate give orders that Jesus' tomb should be sealed and guarded for three days?

11. In John's Gospel, to which group does Jesus say, "If you were blind, you would not be guilty of sin; but now that you claim you can see, your guilt remains"?

12. What reason did the Jews give for wanting to stone Jesus?

13. Why did the Israelites want to stone Joshua and Caleb after they had returned from exploring the Promised Land?

14. Who pelted King David and his officials with stones, but was not reprimanded by David?

15. According to Paul, what is the fate of someone who preaches a gospel other than the Gospel of Jesus Christ?

Answers

1. 1,000 years 2. Satan 3. They could not enter the promised land but died in the wilderness 4. Reuben 5. A rich man with lots of sheep and cattle, who takes away and kills the only lamb belonging to a poor man 6. Proverbs 7. The man was to be expelled from the church 8. The priest and the Levite 9. The tongue 10. It was thought the disciples would steal the body and claim Jesus had risen from the dead 11. Pharisees 12. Blasphemy 13. Because the two men accused the Israelites of rebelling against God 14. Shimei, son of Gera, a man from the same clan as Saul's family 15. Eternal condemnation

Quiz #11

CRIME AND PUNISHMENT

1. Which Old Testament character refused to curse God and turn away from him, even though Satan brought all manner of evil and disaster upon him?

2. When a man said that he had killed King Saul, what did David do?

3. Which priest from the Old Testament had two sons, Hophni and Phinehas, who were killed by the Lord because of their wicked ways?

4. What crime did Joseph claim his brother Benjamin had committed?

5. What was Cain's motive for murdering Abel?

6. To whom was Paul writing when he said people should, "submit to the authorities, not only because of possible punishment but also because of conscience"?

7. Which New Testament writer tells his readers, "For whoever keeps the whole law and yet stumbles at just one point is guilty of breaking all of it"?

8. Why was Miriam, Moses' sister, struck with leprosy?

9. When God asked Cain where his brother Abel was, Cain lied and said, "I don't know." What did Cain then ask God?

10. In the parable about the landowner who leased a vineyard to tenants, what did the tenants do when the landowner's son went to collect his father's harvest?

11. Why did the Jews have Jesus tried by the Romans instead of judging him themselves?

12. According to John's Gospel, when did Satan enter Judas?

13. To whom did Paul say, "May your money perish with you because you thought you could buy the gift of God with money"?

14. True or false? The Law of Moses forbade the oppression of a foreigner.

15. Why did the Roman commander have the prisoner Paul transferred from Jerusalem to Caesarea?

Facts 1

CRIME AND PUNISHMENT

It was common practice among the nations of the ancient world to make two copies of a covenant or agreement. Each party then stored its copy in a holy place. This may be why the Ten Commandments were written on two tablets and kept in the ark of the covenant, the holy place of both God and Israel.

The idea of a "scapegoat" comes from the ceremony performed on the annual Day of Atonement. The high priest first laid both hands on the goat, symbolically putting on it all the sins of the people. Then he sent the goat into the desert as a sign that the people's sins had been taken away.

The Law of Moses stated that capital punishment was appropriate for eighteen different offences, including some, such as rape, that did not involve murder.

God's law was different from that of other nations, notably because it treated all people as equal - kings and rulers, as well as citizens, had to obey it.

The Law of Moses instituted cities of refuge to which murderers could flee until a trial could be held. They could remain in the city and be protected from anyone seeking vengeance.

The gallows mentioned in Esther was probably not scaffolding and rope, but a pole or stake upon which the criminal was impaled. This was a common method of execution in nations in the Near East at that time.

The Romans favored crucifixion when executing military and political criminals, but they never executed a Roman citizen in this way.

The Law of Moses decreed "an eye for an eye" in order to avoid excessive punishment. The point was that the punishment had to fit the crime.

Jeremiah was imprisoned in a private house, and later in a cistern, because there were no prisons in Israel before Roman times.

The Jews found Jesus guilty of blasphemy, but as they could not authorize a death penalty, they had to convince the Romans he had broken one of their laws. He was therefore charged with sedition because of his talk about the kingdom of God.

The authorities were pleased when Judas came forward to betray Jesus because they needed to arrest Jesus away from the crowds. Since Judas was a disciple, he knew the quiet places where Jesus went to be alone with his friends.

Facts 2

CRIME AND PUNISHMENT

There was no police force in Palestine. In Roman times, order was kept by the Roman army. The Jews, however, had their own guards, chosen from among the Levites, to keep order in the Temple.

The name of the place where Jesus was crucified was called, "Golgotha," which means "the place of a skull." The name may have arisen because it was a place of execution, or the hill where it was located may have been shaped like a skull.

In Israel, the main form of execution was by stoning. This was seen as the responsibility of the whole community (Leviticus 24:14).

Traditionally, criminals who had been executed were buried outside the city and had stones flung on top of their graves. This is how Absalom was buried by Joab.

The cities of Sodom and Gomorrah were located in an area where the soil was full of bitumen, which burns easily. One school of thought suggests the cities were destroyed when this bitumen was set alight, perhaps by a meteoric thunderstorm.

The cities of Sodom and Gomorrah may be buried under the water at the southern end of the Dead Sea.

The first plague God sent the Egyptians turned the Nile into blood. This would have had a major religious significance as Egyptians held the Nile and certain species of fish and crocodile to be sacred.

Frogs were sacred to the Egyptians and it was forbidden to kill them. They would therefore have suffered intensely during the second plague.

The Egyptians deified cattle, so when God sent a disease which killed their cows, it would have been clear to the Egyptians that he was attacking their religion.

Facts 3

CRIME AND PUNISHMENT

A unique feature of Hebrew law was that a master had to release a slave that he had harmed, thereby placing emphasis on the humane treatment of all people, regardless of rank or status.

If a woman was raped, the rapist had to pay compensation to her father because she was considered to be his property. Since the father had lost an eligible virgin, the payment had to be the amount he would have received as a bride-price.

In the Old Testament, the crime of negligence was considered as serious as murder or stealing. A goring ox that killed a person was itself killed. However, if the owner knew of its habit, and had neglected to tie it up, then the owner was also put to death.

In early Old Testament times, justice was administered by the chief of the tribe or clan, later by local or circuit judges. During the time of the monarchy, the elders of a town acted as judges at the town gate. The king was an appeal judge.

In New Testament times, the highest court in the land was the Sanhedrin. It had seventy-one members, which acted as a parliament and a court of law. The president of the Sanhedrin was the high priest.

No crucifixions are recorded in the Old Testament, although corpses were sometimes hung on a tree as a warning to others. This symbol of humiliation, with the body regarded as cursed, is described in Isaiah when he foretells Jesus' death.

The possession of animals in a semi-nomadic society was of prime importance, which may explain why the penalty for stealing animals involved a four or five-fold restitution rather than like for like, thereby acting as a deterrent to others.

It was common for Romans to chain guards to prisoners, especially those under house arrest.

Pontius Pilate was the Roman procurator (governor) of Judea during the time of Jesus' ministry. In 36 A.D. he was recalled to Rome because he had used Roman troops to massacre a religious gathering in Samaria.

As well as places of worship, synagogues served as schools, and local law courts. Offenders were sometimes excommunicated, which was a serious punishment, since a synagogue was the center of the community.

Jewish law laid down that the number of strokes in a whipping should not exceed thirty-nine.

Facts 4

CRIME AND PUNISHMENT

In the Law of Moses, there are six hundred and thirteen rules and laws. As time passed, the Jews added many thousands of minute extra laws to explain and elaborate on the written Law.

The word "Satan" is a proper name meaning "opponent" or "adversary." It is the name given in the Bible to the devil.

In accordance with the Ten Commandments, Jews were forbidden to work on the Sabbath. They had many hundreds of laws to explain what "work" meant. Medical treatment could be given only if a life was in danger. A bandage could therefore be put on a wound, but not ointment, since ointment brought about healing.

Some Jewish teachers said that eggs that had been laid on the Sabbath, could not be eaten since the hen had been working.

In Philippi Paul and Silas were put in the "inner cell" of a Roman prison. These cells had no windows, no ventilation or heating. Prisoners were chained to a wall, or their feet were fastened in stocks.

In New Testament times, prisons were places where prisoners were kept waiting for a trial or punishment. Being put in prison was not in itself n punishment.

A frequent punishment was flogging. It was carried out with the use of a scourge, which was a whip made up of many leather thongs studded with bone or lead.

In a Roman prison, the jailer was responsible for the prisoners. If they escaped, the jailer's life would be taken.

War and Peace

Quiz #1
WAR AND PEACE

1. How were the Israelites who took part in a war paid?

2. Who was the only judge who was also a prophetess?

3. Who said, "All who draw the sword will die by the sword"?

4. Which Philistine champion was over nine feet tall?

5. Gideon started with an army of 32,000 men. How many people did he allow to go home?

6. Which judge sang about the time when the Israelites did not have a shield or spear among 40,000 of them?

7. Who made this famous lament over the death in battle of Saul and Jonathan: "Your glory, O Israel, lies slain on your heights. How the mighty have fallen!"?

8. When the spies returned from exploring Canaan what was it about their cities that worried them?

9. Which New Testament letter talks about God's "armor of light"?

10. Speaking of the future glory of Zion who prophesied, "I will make your battlements of rubies, your gates of sparkling jewels, and all your walls of precious stones"?

11. Which Old Testament prophet described the penetrating characteristic of God's word as follows: "He made my mouth like a sharpened sword... he made me into a polished arrow"?

12. Which Old Testament prophet wrote, "I will make a covenant of peace with them; it shall be an everlasting covenant"? (KJV)

13. Who is referred to as "Lord of lords and King of kings" in the book of Revelation?

14. Which king of Judah "...made machines designed by skillful men for use on the towers and on the corner defenses to shoot arrows and hurl large stones"?

15. Manoah was the father of which famous Israelite champion?

Answers

1. By sharing the spoils 2. Deborah 3. Jesus 4. Goliath
5. 31,700, so he was left with just 300 men in his army 6. Deborah 7. David
8. They were fortified and very large 9. The letter to the Romans 10. Isaiah 11. Isaiah
12. Ezekiel 13. The Lord Jesus Christ 14. Uzziah 15. Samson

Quiz #2

WAR AND PEACE

1. What was the name of the Galilean who led an armed revolt against the Romans when Jesus was a boy?

2. True or false? A Roman centurion was an officer in charge of one hundred men.

3. Why did the Israelites give a "long blast" on their trumpets just before they advanced on Jericho?

4. When some soldiers asked John the Baptist, "And what should we do?" how did John reply?

5. After the Israelites crossed the Red Sea why did God say he would not lead them through the Philistine country?

6. Which Israelite leader said that if God was with you then you could rout a thousand people?

7. What happened to all of Pharaoh's chariots as they chased the Israelites?

8. Who told people living in Jerusalem, "Don't be afraid of them: Remember the Lord, who is great and awesome and fight for your brethren, your sons, and your daughters, your wives, and your homes"?

9. Which Psalm speaks about kings being bound with fetters?

10. Where in the Old Testament does the following verse come from: "Consider the blameless, observe the upright, there is a future for the man of peace"?

11. What, according to Psalm 119:165, do people have to do if they want "great peace"?

12. Who prevented a war by saying to Rehoboam, "You should not fight against your brothers"?

13. In which Psalm is it written, "He makes wars cease to the ends of the earth; he breaks the bow, and shatters the spear in sunder; he burns the shields with fire"?

14. Who said, "Blessed are the peacemakers: for they shall be called sons of God"?

15. Who gave this piece of advice in one of his New Testament letters: "Do not let not the sun go down on your anger"?

Quiz #3

WAR AND PEACE

1. The message of which Old Testament book can be summed up by the words, "everyone did as he saw fit"?

2. Who imposed a levy of 100 talents of silver and a talent of gold on Judah?

3. Where in the Old Testament is wisdom described as follows: "Her ways are ways of pleasantness, and all her paths are peace"?

4. What work were the men described in the following verse engaged in: "From that day on, half of my men did the work, while the other half were equipped with spears, shields, bows and armor"?

5. As Moses arrived with the Ten Commandments what did Joshua say to him about the noise in the Israelite camp?

6. Who was the first person to meet Abraham after he returned from defeating Kedorlaomer?

7. True or false? David killed Goliath with a bow and arrow.

8. Which Old Testament book contains this practical advice: "A soft answer turneth away wrath: but grievous words stir up anger"? (KJV)

9. Which king of Babylon did Ezekiel predict would "direct the blows of his battering rams against the walls of Jerusalem"?

10. Which king of Israel is the seventh most mentioned man in the Old Testament?

11. Who, on several occasions, promised the Israelites that they would be defeated in battle if they violated his covenant?

12. Who spoke to the Israelites after he had defeated Sihon king of the Amorites?

13. Which king of Israel was once King Saul's armor-bearer?

14. Joshua made a surprise attack on the Gibeonites after he had marched all through the night from where?

15. Who defeated Ben-Hadad three times and recovered the Israelite towns?

Answers

1. The book of Judges 2. Pharaoh Neco 3. Proverbs 3:17 4. Rebuilding the walls of Jerusalem. 5. "There is a sound of war in the camp" 6. The King of Sodom 7. False. He used a sling and a stone (1 Samuel 17:49, 51) 8. Proverbs 9. King Nebuchadnezzar 10. Solomon 11. The Lord God 12. Moses 13. King David 14. Gilgal 15. Jehoash

Quiz #4
WAR AND PEACE

1. Who wrote, "We do not wage war as the world does"?

2. True or false? In Old Testament days, spies were usually sent out before starting a battle.

3. Who said, "You come against me with sword and spear and javelin, but I come against you in the name of the Lord Almighty, the God of the armies of Israel, whom you have defiled"?

4. Which defeated enemy did David set to work making bricks?

5. Who said, "Bring out Samson to entertain us"?

6. On what animals did David's cavalry ride?

7. Which commander of the army of the king of Aram was a leper?

8. What is the name of the fortress in Jerusalem where the Roman army had its headquarters?

9. Which king of Israel told Amaziah, king of Judah, that he was arrogant?

10. A trumpet was blown to summon the Israelites to gather for war, as Gideon did when summoning the Abiezrites to follow him. What was the trumpet made from?

11. To which two groups of people did Moses say, "Shall your countrymen go to war while you sit here?"?

12. Which Old Testament book is made up of laments over the destruction of Jerusalem?

13. Which Old Testament book says, "His speech is smooth as butter, yet war is in his heart"?

14. True or false? Miriam was a judge who challenged the Israelites to fight against King Sisera and his 900 iron chariots.

15. When Joshua captured Jericho, who were the only ones spared from being killed?

Answers

1. Paul **2.** True (Joshua 2:1) **3.** David **4.** The Ammonites **5.** The rulers of the Philistines **6.** Mules **7.** Naaman **8.** Antonia Fortress **9.** Jehoash **10.** A ram's horn **11.** The Gadites and Reubenites **12.** The book of Lamentations **13.** The Psalms **14.** False. It was Deborah (Judges 4) **15.** Rahab the prostitute and all who were in her house

Quiz #5

WAR AND PEACE

1. What is the name for the "Sea Peoples" against whom King Saul and David waged war?

2. When the Israelites were conquering Canaan did they ever fight as separate tribes?

3. Which town did Goliath come from?

4. What was Joshua told to hold out in his hand in the direction of Ai before attacking that town?

5. True or false? When laying a siege against an enemy city, the army was not allowed to cut down the enemy's fruit trees growing outside the walls.

6. When there was "war in heaven," what name was given to the ejected dragon?

7. Through whom, according to the apostle Paul, do we have peace with God?

8. Who named one of his daughters Eliezer because, "My father's God was my helper; he saved me from the sword of Pharaoh"?

9. The 32 kings who were once in their tents getting drunk were allies with whom?

10. Why were the Levites excused from military service?

11. Which king of Egypt was defeated by Nebuchadnezzar at Carchemish?

12. Who said, "Peace I leave with you; my peace I give you"?

13. What was the last thing King Zedekiah ever saw?

14. Which Old Testament prophetic book is all about Nineveh's sinfulness?

15. Which false prophet predicted that the Lord would "break the yoke of Nebuchadnezzar king of Babylon off the neck of all the nations within two years"?

Answers

1. The Philistines **2.** Yes they did sometimes. One example is when the men of Judah attacked Jerusalem and took it.
3. Gath **4.** A javelin **5.** True (Deuteronomy 20:20) **6.** The devil, or Satan
7. Our Lord Jesus Christ **8.** Moses **9.** Ben-Hadad **10.** Because they were engaged in the ceremonies in the tabernacle.
11. Pharaoh Neco **12.** Jesus **13.** His sons killed by the Babylonians.
14. The book of Nahum **15.** Hananiah

Quiz #6

WAR AND PEACE

1. "All the Israelites twenty years old or more who were able to serve in Israel's army were counted [by Moses and Aaron and the twelve leaders of Israel] according to their families." What was the total number?

2. Who asked the question, "What causes quarrels and fights among you?"?

3. What answer is given in the second part of the verse which is quoted in the previous question?

4. Why did David decline to wear King Saul's coat of armor and bronze helmet?

5. Who predicted that a time would come when people "would no longer train for war"?

6. Which famous warrior said, "He [God] trains my hands for battle; my arms can bend a bow of bronze"?

7. Which city was "kept under siege until the eleventh year of King Zedekiah"?

8. Which Old Testament prophet predicted that the king of the North would be defeated by the king of the South?

9. In which book of the Bible is this proverb found: "By long forbearing is a prince persuaded, and a soft tongue breaketh the bone"? (KJV)

10. True or false? Samson was a one-man army fighting the Philistine army. But he lost his strength when his hair was cut off.

11. Which two kings only ruled Judah for three months?

12. Who was the last king of Judah?

13. Who mistook the dawn sun shining on the water for blood and so lost a battle against the Israelites?

14. What remarkable event did Joshua record about "the day the Lord gave the Amorites over to Israel"?

15. Which Old Testament prophet identified himself completely with his people when he said, "Since my people are crushed, I am crushed"?

Quiz #7

WAR AND PEACE

1. What, according to Isaiah, would be made into plowshares and what would be made into pruning hooks, as a sign of a time of peace?

2. Who killed an Egyptian for mistreating an Israelite slave?

3. The angel of the Lord met which Israelite judge under the oak in Ophrah?

4. In which Old Testament book is this advice given: "If you wage war, obtain guidance"?

5. Which of the judges ruled Israel for the longest?

6. Which Old Testament book prophesied that war would be no more in the following words, "Bow and sword and battle I will abolish from the land, so that all may lie down in safety"?

7. In which Old Testament book is the following question found: "Has any god ever tried to take for himself one nation out of another nation, by testings, by miraculous signs and wonders, by war...?"?

8. In which of Paul's letters is the following instruction found: "If it is possible, as much as you can, live peaceably with all men"? (KJV)

9. Who was the first king of the northern kingdom of Israel?

10. Of which king did the Lord say, "He will not enter this city or shoot an arrow here"?

11. Who asked the Lord that he might die with the Philistines?

12. Which king took silver and gold from the temple and sent it as a gift to King Tiglath-Pileser?

13. Which king of Assyria imprisoned King Hoshea?

14. Who ruled the northern kingdom of Israel for only one month?

15. How, according to the letter of Hebrews, did the walls of Jericho fall?

Quiz #8

WAR AND PEACE

1. David had three exceptionally brilliant soldiers who are known as "The Three," or, "The Three Mighty Men." What were their names?

2. Who was said to be "as famous as the three mighty men"?

3. Which Old Testament prophet prophesied about a "Prince of Peace"?

4. Which warrior-king of Israel was described as being a man after God's own heart?

5. Which infamous queen is mentioned 23 times in the Old Testament?

6. Who said, "My kingdom is not of this world. If it were, my servants would fight"?

7. Which judge called herself "a mother in Israel"?

8. True or false? Moses fought the battle of Jericho.

9. Which famous Israelite warrior is the ninth most mentioned man in the Old Testament?

10. Which New Testament writer assured his readers that, "The peace of God, which transcemds all understanding, shall keep your hearts and minds in Christ Jesus"?

11. Which soldier did David deliberately get drunk?

12. Which king, who was on the point of death, was told by Isaiah that he would live another 15 years and that he would be delivered from the city of Jerusalem?

13. Who plotted to have all Hebrew people killed?

14. 2 Samuel 15 records one of David's sons leading a revolt against him? Which son?

15. In which New Testament letter is the following instruction given: "Follow peace with all men"? (KJV)

Answers

1. Josheb-Basshebeth, Eleazar, and Shammah 2. Benaiah 3. Isaiah 4. David 5. Jezebel
6. Jesus 7. Deborah 8. False. Joshua fought the battle of Jericho (Joshua 6:2) 9. Joshua
10. Paul 11. Uriah 12. Hezekiah 13. Haman 14. Absalom 15. Hebrews

Quiz #9

WAR AND PEACE

1. Which left-handed judge killed Eglon, King of Moab by plunging his sword into the king's belly?

2. What kind of musical instrument did each of Gideon's 300 men take with them when they fought against an enemy who were camped in the valley with more camels "than sand on the sea shore"?

3. Besides a musical instrument what else did each of Gideon's 300 men take with them when they fought against an enemy who were camped in the valley with more camels "than sand on the sea shore"?

4. Which defeated army did David make lie down on the ground so they could be measured with a length of cord? "Every two lengths of them were put to death, and the third length was allowed to live."

5. Who broke many vows he had made to David and tried to kill him several times?

6. What was King Herod's final command concerning John the Baptist?

7. Who was the first king of Judah?

8. Who ruled Judah for 41 years?

9. Who was Queen Jezebel's husband?

10. Which Old Testament king had an iron bed that measured more than 13 feet long and 6 feet wide?

11. When Evil-Merodach became king of Babylon what did he do for Jehoiachin?

12. Over how many provinces did King Xerxes rule?

13. Where in the Bible is the statement "[There is] a time for war and a time for peace"?

14. Who said to Samson, "You have made a fool of me"?

15. How old was Darius the Mede when he became ruler of Israel?

---

11. He released him from prison 12. 127 13. Ecclesiastes 14. Delilah 15. 62 years old
6. That he should be beheaded 7. Rehoboam 8. Asa 9. King Ahab 10. King Og
1. Ehud 2. A trumpet 3. A torch hidden in a jug 4. The Moabites 5. Saul

Answers

Quiz # 10

WAR AND PEACE

1. When the Israelites attacked the town of Kir Hareseth they successfully deployed "men armed with slings". Who was their enemy?

2. David and some of his men were in the back of a cave when Saul came into the same cave. Why did Saul go into the cave?

3. Which king ruled the northern kingdom of Israel for the longest?

4. Against which army did the Lord give David this instruction: "As soon as you hear the sound of marching in the tops of the balsam trees, move quickly, because that will mean that the Lord has gone in front of you"?

5. Who boasted, "With a donkey's jaw-bone I have killed a thousand men"?

6. Once, when Elisha's servant woke up, he saw the enemy army surrounding his town. Elisha said, "Don't be afraid. Those people who are with us are more than those with them." When the servant looked again, what did he see?

7. Which judge "had thirty sons, who rode thirty donkeys"?

8. Who does Isaiah say will have no peace?

9. Who in the New Testament said, "Glory to God in the highest, and on earth peace, good will toward men"? (KJV)

10. When Jesus sent out 72 disciples ahead of him, what did he tell them to say when they went into someone's house?

11. Which three kings are said in the Bible to have ruled all of Israel?

12. How many priests did Saul have killed at Nob because they helped David?

13. Who carried out David's orders and placed Uriah in the middle of the fiercest fighting and then left him to be killed there?

14. Who took over from Moses as leader of the Israelites?

15. Which Old Testament prophet said, "The work of righteousness shall be peace"? (KJV)

Answers

1. The Moabites 2. To relieve himself 3. Jeroboam 4. The Philistines
5. Samson 6. The hills surrounding the town were full of horses and chariots of fire.
7. Jair 8. The wicked 9. A great company of the heavenly host 10. "Peace be to this house"
11. Saul, David and Solomon 12. 85 13. Joab 14. Joshua 15. Isaiah

Quiz # 11

WAR AND PEACE

1. True or false? Before the Israelites embarked on a "holy war" they often made a sacrifice to God.

2. Some of the strongest and bravest of David's soldiers formed a group known as "The Thirty." But there were more than 30 of them. How many were there?

3. Who described the word of God as, "Living and active. Sharper than any double edged sword, it penetrates even to dividing soul and spirit, joints and marrow"?

4. Which army was completely captured by David except for "four hundred young men who rode off on camels and fled"?

5. When Gideon attacked the Midianite camp what did he tell his soldiers to shout out?

6. In which Old Testament book is the following complaint found, "I am a man of peace; but when I speak, they are for war"?

7. Who once "mobilized twenty-six thousand swordsmen"?

8. Which short Old Testament prophetic book says of the wicked people of Nineveh, "the sword will cut you down and, like grasshoppers, consume you"?

9. Micah 5:5 states, "When the Assyrian invades our land and marches through our fortresses, we will raise against him seven shepherds, even eight leaders of men." What do "seven" and "eight" denote?

10. What happened to Israel's last king, Zedekiah, before he was exiled in Babylon?

11. What does the psalmist call on God to do with nations who delight in war?

12. When Jesus predicted that we would hear of wars and rumors of wars, how did he say we should react to such news?

13. Which Old Testament prophet referred to God as his "war club"?

14. Which Old Testament book describes seven times how the Israelites rejected God and then were delivered when God raised up a military champion?

15. The reigns of how many judges are recorded in the book of Judges?

Facts 1

WAR AND PEACE

Israel did not engage in war like her surrounding neighbors. When Israel fought she fought a "holy war" because she only fought when God told her to fight. One of the names by which God was known to Israel was "the God of the armies of Israel" (1 Samuel 17:45).

Eliakim asked a field commander of the threatening Assyrian army to speak in Aramaic and not in Hebrew as he was in the hearing of the people on the wall of Jerusalem. The Assyrians wanted to demoralize the people of Jerusalem by negotiating in their earshot in their own language.

King Ahab discovered to his cost that the weak parts of armor were its joints. "But someone drew his bow at random and hit the king of Israel between the sections of his armor" (1 Kings 22:34).

Those whom God had appointed to destroy Moab were urged on with these words from Jeremiah, "A curse on him who keeps his sword from bloodshed" (Jeremiah 48:10). Such curses have been open to abuse, as when Pope Gregory VII used it as his motto.

The Israelites often celebrated their victories with a song of praise to God (Exodus 15:1-18) and with singing, and dancing and tambourines.

Gideon said, "I will not rule over you, nor will my son rule over you. The Lord will rule over you" (Judge 8:23). The idea of a theocracy, God ruling over the nation of Israel, is central in the book of Judges. Like Samuel, Gideon rejected the idea of a monarchy.

When David, like Moses and Joshua before him, led Israel into battle he thought of himself as fighting the Lord's battles (1 Samuel 25:28). David's victories over the Philistines were not for his personal advancement but to bring glory to the Lord.

"The Lord Almighty is mustering an army for war" (Isaiah 13:4). In this verse the Hebrew word for "army" is the word for "Almighty" in the singular form. God is the leader of the armies that are going to destroy Babylon.

Amos 2:11 states, "For three sins of Edom, even for four, I will not turn back my wrath. Because he pursued his brother with a sword". "Edom" stands for the descendants of Esau and his "brother" was Israel. Edom continually broke its relationship with Israel by its hostile actions.

Jesus said, "I did not come to bring peace, but a sword" (Matthew 10:34). His coming caused conflict within families, as well as among the religious hierarchy.

Zechariah 9:14 predicts, "I will bend Judah as I bend my bow and fill it with Ephraim." God is depicted as the Divine Warrior. He takes Judah as his bow and the northern kingdom of Ephraim as his arrow.

Facts 2

WAR AND PEACE

Numbers 21:14 is the only place in the Old Testament to mention "the Book of the Wars of the Lord." It no longer exists but was most probably an old collection of songs of war which praised God.

David had a royal bodyguard made up of mercenaries, the Kerethites and Pelethites, who were separate from the regular army. They were freed from doing forced labor and from paying taxes.

Nahum 3:3 describes the Assyrian army as causing "Many casualties, piles of dead, bodies without number, people stumbling over the corpses". The Assyrians tortured and mutilated the leaders of the cities they captured.

When Joshua was faced with an army as numerous as the sand on the seashore God told him not to be afraid and to "hamstring their horses" (Joshua 11:6). This was done by cutting the horses tendon above the hock so that it became lame.

When King of Aram's army surrounded Samaria, and famine threatened Samaria, God made the Aramaen army hear the sound of thousands of chariots and horses. They thought the Hittite and Egyptian armies were marching to save Samaria and so fled.

According to Exodus 15:3, "The Lord is a man of war" (KJV), "The Lord is a warrior". In the Old Testament God is often pictured as a warrior-king leading his people into battle.

Gideon was once asked by the officials of Succoth, "Do you already have the hands of Zebah and Zalmunna in your possession?" (Judges 8:6) The Egyptians and Assyrians amputated the hands of their enemies as proof of their victories.

Psalm 76 celebrates God's mighty power in defending Jerusalem. It recalls God's crushing defeat of Zion's enemies. "There he [God] broke the flashing arrows, the shields and the swords, the weapons of war" (Psalm 76).

When Elisha was dying, Jehoash king of Israel visited him and said, "My father! My father!... The chariots and horsemen of Israel!" (2 Kings 13:14) The king knew that Elisha was more important for Israel's success than any military weapons.

The Old Testament repeatedly teaches that Israel's security does not rest in military strength but in God himself. "When you go to war against your enemies and see horses and chariots and an army greater than yours, do not be afraid of them, because the Lord your God... will be with you" (Deuteronomy 20:1).

Abraham rescued Lot with "318 trained men born in his household" (Genesis 14:14). This demonstrates Abraham's great wealth. The Hebrew word for "trained men" only comes here in the Bible and probably refers to armed retainers.

Facts 3

WAR AND PEACE

Like the ancient Greeks, the Philistines sometimes decided the outcome of a war by choosing a champion from each army. The champions then fought each other on behalf of each army (See 1 Samuel 17:9).

Gideon overheard a Midianite telling his friend his dream in which "a round loaf of barley bread came tumbling into the Midianite camp" (Judges 7:13). God often revealed things in dreams in the Old Testament. The unusual feature here is that both the dreamer and the interpreter were not Israelites.

The minor prophets reminded God's people about the vital principle that God himself should be trusted and not any weapons of war. "I will save them–not by bow, sword or battle, or by horses and horsemen, but by the Lord their God" (Hosea 1:7).

Hezekiah "blocked the upper outlet of the Gihon spring and channeled the water down to the west side of the City of David" (2 Chronicles 32:30). The Siloam Inscription still exists in the middle of the 600 yard long tunnel, describing in Hebrew how the work to build this tunnel began at opposite ends and met in the middle.

After a battle the Israelites often observed a ban, called a herem. This meant that a whole city, including its people and possessions, were set apart for God. Israelites were not allowed to appropriate any spoils for themselves.

God did not want the Israelites to think that their own righteousness enabled them to conquer the Promised Land. "No, it is on account of the wickedness of these nations" (Deuteronomy 9:4).

David, on the run from King Saul, had the opportunity to kill Saul, and was urged to do so by his men, but said that he would not lift his hand against the Lord's anointed. David believed that Saul was king by the sanction of God and had been anointed for this purpose.

In Hebrew poetry the shield is often used as a symbol of the power and security that a believer finds in God. The poet-warrior David wrote, "The Lord is my strength and my shield; my heart trusts in him, and I am helped" (Psalm 28:7).

When the Assyrian army surrounded Jerusalem, God rescued the city in a remarkable way. "An angel of the Lord went out and put to death a 185,000 men in the Assyrian camp" (2 Kings 19:35).

Facts 4

WAR AND PEACE

The Philistines' weapons were far superior to anything the Israelites had because they knew how to work iron and other metals. Hence it says in 1 Samuel 13:19, "Not a blacksmith could be found in the whole land of Israel, because the Philistines had said, 'Otherwise the Hebrews will make swords or spears!'"

The Israelites used wooden shields covered with oiled leather once they settled in Canaan. These leather shields were rubbed with oil to preserve them. Hence Saul's shield was "defiled" because it was "no longer rubbed with oil" (2 Samuel 1:21).

The Israelites asked God if they should fight before waging war. They thought of entering the Promised Land, or defending it as a "holy" activity. "The Israelites went up and wept before the Lord until evening, and they enquired of the Lord. They said, 'shall we go up again to battle...?'" (Judges 20:23)

"The king of Assyria captured Samaria and deported the Israelites" (2 Kings 17:6). The Assyrians generally followed the policy of deporting the people they conquered.

"We have heard that the kings of the house of Israel are merciful" (1 Kings 20:31). In contrast with the Assyrians who inflicted torture on their captured enemies, the Israelite kings had a reputation for being compassionate.

On a number of occasions the Israelites killed everyone in a city they captured. "The city and all that is in it are to be devoted to the Lord" (Joshua 6:17). This refers to giving over things and people to God in an irrevocable way.

Leather-covered shields were sometimes soaked in water as a defense against the enemies burning arrows. Hence Paul writes, "take up the shield of faith, with which you can extinguish all the flaming arrows of the evil one" (Ephesians 6:16).

"The Philistines assembled to offer a great sacrifice to Dagon their god" (Judges 16:23). "Dagon," a popular Philistines god, means "grain" and so was probably a vegetation deity.

Jerusalem was a strongly fortified mountain-top citadel. David needed to use a clever plan to capture it. His men climbed up a secret tunnel—a water shaft leading from the city to a spring outside the city walls.

The Israelites were attacked by a war-like nomadic tribe from the region of Sinai, called the Amalekites. So long as Moses held his hands up the Israelites won the battle. Holding his hands up like this was a symbolic way of appealing to God for help.

1 Samuel 23:9 states, "When David learned that Saul was plotting against him, he said to Abiather the priest, 'Bring the ephod'". He did this because this ephod contained the Urim and Thummin, a divinely appointed means of communicating with God.

Facts 5

WAR AND PEACE

Different types and sizes of shield were used in the Old Testament. In 2 Chronicles some soldiers were equipped with large shields and spears while other soldiers were armed with small shields and bows. The smaller meginah was usually carried by archers and the larger sinah by bowmen.

Psalm 127:5 says "Blessed is the man whose quiver is full of them [sons]". Leather quivers were carried by bowmen and fitted in chariots. Ordinary quivers held about 30 arrows and quivers in chariots about 50 arrows. A quiver full of children would have been a big family.

When Joshua approached Jericho he saw a man with a drawn sword in his hand. Joshua asked him "Are you for us or for our enemies?" "Neither," he replied, "but as commander of the army of the Lord I have come" (Joshua 5:13-14). This figure may have been God, or Jesus or an angel.

Lamentations 1:12 asks, "Is any suffering like my suffering... that the Lord brought on me in the day of his fierce anger?". The author of Lamentations sees that the Babylonians were but human agents and that God himself destroyed his temple and city.

The Lord used the elements of nature as one of his armaments to defeat Israel's enemies. In 1 Samuel 7:10 the "Lord thundered with loud thunder against the Philistines" so they were thrown into such a panic that the Israelites routed them.

After Samson lost his strength the Philistines gouged out his eyes. It was common for prisoners of war to receive such brutal and humiliating treatment.

Psalm 149:6-7 speaks of a double-edged sword inflicting vengeance on the nations. Vengeance was God's just retribution on anyone who attacked God's followers.

As Abimelech besieged a tower at Thebez a woman dropped an upper millstone on his head and cracked his skull. It was a great disgrace for a soldier to be killed by a woman. Hence Abimelech asked his armor-bearer to kill him.

When the Psalmist wrote about Jerusalem's famous fortifications, "Walk about Zion, go round her, count her towers, consider well her ramparts, view her citadels" (Psalm 48:12-13), he was saying that the strength of Jerusalem's towers and ramparts is God's presence.

In the Bible, the sword often symbolizes divine judgment. "Out of his mouth came a sharp double-edged sword" (Revelation 1:16). The double-edge sword was similar to a long, broad Thracian sword.

When God commanded Israel to destroy a nation it was because they were evil. The Amorites were spared until their sin became too great. "The sin of the Amorites has not yet reached its full measure" (Genesis 15:16).

Dollars and Sense

Quiz # 1

DOLLARS AND SENSE

1. In Mark's Gospel, what coin did Jesus ask to be brought to him when he was questioned about the paying of taxes?

2. What is Jesus referring to when he says, "I tell you the truth, you will not get out until you have paid the last penny"?

3. In the Gospel of Matthew, Jesus says, "Are not even the tax collectors doing that?" What is he referring to?

4. How much did Abraham pay for the field that he bought from Ephron the Hittite?

5. Why did Jeremiah buy a field from his cousin Hanamel?

6. According to the Law of Moses in Exodus, what must people not do when lending money to the needy?

7. What gifts was Rebekah given at the well?

8. Who stole gold and silver from the ruins of Jericho?

9. What was the name of the tax collector Jesus met as he was passing through Jericho?

10. Which Old Testament prophet did the Lord use to speak to the Israelites, saying, "You earn wages, only to put them in a purse with holes in it"?

11. In Matthew 17, what did Jesus tell Simon Peter he would find in the mouth of a fish?

12. In John's Gospel, who is said to have stolen money from the disciples' money bag?

13. In 1 Kings, which king attacked Jerusalem and carried off the treasures of the temple and the palace?

14. To whom is Paul writing when he says, "For the love of money is a root of all kinds of evil"?

15. Which one of Jesus' disciples was formerly a tax collector?

Answers

1. A denarius **2.** Settling matters with an adversary **3.** Loving those who love you **4.** 400 shekels of silver **5.** Because he was Hanamel's nearest relative and it was his duty to redeem and possess the field if asked to do so **6.** They must not charge interest **7.** A gold nose ring and two gold bracelets **8.** Achan **9.** Zacchaeus **10.** Haggai **11.** A four-drachma coin **12.** Judas Iscariot **13.** King Shishak of Egypt **14.** Timothy **15.** Matthew (called Levi in Mark and Luke)

Quiz #2

DOLLARS AND SENSE

1. In the New Testament, how much was a day's wage to the hired men in the parable of the workers in the vineyard?

2. In a conversation between Simon Peter and Jesus, who was considered exempt when kings collected duty and taxes?

3. In 1 Kings, who took all the silver and gold left in the temple and persuaded Ben Hadad, to break his treaty with Baasha, King of Israel?

4. Fill in the missing word from Deuteronomy, "At the end of every ___ years you must cancel debts."

5. As recorded in Matthew's Gospel, how many sparrows cost a penny?

6. In Exodus, why did the Israelites have to pay a half-shekel offering to God?

7. Which famous person from the Old Testament owned, "7,000 sheep, 3,000 camels, 500 yoke of oxen, and 500 donkeys and had a large number of servants"?

8. In which Old Testament book is it written, "But remember the Lord your God, for it is he who gives you the ability to produce wealth"?

9. Which Gospel does not mention the money-changers being chased out of the temple by Jesus?

10. Fill in the missing word from Proverbs: "A ___ woman gains respect, but ruthless men gain only wealth."

11. Which disciple said at the feeding of the 5,000 that eight month's wages would not buy enough bread for all the people?

12. In Genesis, why does the Pharaoh of Egypt give Abraham a large quantity of livestock and servants?

13. In the Parable of the Lost Coin, how many does the woman have to begin with?

14. In Mark's Gospel, when Jesus is being questioned about the payment of taxes, whose head is on the coin that Jesus looks at?

15. In the Parable of the Rich Fool, what happens to the man who plans to build bigger barns to store all his crops, so he can take life easy?

Quiz #3

DOLLARS AND SENSE

1. Who does Paul tell to: "command those who are rich in this present world not to be arrogant nor to put their hope in wealth which is so uncertain"?

2. In which book of the Old Testament is it written, "Therefore I command you to be open handed towards your brothers and towards the poor and needy in your land"?

3. In Luke, when Jesus is telling the crowds what to do to become a disciple, he uses an example of a man wanting to build a tower. What does he do before he starts to build?

4. In 2 Kings, who did Mesha, King of Moab, have to supply with 100,000 lambs and the wool of 100,000 rams?

5. What did King Solomon exchange for the cypress trees to build his temple?

6. Which queen gave King Solomon, "120 talents of gold, large quantities of spices, and precious stones"?

7. Fill in the missing word from 1 Kings 16:24: "Omri became king of Israel. He bought the hill of ____ from Shemer for two talents of silver and built a city on the hill."

8. What is the rich young man's response when Jesus tells him to sell all of his possessions?

9. Which Old Testament king gave Hiram, the King of Tyre, 20 towns in Galilee in repayment for the cedar, pine, and gold that he had provided?

10. Which Old Testament person became so rich that the Philistines envied him and blocked up his wells?

11. In the New Testament, who gave two silver coins to an innkeeper on behalf of another?

12. True or false? Matthew the Gospel writer was originally a tax collector.

13. Which Old Testament prophet passes judgment on Israel saying that, "they sell the righteous for silver, and the needy for a pair of sandals"?

14. In the Old Testament, who bought a threshing floor and oxen from Araunah the Jebusite for fifty shekels of silver in order to build an altar on it?

15. After which parable does Jesus say, "There is rejoicing in the presence of the angels of God over one sinner who repents"?

Quiz #4

DOLLARS AND SENSE

1. Who does Jesus tell to visit the lost sheep of Israel, but, "do not take along any gold or silver or copper in your belts"?

2. In Genesis, when Joseph's brothers return to Egypt for a second time to ask for food, how much silver do they take with them?

3. In 2 Kings, where did Hezekiah, king of Judah, get the silver and gold that he needed to pay Sennacherib, King of Assyria?

4. In the Old Testament, who gave Saul a quarter of a silver shekel for a gift to Samuel?

5. In the Parable of the Shrewd Manager, what did the manager do after being told he would lose his job?

6. After Jacob's marriage to Rachel and Leah, he continued to work for his father-in law, Laban. What agreement did he reach with Laban for wages?

7. Which Old Testament king said, "I now give my personal treasures of gold and silver for the temple of my God, over and above everything I have provided for this temple"?

8. Through Moses, what three metals did the Lord ask the Israelites to bring him as an offering for the Tabernacle?

9. Why did Abimelech give Abraham 1,000 shekels of silver?

10. In the Parable of the Pearl, what did the merchant do when he found one of great value?

11. In which Old Testament book does the following command appear: "Do not hold back the wages of a hired man overnight"?

12. The words from Deuteronomy, "There will always be poor people in the land" are repeated by Jesus in which Gospel?

13. In which Gospel is the story of the rich man and Lazarus?

14. Which four groups of people benefited from tithes, according to the book of Deuteronomy?

15. When Jesus says, "Do not let your left hand know what your right hand is doing" what is he referring to?

---

1. The 12 disciples **2.** Double the amount they took first of all **3.** From the temple of the Lord and the palace treasures **4.** Saul's servant **5.** He reduced the debts of his master's debtors **6.** Jacob was to have every dark, speckled, or spotted lamb and goat from Laban's flock **7.** King David **8.** Gold, silver and bronze **9.** As compensation for taking Sarah away from Abraham **10.** He sold everything he had to buy it **11.** Leviticus **12.** Matthew **13.** Luke **14.** The Levite, the alien, the fatherless, and the widow **15.** Giving to the needy

Answers

Quiz #5

DOLLARS AND SENSE

1. Which New Testament writer says "has not God chosen those who are poor in the eyes of the world to be rich in faith and to inherit the kingdom...?"?

2. In the Old Testament, who said that he had taken great pains to provide a hundred thousand talents of gold and a million talents of silver for the Lord's temple?

3. What is "a pledge," as described in the Old Testament in relation to a loan?

4. In 1 Kings, how much weight in gold is Solomon reported to have received yearly?

5. In the book of Job, what cannot be bought, "with the finest gold, nor can its price be weighed in silver" and "neither gold nor crystal can compare with it"?

6. In the book of Nahum, which city is referred to when it says, "Plunder the silver! Plunder the gold! The supply is endless, the wealth from all its treasures"?

7. In the Old Testament, who got wealth and riches and wisdom from God when all he asked for was wisdom?

8. According to Leviticus, in what year does any property sold previously have to be returned to its owner?

9. Did Joseph's brothers sell Joseph to Babylonian or Ishmaelite merchants?

10. During the long siege of Samaria, people began to grow desperate for food. What animal's head sold for eighty shekels of silver?

11. In Acts, to whom did Peter say, "Silver or gold I do not have, but what I have I give you. In the name of Jesus Christ of Nazareth, walk!"?

12. The chief priests bribed the guards guarding Jesus' tomb to tell what lie?

13. In the Parable of the Talents in Matthew's Gospel, how many talents did the master give each of his three servants?

14. At the Last Supper, when Jesus told Judas to do what he had to do quickly, what did the disciples think Judas was going to do?

15. Who said in the New Testament, "provide purses for yourselves that will not wear out"?

Answers

1. James 2. King David 3. Security for a loan 4. 666 talents (about 25 tons; 23 tonnes) 5. Wisdom 6. Nineveh 7. King Solomon 8. The year of Jubilee 9. Ishmaelites (Midianites) (Genesis 37:28) 10. A donkey's 11. A crippled beggar 12. That the disciples stole Jesus' body during the night while they slept 13. He gave five to the first, two to the second and one to the third 14. They thought Jesus was asking Judas to buy things what was needed for the feast or to give something to the poor 15. Jesus

Quiz #6

DOLLARS AND SENSE

1. In 2 Kings, to whom did Naaman give two silver talents after he had been cured of leprosy?

2. Where did the disciples normally keep their money, according to Mark's Gospel?

3. In the Parable of the Talents in Matthew's Gospel, what did the servant who had received one talent do with it?

4. In Genesis, during the famine in Egypt, who was in charge of collecting money and distributing corn?

5. In the New Testament, which couple sold a piece of property, and kept some of the money for themselves, before taking the rest to the apostles?

6. In Acts, who sold their lands and houses and had the money distributed to people as they had need?

7. Who tried to buy the "gift of God" with money in the New Testament?

8. Which governor hoped that Paul might offer him a bribe to get out of prison?

9. In 2 Kings, who were the first to plunder the camp of the Arameans after the siege of Samaria was lifted?

10. True or false? Joseph was sold for 20 shekels of gold.

11. Fill in the missing word from Psalm 112, "Good will come to him who is ___ and lends freely."

12. In Matthew's Gospel, what three things are said to destroy treasures on earth?

13. Which believers did Paul instruct to set aside money, each week, according to their income, for those in Jerusalem?

14. Why didn't the chief priests and elders put Judas' money back into the treasury?

15. In Acts, who made money by fortune-telling in Philippi?

Answers

1. Elisha's servant, Gehazi 2. In their belts 3. The servant dug a hole in the ground and hid it
4. Joseph 5. Ananias and Sapphira 6. The believers 7. Simon the Sorcerer 8. Felix
9. 4 men with leprosy 10. False. He was sold for 20 shekels of silver (Genesis 37:28) 11. Generous
12. Rust, moths, and thieves 13. Those in Corinth and Galatia 14. Because it was blood money 15. A slave girl

Quiz #7

DOLLARS AND SENSE

1. During the famine in Egypt, what two things did the Egyptians and Canaanites sell after they had used up all their money and had sold their livestock?

2. In the New Testament, who dropped down dead after lying to the apostle Peter about the money she and her husband had received from selling some land?

3. In Psalm 112, in which man's house is wealth and riches?

4. For how many silver pieces was Jesus betrayed?

5. In the Old Testament, who is Micah rebuking when he says, "Her leaders judge for a bribe, her priests teach for a price, and her prophets tell fortunes for money"?

6. In the book of Esther, which man tells the king that he will put 10,000 silver talents in the royal treasury for the men who take part in the massacre of the Jews?

7. In 2 Kings, Menahem, king of Israel, exacted 50 shekels of silver from every wealthy man to secure the support of the king of which country?

8. In Numbers, to whom did Moses give the sanctuary shekel?

9. In James' letter, what did he say had happened to the rich people's clothes and money?

10. In the book of Nehemiah, which group of people are accused by the prophet of exacting usury from the Jews?

11. Which three Gospels document the discussion between Jesus and the Pharisees about paying taxes?

12. In Exodus, the law states that a man must pay compensation if an animal he has borrowed is injured or dies. What are the two exceptions?

13. Who did Jesus meet and eat with at Matthew's house?

14. According to the book of Exodus, what payment weighed 20 gerahs?

15. In 2 Kings, to whom did Jehoiakim pay the silver and gold demanded of him?

Quiz #8

DOLLARS AND SENSE

1. Which king wrote a letter to Ezra telling him to take lots of silver and gold and buy livestock and produce for sacrificing in the temple in Jerusalem?

2. In the New Testament, whom does James compare to a mist that appears for a little while and then vanishes?

3. In the book of Exodus, how much was the sanctuary shekel?

4. To the king of which nation did Elisha prophesy, "about this time tomorrow, a seah of flour will sell for a shekel and two seahs of barley for a shekel"?

5. In the time of Elisha, how was the widow of one of Elisha's prophets saved from creditors?

6. In the New Testament, which field was bought with Judas' thirty pieces of silver?

7. After which parable does Jesus say, "so if you have not been trustworthy in handling worldly wealth, who will trust you with true riches"?

8. What was the name of the beggar, in one of Jesus' parables, who was laid at the gate of a rich man?

9. Which church does Paul exhort to, "just as you excel in everything... see that you also excel in this grace of giving"?

10. According to Paul's letter to Timothy what kind of people, "fall into temptation and a trap and into many foolish and harmful desires that plunge men into ruin and destruction"?

11. Who was Jesus talking to when he told the story of the two men who did not have any money to pay off the debts they owed to a moneylender?

12. True or false? Just before they left Egypt, the Israelites asked the Egyptians for articles of silver and gold and clothing and were given them.

13. According to Exodus, if you buy a Hebrew servant, how long should he serve you for before he goes free?

14. According to Proverbs 22, what is more desirable than great riches?

15. When Solomon asked Hiram, King of Tyre, to supply him with cedars for building the temple, what did Hiram ask for in return?

---

14. A good name 15. Food for his royal household

10. People who want to get rich 11. Simon the Pharisee 12. True (Exodus 12:35-36) 13. 6 years

6. The potter's field 7. The Parable of the Shrewd Manager 8. Lazarus 9. The church at Corinth

3. Half a shekel 4. The king of Israel 5. God provided the widow with enough oil to sell and pay off her debts

1. King Artaxerxes 2. Those who boast about the business they will do in the future and the money they will make

Answers

Quiz #9
DOLLARS AND SENSE

1. When Joseph's brothers went to Egypt to buy corn, which brother stayed at home?

2. In the New Testament, what was the field bought with Judas' thirty pieces of silver used for?

3. In which letter is it written, "No immoral, impure or greedy person—such a man is an idolater—has any inheritance in the kingdom of Christ and of God"?

4. In the Parable of the Sower, what did the seeds that fell among the thorns stand for?

5. True or false? In the Parable of the Prodigal Son, it was the older son who squandered his wealth in a distant country.

6. Who is worth far more than rubies in Proverbs 31?

7. As recorded in Paul's letter to Timothy, for what job must a man be, "not violent but gentle, not quarrelsome, not be a lover of money"?

8. In which New Testament letter is it said that in the last days people will be lovers of themselves and of money?

9. In the New Testament, who told Titus that slaves should be taught not to steal from their masters?

10. Who is responsible for receiving tithes in the Temple?

11. Which letter writer in the New Testament exhorts believers not to discriminate against the poor and favor the rich?

12. Fill in the missing words, "Has God not chosen those who are ___ in the eyes of the world to be ___ in faith."

13. Who was angry with Job for saying, amongst other things, that if he had put his trust in gold, or rejoiced over his wealth then he would have sinned against God?

14. In the Old Testament, who did Balak, King of Moab, want to reward handsomely, if only he would put a curse on the Israelites?

15. Which Old Testament prophet, when talking of the daughter of Zion, says, "you were sold for nothing and without money you will be redeemed"?

Quiz # 10

DOLLARS AND SENSE

1. Who did Paul ask Philemon to welcome, saying that if he owed anything, then he, Paul, would pay?

2. Which Old Testament book says that riches and pleasures are meaningless?

3. In James' warning to rich oppressors, who cried out against the rich because their wages were not paid?

4. Which Old Testament prophet writes, "Why spend money on what is not bread, and your labor on what does not satisfy?"?

5. Which New Testament letter states: "Keep your lives free from the love of money and be content with what you have"?

6. Which king did Ezekiel say was the model of perfection but corrupted his wisdom because of his splendor?

7. Who did Peter appeal to in the New Testament, saying that they should not be greedy for money, but eager to serve, not lording it over others, but making examples of themselves?

8. Which Old Testament prophet told a Moabite king that even if he was given a palace filled with silver and gold, he could not do anything the Lord had not commanded?

9. In James chapter 2, who does James say is exploiting the believers by dragging them into court?

10. In the Old Testament, which two nomads had such a large number of flocks and herds and tents that the land could not support both of them, causing them to separate?

11. In the book of Revelation, who is said to be, "wretched, pitiful, poor, blind, and naked" although they think they are rich and wealthy and lack nothing?

12. Who rescued Lot and all of his possessions from captivity?

13. What happens to a thief who cannot compensate his victim, according to the law of Moses?

14. In 2 Thessalonians who are told to settle down and earn the bread they eat?

15. In which Gospel is the parable of the man who plans to build bigger barns to store his crops and goods so that he can take life easy?

Quiz #11
DOLLARS AND SENSE

1. According to the book of Exodus, is a person allowed to kill a thief caught breaking into their property?

2. Fill in the missing word from the book of Ecclesiastes: "Whoever loves money never has money enough; whoever loves wealth is never satisfied with his___."

3. Fill in the missing word from Proverb 23: "Cast but a glance at riches, and they are gone, for they will surely sprout wings and fly off to the sky like an___."

4. Which Old Testament prophet describes the day of Judgment as a day when God will come and sit as a refiner and purifier of silver, purifying the Levites?

5. When Paul received the blessing of the apostles to preach to the Gentiles, they asked him to remember which group of people?

6. Which church does Paul thank for sending him, "aid again and again when I was in need"?

7. What did Laban's sons say about the growth in Jacob's prosperity?

8. Who does Jesus tell to, "stay in that house, eating and drinking whatever they give you, for the worker deserves his wages"?

9. In the New Testament, who was told, "You have been faithful with a few things; I will put you in charge of many things. Come and share your master's happiness"?

10. Fill in the missing word from Romans 16 it says, "If the___ have shared in the Jew's spiritual blessings, they owe it to the Jews to share with them their material blessings"?

11. Who did Abraham refuse to accept anything from so that he could never say that he had made Abraham rich?

12. Who is Jeremiah criticising when he says that, "your eyes and your heart are set only on dishonest gain, on shedding innocent blood and on oppression and extortion"?

13. In the reign of King Artaxerxes, who championed the poor, telling Jewish nobles and officials that they had to stop the exacting of usury from their own countrymen?

14. Which famous Old Testament judge prophesised that if the Israelites had a king he would extort a tenth of their grain, wine, and flocks and give it to his officials?

15. What was the name of the silversmith who caused a riot in Ephesus by telling fellow traders that Paul was damaging their business?

Quiz #12

DOLLARS AND SENSE

1. In the Old Testament, whose palaces were filled with gold, as, "nothing was made of silver, because silver was considered of little value"?

2. In one of Jesus' parables, what is likened to treasure found in a field?

3. In Luke's Gospel, what did Jesus see the widow put in the collection box?

4. Who should not be in pursuit of dishonest gain according to Paul's letter to Timothy?

5. What do the rich and the poor have in common according to Proverbs 22?

6. To whom did Abraham give a tenth of everything in Genesis 14?

7. In the Old Testament, who cheated who by changing his wages ten times?

8. What happened to Jesus to cause him to say to his followers, "You will always have the poor among you, but you will not always have me"?

9. Which wealthy old man provided for King David during his stay in Mahanaim?

10. Which churches does Paul praise, saying, "out of the most severe trial, their overflowing joy and their extreme poverty welled up in rich generosity"?

11. In 1 Samuel, who overcharged the Israelites for sharpening their axes and plowshares, because there were no blacksmiths in Israel?

12. "Let no ____ remain outstanding, except the continuing ____ to love one another." Which one word is repeated twice in this passage from Romans 13?

13. In Judges, whose mother paid 200 shekels of silver to make him a silver image and idol, which was later stolen by the Danites?

14. In the Old Testament, who did the Lord tell to return to his country and relatives and he would make them prosper?

15. Which Psalm says, "Do not be overawed when a man grows rich... for he will take nothing with him when he dies, his splendor will not descend with him"?

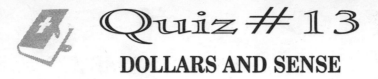

Quiz #13
DOLLARS AND SENSE

1. In the Old Testament, who became poverty-stricken because of Satan?

2. How was the prodigal son reduced to poverty?

3. Which person from the Old Testament prepared a large peace offering of livestock for his brother and sent it ahead of him as he traveled to Seir?

4. Why should you not invite your rich neighbors to lunch or dinner according to Luke's Gospel?

5. What did the prodigal son do when he found himself penniless?

6. To whom did Paul give the rule, "If a man will not work, he shall not eat"?

7. Which Old Testament woman praised God in a psalm, saying, "The Lord sends poverty and wealth; he humbles and he exalts. He raises the poor from the dust"?

8. Which New Testament writer says, "If anyone has material possessions and sees his brother in need but has no pity on him, how can the love of God be in him?"?

9. Which two Gospels record the beatitudes?

10. According to the law of Moses, what were the Israelites told to do if their tithe was too large to carry to "the place the Lord will choose to put his name"?

11. Which New Testament writer forbids favoring a rich man over a poor man?

12. Fill in the missing word, "Watch out! Be on your guard against all kinds of___; a man's life does not consist in the abundance of his possessions."

13. What advice does Jesus give to the rich fool who wants to inherit eternal life?

14. Which prophet quotes Ephraim who boasts, "I am very rich; I have become wealthy. With all my wealth they will not find in me any iniquity or sin"?

15. What event is Jesus referring to in Luke's Gospel when he says, "all these people gave their gifts out of their wealth; but she out of her poverty put in all she had to live on"?

Quiz # 14
DOLLARS AND SENSE

1. Complete the verse from Ecclesiastes, "Wisdom is a shelter as ___ is a shelter, but the advantage of knowledge is this: that wisdom preserves the life of its possessor."

2. The writer of Proverbs 30 asked the Lord to give him neither poverty or riches. If he was poor he might shame God. What did he fear he would do if he was rich?

3. In which Old Testament book are the rules for the redemption of property laid out?

4. In the time of King Joash, which priest bored a hole in a chest, giving instructions that all the money brought to the temple was to be placed inside, to pay the temple workmen?

5. Where in the Old Testament is it written, "Better a poor man whose walk is blameless, than a rich man whose ways are perverse"?

6. If a man redeems any of his tithe, how much must he add to the value of it, according to the book of Leviticus?

7. In the Parable of the Great Banquet in Luke's Gospel, what excuses did three of the guests give for not being able to come to the wedding?

8. Who bribed Delilah with silver so that she would betray her husband?

9. Whose sons, Joel and Abijah, were appointed judges but, "turned aside after dishonest gain and accepted bribes and perverted justice"?

10. In 2 Kings, what did the King of Assyria do after King Ahaz had sent him silver and gold from the Lord's temple and the palace treasuries?

11. During the temptation in the desert, what was Jesus's reply when Satan offered him all the kingdoms of the world and their splendor, if only Jesus would worship him?

12. What is the first instance recorded in the Bible of someone buying something?

13. Who is Paul writing to when he says that slaves should be taught to be trustworthy rather than steal?

14. When Jericho was attacked by Joshua and his people, what did they do with all the gold and silver they found there?

15. Why did David make plans for building the temple but then leave the building of it to Solomon?

Answers

1. Money 2. He feared he might disown God 3. The book of Leviticus 4. Jehoiada 5. The book of Proverbs 6. Fifth 7. One had just bought a field, one had just bought some oxen, and one had just got married 8. The Philistines 9. Samuel's 10. He captured Damascus, deported its inhabitants and killed Rezin, King of Aram 11. "Away from me Satan! For it is written: Worship the Lord your God, and serve him only." 12. Abraham buying a tomb for Sarah 13. Titus 14. They put it in the temple treasury 15. God had told him not to build the temple himself because he was a warrior and had shed blood

Quiz # 15

DOLLARS AND SENSE

1. What name did Jacob give to the land that he bought from the sons of Hamor for a hundred pieces of silver?

2. In Ecclesiastes, what turns a wise man into a fool?

3. According to Proverbs 22, what will the man who oppresses the poor to increase his wealth have in common with the man who gives gifts to the rich?

4. What was the value of a male between the ages of twenty and sixty in terms of being dedicated to the Lord?

5. Which New Testament letter states, "the world and its desires pass away, but the man who does the will of God lives for ever"?

6. In Nehemiah, the Israelites promised God they would not buy things on which days?

7. Fill in the missing word, "_____ is the man who accepts a bribe to kill an innocent person."

8. In John's account of Jesus overturning the moneychangers' tables in the temple, what animals were also ejected?

9. True or false? Jesus met and talked with tax collectors, but never ate and drank with them.

10. Who, according to Jesus, announced their gifts to the needy with trumpets in the synagogues and on the streets?

11. According to Matthew's Gospel, what should a person do if they are offering a gift at the alter and then remember that their brother has something against them?

12. According to Proverbs 11, what happens to the one who withholds his riches unduly?

13. Moses and the Israelites were commanded by God to bring offerings for the Tabernacle. What precious metal was offered in the form of jewellery?

14. In Deuteronomy, who is said to give the ability to produce wealth?

15. True or false? Talents could be made of gold, silver, bronze or iron.

Answers

1. El Elohe Israel **2.** Extortion **3.** They both come to poverty **4.** 50 shekels of silver
5. 1 John (2) **6.** On Sabbath days and holy days **7.** "Cursed" **8.** Doves, sheep, and cattle
9. False, Jesus did dine with them (Luke 15:2) **10.** The hypocrites (Pharisees) **11.** They should go and be reconciled with their brother and then return and offer the gift **12.** He comes to poverty
13. Gold **14.** God **15.** True (1 Chronicles 29:7)

Quiz # 16
DOLLARS AND SENSE

1. Who levied a tax of 100 talents of silver and one talent of gold on Judea and dethroned King Jehoahaz?

2. Which area in the Old Testament was famous for the gold it produced?

3. Which Old Testament king from Babylon stole articles from the temple and put them in his own temple?

4. Which wealthy Old Testament king ruled over 127 provinces stretching from India to Cush?

5. Which king of Judah defeated the Ammonites and forced them to pay him silver, wheat, and barley for three years?

6. Fill in the missing word, "Of what use is money in the hand of a fool, since he has no desire to get____."

7. In the book of Judges, who hired "reckless adventurers" to kill Jerub-Baal's sons for 70 silver shekels?

8. In the Old Testament, if someone wanted to make a special vow to dedicate a person to the Lord, but was too poor to pay the specified amount, what could he do?

9. As recorded in Numbers, how old did a baby have to be before it was redeemed at the temple for the price of five shekels of silver?

10. Who received a tithe from the Levites' tithe?

11. Who settled in the hill country of Seir because his possessions were too great to live in the same place as Jacob?

12. Why should you not take millstones as security for a debt?

13. In the Old Testament, who received a piece of silver and a gold ring from each of his friends and family after suffering great hardships?

14. Under what circumstances could an Israelite charge another Israelite interest?

15. True or false? According to Deuteronomy 24, you should pay the wages of a hired Israelite each day before sunset, but not the wages of an alien.

Quiz # 17

DOLLARS AND SENSE

1. Which Old Testament king said to his official Haman, "Keep the money, and do with the people as you please"?

2. In the book of Judges, who asked each of the Israelites to give him an earring from their plunder after the defeat of the Midianites?

3. Moses and Eleazar the priest led the Israelites into battle, after which the commanders offered to the Lord all the gold they had plundered. Against whom did they battle?

4. In the Old Testament which prophet bought his wife for fifteen shekels of silver and some barley?

5. True or false? After all the trials that Job went through, God made him more prosperous that he had been before.

6. In the book of Joel the nations are condemned for selling the people of Judea and Israel to whom?

7. Who, according to Jesus, had to depend on the generosity of the people in the towns and villages that they passsed through?

8. True or false? Jesus overturned the moneychanger's tables in the temple because he disagreed with paying the temple tax.

9. Who told Jacob to leave Laban's household when arguments about his wealth and wages began to surface?

10. What is the "work" referred to in the following passage, "The expenses of these men are to be fully paid out of the royal treasury, from the revenues of Trans-Euphrates, so that the work will not stop"?

11. In the New Testament, why is it said that God and Money cannot be served at the same time?

12. In the Old Testament, who paid who to nurse her own child?

13. In Malachi, on the Day of Judgment who will testify against those who defraud laborers of their wages?

14. Where did Jeremiah store his deeds of purchase for the field he had acquired from his cousin?

15. How did the gold that Gideon requested from the Israelites become a snare to him and his family?

---

15. He had the gold made into an ephod, which the Israelites worshiped
. 12. Pharaoh's daughter paid Moses' mother 13. The Lord 14. In a clay jar
11. Because you cannot serve two masters. You will hate one and love the other
9. God 10. The rebuilding of the temple in Jerusalem
6. Greeks 7. The apostles 8. False. He is recorded as paying the temple tax willingly (Matthew 17:27)
1. King Xerxes 2. Gideon 3. The Midianites 4. Hosea 5. True (Job 1:1-3; 42:12-15)

Answers

298

Quiz #18

DOLLARS AND SENSE

1. Which Old Testament prophet prophesised that where there were a thousand vines worth a thousand silver shekels, there would be only briers and arrows?

2. What reason did Abraham give the Hittites for wanting to buy a field from them?

3. Who in the Old Testament, "collected all the money that was to be found in Egypt and Canaan in payment for the corn they were buying"?

4. If a man gave a neighbor his silver or goods for safekeeping and they were stolen and then the thief was caught, what must the thief do?

5. Levites were entitled to sell their houses, but what were they not allowed to sell, according to the book of Leviticus?

6. Who betrayed Samson for a fortune in silver shekels?

7. From whom did King Ahab try to buy a vineyard, so he could use it as a vegetable garden?

8. In the Old Testament, why did Naomi's kinsman redeemer decline to buy the land she was selling?

9. In the reign of Joash, what was done with the money offerings that were left over after the temple had been rebuilt?

10. In the book of Ezra, what did the Lord ask the Israelites to do with the money that they received from Babylon once they had returned to Jerusalem?

11. In Luke, Jesus tells a parable about two men who owed money to a moneylender. One owed 500 denarii and the other 50. How did the parable end?

12. Who claimed in the New Testament that he had not coveted anyone's silver, gold, or clothing and had used his own hands to supply all that he and his companions needed?

13. What was the other name for half a shekel, as described in the book of Exodus?

14. Who supplied Solomon with gold?

15. According to the book of Leviticus, if a man dedicated part of his land to the Lord, how was the value of it determined?

Quiz # 19
DOLLARS AND SENSE

1. True or false? Slaves could be part of an inheritance as they were the property of their owner.

2. For what job did Jethro tell Moses to select capable men, "men who fear God, trustworthy men who hate dishonest gain"?

3. Complete the following verse from Deuteronomy, "Do not have two differing ____ in your bag—one heavy, one light."

4. How were the disciples expected to survive without money as they preached the Gospel throughout the land?

5. Where did the buying and selling of goods take place in Jerusalem?

6. Who wrote to the church in Smyrna telling them that although they were afflicted and poor, they were, in fact, rich?

7. According to Mark's Gospel, who was begging for money by the roadside as Jesus and his disciples approached Jericho?

8. In the book of Ruth, who wanted to sell land that had belonged to Elimelech?

9. What parable does Jesus tell to illustrate how hard it is for the rich to enter the kingdom of God?

10. Which group of people in the New Testament are described as lovers of money?

11. In which Old Testament book is it written, "The sleep of a laborer is sweet, whether he eats little or much, but the abundance of a rich man permits him no sleep"?

12. In Matthew's Gospel, to whom did Jesus tell Simon Peter to give a four-drachma coin?

13. Which prophet at the end of the Old Testament admonishes the Israelites for robbing God of his tithes and offerings?

14. According to the Law of Moses what were masters required to give their servants when they were released from service?

15. Who pleaded in the Old Testament, "Give me, O God, the pledge you demand. Who else will put up security for me?"?

Answers

1. True (Leviticus 25:46) 2. Judges 3. Weights 4. They were to rely on the hospitality of the places they visited 5. Outside the temple and at the city gates 6. John 7. Bartimaeus 8. Naomi (his widow) 9. The Parable of the Rich Ruler (Rich man in other gospels) 10. The Pharisees 11. Ecclesiastes 12. The collectors of the temple tax 13. Malachi 14. They were required to give liberally from their flocks, threshing floor, and winepress 15. Job

Quiz #20

DOLLARS AND SENSE

1. In the New Testament, which nation is said to have made merchants grow rich from its excessive luxuries?

2. Zephaniah prophesied to which nation, saying, "Wail, you who live in the market district; all your merchants will be wiped out, all who trade with silver will be ruined"?

3. Fill in the missing word. Paul in his letter to Timothy recommends that the wealthy be, "____ in good deeds."

4. In Genesis 37, who bought Joseph from his brothers?

5. What is the city pictured in Revelation chapter 21 made of?

6. After Ezra and the exiled Israelites had left Babylon and returned to Jerusalem, they rested for three days. What did they do on the fourth day?

7. Who redeemed Ruth and her father-in-law's land in the book of Ruth?

8. In the Old Testament, who went to the King of Israel laden with silver talents, gold shekels, and clothing in the hope that he might be cured of leprosy.

9. In Old Testament times, could an Israelite sell himself to another as a slave?

10. In the book of Revelation who does John counsel to, "buy from me gold refined in the fire, so that you can become rich"?

11. In which Old Testament book is there a chapter that begins, "The Lord abhors dishonest scales, but accurate weights are his delight"?

12. True or false? Abraham brought a field from the Hittites because it contained a cave that he wished to bury Sarah in.

13. Who in the Old Testament gave his three daughters the same inheritance as his seven sons?

14. Fill in the missing word from Exodus 30:16, "Receive the _____ money from the Israelites, and use it for the service of the Tent of Meeting."

15. In the book of Esther, who boasted to his wife and friends about his vast wealth, his many sons, and his close relationship with the king?

Quiz #21
DOLLARS AND SENSE

1. What was Jesus' reply to those who asked him, "Is it right to pay taxes to Caesar or not? Should we pay or shouldn't we?"?

2. What New Testament parable ends with the protagonist saying, "Don't I have the right to do what I want with my own money?"?

3. Who said, after he met Jesus, "Here and now I give half of my possessions to the poor, and if I have cheated anybody out of anything, I will pay back four times the amount"?

4. Which Old Testament figure grew prosperous as a rearer of livestock and came to own large flocks of sheep and goats?

5. In Matthew's Parable of the Talents, when the master spoke to the servant who had received only one talent, what did he tell him he should have done with it?

6. In Exodus, what is a man told to do if, through no fault of his own, his bull injures another bull, which then dies?

7. According to Exodus, if you take your neighbor's cloak as a pledge, when should you return it to him?

8. In which Gospel are we told to love our enemies and lend to them without expecting repayment?

9. What was Jesus doing when he said, "It is not the healthy who need a doctor, but the sick"?

10. Which Old Testament king "made silver as common in Jerusalem as stones"?

11. Which Old Testament book laments that gold had lost its luster?

12. In 2 Kings, how did Jehoiakim find the money to pay the tribute tax demanded of him?

13. In 2 Kings, why did the widow of one of Elisha's prophets come to Elisha for help?

14. In the book of Revelation, what was the rider of the third horse holding?

15. What was the name of the field that the priests and elders bought with Judas' money?

Answers

1. "Give to Caesar what is Caesar's and to God what is God's" (Mark 12:17).
2. The Parable of the Workers in the Vineyard 3. Zacchaeus 4. Jacob 5. He should have put it on deposit with the bankers so that it earned interest 6. Sell the live bull, then divide up the dead bull and money equally between owners 7. By sunset 8. Luke's Gospel 9. When he sat and ate with Matthew and other tax collectors and sinners. 10. King Solomon 11. The book of Lamentations 12. He taxed people for the land they owned 13. Her husbands creditors were threatening to take her boys as his slaves 14. A pair of scales 15. The field of blood

Facts 1

DOLLARS AND SENSE

In the Old Testmant, Abraham was considered a very wealthy man (Genesis 13:2). A person's wealth was measured by the number of livestock they owned and the amount of precious metal they had.

Silver was the most common precious metal in the Near East during biblical times.

Money changers were a common but necessary sight in the outer areas of the temple in Jerusalem, as the temple tax had to be paid with a Tyrian silver half-shekel although there were coins of several different origins in circulation in the city.

The Jewish temple tax had to be paid in coins from Tyre (Matthew 21:12), as the coins from Antioch did not have enough silver in them.

King Solomon's wealth was apparent in the many gold articles he owned, such as 200 gold shields, each containing 600 bekas of gold, which amounts to approximately seven and a half pounds (3.5 kilograms) of gold per shield.

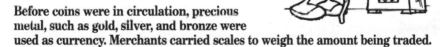

Before coins were in circulation, precious metal, such as gold, silver, and bronze were used as currency. Merchants carried scales to weigh the amount being traded.

Jewish coins had scenes from Israel's history and pictures of plants on them instead of people's heads as the second commandment forbade the making of idols or use of images.

In the account of the widow's mite in Mark's Gospel, the word "mite" refers not to a unit of currency but to a very small amount of money. The widow put in two small copper coins called "leptons", which amounted to a Roman "quadrans", or penny.

A shekel was originally just a unit of weight rather than a unit of currency ("shekel" comes from the Hebrew word for "weight"). King Solomon imported a chariot from Egypt for 600 shekels of silver, which weighed approximately 7 kilograms.

In Biblical times the Israelites had to pay a temple tax of two drachmas. In Matthew, Jesus asked Simon Peter to pay both of their temple taxes with a four-drachma coin, a "stater". This coin was more common than a two-drachma coin, so people may often have paid their tax in pairs.

Facts 2

DOLLARS AND SENSE

The Roman word for money was *"pecunia"*, from the word "pecus" meaning cow or cattle, reflecting the importance of livestock as a sign of wealth and as a item of barter before money was in common usage.

In the account of Jesus' anointing with perfume in Bethany (Mark 14), the jar of perfume is said to be worth more than a year's wages. The Greek translation puts this as more than 300 denarii, the basic Roman coin, made of silver.

A tribute-tax, such as that paid by several kings of Israel and Judea to Assyrian kings, was levied by a conqueror in order to subdue and weaken hostile nations.

There are few references in the Old Testament of an Israelite king receiving tribute-tax, possibly because it was rare for the Israelites to be powerful enough to exact it. One exception is King David who in 2 Samuel 8:9-11 dedicated the tax to the Lord.

Jews did not just hate tax collectors because of their habit of extorting money, but because their regular contact with Gentiles made them unclean.

Tithes, the giving of one-tenth of your income or produce for religious purposes, was practised by many nations before it was included in the Law of Moses (Genesis 14:18; Gen 28:22).

Tithes were given by the Israelites to the Levites as payment for their duties to the Tabernacle, as the Levites had no income of their own. The Levites then had to pay a tenth of this payment to the priests (Numbers 18:26).

"Numbered, weighed, and divided" is a literal translation of the writing on the wall in Daniel. It could have a double meaning; "Mene" also means mina, or about 50 shekels, "Tekel" can mean a shekel, and "Parsin", the plural of "Peres", can mean a half shekel.

In the famous Pauline saying, " the love of money is the root of all kinds of evil" the word translated as "money" in the NIV is the Greek word for "silver". Silver was used so often to buy things that the Hebrew word for "silver", "kesep", came to mean "money".

Because silver was so commonly used, the word was often omitted from the text and just the weight of it, in shekels, was recorded, as in 2 Kings 7:1.

The word "talent" comes from the Latin word "talenta" meaning sum of money, and the Greek word "talanton" which means weight or unit of money.

Facts 3

DOLLARS AND SENSE

In Leviticus and Deuteronomy, the Lord tells the Israelites not to use dishonest weights when measuring metals. To ensure there was no cheating, the purchaser usually weighed out the metal and the vendor checked it in front of witnesses, as mentioned in Genesis 23:16.

Throughout the Bible there are repeated references to dishonesty in weighing, such as in Micah 6. It could be comparatively easy to use false weights. Hebrew weights inscribed with the same standard have been found to vary in weight, with an error margin of up to 6%.

Egyptian monuments from biblical times show gold in the form of rings being weighed.

"*Nechosheth*" is translated as "brass" in the KJV and "bronze" in the NIV, but usually refers to copper. Copper was used as currency in the Old Testament. It is listed beside gold and silver as a suitable offering to the Lord for the Tabernacle.

Ancient weights used for measuring metal were made of carved stone and carried in pouches (Deuteronomy 25:13). Purchasers could check the weights of the merchants to see if they were getting a fair deal.

Gold was commonly kept in the form of jewellery or ingots, whereas silver was used in pieces or lumps.

Perfumes and ointments were of great value, hence the inclusion of myrrh and frankincense with the gold brought to Jesus by the Magi.

Each city or nation set its own standards of weights and measures. For example, there were heavy and light Phoenican shekels made of silver and heavy and light Babylonian shekels made of gold.

Although gold was rarely used as currency in transactions, it was highly prized and was symbolic of great wealth and riches in the Old Testament. It is mentioned more than any other metal in the Bible with more than 500 references in all.

The belt that the disciples were told not to fill with money was probably a sash, a piece of folded cloth that would have been wound several times around the waist. It not only served for carrying money, but for carrying other valuables, even food.

Canaan, the land of "milk and honey", was an ideal location for the Israelites to settle in as it was situated on the main trade routes between Egypt in the south, Syria and Phoenicia in the north, and the Babylonian empire in the east.

Facts 4

DOLLARS AND SENSE

The word "dross" refers to the residue left after a metal ore has been smelted to separate the impurities from the pure metal. It is used in the Bible to signify Israel's sinfulness (Isaiah 1:25).

Wages were more commonly paid in livestock, property, or services rather than in money in Old Testament times. Jacob, for example, was paid in livestock by Laban. This kind of payment was more suited to a semi-nomadic lifestyle.

The Hittites, Semites, and early Egyptians shaped the precious metals they were trading into nodules, rings, or bars, which were easier to transport.

Even after coins had been introduced, they were still weighed to ensure that they had not been filed or tampered with in any way.

Among the earliest known coins are ones made in Lydia by King Croesus, famous for his Anatolian gold and silver mines. Cyrus the Great probably brought the idea of coins back to Persia after conquering Croesus.

Israel did not have many natural resources, but the major trading routes that crossed its territory gave access to precious metals that the people could use as currency.

The first mention of the Jews minting their own coins comes in the Apocrypha, in 1 Maccabees 15:6 when Simon Maccabaeus is granted permission to issue coins by the reigning Roman emperor, Antiochus VII.

Cloth and clothing are often mentioned in Biblical passages about treasure on earth, alongside silver and gold. Israel had a thriving textile industry and was famous for its rich purple cloth manufactured in Tyre that was popular throughout the Mediterranean region.

Israel's wealth was further enhanced by the trade routes that passed through Isrealite territory, especially during the reigns of David and Solomon Israelite territory. This meant the Israelites could impose large import and export duties, and excise tax, on merchants.

In God's Garden

Quiz # 1

IN GOD'S GARDEN

1. In John 15, who did Jesus say was the gardener?

2. What name is given to the festival that celebrated the gathering in of the wheat harvest?.

3. By which trees was Abraham sitting when he was visited by angels?

4. Why did Jesus curse a fig-tree?

5. In the parable, what kind of seed, when it is full grown, offers shelter to birds?

6. Who died in the Field of Blood?

7. In the Parable of the Vineyard Workers, how much was each worker paid?

8. When Adam and Eve were banished from the garden, the land was cursed to produce what?

9. According to the parable, why did the farmer allow the wheat and the weeds to grow together until harvest?

10. Who allowed Ruth to glean in his fields?

11. Who wore a crown of thorns?

12. From which tree were Adam and Eve not allowed to eat?

13. In what way was an oak tree instrumental in the death of Absalom?

14. Whose barley crop was set on fire because he refused to meet with Absalom?

15. Which king wanted possession of Naboth's vineyard?

Answers

1. His Father. **2.** Pentecost **3.** The great trees of Mare **4.** It had no fruit **5.** Mustard **6.** Judas **7.** A denarius (the usual daily wage) **8.** Thorns and thistles **9.** By picking out the weeds, he may have picked the wheat too **10.** Boaz **11.** Jesus **12.** The tree of the knowledge of good and evil **13.** Absalom's head got caught in the branches as he was escaping from his enemies on his mule **14.** Joab **15.** Ahab

Quiz #2

IN GOD'S GARDEN

1. According to John's Gospel, who mistook Jesus for a gardener?

2. Which of the ten plagues of Egypt consisted of hail and lightning that destroyed vegetation?

3. Who had a vision of an angel standing among the myrtle trees?

4. Which fruit, the size of an orange, is embroidered round the edge of the high priest's robe?

5. According to the parable in Matthew 21, who did the landowner eventually send to his vineyard?

6. Palm Sunday commemorates which event in the life of Jesus?

7. What caused the plant that was shading Jonah to die?

8. Which Old Testament character said, "At least there is hope for a tree. If it is cut down, it will sprout again"?

9. In the Song of Songs, which animals are said to ruin the vineyards?

10. Who had a dream of a tree that grew large and strong and touched the sky?

11. According to Matthew's Gospel, who bought the Potter's Field?

12. In ancient Israel, with which oil were kings and priests anointed?

13. Who had an almond rod that flowered and produced fruit overnight?

14. In the book of Genesis, who had a dream that there would be seven years of plenty followed by seven years of famine?

15. In which book of the Bible do we find the words, "I am a rose of Sharon, a lily of the valleys"?

---

12. Olive oil 13. Aaron 14. Pharaoh 15. Song of Songs
7. A worm 8. Job 9. Foxes 10. Nebuchadnezzar 11. The chief priests
6. Jesus entering Jerusalem on a donkey
1. Mary 2. Seventh 3. The prophet Zechariah 4. Pomegranate 5. His son

Answers

Quiz #3

IN GOD'S GARDEN

1. In the Parable of the Sower, what happened to the seed that fell on the path?

2. The river in the Garden of Eden separated into four rivers, the Euphrates and the Tigris are two them, name one of the other two.

3. True or false? Abel kept flocks and Cain worked the soil.

4. Who planted crops in the land and reaped a hundredfold because of the Lord's blessing?

5. According to Paul's teaching to Timothy, who should be the first to receive a share of the crops?

6. What name is given to the last tree mentioned in the Bible?

7. True or false? There are no oak trees in the Bible.

8. In Isaiah 32, what is poured out to make the desert a fertile field and the fertile field seem like a forest?

9. In Psalm 23, what type of pastures does the Lord make the writer lie down in?

10. In which of Paul's letters is there a list of nine characteristics described as the fruit of the Spirit?

11. From James 5, name the two kinds of rain the patient farmer waits for.

12. In Peter's first letter, he wrote, "The grass withers and the flowers fall," but what did he say would last for ever?

13. What did the serpent tell Eve would happen if she ate the forbidden fruit?

14. In which garden was Jesus arrested?

15. Finish off this sentence from Paul's letter to the Galatians, "Do not be deceived. God is not mocked. A man reaps..."

Quiz #4

IN GOD'S GARDEN

1. According to Isaiah, what building stands in the vineyard?

2. True or false? Jesus' tomb was in a garden.

3. In how many Gospels does the Parable of the Sower appear?

4. Talking of the church, Paul says, "I planted the seed." Who does he say watered it?

5. If you have faith, what type of tree can you tell to be uprooted and planted in the sea?

6. Which Old Testament prophet was appointed to uproot and tear down, destroy and overthrow, to build and to plant?

7. Who sold a field and gave all the money to the apostles?

8. In which Old Testament book do we find the words, "a time to plant and a time to uproot"?

9. Who in the Garden of Eden called out, "Where are you?'"?

10. In Genesis, a cherubim and a flaming flashing sword guard the way to which tree?

11. What type of tree is Gethsemane most famous for?

12. In the vision of Ezekiel 47, the leaves of the trees served what purpose?

13. According to John the Baptist, what will happen to trees that fail to bear good fruit?

14. Who asked, "Do people pick grapes from thorn bushes, or figs from thistles?'"?

15. Fill in the missing word in this verse taken from the book of Job: "They skim past like boats of ___."

Quiz #5

IN GOD'S GARDEN

1. True or false? The Bible tells us that the fruit Eve ate in the Garden of Eden was an apple.

2. When Abram and Lot separated, which way did Lot go?

3. Who in the book of Genesis, took fresh cut branches and made white stripes on them by peeling back the bark and exposing the inner wood?

4. Which king of the Philistines did Isaac go to during a time of famine?

5. To what use did the king of Samaria want to put Naboth's vineyard?

6. In John 12, what must a grain of wheat do to produce many seeds?

7. The roots of which tree produce charcoal to make incendiary arrows?

8. Which prophet wrote these words: "The harvest is past, the summer has ended, and we are not saved"?

9. In Hosea, what will you reap if you sow the wind?

10. In the Parable of the Sower, where did the third lot of seed land?

11. At the Passover, what plant did Moses use to sprinkle blood on the doorposts of houses?

12. What type of fungus, regarded as God's punishment on the disobedient, did Solomon pray for deliverance from in his prayer at the dedication of the temple?

13. True or false? Jesus asked the people whether they had gone out into the desert to see sand blown by the wind.

14. In Isaiah 42, what kind of reed will the servant of the Lord not break?

15. Who said, "I knew that you are a hard man, harvesting where you have not sown and gathering where you have not scattered seed"?

Answers

1. False. The fruit is not named (Genesis 2:17) 2. Lot went to the plain of Jordan, which was "well watered, like the garden of the Lord" 3. Jacob 4. Abimelech 5. Vegetable garden 6. Fall in the ground and die 7. Broom tree 8. Jeremiah 9. The whirlwind 10. Among thorns 11. Hyssop 12. Mildew 13. False. Jesus said, "a reed swayed by the wind" (Matthew 11:7) 14. A bruised (bent) reed 15. The servant who hid his one talent in the ground

Quiz #6

IN GOD'S GARDEN

1. In Psalm 92, who spring up like grass?

2. Which king was driven away from his people and ate grass like cattle?

3. In the parable, what is the mustard seed likened to?

4. Complete the sentence: "A king's rage is like the roar of a lion, but his _____ is like dew on the grass."

5. In the feeding of the 5,000, what special detail does Mark tell us about the grass?

6. In the Parable of the Weeds, the weeds are burned. What happens to the wheat?

7. During the wheat harvest, who went out and found some mandrake plants for his mother Leah?

8. True or false? In Exodus 34, keeping the Sabbath instructions did not apply during harvest time.

9. In the Parable of the Weeds, who came when everyone was sleeping and sowed weeds among the wheat?

10. Complete the sentence: "Do not plant your field with _____ kinds of seed."

11. In the New Testament, who said, "The ax is already at the root of the trees"?

12. According to the Sermon on the Mount, what kind of fruit does a good tree bear?

13. In Deuteronomy 24, the Israelites were told not to over-harvest their vines, but to leave grapes for three types of people, the alien (foreigner) and two others. Who were they?

14. Where was the cave where thirty chief men visited David during the harvest?

15. Complete the sentence: "He who sleeps during harvest is a disgraceful ___."

Answers

1. The wicked **2.** Nebuchadnezzar **3.** The kingdom of God **4.** Favor **5.** It was green **6.** The wheat is gathered and put into the barn **7.** Reuben **8.** False (Exodus 34:21) **9.** An enemy **10.** Two **11.** John the Baptist **12.** Good fruit **13.** The fatherless and the widow **14.** Adullam **15.** Son

Quiz #7

IN GOD'S GARDEN

1. In Matthew 13, who are the harvesters at the end of the age?

2. To whom in Luke's Gospel does Jesus say, "The harvest is plentiful"?

3. Which Old Testament prophet spoke of the purchase of a field for thirty silver coins?

4. Who in the New Testament said of Jesus, "His winnowing fork is in his hand"?

5. In Matthew 24, Jesus speaks of two men in a field, what happens to them?

6. According to Leviticus 19, when entering a new land, in which year is the fruit of a new tree allowed to be eaten?

7. In the Old Testament, what name is given to the fiftieth year, when no sowing or reaping was allowed?

8. Which Old Testament prophet bought a field from his cousin Hanamel?

9. In Genesis 4, who was killed in a field?

10. At the threshing floor of Atad, who observed a seven-day period of mourning for his father Jacob?

11. True or false? Seed that fell on good soil produced a crop of a 100, 60 or 30 times what was sown.

12. Which Old Testament prophet spoke of untold destruction by swarms of locusts?

13. In Mark's Gospel, who found himself naked in a garden?

14. Who placed a wool fleece on a threshing-floor to get guidance from God?

15. At the instruction of her mother-in-law, who went to a threshing-floor to meet her future husband?

Quiz #8
IN GOD'S GARDEN

1. In the book of Judges, who told the story of trees anointing a king for themselves?

2. In 2 Kings 6, when a man was cutting down a tree, what fell in the water?

3. In Matthew 9, who are the disciples to ask to send workers into the harvest field?

4. Complete the sentence, "The harvest is plentiful but the workers are ____."

5. True or false? The fruit of the righteous is a tree of life.

6. Who saw a vision of an almond tree?

7. In which parable do we find the excuse of just having bought a field?

8. Which king could describe all types of plant life?

9. Name one of two animals that should not be yoked together for plowing?

10. Complete the sentence, "No one who puts his hand to the plow and looks back is fit for service in the ____."

11. Who had a dream about sheaves of grain bowing down?

12. True or false? Boaz grew barley and wheat.

13. Why did Zacchaeus climb a tree to see Jesus?

14. In support of whom does Paul write to the Corinthians quoting from the Old Testament, "Do not muzzle the ox while it is treading out the grain"?

15. Who in Genesis is called a man of the soil?

Answers

1. Jotham 2. An ax head 3. The Lord of the harvest (God) 4. Few 5. True (Proverbs 11:30)
6. Jeremiah 7. The Parable of the Great Banquet 8. Solomon 9. Ox or donkey 10. Kingdom of God
11. Joseph 12. True (Ruth 2:23) 13. He was a little man
14. The elders who were leaders, preachers and teachers in a church 15. Noah

Quiz #9
IN GOD'S GARDEN

1. Which of Job's companions said that the man who forgets God is like a well-watered plant in the sunshine, which entwines its roots around rocks?

2. The word "orchard" or "orchards" only appear in three books of the Bible, name one of them.

3. Complete the sentence: "A shoot will come up from the stump of _____ ; from his roots a Branch will bear fruit."

4. True or false? During the Passover Festival, the Jews were not allowed to eat bread.

5. Who did the Lord call "a thriving olive tree with fruit beautiful in form"?

6. In the parable, how long was the fig-tree given to bear fruit before it would be cut down?

7. Who said, "The man who plants and the man who waters have one purpose"?

8. Complete the sentence from 1 Corinthians: "Who plants a vineyard and does not eat of its _____"?

9. According to Job 40, what lies under the lotus plant and is hidden among the reeds in the marsh?

10. According to Proverbs 31, what sort of wife plants a vineyard?

11. In the Parable of the Sower, why were some plants scorched when the sun came up?

12. How would God provide for the Israelites during every seventh year when they neither sowed nor harvested?

13. In Exodus 10, what covered the ground until it was black and devoured everything left in the fields and on the trees?

14. The spies who Moses sent to explore the promised land returned with grapes and two other types of fruit. Name one of the other two.

15. According to 1 Kings 4, where would you find hyssop growing?

Answers

1. Bildad **2.** Isaiah or Jeremiah or Song of Songs **3.** Jesse **4.** False. They could eat bread, but it had to be made without yeast (Deuteronomy 16:3) **5.** The people of Judah **6.** 12 months **7.** The apostle Paul **8.** Grapes **9.** The behemoth (or hippopotamus or elephant) **10.** A wife of noble character **11.** The ground was rocky, and the soil was shallow, so they had no roots **12.** There would be a threefold harvest in the sixth year **13.** Locusts **14.** Pomegranates and figs **15.** Out of walls

Quiz #10
IN GOD'S GARDEN

1. In the Parable of the Sower, who went out to sow the seed?

2. Who was responsible for a servant losing his ear in a garden?

3. Who said, "Take my yoke upon you and learn from me"?

4. What did Solomon want to do with the cedar and pine logs that he bought from King Hiram?

5. In Genesis 2, how was the ground watered?

6. Who beat out wheat in a winepress to hide it from the Midianites?

7. In the ancient world, which biblical city was famed for its hanging gardens?

8. Why did God bring all the animals to Adam in the garden?

9. True or false? The first people were vegetarians.

10. In the Old Testament, what plant is Israel compared to?

11. In Matthew 15, which plants will be pulled up by their roots?

12. When Jesus was on the cross, on the stalk of which plant was a sponge of wine vinegar placed to give Jesus a drink?

13. In 1 Chronicles 27, who was in charge of the vineyards?

14. Complete this verse from the psalms: "He who goes out weeping, carrying seeds to sow, will return with songs of joy, carrying ____ with him."

15. In the book of which prophet do we find the question, "Is there yet any seed left in the barn?"?

Quiz #11
IN GOD'S GARDEN

1. In Nebuchadnezzar's dream, what did the command to leave the stump of the tree with its roots in the ground signify?

2. In Mark 11, what happened to the fig-tree cursed by Jesus?

3. Who in the New Testament is said to come from the root of Jesse?

4. In which of his letters does Paul write, "If the root is holy, so are the branches"?

5. What is the root of all kinds of evil?

6. In Genesis 41, what came out of the river and grazed among the reeds?

7. In Revelation 11, what was John told to measure with a reed?

8. Jesus said the Pharisees gave a tenth of their spices. One spice was dill. What were the other two?

9. Who, according to the book of Acts, declared, "He has shown kindness by giving you rain from heaven and crops in their seasons"?

10. Fill in the gap: the spies reported that the Promised Land flowed "with milk and ___."

11. True or false? God told the Israelites to add salt to all their grain offerings.

12. In which book of the Bible do we find the words, "There is a time for everything, and a season for every activity under heaven"?

13. Which Old Testament prophet records the words, "Sow for yourselves righteousness, reap the fruit of unfailing love"?

14. When Jesus cursed the fig tree, which Gospel records the fact that it was not the season for figs?

15. True or false? When the disciples saw the fig tree Jesus had cursed, Jesus said "Have faith in yourselves."

Quiz # 12

IN GOD'S GARDEN

1. In the purification rites of Leviticus 14, what plant was used?

2. Fill in the missing word in David's prayer in Psalm 51, "Cleanse me with ___, and I will be clean."

3. Which New Testament writer heard a sound like a voice saying, "A quart of wheat for a day's wages, and three quarts of barley for a day's wages, and do not damage the oil and wine!'"?

4. In order to stop him becoming conceited, what does Paul say he was given?

5. In Numbers 33, who would become barbs in the eyes of the Israelites and thorns in their sides?

6. In Luke 13, what type of seed did a man plant in his garden?

7. In 1 Samuel 6, when harvesting the wheat, what did the people of Beth Shemesh see to make them rejoice?

8. True or false? The first people in the Bible were builders.

9. In the book of Judges, who burned down a field of corn?

10. What plant did Jesus say he was?

11. In 1 Chronicles 21, what did Araunah see when threshing wheat?

12. What wood did Noah use to build his ark?

13. In which Old Testament book is there a reference to trees clapping?

14. Who was told in Jeremiah 41, "Don't kill us! We have wheat and barley, oil and honey, hidden in a field"?

15. To whom did Jesus say, "Satan has asked to sift you as wheat"?

Answers

1. Hyssop **2.** Hyssop **3.** John in the book of Revelation **4.** A thorn in the flesh **5.** People who had been living in the Promised Land before the Israelites arrived and had been allowed to stay on in the land **6.** A mustard seed **7.** The ark of the covenant **8.** False. They were gardeners (Genesis 2:15) **9.** Samson **10.** Vine **11.** An angel **12.** Cypress wood (or gopher wood) **13.** Isaiah **14.** Ishmael **15.** Peter

Quiz # 13

IN GOD'S GARDEN

1. In the Parable of the Sower, what metaphor is used to describe Satan taking away the word that was sown?

2. Complete the sentence from the Song of Songs, "Like a _____ among thorns."

3. In Genesis, who was told, "When you work the ground, it will no longer yield its crops for you"?

4. In which book of the Bible do we find the words, "Flowers appear on the earth, the season of singing has come"?

5. Fill in the missing word: on every ___ year the people were not to sow their fields or prune their vineyards because the land had to have a year of rest.

6. In the interpretation of the Parable of the Sower, what does the seed represent?

7. In the book of Esther, who gave a party in his garden lasting for seven days?

8. In Genesis, what did Jacob buy from the sons of Hamor?

9. When the Israelites were in the wilderness, what appeared on the ground like flakes of thin frost?

10. True or false? It was Elisha, not Elijah, who features in the account of Naboth's vineyard.

11. True or false? After the flood, Noah first of all sowed seed in the ground.

12. Fill in the name of the flower: "The wilderness will rejoice and blossom. Like the ___ it will burst into bloom."

13. In which Old Testament book do we find the words, "I will pour water on the thirsty land, and streams on the dry ground; I will pour out my Spirit on your offspring"?

14. In John's Gospel, who did Jesus see under a fig tree?

15. True or false? Zacchaeus climbed a sycamore tree.

Quiz #14

IN GOD'S GARDEN

1. In Haggai, what had the people neglected to do, causing God to withhold dew from heaven and crops from the earth?

2. In the Parable of the Rich Fool, why did the farmer decide to pull down his barns?

3. True or false? Jesus told the Parable of the Rich Fool to warn the people to be on their guard against worry.

4. In Exodus, what was on fire and not burning up?

5. On the Egyptian building site, what was mixed with clay and water to make bricks?

6. Who wandered around in the fields of Shechem looking for his brothers, before finding them near Dothan?

7. In Genesis 47, why did the Egyptians have to sell their land?

8. True or false? Before the famine began in Egypt, Joseph stored up huge quantities of rice.

9. In Genesis 47, what percentage of their crop did the Egyptians have to give to Pharaoh?

10. What percentage of their crops did God ask of the Israelites?

11. Why did Abraham and Sarah travel down to Egypt?

12. Who learnt that the portions of grain, wine and oil assigned to the Levites had not been given and that the Levites and singers had therefore returned to their fields?

13. Which book of the Bible gives the advice, "Finish your outdoor work and get your fields ready; after that, build your house"?

14. Which Old Testament prophet would rejoice, even though "the fig tree does not bud and there are no grapes on the vines"?

15. In the parable, what did the man find hidden in a field?

Quiz # 15

IN GOD'S GARDEN

1. Complete the phrase from John 4, "_____ months more and then the harvest."

2. In the account of creation, on what day did God make all the plants and trees?

3. Houses were lit by lamplight: what oil was used?

4. In Isaiah's image of peace, what will spears be turned into?

5. True or false? When harvesting, the Israelites were told to reap to the very edge of their fields.

6. In Jeremiah's vision of two baskets of fruit, what was the fruit?

7. True or false? As a result of the Fall, farming became hard work.

8. According to the book of Joshua, who gave his daughter the "upper and lower springs"?

9. Who shot an arrow in a field, as a sign that David's life was in danger?

10. Who told his servants to burn Joab's field of barley?

11. Near a field full of lentils, from whom did the Israelites flee?

12. True or false? Joseph had a dream in which he and his brothers were harvesting grain.

13. In 2 Kings 19, of which nation is it said, "They are like plants in the field, like tender green shoots, like grass sprouting on the roof, scorched before it grows up"?

14. Which Old Testament prophet records, "All the trees of the field will know that I the Lord bring down the tall tree and make the low tree grow tall"?

15. A leaf from which plant was brought by the dove to Noah as a sign that the flood water had receded?

Answers

1. Four 2. The third day 3. Olive oil 4. Pruning hooks 5. False (Leviticus 19:9)
6. Figs 7. True (Genesis 3:17-19) 8. Caleb 9. Jonathan 10. Absalom
11. The Philistines 12. True (Genesis 37:7)
13. Assyria 14. Ezekiel 15. Olive

Quiz #16

IN GOD'S GARDEN

1. Which two Old Testament prophets both spoke of a tree with the birds of the air nesting in its boughs?

2. Which Old Testament prophet declared that Zion would be plowed like a field and thickets would grow over the temple mound?

3. The wild flowers are dressed more beautifully than which king?

4. In the Parable of the Weeds, what does the field represent?

5. From which Old Testament book is the following quotation: "I will make Samaria a heap of rubble, a place for planting vineyards"?

6. True or false? Luke writes that Ananias and Sapphira sold a field.

7. In Judges 6, what remained dry when all the ground around it was covered in dew?

8. Fill in the missing word: "During Solomon's time Judah and Israel lived in safety, each man under his own vine and ___."

9. According to Acts 1, did Judas or the priests buy a field?

10. True or false? The law of Moses allowed an Israelite to eat as many grapes as he wanted from his neighbor's vineyard, but not to take any away in a container.

11. True or false? The vineyard in Isaiah 5 yielded only bad grapes.

12. In Luke 13, what type of tree was growing in the man's vineyard?

13. Which Old Testament prophet records, "There I will give her back her vineyards, and will make the Valley of Achor a door of hope"?

14. In the Parable of the Two Sons, which son, when asked by his father, went and worked in the vineyard?

15. According to Proverbs, what sweeps away the abundant food from a poor man's field?

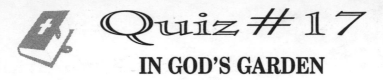

Quiz #17
IN GOD'S GARDEN

1. A Nazirite must not eat the seeds or skin of which fruit?

2. In Isaiah 32, when justice dwells in the desert, what will live in the fertile field?

3. True or false? Cinnamon was mixed with olive oil for anointing priests.

4. What natural disaster made Amos cry out, "How can Jacob survive? He is so small!"

5. In Numbers 22, what appeared standing in a narrow path between two vineyards?

6. Having created all vegetation, how, in one word, did God describe it?

7. In Deuteronomy 28, what will eat the grapes from the vineyards?

8. True or false? Lebanon was famous for its fine pine trees.

9. Fill in the missing word from Ezekiel's prophecy, "He took some of the seed of your land and put it in fertile soil. He planted it like a ___ by abundant waters."

10. According to Matthew 24, what does it mean when the fig tree becomes green and puts out its leaves?

11. In 1 Samuel 4, why did the ground shake when the ark of the covenant entered the camp?

12. Who found Elisha plowing with twelve yoke of oxen?

13. Who was told, in the first chapter of his book, "The oxen were plowing and the donkeys were grazing nearby, when the Sabeans attacked"?

14. In Judges 21, what did the Benjamites watch for when hiding in the vineyards?

15. Who said, "If you had not plowed with my heifer, you would not have solved my riddle"?

---

11. The Israelites shouted 12. Elijah 13. Job 14. Girls (or future wives) 15. Samson
6. Good 7. Worms 8. False. It was cedar trees (1 Kings 5:6) 9. Willow 10. Summer is near
1. Grape 2. Righteousness 3. True (Exodus 30:24) 4. A swarm of locusts 5. The angel of the Lord

Answers

Quiz # 18

IN GOD'S GARDEN

1. In Isaiah 1, who is left like a hut in a field of melons?

2. According to Proverbs, why does the sluggard find nothing at harvest time?

3. True or false? Jesus called his Father a gardener.

4. In the words of Jesus, who do not sow or reap or store away in barns?

5. Which Bible book has the most references to gleaning?

6. Naboth's vineyard was in Jezreel close to which building?

7. In Gethsemane, who did Jesus ask to keep watch with him?

8. According to Isaiah 2, where do oaks come from?

9. Name one of the things that Jacob buried under the oak at Shechem?

10. In John's vision in the book of Revelation, what stood on each side of the river that flowed down from the throne?

11. What sort of tree did Abraham plant at Beersheba?

12. True or false? According to Moses, the gardens of Egypt were watered by hand.

13. Who was buried in his palace garden?

14. In 1 Chronicles 27, what was Zabdi in charge of?

15. Where did the old prophet live who met a man of God under an oak tree?

Quiz #19

IN GOD'S GARDEN

1. According to Psalm 104, in which kind of tree does the stork nest?

2. Which Old Testament prophet urged the pine and oak to wail?

3. According to Psalm 92, who will flourish like a palm tree?

4. Who said, "I made gardens and parks and planted all kinds of fruit trees in them"?

5. In the account of the trees in Judges 9, what can come out of the thornbush to consume the cedars of Lebanon?

6. True or false? Jesus said that if you have faith as small as a mustard seed you can tell a mulberry tree to go into the sea and it will?

7. In Revelation 8, how much of the tree was burned up at the sound of the first trumpet?

8. To cover their nakedness, what type of leaves did Adam and Eve sew together?

9. In the book of Numbers, who said that the Israelites were spread out like gardens beside a river?

10. Who said, "To each kind of seed he [God] gives its own body"?

11. Complete this phrase quoted in Galatians, "_____ is everyone who is hung on a tree."

12. From Revelation, name the tree that bore its fruit every month.

13. According to Hosea, what tree is God like?

14. In Psalm 1, who is like a tree planted by streams of water?

15. Which two cereal crops are usually intended by the use of the term "grain"?

---

12. The tree of life **13.** A green pine tree **14.** Someone who studies God's word **15.** Barley and wheat

5. Fire **6.** True (Luke 17:6) **7.** One third **8.** Fig **9.** Balaam **10.** Paul **11.** Cursed

1. The pine (or fir) **2.** Zechariah **3.** The righteous **4.** The teacher (Solomon, the writer of Ecclesiastes)

Answers

326

Quiz #20
IN GOD'S GARDEN

1. In which garden did Adam and Eve live?

2. Why did Jesus stop under a sycamore-fig tree?

3. Under the shelter of what tree did the angel sit when visiting Gideon?

4. In the thunderstorm described in Psalm 29, what tree is twisted by the voice of the Lord?

5. In the Garden of Gethsemane, how many times did Jesus return to find his disciples asleep?

6. In which of the four Gospels is the Parable of the Growing Seed?

7. Who wrote, "All over the world this gospel is bearing fruit and growing"?

8. Is the Mount of Olives nearer Bethlehem or Jerusalem?

9. Who left Jerusalem at night, by way of the king's garden?

10. In the parable of Luke 20, how many servants did the owner send to his vineyard?

11. True or false? The Garden of Gethsemane was on the Mount of Olives.

12. To whom did Jesus say, "For if men do these things when the tree is green, what will happen when it is dry"?

13. Complete this promise from Isaiah, "You will be like a ___ garden."

14. In the seven "I am" sayings of Jesus in John's Gospel, how many refer to a plant or tree?

15. What common form of vegetation is used in the Bible to describe both the flourishing and the mortality of people?

Answers

1. Eden 2. To speak to Zacchaeus in the branches of the tree 3. Oak 4. Oak
5. 3 6. Mark 7. The apostle Paul 8. Jerusalem 9. King Zedekiah 10. 3 11. True (Luke 22:39)
12. Women of Jerusalem 13. Well-watered 14. 1. "I am the vine" 15. Grass

Quiz #21
IN GOD'S GARDEN

1. True or false? There were only two trees in the Garden of Eden.

2. Who wrote to the Jews in Babylon, "Plant gardens and eat what they produce"?

3. In the New Testament, who wrote that the rich man would pass away "like a wild flower"?

4. In Jesus' illustration of the vine, who are the branches?

5. According to the book of Job, what can revive a dead tree stump?

6. True or false? Naboth sold his vineyard for a great price.

7. In Jesus' illustration of the vine, what does the gardener do to fruitful branches?

8. Fill in the missing word, "Like the coolness of ____ at harvest time is a trustworthy messenger."

9. In Ecclesiastes 11, when are you told to sow your seed?

10. In which Bible book is a locked garden used as an analogy?

11. How is the garden in the Song of Songs shared?

12. In Isaiah 2, which two gardening tasks will replace warfare?

13. Pentecost celebrates the wheat harvest. What is the festival that celebrates the end of the fruit harvest?

14. For what virtue does James praise the farmer?

15. In Hosea, what is likened to poisonous weeds?

Facts 1

IN GOD'S GARDEN

Many burial chambers belonging to wealthy families have been found on the sides of the hills to the north, south and east of Jerusalem. The tombs were cut out of the soft limestone rock, and often a garden was made in front of the tombs.

When the grapes were being harvested, vineyard workers camped in a stone watchtower in the orchard or slept in the open. By doing this, they were able to guard the grapes against thieves.

Vineyard watchtowers were expensive to build. Jesus told a parable about a farmer who started to build a watchtower, but could not afford to finish it.

In the towns, houses were crowded together, and there were not many gardens. Sometimes a rich person would have a walled courtyard garden, with a fountain and flowering trees.

The well-to-do had shady gardens on the hills outside the city walls. These were orchards rather than flower gardens.

Large solitary oak trees often became landmarks. They were a favorite place to sit beneath (Judges 6:19), and were also used as burial sites (Genesis 35:8).

Summer houses were a regular feature of most royal gardens.

In the early stages of growth, it is hard to distinguish wheat from a poisonous weed, the darnel grass. This explains Jesus' parable about allowing the wheat and the weeds to grow together until harvest, when they are clearly distinguishable.

When Jesus spoke of the "lilies of the field," he was speaking of wild flowers such as the blue hyacinth, the poppy, anemone and crown daisy.

Straw is the stubble that remains after harvesting wheat. It was mainly used as bedding for animals and people and for animal fodder. Isaiah likens Moab's fate to straw being trampled down among dung (Isaiah 25:10).

Facts 2
IN GOD'S GARDEN

When there was no space for a vegetable garden, vegetables were planted between the rows of vines in the vineyard.

In Egypt, ditches, filled with water by hand, would criss-cross vegetable gardens. Irrigation of small plots was achieved simply by breaking the ditch wall with one's foot (Deuteronomy 11:10).

The exact location of Eden is unknown: some say it was in the land between the Tigris and Euphrates rivers, others that it was in the Arabian peninsula.

The palm trees referred to in the Bible were date palms. They were tall, slender trees, and were seen as gracious and elegant. The Hebrew word for palm, *tamar*, was often used as a girl's name.

Palm trees were a national symbol of victory and rejoicing. The people who waved palm branches as Jesus entered Jerusalem were therefore making a political statement.

Cedar wood was prized for its durability and was used in major building projects. Ships' masts were also made of cedar wood. The finest cedar wood came from the cedars of Lebanon (Song of Songs 5:15).

Pharisees referred to those with no religious education as "people of the land," suggesting that those who tended gardens and farmed were not held in high regard.

The village threshing floor was located in a windy spot to help with the winnowing. After the grain had been threshed, it was thrown into the air with a winnowing fork. The wind blew away the lighter straw and chaff while the grain fell to the ground.

In Bible times, flax was the only plant grown for cloth. Flax plants were pulled up by the root, and laid out to dry, often on the flat roofs of houses (Joshua 2:6). Linen cloth was made from the stems of the plants.

Identifying plants in the Bible is difficult because the plants found in the Middle East today were not necessarily native to the region in biblical times.

Facts 3

IN GOD'S GARDEN

Acacia trees flourished in the desert, providing the Israelites with timber for the construction of the tabernacle and its furnishings.

Several times a fruit is mentioned which has characteristics similar to an apple. It has been suggested that Proverbs' "apples of gold" could be apricots, and this should be the translation elsewhere. There is no evidence that the apricot was known in biblical times.

Grapes, melons and cucumbers were a source of much needed liquid during the dry summer months.

God's agricultural principles laid down in Leviticus are proven practice to this day. These include leaving a field fallow every seven years to aid conservation of the soil Another principle was not to plant two different crops in one field.

When poorer people had gardens in the villages, they used them to grow vegetables and herbs.

Green pastures are not a permanent sight in Israel, but last only for a short while after rain. Grass is thus a fitting symbol for the temporary nature of human life (Psalm 90:5-6).

The biblical description and use of hyssop indicates that it is not the plant we now know as hyssop, which does not grow in Palestine.

The hyssop used in Jewish cleansing ceremonies was probably the white Syrian marjoram. It belongs to the mint family and is scented like mint. Its hairy stems hold water, making it a good sprinkler (Exodus 12:22).

The "hyssop that grows out of walls," referred to in 1 Kings 4:33, may be the prickly caper, which grows in the crannies of walls in Palestine.

According to John, when Jesus was on the cross, a man fixed a sponge soaked in wine- vinegar on the stalk of a hyssop and gave it to Jesus. But a hyssop stalk was too feeble to hold a sponge. It has been suggested that the Greek word *hussopo*, has at some point been copied in error, and the word should be *hysso*, which means "lance."

Facts 4

IN GOD'S GARDEN

A number of different Hebrew words are used for briars, brambles, nettles, thistles, and thorns, and no one is sure of the exact plant indicated by each Hebrew word. They all represent fruitlessness and evil.

Thorn hedges were sometimes grown to make defensive barriers (Hosea 2:6).

Exemption from military service was granted for men working in a vineyard.

In Mark's account of the feeding of the five thousand, the unique detail that the grass was "green," is a reference to the time of the year in which the miracle occurred—shortly after the rains.

Mildew is a common form of fungus that attacks plants and was seen in biblical times as a punishment from God for disobedience.

Plows were made of light wood so that farmers could lift them easily over the numerous stones and rocks in their fields.

Wormwood is a small shrub with a bitter, poisonous taste which grows in dry places. The Hebrew name means "accursed plant," and wormwood symbolized calamity and punishment (Lamentations 3:19).

Mulberry trees grow near water, very often on river banks, which makes sense of Jesus' statement that faith the size of a mustard seed is enough to send a mulberry tree into the sea.

Passers-by could, by law, eat ears of grain as they passed by fields of grain—but not on the Sabbath, since the plucking and breaking was thought to be threshing and winnowing, which was forbidden work.

The pink blossom of the almond tree appears at the end of January, before the leaves. Its Hebrew name, *shaqed*, sounds like the Hebrew word for "be wakeful," "watch over." It is as if the tree is keeping watch to announce the coming of spring (Jeremiah 1:11-12).

The small tree that is a variety of the pistachio tree grew wild in Canaan, but not in Egypt. The small round pistachio nuts that Jacob sent as a gift to the governor of Egypt would have been a rare delicacy (Genesis 43:11).

Facts 5

IN GOD'S GARDEN

The most important crop was grain, which comes first in the lists of the main crops: grain, grapes and olives. Wheat and barley were the major grain crops. Millet was also grown, but not corn or maize.

Wheat was grown in the better soil and made into very fine and expensive white flour: the best of foods (Psalm 81:16). When thank-offerings of grain were given to God, it was wheat that had to be offered.

Barley could be grown on poorer soil, and had a shorter growing period. Loaves made from barley were a poor man's food and animal fodder. The flour was coarser than wheat flour and two or three times cheaper.

When confessing to jealousy, whether legitimate or groundless, a man was to take his wife to the priests for cleansing, together with an offering of barley. He could not add oil or incense to this offering.

Millet provided food for animals and for the very poor. Bread made from millet was rather like rye bread.

The main obstacles to working the land were: drought, strong winds which could lift and take away vast quantities of dry soil, locusts and invading armies.

The costly ointment lavished upon Jesus (Mark 14:1-11) was nard from India. It was imported in sealed alabaster jars to preserve its perfume.

The "first rains" came in October to November, and without these there could be no crop. Winter was the rainy season, and the winter rains kept the ground fertile. The rains stopped in March.

The "latter rains" came in April when the ear of grain was beginning to grow. For a good crop it was important that these rains came in early April. According to the Talmud, the latter rains brought more blessing than the ox and the yoke.

When Jesus told the parable about a man's enemy sowing weeds into his field of wheat, he probably knew that Roman law specified this was a criminal activity.

Facts 6

IN GOD'S GARDEN

The rose was not known in Israel in Old Testament times. In some translations of Solomon's Song of Songs, the loved one's lips are compared to a "rose of Sharon." The red tulip or scarlet anemone may be the reference to that flower.

The rose seems to have been introduced into Palestine just before the Christian era. In Acts, Luke talks of a servant girl called Rose (Rhoda).

Olives were cooked, or pickled in salt water; the juice was extracted for cooking, for burning in lamps, for putting on wounds, for rubbing into the skin and hair (as a refreshing beauty treatment), for pouring on offerings given to God and for anointing kings and priests.

Olive wood was hard and could be rubbed into a high polish. The cherubim in the temple were made of wild olive wood.

The fig-tree was often grown with the vine (1 Kings 4:25), and its broad leaves gave a welcome shade. A fig-tree stood for peace, and it was customary to sit and meditate under its branches (John 1:48).

Papyrus is a marsh plant that grows in the Huleh swamp in northern Palestine, and used to grow in the Nile delta. Not only was paper made from papyrus, but also boats (Isaiah 18:2).

The land of Canaan was God's gift to the Israelites. The land was allocated to the tribes by lot. God determined the fall of the lot, so each tribe's area of land was God-given.

Within the tribes, each family was given its own plot of land which was to be treasured by the family for all generations (Isaiah 34:17).

When Naboth refused to sell his land to King Ahab, he was not being churlish. To sell would have been to rebel against God, who had given the land. Queen Jezebel, who was a foreigner, did not understand this.

If a family fell into debt and had to sell its land, the nearest relative bought it, to keep it within the family. Every fifty years all land had to be returned to the family. This preserved equality.

In the time of the kings, rich families bought the lands of poor people, and built up large estates, while the poor, unable to grow their own crops, became very poor. The prophets spoke out against this (Micah 2:2).

Facts 7

IN GOD'S GARDEN

When a man was plowing a field, he had to keep his eyes straight ahead and not look back (Luke 9:62). This was not only to keep a straight furrow, but because the ground was often hard, in spite of the rains, and full of stones.

The roots of the broom tree were an excellent source of charcoal (Psalm 120:4).

The gardens of Assyrian and Babylonian kings were famous for their many varieties of trees and shrubs.

The plant that grew up to shelter Jonah from the sun was probably a castor oil plant, which is noted for the rapidity of its growth.

Boundary stones marked the edges of land belonging to one family. The Israelites were to resist the temptation to move an ancient boundary stone in an attempt to grab more land for themselves (Deuteronomy 19:14).

Frankincense is a resin obtained from the gum of trees in the Boswellia family, which grow in Arabia, Ethiopia, and India. When the bark is cut, the resin oozes out and hardens into whitish drops which are then collected and processed.

Frankincense was often carried by camels along the ancient spice routes. The traders added their overheads, and frankincense was very expensive by the time it reached Jerusalem.

Frankincense was the most important ingredient in the incense which priests burnt on the altar to make a sweet-smelling smoke. It was also added to the olive oil with which priests were anointed, and was made into a perfume.

Myrrh is an aromatic resin collected from a prickly shrub which grows in the deserts of north-east Africa and southern Arabia. When the branches are cut the brownish resin oozes out and hardens.

Like frankincense, myrrh was very expensive. It was made into a perfume (Song of Songs 3:6) and was added to oil for anointing priests. Myrrh was also one of the aromatic substances that was rubbed on a corpse in preparation for burial.

Miraculous Events

Quiz # 1

MIRACULOUS EVENTS

1. Who was struck blind on the road to Damascus as he sought to persecute Christians?

2. Who did Paul strike blind as a punishment?

3. How many of Jesus' recorded miracles took place on the Sabbath?

4. In the Old Testament who was told that the Lord would take away all sickness from them?

5. When the Israelites were fleeing from the Egyptians, what happened when Moses raised his staff and stretched his hand over the sea?

6. True or false? The word "miracle" never occurs in the New Testament outside the four Gospels.

7. Who saw a bush on fire that did not burn?

8. How long had Lazarus been dead when Jesus raised him to life?

9. When did the sun and moon stand still?

10. True or false? Elijah went up to heaven in a chariot of fire.

11. Who wrote that the apostles did many wonders and miraculous signs?

12. When Philip the deacon cast out evil spirits what noise was heard?

13. Which of Jesus' half-brothers experienced a resurrection appearance of the risen Lord Jesus Christ?

14. Who did an angel of the Lord tell to go to the desert road that links Gaza and Jerusalem?

15. As they had no boats, how were the Israelites able to cross the river Jordan?

---

13. James **14.** Philip **15.** The waters stopped flowing
10. False. Elijah went up in a whirlwind (2 Kings 2:11) **11.** Luke **12.** Shrieking
6. False (Galatians 3:5) **7.** Moses **8.** 4 days **9.** When Joshua defeated the Amorites
1. Saul who was later called Paul **2.** Elymas **3.** 7 **4.** The Israelites **5.** The waters divided

Answers

Quiz #2
MIRACULOUS EVENTS

1. True or false? Jesus never healed a woman.

2. What happened when Elijah struck the waters of the river Jordan with his cloak?

3. Which famous general was healed of his leprosy by dipping himself in a river?

4. How many times did this general dip himself in the river?

5. What was the first thing the general said after he was healed?

6. Which Old Testament prophet had a vision in which he was lifted up by the hair of his head?

7. True or false? Jairus' daughter was twelve years old when Jesus brought her back to life.

8. Which of Jesus' apostles walked on water?

9. Which Old Testament book mentions twice, "miracles that cannot be counted"?

10. Who became silent when Barnabas and Paul recounted the miracles they had performed among the Gentiles?

11. Which Gospel writer records the healing of the official's son as the second miraculous sign Jesus did?

12. After Elijah prayed, how long did the drought last?

13. The first miracle the Bible records is the creation of the world by God. Which Bible book is this in?

14. What happened to Moses' hand when he put it inside his cloak to perform a miraculous sign?

15. What was the first of the plagues with which God punished Pharaoh?

Answers

1. False (Matthew 8:14-15) 2. The waters divided 3. Naaman 4. 7 times
5. "Now I know that there is no God in all the world except in Israel!" 6. Ezekiel
7. True (Luke 8:42) 8. Peter 9. Job 10. The council at Jerusalem 11. John 12. Three and a half years
13. Genesis 14. It became leprous 15. The water of the river Nile was turned into blood

Quiz #3

MIRACULOUS EVENTS

1. Luke 9:1-2 records Jesus sending out his twelve disciples to preach about the kingdom of God. What else did Jesus tell them to do?

2. True or false? When a blind beggar kept calling out to Jesus, those around Jesus told him to be quiet.

3. If the Greeks looked for wisdom, what did Jews demand?

4. When James' letter refers to the miraculous drought in Elijah's time, what in particular about Elijah does James remind his readers about?

5. Who was promised, "The jar of flour will not be used up and the jug of oil will not run dry until the day of the Lord gives rain on the land"?

6. Which Old Testament prophet likened the glory of God to a rainbow on a rainy day?

7. On which day did the religious leaders object to Jesus healing people?

8. Who raised the son of the widow of Zarephath from the dead?

9. Who was healed after she touched the edge of Jesus' cloak?

10. What was the second of the plagues God punished Pharaoh with?

11. Against the people of which town did God send an outbreak of tumors?

12. True or false? Jesus never told his disciples to heal the sick and to raise the dead.

13. Which New Testament book, outside the Gospels, mentions at least four resurrection appearances of Jesus?

14. Why did Jesus do so few miracles among the people of his own home town?

15. Matthew explains in his Gospel that Jesus' conception was miraculous. Which Old Testament prophet does he quote in support of this?

Quiz #4
MIRACULOUS EVENTS

1. True or false? According to John very few believed in Jesus when they saw his miracles.

2. After being cursed by Elisha how many youths were killed by two bears?

3. True or false? Peter went into the empty tomb, where Jesus had been, before John did.

4. How many of Jesus' miracles are linked to him having authority over the forces of nature?

5. Who visited Jesus at night and said that nobody could do the miracles Jesus did if he was not from God?

6. After Elijah was taken to heaven in a whirlwind what was the first thing Elisha did?

7. What was the third of the plagues with which God punished Pharaoh?

8. Where was the angel of the Lord standing when the plague that killed 70,000 Israelites stopped?

9. Who said that it was impossible for anyone to do a miracle in his name and then say something bad about him?

10. Whose son did Elisha raise from the dead?

11. What happened to King Jeroboam's arm when he ordered that a man of God should be seized?

12. About whom was this question asked, "Why do you look for the living among the dead"?

13. What musical instrument was being played when Elisha had a vision about water being supplied for armies and cattle?

14. When Jesus visited the place where Lazarus had been buried, what did he do?

15. Which married couple dropped down dead after lying about the price they sold a piece of property for?

Quiz #5

MIRACULOUS EVENTS

1. True or false? Jesus healed Peter's father-in-law.

2. When Moses, Aaron, Aaron's two eldest sons and seventy of Israel's elders saw the God of Israel, what did they see under God's feet?

3. Who said that he had to boast about visions and revelations he had from God?

4. What happened to some of the immoral men of Sodom just before Lot was rescued?

5. If a Christian is ill in bed who should be called in, according to James?

6. Who saw amazing visions when he was in the Spirit on the Lord's day?

7. True or false? There are more miracles in the New Testament linked to Paul than to Peter.

8. Which Old Testament king was told that he would be healed and that the shadow of the sun would go backwards?

9. How many of Jesus' miracles in John's Gospel took place on the Sabbath?

10. Whose staff did Gehazi lay on a dead boy in a vain attempt to bring him back to life?

11. What were the names of the two people the risen Jesus spoke to on the road to Emmaus?

12. God promised that a married couple would miraculously have a child. The husband was a hundred years old and the wife ninety years old. What were their names?

13. Who was turned into a pillar of salt for looking back at the cities of Sodom and Gomorrah?

14. Isaac prayed to the Lord that his barren wife might become pregnant. God miraculously answered this prayer and Rebekah had twins. What were the names of the twins?

15. About whom is it said in the book of Genesis that God remembered her, listened to her and opened her womb?

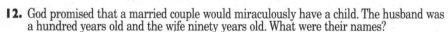

Answers

1. False. It was Peter's mother-in-law (Mark 1:30) **2.** Something like a pavement **3.** Paul **4.** They were blinded **5.** The elders **6.** John, the writer of the book of Revelation **7.** True **8.** Hezekiah **9.** 2 **10.** Elisha's **11.** We are only told the name of one of them: Cleopas **12.** Abraham and Sarah **13.** Lot's wife **14.** Esau and Jacob **15.** Rachel

Quiz #6
MIRACULOUS EVENTS

1. In John's Gospel, just before the feeding of the 5,000, a great crowd followed Jesus because of the miracles he had performed on whom?

2. Which Old Testament prophet promised that "the ears of the deaf would be unstopped"?

3. Who, in Genesis 38, did the Lord kill because of his wickedness?

4. True or false? Anybody who saw Jesus' miracles automatically became a believer in Jesus.

5. Who did Paul predict would display all kinds of counterfeit miracles?

6. Who was killed in the tenth and final plague that struck Egypt?

7. True or false? Four times in his letters Paul mentions that ill Christians should be anointed with oil.

8. Which Old Testament prophet made bad spring water wholesome?

9. Just before he became the first Christian martyr, who saw a vision of God's glory with Jesus standing at God's right hand?

10. What did God do as a result of people trying to make a name for themselves by building the tower of Babel?

11. What was the fourth of the plagues with which God punished Pharaoh?

12. Which Old Testament prophet increased a widow's supply of oil?

13. Which two people from the Old Testament appeared with Jesus at his transfiguration?

14. After Jesus healed a man who was blind and mute, who did the Pharisees say Jesus used to drive out demons?

15. Which Old Testament prophet had a dream about four beasts?

---

12. Elisha **13.** Moses and Elijah **14.** Beelzebub **15.** Daniel
8. Elisha **9.** Stephen **10.** The Lord confused the language of the whole world **11.** A plague of flies
5. The lawless one **6.** All the firstborn of Egypt **7.** False. This is only mentioned in James' letter (James 5:14)
4. False. Many people did not believe in Jesus, even though they witnessed his miracles
1. The sick **2.** Isaiah **3.** Er

Answers

343

Quiz #7

MIRACULOUS EVENTS

1. To whom did Jesus say, "Daughter your faith has healed you. Go in peace and be freed from your suffering"?

2. The three women who went to Jesus' tomb wondered who would roll the stone away for them. Who, according to Matthew, did this?

3. True or false? Miraculous powers are included by Paul in his list of spiritual gifts.

4. Which Old Testament prophet was credited with the ability of knowing the words the king of Aram spoke in his bedroom?

5. Where was Paul when the islanders thought he was a god because he did not die after being bitten by a snake?

6. Which is the only miracle of Jesus recorded in all four Gospels?

7. What was the fifth of the plagues with which God punished Pharaoh?

8. Which army did Elisha strike blind?

9. True or false? After appearing to the two people on the road to Emmaus, the risen Jesus appeared to the eleven disciples who thought he was a ghost.

10. Who was seen in the fiery furnace with Shadrach, Meshach, and Abednego?

11. What explanation did Daniel give for not being mauled to death when he was in the lions' pit?

12. When Jonah was thrown overboard into a raging sea, what happened to the sea?

13. What did God send to rescue Jonah from the sea?

14. What did God provide Jonah with as he sat in the sun, east of the city of Nineveh?

15. Where did Jesus' ascension take place according to Luke's Gospel?

---

14. A vine (NIV), gourd (KJV) **15.** The vicinity of Bethany

11. Because God sent his angel to shut the mouths of the lions **12.** The sea became calm **13.** A great fish

8. The Syrian army **9.** True (Luke 24:37) **10.** One who looked like the son of the gods

3. True (1 Corinthians 12:10) **4.** Elisha **5.** Malta **6.** The feeding of the 5,000 **7.** A plague of livestock

1. The woman who had been suffering from bleeding for twelve years **2.** An angel of the Lord

Answers

344

Quiz #8

MIRACULOUS EVENTS

1. True or false? The woman Jesus cured of bleeding had been ill in this way for twelve years.

2. Who, according to Paul in 2 Thessalonians 2:10, would be deceived by counterfeit miracles?

3. Some Jews said that since Jesus had opened the eyes of the blind could he not have prevented a friend of his from dying Jesus went on to raise his friend to life. Who was the friend?

4. What was the sixth of the plagues with which God punished Pharaoh?

5. True or false? More than thirty miracles are associated with Moses.

6. True or false? When Mary Magdalene first saw the risen Jesus she mistook him for a shepherd.

7. While listening to Paul speaking Eutychus fell out of a window and died. What did Paul do?

8. How did Joseph know that he had to take Jesus and Mary and flee to Egypt?

9. Who did Jesus heal because of Peter's action?

10. Who stopped a man from driving out demons in Jesus' name?

11. What was the result of Peter healing Aeneas?

12. What did Paul do to a slave girl who was able to predict the future?

13. What did the psalmist tell the descendants of Abraham and the sons of Jacob to remember?

14. When the risen Jesus told some of his disciples to throw their nets into the water to catch fish, did he say to throw the nets over the right or the left hand side of the boat?

15. How many baskets full of broken pieces were left over after Jesus fed 4,000 people?

---

14. The right hand side of the boat 15. 7

8. The Lord appeared to him in a dream 9. Malchus 10. John 11. The people who lived in Lydda and Sharon turned to the Lord 12. Commanded the spirit in her to come out of her 13. God's wonders and miracles

5. True 6. False. She mistook him for the gardener (John 20:15) 7. Paul brought him back to life

1. True (Luke 8:43) 2. Those who are perishing 3. Lazarus 4. A plague of boils

Answers

345

Quiz #9

MIRACULOUS EVENTS

1. How many extra years of life was King Hezekiah given by the Lord?

2. What was the seventh of the plagues with which God punished Pharaoh?

3. When Elijah and the prophets of Baal opposed each other it was agreed that the God who answered in what way would be the true God?

4. Who said, "If only my master would see the prophet who is in Samaria! He would cure him of his leprosy"?

5. Which prophet was instrumental in a commander of the army of the king of Aram being healed of his leprosy?

6. Where was Moses when the Lord met him in a dense cloud?

7. What kind of people did Isaiah predict would leap like deers?

8. How many of Jesus' miracles recorded in Luke's Gospel took place on the Sabbath?

9. Who said "Nothing will be impossible for you"?

10. True or false? Jesus spat on a blind man's eyes. Then the man said he could see people, but they looked like clouds in the sky.

11. True or false? The first word Mary Magdalene said to the risen Jesus, once she recognized him, was the Aramaic word, "Rabboni."

12. What did Jesus say his disciples would need if they were going to do greater deeds that he had done?

13. What came down from heaven when Solomon finished praying at the dedication of the temple?

14. Which three disciples of Jesus witnessed his transfiguration?

15. True or false? There are more than ten miracles recorded in the New Testament linked to Paul.

Answers

1. 15 years 2. A plague of hail 3. The God who answers by fire
4. A young girl who served the wife of Naaman 5. Elisha 6. On Mount Sinai 7. The lame
8. 5 9. Jesus 10. False. He said taht people looked like walking trees (Mark 8:24)
11. True (John 20:16) 12. Faith in Jesus 13. Fire 14. Peter, James and John 15. True (Acts 28:8)

346

Quiz #10
MIRACULOUS EVENTS

1. When Moses threw his staff to the ground at the Lord's command what did it turn into?

2. When the Egyptian sorcerers turned their staffs into snakes what did Aaron's staff do to their staffs?

3. After Jesus had applied some mud on a blind man's eyes to which pool did he send him to wash his eyes?

4. What was the eighth plague with which God punished Pharaoh?

5. Which seven non-Christians tried to cast out demons in the name of the Lord Jesus?

6. What did the demon-possessed man do to the seven people trying to exorcize him?

7. In what memorable way did the seven people attempting the exorcism leave the house?

8. When the risen Jesus appeared to his ten disciples why were the disciples meeting in a locked room?

9. True or false? Jesus was transfigured on the shore of the Dead Sea.

10. What did Paul tell a man who had been a cripple from birth to do at Lystra?

11. When the crowds saw Paul perform a miracle at Lystra, what name did they give Barnabas?

12. When the crowds saw Paul perform a miracle at Lystra what name did they give Paul?

13. In which town does the book of Acts state that God did extraordinary miracles through Paul?

14. In Luke's Gospel, what did Jesus' clothes resemble during his transfiguration?

15. Who struck Peter on the side to wake him up when he was in prison?

---

14. A flash of lightning **15.** An angel

transfiguration (Matthew 17:1) **10.** To stand up on his feet **11.** Zeus **12.** Hermes **13.** Ephesus

7. They ran out naked and bleeding **8.** They were frightened of the Jews **9.** False. Jesus went up a mountain for his

them

5. Seven sons of Sceva **6.** He jumped on them, overpowered them and beat them

1. A snake **2.** Aaron's staff swallowed their staffs **3.** Pool of Siloam **4.** A plague of locusts

Answers

Quiz # 11
MIRACULOUS EVENTS

1. What was the ninth plague with which God punished Pharaoh?

2. Who met Moses in the desert, kissed him and then was told by Moses about all the miraculous signs God had commanded him to perform?

3. Who did Paul write to telling him not to ignore his gift?

4. As he was holding two stone tablets whose face was seen to be radiant because he had been in the Lord's presence?

5. During Jesus' transfiguration, what did Peter suggest they should assemble?

6. During Jesus' transfiguration, what did he speak about?

7. After one person was healed on a certain island, all the people came to be healed by whom, according to Dr. Luke?

8. Who gave an interpretation which came true about a dream concerning seven fat cows and seven lean cows?

9. Who said, "If you forgive anyone his sins, they are forgiven"?

10. During Jesus' transfiguration, what words did the three disciples hear?

11. Which Old Testament prophet told a king that there "is a God in heaven who reveals mysteries"?

12. What miracle took place after Jesus' transfiguration?

13. Who demanded that his dream should be interpreted but would not say what his dream was?

14. Through what kind of message did Timothy receive his spiritual gift?

15. To whom did Jesus say, "Everything is possible for him who believes."?

Answers

1. A plague of darkness 2. Aaron 3. Timothy 4. Moses 5. 3 shelters 6. His departure 7. Paul 8. Joseph 9. The risen Jesus 10. "This is my Son, whom I have chosen; listen to him" (NIV) 11. Daniel 12. The healing of a boy with an evil spirit 13. Nebuchadnezzar 14. Prophetic 15. The father of a boy who had an evil spirit in him

Quiz # 12

MIRACULOUS EVENTS

1. What did the Lord tell Moses to do to a rock so water would come out of it for the Israelites to drink?

2. Who was involved when Timothy received his spiritual gift?

3. Who prayed in the New Testament, "Stretch our your hand to heal and perform miraculous signs and wonders through the name of your holy servant Jesus"?

4. To whom did Jesus give authority to drive out demons?

5. At the end of Mark's Gospel, how many signs are mentioned which will accompany those who believe?

6. True or false? Jesus went up to an apple tree, expecting to pick and eat an apple. When there was no fruit on the tree, he said, "May you never bear fruit again."

7. Who said that he would never believe in Jesus' resurrection unless he put his finger in the nail marks on Jesus' hands?

8. At the end of Mark's Gospel, what is the first of the signs mentioned which will accompany those who believe?

9. True or false? Peter healed a man called Aeneas who had been a paralytic for eight years.

10. At the end of Mark's Gospel, what is the second of the signs mentioned which will accompany those who believe?

11. Which Old Testament prophet prayed, "You performed miraculous signs and wonders in Egypt and have continued them to this day, both in Israel and among all mankind"?

12. At the end of Mark's Gospel, what is the third of the signs mentioned which will accompany those who believe?

13. True or false? The risen Jesus never appeared to more than eleven at the same time.

14. At the end of Mark's Gospel, what is the fourth of the signs mentioned which will accompany those who believe?

15. While Daniel pondered about the meaning of a vision he had seen, who was told to tell him its meaning?

Answers

1. Strike it with his staff **2.** Elders who laid their hands on him **3.** Peter and John and other believers **4.** His 12 apostles **5.** 5 signs **6.** False It was a fig tree (Matthew 21:19) **7.** Thomas **8.** They will drive out demons **9.** True (Acts 9:34) **10.** They will speak in new tongues **11.** Jeremiah **12.** They will pick up snakes with their hands **13.** False. He appeared to more than 500 people at one time (1 Corinthians 15:6) **14.** They will not be harmed by drinking deadly poison **15.** Gabriel

349

Quiz #13

MIRACULOUS EVENTS

1. Which king said to Daniel, "Surely your God is the God of gods and the Lord of kings and a revealer of mysteries, for you were able to reveal this mystery"?

2. Which New Testament writer lists "miraculous powers" as one of the spiritual gifts?

3. True or false? "Gifts of healing" are one of the spiritual gifts.

4. Which ruler was pleased to have Jesus brought before him because he wanted to see Jesus perform a miracle?

5. Who said, "But if I drive out demons by the Spirit of God, then the kingdom of God has come upon you"?

6. What did Pharaoh's sorcerers use in order to copy Aaron when his staff was turned into a snake?

7. Where did the risen Jesus say that his disciples should wait until they received the gift promised by the Father?

8. Jesus predicted that many people would falsely claim to do three things in his name. What was the first thing?

9. What was the revelation about which Daniel saw in the third year of King Darius?

10. What were Thomas' first words on encountering the risen Jesus?

11. On which day were the disciples baptized with the Holy Spirit?

12. When the Holy Spirit came on the disciples, what sound came from heaven?

13. When the Holy Spirit came on the disciples, what did they see?

14. Which two Old Testament prophets described a man in linen?

15. When the Holy Spirit came on the disciples what was unusual about their speech?

Quiz # 14

MIRACULOUS EVENTS

1. Which New Testament preacher touched handkerchiefs and aprons that were then used to heal people?

2. Which is the first miraculous sign recorded in John's Gospel?

3. Jesus predicted that many people would falsely claim to do three things in his name. What was the second thing?

4. Which king said about the God of Daniel, "He rescues and saves; he performs signs and wonders in the heavens and on the earth. He has rescued Daniel from the power of the lions"?

5. Jesus predicted that many people would falsely claim to do three things in his name. What was the third thing?

6. What did Jesus find amazing about the faith of a Roman centurion who came to him?

7. Paul wrote that when the lawless one comes he would display four things. What is the first thing?

8. To whom did Jesus send this report, "The blind receive sight, the lame walk, those who have leprosy are cured, the deaf hear, the dead are raised, and the good news is preached to the poor"?

9. Who wrote that Jesus performed many miracles which are not recorded in his Gospel?

10. Paul wrote that when the lawless one comes he would display four things. What is the second thing?

11. Who were amazed, praised God, and said, "We have never seen anything like this!"?

12. Paul wrote that when the lawless one comes he would display four things. What is the third thing?

13. In the first recorded Christian sermon who said, "Jesus of Nazareth was a man accredited by God to you by miracles, wonders and signs"?

14. To how many of his disciples did the risen Jesus appear by the Sea of Tiberias?

15. Paul wrote that when the lawless one comes he would display four things. What is the fourth thing?

Answers

1. Paul **2.** Changing water into wine at Cana **3.** They would drive out demons in his name **4.** Darius **5.** They would perform miracles **6.** The centurion believed that Jesus could heal from a distance, simply by speaking a word of command **7.** All kinds of counterfeit miracles **8.** John the Baptist **9.** John **10.** Counterfeit miracles **11.** Everyone who saw Jesus heal the paralytic who was lowered through the roof **12.** Counterfeit signs **13.** Peter **14.** 7 **15.** Counterfeit wonders

Quiz # 15

MIRACULOUS EVENTS

1. What kind of prayer, according to James' letter, will make a sick person better?

2. Who saw Peter and John laying hands on people and asked if he could buy this ability to give the Spirit?

3. How many days, according to Daniel's vision, would there be between the daily sacrifice being abolished and the setting up of the abomination that caused desolation?

4. Which Old Testament king wrote, "It is my pleasure to tell you about the miraculous signs and wonders that the Most High God has performed for me"?

5. After the disciples had caught no fish all night long Jesus told them to go out into the deep and let down their nets. What happened?

6. What did Peter say to Simon the sorcerer as he tried to buy the Holy Spirit?

7. True or false? When Jesus healed ten lepers, only two came back to thank Jesus.

8. How many of Jesus' miraculous signs are recorded in John's Gospel?

9. What was distinctive about the healed leper who returned to thank Jesus?

10. What did the Psalmist say took place in the land of Egypt, in the region of Zoan?

11. At what time of day did the first miracle recorded in the book of Acts take place?

12. How old was the man who was the first person to be healed in the book of Acts?

13. According to Deuteronomy, if a prophet predicts a miraculous sign that does take place, how can you tell if he is false prophet?

14. When Jesus turned water into wine at Cana, John says that the master of the banquet was unaware of this. But who was aware?

15. When false messiahs come what did Jesus say they would do?

Answers

1. The prayer offered in faith **2.** Simon **3.** 1,290 days **4.** Nebuchadnezzar
5. They caught so many fish that their nets began to break. **6.** May your money perish with you, because you thought that you could buy the gift of God with money **7.** False. Only one came back to thank Jesus (Luke 17:16)
8. Eight **9.** He was a Samaritan **10.** Miracles **11.** At three in the afternoon **12.** Over 40 years old
13. He is a false prophet if he says, "Let us follow other gods"
14. The servants who had filled the six stone water jars **15.** Perform signs and miracles

Quiz # 16
MIRACULOUS EVENTS

1. When the Jews asked Jesus for a miraculous sign to validate his authority, how did Jesus reply?

2. Who was given authority by Jesus to drive out evil spirits and to heal all kinds of diseases?

3. Who did God say he would heal because he had seen his tears and heard his prayers?

4. Who became leprous, like snow, because she spoke against Moses?

5. Which Gospel does not record Jesus walking on water?

6. True or false? The New Testament records at least nine miracles associated with Peter?

7. How many miracles linked to Elijah and Elisha are recorded in the Bible?

8. Who in the New Testament healed a man who was suffering from dysentery?

9. True or false? Because of something the risen Jesus said to Peter a rumor spread that the "disciple whom Jesus loved" would never die until Jesus returned.

10. True or false? The invalid at the pool of Bethesda had been ill for thirty-eight years.

11. To whom did Jesus say, "Your sins are forgiven. Get up, take your mat and walk"?

12. When Peter preached in Cornelius' house, what astonished the circumcised believers who had come with Peter?

13. How did Cornelius and his household respond when the Holy Spirit came on them?

14. To whom did Jesus say, "Unless you people see miraculous signs and wonders you will never believe"?

15. When Peter and John arrived in Samaria from Jerusalem what did they pray about?

Quiz #17
MIRACULOUS EVENTS

1. Which Old Testament prophet said, "I will pour out my Spirit on all people"?

2. When God's Spirit is poured out on all people what will sons and daughters do?

3. When God's Spirit is poured out on all people what will old men do?

4. When God's Spirit is poured out on all people who will see visions?

5. After Jesus called out, "Lazarus, come out!" what is the very next thing that happened according to John's Gospel?

6. After Jesus had raised Lazarus from the dead what did the chief priests plan to do to Lazarus?

7. After Philip had baptized the Ethiopian eunuch why did he not see Philip again?

8. When Paul asked the disciples at Ephesus if they had received the Holy Spirit how did they reply?

9. What outward sign did Paul use as the Holy Spirit came on the disciples at Ephesus?

10. When the crowds saw the miraculous signs Philip did in the city of Samaria how did they respond?

11. True or false? When the disciples at Ephesus received the Holy Spirit they spoke in tongues.

12. True or false? When the disciples at Ephesus received the Holy Spirit they prophesied.

13. Approximately how many disciples at Ephesus received the Holy Spirit through Paul's ministry?

14. What did the people of Lydda and Sharon do when they saw the man who had been healed by Peter?

15. Jesus predicted that with false 'Christs' another group of people would also appear? Who would they be?

Answers

1. Joel **2.** Prophesy **3.** Dream dreams **4.** Young men **5.** The dead man came out **6.** Kill him **7.** Because Philip was suddenly taken away by the Spirit of the Lord **8.** They said that they had never heard of the Holy Spirit **9.** He placed his hands on them **10.** They paid close attention to everything Philip said **11.** True (Acts 19:6) **12.** True (Acts 19:6) **13.** About 12 men **14.** They turned to the Lord **15.** False prophets

Quiz # 18
MIRACULOUS EVENTS

1. Why did God kill Uzzah?

2. True or false? John records more of Jesus' miracles than the other three Gospel writers put together.

3. What, according to the last verse in Mark's Gospel, confirmed the disciples' preaching?

4. Where were Paul and Barnabas when their preaching was confirmed by miraculous signs and wonders?

5. True or false? Matthew does not record any miracles of Jesus in the first seven chapters of his Gospel.

6. When the proconsul of Paphos saw Paul make a sorcerer blind what did the proconsul do?

7. Why were 14,700 Israelites killed by a plague?

8. How many healing miracles of Jesus are recorded in which Jesus healed women?

9. True or false? Doubting Thomas walked on water to Jesus, but doubted and so began to oink in the water.

10. Which is the only Gospel to record the raising of Lazarus?

11. Which is the only Gospel to record the raising of the widow's son at Nain?

12. Which is the only Gospel to record the coin being found in a fish's mouth?

13. Who wrote that he would not speak except "by the power of signs and miracles, through the power of the Spirit"?

14. Which is the only Gospel to record the healing of the man who had dropsy?

15. True or false? On one occasion Jesus healed eleven lepers.

Quiz # 19
MIRACULOUS EVENTS

1. According to the apostle Paul why was each Christian given a manifestation of the Spirit?

2. There are only two miracles of Jesus recorded by Mark which are not found in any of the other Gospels. Which is the first of these miracles?

3. Who said to Moses that he knew that the king of Egypt would not let the Israelites go unless a strong hand forced him?

4. True or false? Paul said that the Christians at Corinth had no interest in the gifts of the Holy Spirit.

5. Which gifts did Paul say the Christians at Corinth should excel in?

6. What did Paul say that a Corinthian Christian who spoke in tongues should pray for?

7. True or false? Paul said that he spoke in tongues more than all the Corinthian Christians.

8. True or false? Paul said that tongues were not a sign for believers but for unbelievers.

9. True or false? After Jesus' resurrection he enabled some of his disciples to catch fish in a miraculous way.

10. Who in the New Testament was struck dumb for about nine months?

11. How many people were not killed by the great flood in Noah's time?

12. True or false? Paul said that prophecy was not a sign for believers but for unbelievers.

13. Who wrote, "The spirits of prophets are subject to the control of prophets"?

14. What kind of spiritual gifts did Paul encourage the Corinthian Christians to seek after?

15. Paul mentioned one particular gift the Corinthian Christians should seek after. What was it?

Quiz #20
MIRACULOUS EVENTS

1. True or false? Peter cut off the index finger of the High Priest's servant but Jesus immediately healed it.

2. Why did God kill 70,000 Israelites with a plague?

3. Who saw God's back?

4. Who had a staff that miraculously produced almonds?

5. Which Old Testament prophet saw God sitting on his throne with the host of heaven sitting on both of God's hands?

6. Because the Israelites grumbled in the desert the Lord punished them. What did he send that hit them so hard they died?

7. The Lord told Moses to erect a bronze snake on a pole. What did any Israelite bitten by a snake have to do in order to be healed?

8. In contrast to love that never fails, what did Paul say would happen to prophecies?

9. What does the number 153 refer to in John 21:11?

10. At which temple gate did Peter heal a man?

11. True or false? Paul was delivered from prison by an angel.

12. In contrast to love that never fails, what did Paul say would happen to tongues?

13. There are only two miracles of Jesus recorded by Mark which are not found in any of the other Gospels. Which is the second of these miracles?

14. True or false? Over 30 of Jesus' miracles are recorded in the New Testament.

15. Isaiah's a vision of God with the train of God's robe filling the temple was received in the same year as which king's death?

Quiz #21
MIRACULOUS EVENTS

1. In order to tell a mountain to move what did Jesus say was necessary?

2. At Nain Jesus saw a funeral procession. Men were carrying the body of the only son of a widow. What were Jesus' first words to the widow?

3. Who did the prophet Malachi say had healing in his wings?

4. When Peter was miraculously delivered from prison what happened when he came to the iron gate which led to the city?

5. True or false? All four Gospels record Jesus turning water into wine.

6. Who wrote, "He rained meat down on them [the Israelites] like dust"?

7. Who is being described here, "Paul looked directly at him, saw that he had faith to be healed…"?

8. At the end of Mark's gospel what is the fifth of the signs mentioned which will accompany those who believe?

9. To whom did Jesus say, "A wicked and adulterous generation asks for a miraculous sign!"?

10. Which king said, "Praise be to the God of Shadrach, Meshach and Abednego, who has sent his angel and rescued his servants!"?

11. How did some people who witnessed the Holy Spirit coming on the disciples make fun of them?

12. True or false? Jesus told a storm at sea to be quiet and it obeyed him.

13. What, according to the book of Revelation, will three evil spirits that look like frogs do?

14. Who prophesied, "Then will the eyes of the blind be opened and the ears of the deaf unstopped"?

15. Who was told by the risen Jesus to feed Jesus' sheep?

Answers

1. Faith **2.** "Don't cry" **3.** The sun of righteousness **4.** It opened by itself
5. False. Only John's Gospel records it (John 2:1-11) **6.** The Psalmist **7.** A cripple in Lystra
8. They will place their hands on sick people and heal them **9.** The Pharisees and the teachers of the Law
10. Nebuchadnezzar **11.** They were drunk **12.** True (Mark 4:39)
13. Perform miraculous signs **14.** Isaiah **15.** Peter

Facts 1

MIRACULOUS EVENTS

After being involved in the miraculous incident with Eutychus Paul did not comment on the miracle. He carried on teaching until dawn as his overriding concern was to build up the believers at Troas.

The temple tax which Jesus told Peter to find in a fish's mouth (Matthew 17:24-27) was the tax that every male from the age of 20 had to pay each year and was used to pay for looking after the temple.

Jesus told his 72 disciples that he saw Satan fall as a result of them exorcizing demons. This was a clear indication that Satan was being defeated.

In Jacob's dream at Bethel he saw a "ladder" (KJV) extending from earth to heaven. Angels were able to go up and down it because it was not a ladder with rungs, but rather a stairway as would have been found at the side of ziggurats.

Jesus said that his followers would do greater miracles than he had done (John 14:12). Once Jesus returned to the Father, he would send the Holy Spirit in whose power these miracles would be performed.

Miracles often appear in clusters in the Bible. For example, as Ahab and Jezebel tried to make Baal the official deity of Israel the miraculous ministries of Elijah and Elisha were empowered by the Lord.

One of the Greek words used for miracles in the New Testament is *dunamis* (Acts 2:22) from which we derive the word "dynamite".

When the Pharisees accused Jesus of driving out demons using Beelzebub's power Jesus said that the Pharisees were guilty of blasphemy against the Spirit. Beelzebub, the prince of the demons, was the name used of Satan.

When Jonathan and his armor-bearer won a victory over the Philistines, the Israelites gave God the credit for a miraculous deliverance. Even the panic that overtook the Philistines was attributed to the Lord.

General Naaman was told to dip himself in the river Jordan. He was upset at the thought of a 25 mile journey to a muddy, meandering river. He considered the rivers of Damascus, Abana and Pharpar, superior to any waters of Israel.

Facts 2

MIRACULOUS EVENTS

One of the greatest groupings of miracles in the Bible are the twenty-one miracles associated with Elijah and Elisha. They witnessed to God's power as the Israelites were called back to the Lord, the true God.

Paul wrote that he was once caught up into the "third heaven" (2 Corinthians 12:2-3). If the first heaven is the earth's atmosphere, and the second heaven is the heaven of space, the "third" heaven is God's presence.

Jesus performed his miracles in a different way from anybody else. Prophets healed in the name of God. Jesus healed with the same authority that he forgave sins.

When the Israelites fled from Egypt, all night long a strong east wind drove the water back so Moses and the Israelites could cross over the sea on dry land. This natural phenomena is said to be the work of the Lord as it happened at the precise moment that it was so desperately needed.

Two of the wise men, sorcerers and Egyptian magicians who opposed Moses (Exodus 7:11) are, according to tradition, named by Paul in 2 Timothy 3:8 as Jannes and Jambres.

Mark 16:18 speaks about people being able to pick up snakes in the hands, drink poison and be unharmed and heal the sick. There is serious doubt about the authenticity of Mark 16:9-20 as it is missing in the earliest manuscripts of Mark's Gospel.

When a dead man's body touched the bones of the prophet Elisha the dead man came alive. The was the final time that Elisha demonstrated God's life-giving power.

The first thing Matthew's Gospel records after Jesus died is that the curtain in the temple was torn from top to bottom. This was a vivid symbol of Jesus' death providing access to God, as this curtain cut everyone off from God's presence.

Jesus' miracles did not always create faith. They gave people the opportunity to choose between faith and unbelief. After Lazarus was brought back to life some Jews believed while other Jews reported the matter to the Pharisees.

A mother from outside Palestine asked Jesus to help her demon-possessed daughter. Jesus said, "It is not right to take the children's bread and toss it to the dogs." This suggests that the the gospel was for the Jews first of all.

Facts 3

MIRACULOUS EVENTS

In the Old Testament one of the purposes of the miracles was to demonstrate that the God of Israel was completely different from the local gods. He was the one and only true and living God.

The letter to the Hebrews states that miracles, such as the supernatural healing of the sick, as well as signs and wonders, confirm the gospel message of salvation (Hebrews 2:3-4).

Mark states that Jesus touched and healed a leper. According to the Mosaic law you became defiled if you touched a leper. However, Jesus' great compassion for the leper overrode any ceremonial traditions.

When Jesus forgave the sins of the paralytic who had been let down by his four friends from the roof, the teachers of the law objected. Jesus had dealt with his greatest need. To show his authority to do this Jesus healed the paralytic.

After the miraculous catch of fish Jesus called his first disciples to follow him. Only great rabbis had the prerogative to gather round them a group of disciples. This was seen as a claim to authority and angered the Pharisees.

Jesus' resurrection was quite different from the raising to life of other people in the New Testament. They all died again. Jesus was raised to life and now lives for ever.

In the Old Testament a miracle is never an isolated fact. It is linked to other events. God's extraordinary interventions always said or announced something. To an Israelite the question to ask was, "What is the meaning of the miracle?"

When Jesus healed Peter's mother-in-law's fever he held her hand. Her healing was instantaneous and complete so she was able to serve them food immediately.

Jesus told his 12 disciples not to rejoice so much that the spirits were subject to them but to rejoice that their names were written in heaven. Jesus taught that salvation is more important than having miraculous power.

After Abraham's servant had found Rebekah he worshiped God. He took this meeting as a sign of God's intervention believing he had been divinely led on his journey to the house of his master's relatives.

Facts 4

MIRACULOUS EVENTS

When Jesus exorcized a demon from a man in the Capernaum synagogue the evil spirit cried out, "What have you to do with us" (Mark 1:24)? The demons meant, "Why are you interfering with us?" Jesus' arrival signaled their end.

Jesus taught that the three miracles of him raising the dead in the Gospels: the son of the widow of Nain, Jairus' daughter and Lazarus, were one of the signs that he was the Messiah. "The dead are raised" (Luke 7:22).

Jesus healed a number of people who were possessed by demons. While pagans thought of demons as being both good and bad, Luke states that they are evil spirits which cause mental illness, physical disease and rebellion against God.

When Jesus healed the man with the withered hand the Pharisees thought he broke the Sabbath law. Jesus pointed out to them that if he had not healed the man he would, technically speaking, be "working" by doing evil and killing the man.

The writers of the New Testament saw Jesus' birth as a miracle. Luke records that God's power would overshadow Mary. Mark and Paul do not mention the virgin birth, but to deduce anything from this silence is a weak argument.

The only exorcism where Jesus laid his hands on the person is on a woman who had been crippled for 18 years and who probably had some bones in her spine fused together so she could not even stand up straight.

Dr Luke describes the healing of a man who had dropsy. The medical term "dropsy," an accumulation of fluid, is not found anywhere else in the New Testament. Dropsy indicated illness in more than one part of the body.

Miracles do not necessarily prove divine intervention. In the Old Testament false prophets were able to delude people with signs and wonders (Deuteronomy 13:1), and similar signs are predicted in the New Testament (2 Thessaloninans 2:8-9)

When Jesus healed the man with many demons he may have allowed the demons to enter the pigs to help the healed man understand that he really was released from their grip.

Facts 5

MIRACULOUS EVENTS

The appearance of Moses and Elijah at Jesus' transfiguration are taken to represent the law and the prophets, and that Jesus was now fulfilling everything spoken in them.

Matthew's Gospel is the only one to record that just after Jesus died tombs broke open and holy people were brought to life. If an earthquake opened the tombs, Jesus' resurrection made the rising of these people possible.

Matthew 9:27-31 records Jesus healing two blind men. He told them not to tell anyone about it. Jesus would choose when the time was right for his miracles to be made public.

When Jesus told his 72 disciples that he had given them power over snakes and scorpions he may have been referring to evil spirits as he went on to say that they would overcome the enemy, who was Satan.

In the New Testament a divine action which might have an ordinary outward appearance, is seen, through the eye of faith, as a miracle. But an extraordinary phenomenon, unrelated to faith, is not a miracle.

The earliest form of ministry in the New Testament was charismatic. It was a supernatural gift or endowment and bore witness to the power and presence of the Holy Spirit.

Many of the miracles recorded in the Bible were meant for the encouragement of God's people and were not primarily for unbelievers.

When Jesus healed Jairus' daughter he said in Aramaic, "Talitha koum!" ("Little girl, I say to you, get up!" Mark 5:41), Aramaic was probably the language Jesus spoke.

The healing of the blind man at Bethsaida is the only miracle of Jesus that happened in two stages. With Jesus' first touch the blind man saw but he needed Jesus' second touch to see things as they really were.

Isaiah ordered that a poultice made from figs should be applied to King Hezekiah's boil. This healed him. God uses ordinary remedies but remains the divine healer.

Facts 6

MIRACULOUS EVENTS

The Bible offers no explanation about how King Hezekiah was able to see the shadow of the sun go back ten steps on a stairway. It was a dramatic symbol of extra time being given.

The Pharisees accused Jesus of breaking the Sabbath because when he healed a blind man he applied mud to his eyes. This involved mixing saliva and mud from the ground and the Pharisees said this was work.

In the book of Acts the first person to have performed great wonders and miraculous signs who was not an apostle was Stephen. The working of miracles was not exclusive to the apostles.

Jesus went up to a fig tree to see if it had any fruit in mid-April. The leaves of the fig trees in Palestine appear in March accompanied by a crop of edible knobs called *taksh*. If there are no *taksh*, there will be no edible fruit that year.

When Jesus cursed the fig tree for having no fruit he enacted out a piece of dramatic symbolism. Just as the fig tree had leaves but no fruit, so the Jews made a great show of outward religious observance but produced no spiritual fruit.

Among the spiritual gifts Paul lists is healing. Paul actually uses a double plural "gifts of healings" (1 Corinthians 12:9). This suggests a variety of healings to deal with a variety of diseases.

When Mary Magdalene, Mary the mother of James, and Salome went to Jesus' tomb they found that the stone across the entrance of the cave had already been rolled back. This was not to let Jesus out, but to let the women in.

People who do not have faith in God nearly always missed God's miraculous interventions. So Pharaoh, despite the extraordinary plagues in his land, saw nothing divine in them. They only hardened his heart against God.

When Jesus started his ministry it was a time when the Jews were running after people who performed miracles. Jesus, however, rejected the temptation to be a wonder-worker (Matthew 4:5-6).

Most of the miracles recorded in the Bible took place at critical times in the history of God's people. They took place leading up to and during the Exodus, in the days of Elijah and Elisha, and in the ministry of Jesus.

Facts 7

MIRACULOUS EVENTS

2 Kings 4:42-44 records how 20 loaves of bread, similar to our rolls, miraculously feed 100 men. The loaves were multiplied as a result of God's word without Elisha doing anything.

An ax-head fell into a river so Elisha threw a stick after it and it floated. As the ax-head was expensive and was borrowed the prophet who used it might have had to become a bond-slave until he had paid back the value of the ax-head.

In Isaiah's vision of the Lord the prophet also saw seraphs. Only in this place in the Bible are they mentioned. The root meaning of seraphs in Hebrew is "burn" indicating their purity as they ministered in God's presence.

The miracles of the Bible had a specific purpose. For example, the plagues in Egypt were performed by the Lord as "wonders" so that the Israelites would be freed.

On the Day of Pentecost Peter said in his sermon that "Jesus of Nazareth was a man accredited by God to you by miracles, wonders and signs" (Acts 2:22). Peter meant that such miracles demonstrated that Jesus was the Messiah.

When Jesus healed a deaf and mute man he put his fingers in the man's ears and spat and touched the man's tongue. In this way Jesus communicated to the deaf and mute man what he was about to do. Saliva was thought to have healing properties.

Some modern writers accuse Jesus and the Gospel writers of confusing mental illness with demon possession. Mark clearly distinguishes (1:32-34) between the sick and the demon-possessed, who were both healed by Jesus.

When Elisha was told in a vision that the Lord would provide water for the kings of Israel, Judah and Edom, the Lord also told him what to do. He was told to make the valley full of ditches. God provided water through flash floods because of Elisha's obedience.

Joshua 10:13 records that the sun stopped and delayed going down. Many possible interpretations have been suggested but the Bible offers no explanation, beyond it being a dramatic sign of divine intervention.

When Jesus gave sight it was a sign that he was fulfilling what God had promised his Messiah would do. "Then the eyes of the blind will be opened" (Isaiah 35:5).

Facts 8
MIRACULOUS EVENTS

Simon the sorcerer (Acts 8:9-24) managed to amaze many people because of his magic. Some very early Christian teachers thought that Simon was responsible for Gnostic teaching in the church and labeled him the "arch-heretic."

Absence of healing does not necessarily mean that God's miraculous power has been thwarted. Paul spoke about God's power, despite his continuing illness which he asked God to remove three times (2 Corinthians 12:7-10).

Sick people were laid in streets hoping to be healed as Peter's shadow fell on them. The shadow itself was not important except that it served as a medium for faith.

Jesus walked on the water towards his disciples "during the fourth watch of the night" (Matthew 14:25). The Romans divided the night up into four watches, and the fourth one was 3:00–6:00 a.m. The Jews divided the night into three watches.

Jesus' ascension is recorded as a miraculous event. A cloud, the symbol of God's presence, hid Jesus from the sight of the apostles and they were left staring at two men dressed in white, who were angelic messengers.

Counterfeit miracles are often encountered in the Bible. It is not that so-called miracles did not take place, but that they produced a false and misleading impression because they were ultimately empowered by Satan.

God guided the Israelites by a pillar of cloud and a pillar of fire. These were the symbols of God's presence. God often revealed himself in fire, as he did to Moses, and as he did on the Day of Pentecost.

Natural events, such as a strong east wind (Exodus 14:21), are miraculous for God's believing people, because they would not have taken place apart from divine intervention.

Angels Among Us

Quiz # 1

ANGELS AMONG US

1. How many angels persuaded Lot to leave the city of Sodom before it was destroyed?

2. Which animals had their mouths shut by an angel in the book of Daniel?

3. The Old Testament prophet Zechariah met an angel among which type of tree?

4. Which prophetic book records the destruction of Sennacherib's army by an angel of God?

5. How many angels appeared to the shepherds at the time of Jesus' birth?

6. In the Old Testament, how many men were killed by an angel following David's census of his fighting men?

7. Who, according to Paul in his letter to Timothy, was "vindicated by the Spirit and seen by angels"?

8. When an angel appeared to Peter in prison how did he wake the apostle?

9. An angel appeared to Hagar, concerning her son. What was the name of her son?

10. According to Acts which believer had the face of an angel?

11. True or false? Jesus never spoke about angels.

12. In Galatians, what does Paul say was put into effect through the mediation of angels?

13. During his escape from prison in Acts how many guards did the angel lead Peter past?

14. In Revelation 8 an angel fills a censer with fire and flings it where?

15. According to Luke what proof did the angel give to Mary that his words were true?

Answers

1. 2 **2.** Lions **3.** Myrtle **4.** Isaiah **5.** A multitude of the heavenly host **6.** 70,000 **7.** Jesus **8.** He struck him in the side **9.** Ishmael **10.** Stephen **11.** False (Matthew 18:10) **12.** The law **13.** 2 guards **14.** On earth **15.** The fact that her cousin Elizabeth was pregnant

Quiz #2
ANGELS AMONG US

1. What was the name of the angel who told Mary she was going to have a baby?

2. After his confrontation with the prophets of Baal, Elijah fell asleep only to be woken by an angel who told him to do what?

3. An angel appeared to Mary in the sixth month of what?

4. How did angels help Jesus during and after his temptation in the desert?

5. In the book of Kings an angel found Elijah sleeping under which type of tree?

6. In the Old Testament, who claimed an angel had rescued Shadrach, Meshach and Abednego from the fiery furnace?

7. According to the Gospels, where did the angel tell the women Jesus had gone after his resurrection?

8. True or false? Paul says that nothing can separate Christians from God's love, not even angels.

9. To whom did an angel say, "Greetings, you who are highly favored!"?

10. What sort of angel is Michael?

11. According to Psalm 34, whom does the angel of the Lord encamp around?

12. In Acts an angel appears to Paul during a storm telling him he would stand trial before whom?

13. In Judges, what did an angel ask Gideon to place on a rock?

14. In Revelation 20, an angel is seen holding what?

15. In Acts, where was Stephen when his face was said to be like that of an angel?

Answers

1. Gabriel 2. To get up and eat some food 3. Of Elizabeth's pregnancy
4. They attended him 5. A broom tree 6. Nebuchadnezzar 7. To Galilee 8. True (Romans 8:38-40)
9. Mary, the mother of Jesus 10. An archangel 11. Those who fear him 12. Caesar
13. Meat and unleavened bread 14. The key to the abyss 15. In the Sanhedrin

Quiz #3

ANGELS AMONG US

1. When Zechariah refused to believe his wife was going to have a son how did the angel punish him?

2. True or false? When he was arrested, Jesus told his followers that if necessary he could call upon more than ten legions of angels to help him.

3. After his meeting with the angel in 1 Kings, where did Elijah travel to?

4. Where was Gideon when he was visited by an Angel?

5. According to Matthew, how many times did an angel appear to Joseph?

6. In Revelation 8, how many angels were given trumpets?

7. In Luke, what did the angel say that Zechariah's son must not do?

8. In Matthew 28, to whom did the angels tell the women to go?

9. Which angel's name means "Who is like God"?

10. True of false? The angels who came to rescue Lot and his family from Sodom spent the night in the town square.

11. The angel Gabriel told Mary that her child would be called the son of whom?

12. In Matthew 25, what does Jesus say is prepared for the devil and all his angels?

13. According to Matthew what noise will accompany the sending of angels when the Son of Man appears?

14. In Genesis 16, what did the angel tell Hagar to do?

15. In the Old Testament where was Lot sitting when the angels appeared to him?

Answers

1. He made him unable to speak until the child was born **2.** False. Jesus said more than 12 legions (Matthew 26:53) **3.** Horeb **4.** At the threshing floor of Araunah the Jebusite **5.** 3 times **6.** 7 angels **7.** Drink wine or fermented drink **8.** To the disciples **9.** Michael **10.** False, they stayed in his house **11.** Son of the Most High **12.** The eternal fire **13.** A loud trumpet call **14.** Return to Sarah **15.** In the gateway of the city of Sodom

Quiz #4

ANGELS AMONG US

1. In Genesis as Jacob set out to meet Esau where did he encounter the angels of God?

2. In the New Testament, what name did the angel tell Zechariah to give to his son?

3. True or false? In Psalm 78 the manna eaten by the Israelites is called the bread of angels.

4. In Matthew's Gospel, where was the angel when he addressed the women after the resurrection?

5. According to Luke, why did Zechariah doubt the angel's words?

6. According to Revelation 16, angels held bowls containing what?

7. In Acts what did the angel rescuing Peter from prison tell him to put on?

8. At what point after his rescue from prison did the angel leave the apostle Peter?

9. What did Paul charge Timothy to do in the sight of the elect angels?

10. In Genesis, why did angels come to Sodom?

11. True or false? Mary did not question the pronouncement made by the angel Gabriel.

12. According to the apostle Paul, what should be the fate of an angel who attempts to preach a different gospel?

13. In Revelation 8, which musical instruments were given to the angels?

14. In Judges, when Manoah the father of Samson asked an angel for his name, what was the angel's reply?

15. What fact, according to Jesus in Matthew 24, are angels ignorant of?

Answers

1. Mahanaim **2.** John **3.** True (Psalm 78:25) **4.** Sitting on the rolled back entrance stone **5.** He and Elizabeth were old **6.** God's wrath **7.** His clothes and sandals **8.** After they had walked the length of one street **9.** To keep the instructions he had given him, without partiality **10.** To destroy it **11.** False, Mary asked how, as a virgin, she could have a child (Luke 1:34) **12.** Eternal condemnation **13.** Trumpets **14.** It is beyond understanding **15.** The day of Christ's return

Quiz #5

ANGELS AMONG US

1. How does Paul describe Satan in his second letter to the Corinthians?

2. As recorded by Deborah's song in Judges, who did the angel command to be cursed?

3. Who were told of the birth of Jesus by a huge number of angels?

4. At Jesus' birth, where did the shepherds go when the angels had left them?

5. In 2 Kings 1 an angel appears to Elijah with a message for which king?

6. In Genesis, an angel likened Hagar's son to which animal?

7. What did the angel that Balaam saw have in his hand?

8. True or false? Paul says that a destroying angel killed some people for grumbling.

9. True or false? In Numbers the angel told Balaam to return home.

10. What happened to Jesus when Satan left him after tempting him in the wilderness?

11. The angel told Zechariah that his son would come in the power of which Old Testament prophet?

12. In John's Gospel, when a voice from heaven was heard, who thought it was an angel?

13. True or false? Cherubim are angels.

14. Who, did Paul say, were a spectacle to the whole universe, including angels?

15. Who, according to Psalm 8, was made a little lower than the angels?

Quiz #6

ANGELS AMONG US

1. In Genesis, which crying mother was found by an angel of the Lord in the desert of Beersheba?

2. Which apostle was rescued by an angel the night before he was due to stand trial?

3. According to the book of Jude, which angel argued with the devil concerning the body of Moses?

4. True or false? Two angels appeared to Jesus as he prayed on the Mount of Olives.

5. True or false? The Galatians welcomed Paul as if he were an angel.

6. In Numbers, when Balaam met with an angel, who was he on his way to see?

7. "For he will command his angels concerning you" comes from which Psalm?

8. In 1 Kings, what did an angel tell the exhausted Elijah to eat?

9. In Genesis, what did the angel of the Lord do when Pharaoh's army approached the fleeing Israelites?

10. In Genesis, Lot asked angels if he could flee to which city?

11. According to Revelation 16, how many angels held bowls containing God's wrath?

12. Who stopped Abraham from slaying his son Isaac?

13. True or false? An angel said that Ishmael would live in peace with his brothers.

14. According to Hebrews 1, what is the task of angels?

15. After his meeting with the angel in 1 Kings, how long did Elijah travel for?

---

14. To worship God's Son **15.** 40 days and 40 nights

10. Zoar **11.** Seven **12.** An angel calling from heaven **13.** False, he said he would live in hostility (Genesis 16:12)

5. True (Galatians 4:14) **6.** Balak **7.** Psalm 91 **8.** A cake of bread **9.** He moved behind the Israelites

1. Hagar **2.** Peter **3.** The archangel Michael **4.** False, only one angel appeared (Luke 22:43)

Answers

Quiz #7

ANGELS AMONG US

1. According to the prophet Hosea, who struggled with an angel and overcame him?

2. What was the name of the Roman centurion who saw an angel at Caesarea?

3. In Chronicles God sent an angel to destroy which city?

4. According to the book of Job, what did the angels do at the act of creation?

5. What attitude towards angels is condemned by Paul in Colossians chapter 1?

6. In Genesis chapter 24, Abraham told his servant that an angel would go before him. For what purpose?

7. In which of his temptations of Jesus does Satan mentions angels?

8. Who is the first person in the New Testament who sees an angel?

9. In Numbers, what did the angel say he would have done to Balaam if his donkey had not seen him?

10. In Matthew 1, what did an angel prevent Joseph from doing?

11. In Genesis, when Hagar fled from Sarah, an angel found her beside which geographical feature?

12. According to the apostle Paul who will judge the angels?

13. Why did an angel call out to Abraham in the region of Moriah?

14. Where was the angel standing when Balaam's donkey saw it the second time?

15. According to Matthew, when did an angel appear to Joseph for the last time?

Answers

1. Jacob 2. Cornelius 3. Jerusalem 4. Shout for joy 5. Angel worship 6. To find a wife for Isaac
7. The second temptation 8. Zecheriah 9. He would have killed him
10. Divorcing Mary 11. A spring
12. Christians 13. To stop him killing his son Isaac
14. Between two vineyards 15. After Herod's death

Quiz #8

ANGELS AMONG US

1. How did an angel of the Lord first appear to Moses?

2. How did an angel appear to Joseph telling him not to divorce Mary?

3. An angel appeared to Gideon under which type of tree in Ophrah?

4. In Acts, Cornelius was told by an angel to send messengers to which city?

5. In which chapter of Isaiah does the prophet see seraphim and receive his call?

6. In Revelation 15 the plagues are held by how many angels?

7. In the Parable of the Weeds in Matthew 13, who does Jesus say represents angels?

8. According to Revelation 15 what did the angels hold?

9. According to Matthew what phenomenon was caused by the angel at the tomb of Jesus?

10. Who thought she saw Peter's angel when the apostle arrived at Mary's house after his escape from prison?

11. In Judges, how does the angel address Gideon when he first appears?

12. What did Manoah the father of Samson sacrifice to the angel?

13. True or false? In Luke's Gospel, the angel which appeared to Zechariah was standing on the left-hand side of the altar of incense.

14. In Genesis 16 what did Hagar name the place where she met an angel?

15. According to the angel why should Joseph and his family flee to Egypt?

---

14. Beer Lahai Roi, Well of the Living One Who Sees Me 15. Herod was trying to kill Jesus

12. A goat 13. False. The angel was standing at the right hand side (Luke 1:11)

6. Seven 7. The harvesters 8. Plagues 9. An earthquake 10. Rhoda 11. Mighty Warrior

1. In a burning bush 2. In a dream 3. An oak tree 4. Joppa 5. Isaiah 6

Answers

Quiz #9

ANGELS AMONG US

1. In the book of Acts, Philip is told to go where by an angel?

2. The writer to the Hebrews describes someone who is far greater than angels. Who is this person?

3. In Genesis, what do angels inflict upon the men of Sodom?

4. What did David do that caused God to send an angel to destroy Israel?

5. How many times did an angel appear to Elijah after his ordeal with the prophets of Baal?

6. What happened to the meat and unleavened bread which the angel told Gideon to place on the altar?

7. True or false? According to Jesus in Matthew 22, angels do not marry.

8. What name did Abraham give to the place where an angel of the Lord stopped him from killing Isaac?

9. In Zechariah 5, what does the angel show the prophet?

10. What did Gabriel say about himself to Mary?

11. In which month of Elizabeth's pregnancy did God send the angel Gabriel to Mary?

12. In his speech in Acts what did Stephen say was put into effect by angels?

13. According to Matthew where did the angel tell Joseph to take Mary and Jesus?

14. Fill in the missing word: "If I speak in the tongues of ____ and of angels, but have not love..."

15. According to the angel, Zechariah's son would be filled with what from birth?

---

13. To Egypt **14.** Men **15.** The Holy Spirit

9. A measuring basket **10.** "I am Gabriel. I stand in the presence of god" **11.** The sixth month **12.** The Law

5. Twice **6.** It was consumed by fire **7.** True (Matthew 22:30) **8.** The Lord will provide

1. South, to the Jerusalem to Gaza road **2.** Jesus **3.** Blindness **4.** David took a census of the fighting men

Answers

376

Facts 1

ANGELS AMONG US

The Greek word *"angelos"* really means "messenger." It is translated in this way in the New Testament when it refers to a human being (e.g. Luke 7:24). However the word usually refers to a separately created order of heavenly beings.

"Cherubim" comes from the Hebrew *"kerub"* and probably means "fullness of knowledge" or "one who intercedes."

The name Gabriel means "hero of God" or "mighty one."

The idea that angels had wings evolved in the fourth century. Prior to that they were usually considered to be wingless.

Mark is the only gospel not to mention angels.

According to 2 Kings 19, the angel of the Lord killed 185,000 Assyrians.

Thanks to the intervention of the angels three people survived the destruction of Sodom: Lot and his two daughters.

There is nothing in the Bible to suggest that angels were ever human beings elevated to angelic status. Rather, angels are spiritual beings who were specially created by God (Hebrews 1:7).

In the time of Jesus the Sadducees did not believe in angels but the Pharisees did.

In both the Old and New Testaments the first accounts of visits from angels are to women – Hagar and Mary.

The idea of guardian angels describes God's watchful care over his people and this is mentioned occasionally in the Bible (Matthew 18:10; Hebrews 1:13-14). There are many examples of God's followers being helped by angels. Jesus himself was frequently helped by them.

Dreams, Visions and Prophecies

Quiz # 1

DREAMS, VISIONS AND PROPHECIES

1. According to Genesis, who did God promise to make the father of a great nation?

2. In the book of Revelation, which is the first Church that is given a prophetic message?

3. In Numbers, who did Balak ask to prophesy against the Israelites?

4. In which chapter of Deuteronomy does Moses predict the coming of another prophet?

5. According to Matthew, how did an angel first appear to Joseph?

6. In Isaiah 5 there is a song concerning what?

7. Which prophet was the son of Hilkiah?

8. In the Old Testament, which child received a prophesy concerning the sons of Eli the priest?

9. In his address on the day of Pentecost, Peter begins by quoting from which prophetic book?

10. What was the profession of Cornelius who was given a vision in Acts 10?

11. How many baskets did Pharaoh's baker see in a dream?

12. Which chapter of Ezekiel records the prophet's call?

13. In which chapter of Luke is Jesus met by a prophetess?

14. True or false? Elijah prophesied that there would be no rain in Israel for five years.

15. How many chapters are there in the book of the prophet Jeremiah?

Answers

1. Abram **2.** The Church at Ephesus **3.** Balaam **4.** Chapter 18 **5.** In a dream
6. A vineyard **7.** Jeremiah **8.** Samuel **9.** Joel **10.** Soldier **11.** 3 **12.** Chapter 12
13. Chapter 2 **14.** False, he prophesied there would be a drought for three and a half years (James 5:17)
15. 52

Quiz #2

DREAMS, VISIONS AND PROPHECIES

1. In Genesis, what does Joseph see in his first dream?

2. Who, according to Peter on the day of Pentecost, will prophesy?

3. According to Revelation, where was John when he received the heavenly vision?

4. In the New Testament, who imprisoned the prophet John the Baptist?

5. According to Ezekiel 14, how many days was the prophet to bear the sin of Israel?

6. True or false? Jesus considered the Old Testament character Abel a prophet.

7. Which Old Testament character, who excelled in interpreting dreams, refused to eat from the king's table?

8. According to Isaiah's prophecy, what name would the virgin give to the child?

9. What is the name of the angel seen in Daniel 8?

10. In the Old Testament, whilst he was in prison, what interpretation did Joseph give to the baker's dream?

11. In which chapter of his prophecy does Ezekiel talk of shepherds and sheep?

12. Which Old Testament prophet had a father called Beeri?

13. According to 1 Kings 14, who prophesies against King Ahab?

14. Who was told to draw a picture representing Jerusalem on a clay tablet?

15. How many chapters are there in the book of Zechariah?

Answers

1. Sheaves of corn **2.** Your sons and daughters **3.** On the island of Patmos **4.** Herod **5.** 390 days **6.** True (Luke 11:50,51) **7.** Daniel **8.** Immanuel **9.** Gabriel **10.** He would be killed and hung on a tree, where the birds would eat his flesh **11.** Chapter 34 **12.** Hosea **13.** Micaiah **14.** Ezekiel **15.** 12

Quiz #3
DREAMS, VISIONS AND PROPHECIES

1. According to 1 Samuel 2, a man of God gave a prophecy concerning whose wicked sons?

2. True or false? Matthew tells us that an angel warned the wise men not to return to Herod in a dream.

3. In chapter 10 of his book, Daniel is standing by a river when he has a vision. Which river is it?

4. In which chapter of Genesis does God first promise to make Abram the father of a great nation?

5. True or false? According to 1 Kings 14 the house of king Jeroboam was destined to be burnt as if it were dung.

6. What does Nebuchadnezzar dream about in Daniel 4?

7. How many chapters are there in the prophecy of Ezekiel?

8. In the book of Revelation which is the last Church to receive a prophetic message?

9. True or false? The prophet Amos sees a tree of ripe fruit in the eighth chapter of his prophesy.

10. In which chapter of Isaiah do we find the question, "Who has believed our message?"?

11. How many chapters are there in the Old Testament prophecy of Obadiah?

12. According to the Old Testament, what new name was given to Daniel?

13. In 1 Kings 14 Ahijah prophesies against which evil king of Judah?

14. Which two birds are seen in Ezekiel 17?

15. According to Joseph what was the correct interpretation of Pharaoh's dreams?

Answers

1. Eli's **2.** False, there is no mention of an angel in their dream (Matthew 2:12) **3.** The Tigris **4.** Genesis 12 **5.** True (1 Kings 14:10) **6.** A tree **7.** 48 **8.** The Church at Laodicea **9.** False, he sees a basket of ripe fruit (Amos 8:1) **10.** Chapter 53 **11.** 1 **12.** Belteshazzar **13.** Jeroboam **14.** 2 eagles **15.** 7 years of plenty would be followed by 7 years of famine

382

Quiz #4

DREAMS, VISIONS AND PROPHECIES

1. In Genesis, which officials of Pharaoh had dreams when they were in prison?

2. What is burnt in Jeremiah 36?

3. Who burnt the prophet's property in Jeremiah 36?

4. Which prophet saw visions in the "thirtieth year, in the fourth month on the fifth day"?

5. Who was the father of the prophet Joel?

6. In the Old Testament, Elijah defeated the prophets of which false god?

7. True or false? The book of Obadiah contains a prophecy for Midian.

8. When Jesus rode into Jerusalem on a donkey, whose words was he fulfilling?

9. Which prophetic book of the Old Testament begins with an invasion of locusts?

10. In Ezekiel 37 the prophet sees a valley of dry what?

11. In the vision of Revelation, which Church is described as being neither hot nor cold?

12. Which reluctant Old Testament prophet was the son of Amittai?

13. In the Old Testament what is the fate of the tree in Nebuchadnezzar's dream?

14. According to Luke, with what words did the prophet John the Baptist welcome those who came to him to be baptised?

15. In the Old Testament, Daniel has a vision of a man during the reign of which king?

Answers

1. Cup bearer and Baker 2. Jeremiah's scroll 3. Jehoiakim 4. Ezekiel
5. Pethuel 6. Baal 7. False, for Edom (Obadiah 1) 8. Zachariah's 9. Joel
10. Bones 11. The Church at Laodicea 12. Jonah 13. It is cut down
14. "You brood of vipers" 15. Cyrus

Quiz #5

DREAMS, VISIONS AND PROPHECIES

1. What "geographical feature" does John see in Revelation 22?

2. In the Old Testament when Joseph was questioned concerning Pharaoh's dreams he said only one person could interpret them. Who was that person?

3. In Acts 10, at whose house was the apostle Peter staying when he had a vision?

4. Who did Stephen see in a vision at his trial?

5. When the prophet Ezekiel lay on his left hand side, what did this action signify?

6. According to God's promise to Abram his descendants would be ill-treated in a strange country for how many years?

7. In which chapter of Isaiah does the prophet receive his commission?

8. True or false? In the book of Daniel when Nebuchadnezzar told his wise men his dream they were unable to interpret it.

9. Which Old Testament prophet had a wife called Gomer?

10. According to Numbers what did the donkey of Balaam the prophet see?

11. In Ezekiel 37 what is the prophet told to do to the dry bones?

12. True or false? The prophet Jonah boarded a ship bound for Joppa.

13. In which chapter of the book of Revelation does John see a vision of the scroll and the lamb?

14. Cushi was the father of which Old Testament prophet?

15. In the Old Testament Daniel has a vision of a man wearing a belt made of what material?

Answers

1. The river of life **2.** God **3.** Simon the Tanner **4.** Jesus **5.** The sin of the house of Israel **6.** 400 **7.** Chapter 6 **8.** False, the king refused to tell them what had happened in the dream (Daniel 2:5) **9.** Hosea **10.** An angel **11.** Prophesy to them **12.** False, it was bound for Tarshish (Jonah 1:3) **13.** Chapter 5 **14.** Zephaniah **15.** Gold

384

Quiz #6

DREAMS, VISIONS AND PROPHECIES

1. True or false? On his release from prison Pharaoh's cup bearer immediately informed his master of Joseph's ability to interpret dreams.

2. "For to us a child is born, to us a son is given." Who wrote these words?

3. Which Old Testament prophet was called with the words, "Before I formed you in the womb I knew you"?

4. In which chapter of Zechariah's prophecy does a flying scroll appear?

5. In Revelation 6, how many seals does John see in his vision?

6. According to Matthew, what were the wise men advised to do in a dream, after they had seen the baby Jesus?

7. Which prophetic book lies between Obadiah and Micah?

8. According to Jeremiah 31, the fathers have eaten which sour fruit?

9. Which prophetic book of the Old Testament promises the outpouring of the Spirit?

10. According to Daniel's interpretation of Nebuchadnezzar's dream of a tree, what would the king soon be eating?

11. How many Churches receive heavenly messages in the book or Revelation?

12. According to Acts 10, at what time of day did Peter receive his vision?

13. According to Hosea 1, what name did the prophet give to his first child?

14. What is the name of the prophetess who greets Mary and Joseph in Luke 2?

15. According to Daniel's prophecy at the end of his book what is the name of the great prince?

---

10. Grass 11. 7 12. About noon (Acts 10:9) 13. Jezreel 14. Anna 15. Michael
4. Chapter 5 5. 7 6. Not to return to Herod 7. Jonah 8. Grapes 9. Joel
1. False. He forgot about Joseph (Genesis 40:23) 2. Isaiah 3. Jeremiah

Answers

Quiz #7

DREAMS, VISIONS AND PROPHECIES

1. What, according to Pharaoh's dream in Genesis 41, scorched the seven thin ears of corn?

2. In his prophetic message John the Baptist said that God could make the children of Abraham from what?

3. Who was the father of the prophet Isaiah?

4. According to Revelation 22, what is heaven's light source?

5. In Genesis 40, what plant did the cup bearer see in his dream?

6. In the New Testament, who saw Nathaniel while he was sitting under a fig tree?

7. In the Old Testament, who took Daniel to Nebuchadnezzar so he could interpret the king's dream?

8. God told Abram his people would return to the Promised Land when the sin of which people reached full measure?

9. In the book of Revelation, which Church was told to open the door to Christ?

10. In Acts, when Philip met the Ethiopian eunuch, from which prophetic book was he reading?

11. Who was the father of the Old Testament prophet Zechariah?

12. In Revelation 6, what did John see when the first seal was opened?

13. What was the occupation of the prophet Amos?

14. According to Acts 10, what did Peter see being dropped down from heaven?

15. Which prophet received his commission in the year King Uzziah died?

Answers

1. The east wind 2. Stones 3. Amoz 4. God himself 5. A vine
6. Jesus 7. Arioch, the commander of the king's guard 8. The Amorites
9. The Church at Laodicea 10. Isaiah 53 11. Berekiah 12. A white horse 13. Shepherd
14. A large sheet 15. Isaiah

Quiz #8

DREAMS, VISIONS AND PROPHECIES

1. What is the last word recorded in John's vision of heaven in the book of Revelation?

2. What did the prophet purchase in Jeremiah 32?

3. What color did Jesus' clothes appear when he was transfigured?

4. In Genesis 28, what does Jacob name the place where he had a dream?

5. In Jeremiah 1 the prophet sees a branch of which tree?

6. Where was Saul traveling from when he had a vision?

7. True or false? In Daniel 7, Daniel has a dream of three ferocious beasts.

8. When in prison with Joseph, the cup bearer dreams about a vine with how many branches?

9. Which prophetic book of the Old Testament has the greatest number of chapters?

10. In Ezekiel's vision of dry bones what do the bones eventually become?

11. According to Isaiah 53, someone was "led like a lamb to the____"

12. To which king did Elijah prophesy there would be a drought?

13. By which river was Ezekiel when he saw visions of God?

14. God told Hosea to name his daughter Lo-Ruhamah. What does this name mean?

15. According to his vision received in Acts 10 a voice told Peter to do what?

Quiz #9

DREAMS, VISIONS AND PROPHECIES

1. In John's vision in Revelation 7 what do four angels hold back?

2. According to Daniel 2, what did Nebuchadnezzar see in his dream?

3. True or false? The Church at Thyatira is the third one to receive a message in the book of Revelation.

4. According to Peter on the day of Pentecost, who will see visions?

5. God asked Jonah to prophesy in which city?

6. Daniel had a dream of four beasts during the reign of which king?

7. According to Genesis, what was the first thing Pharaoh saw in his second dream?

8. Which is the last prophetic book of the Old Testament?

9. How many adulterous women are seen in Ezekiel 23?

10. God told Abram that his people would return to the Promised Land after how many generations?

11. In his confrontation with the prophets of Baal how many large jars did Elijah use?

12. What was the head of the statue in Nebuchadnezzar's dream made of?

13. According to the book of Numbers how many oracles did the prophet Balaam speak?

14. According to the book of Jonah how many people lived in Nineveh?

15. Where did the Old Testament prophet Amos live?

Answers

1. The four winds **2.** A statue **3.** False, it is the fourth one (Revelation 2:18)
4. Young men **5.** Nineveh **6.** Belshazzar **7.** 7 healthy ears of corn **8.** Malachi
9. 2 **10.** 4 **11.** 4 **12.** Gold **13.** 7 **14.** Over 120,000 **15.** Tekoa

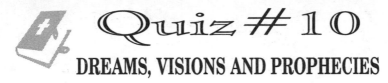

Quiz #10

DREAMS, VISIONS AND PROPHECIES

1. Fill in the missing word: "This is none other than the house of God; this is the ____ of heaven," exclaimed Jacob after his dream at Bethel.

2. Complete the exclamation of the prophet Isaiah, "I am a man of unclean ____"

3. In the Old Testament, which prophetic book lies between Daniel and Joel?

4. How many times did Peter hear a voice in his vision recorded in Acts 10?

5. In Ezekiel 38, which chief priest does the prophet speak against?

6. Which Old Testament prophet's ministry stopped in the 11th year of king Zedekiah?

7. In which chapter of Isaiah are the words, "Of the increase of his government and peace there will be no end" written?

8. According to Daniel's interpretation of Nebuchadnezzar's dream, which part of the statue was made of silver?

9. To which tribe did the prophetess Anna who met Mary and Joseph in the temple, belong?

10. In Ezekiel 4, why was the prophet told to lie on his right hand side?

11. Amos prophesied two years before what natural event?

12. From where did the Old Testament prophet Micah originate?

13. True or false? The Church at Sardis received the fifth prophetic message in Revelation.

14. Name the false prophet who opposed the prophet in Jeremiah 28.

15. What was the fate of this false prophet who opposed Jeremiah?

Answers

1. Gate 2. Lips 3. Hosea 4. 3 times 5. Gog 6. Jeremiah 7. Chapter 9
8. Its chest and arms 9. Asher 10. To signify bearing the sin of the house of Judah
11. An earthquake 12. Moresheth 13. True (Revelation 3:1) 14. Hananiah 15. Death

Quiz # 11

DREAMS, VISIONS AND PROPHECIES

1. According to Joseph, who would be killed by Pharaoh, the cup bearer or the baker?

2. Who had a show of strength with the prophets of Baal in 1 Kings?

3. In the Old Testament Isaiah records his vision during the reign of how many kings?

4. Which woman laughed when it was prophesied that she would have a son in her old age?

5. True or false? According to Revelation the temple in heaven is more glorious than the earthly temple.

6. What was the first beast seen in Daniel 7?

7. The first beast seen in Daniel 7 had wings of which bird?

8. Who was Ezekiel among when he first saw visions of God?

9. According to the prophetic book of Jonah, who declared a fast at the city of Nineveh?

10. In his dream at Bethel God tells Jacob that his descendants will be like what?

11. In his dream what does Pharaoh's cup bearer do?

12. Which name, meaning "Not my people," did God tell the prophet Hosea to give to his child?

13. According to Daniel 2, what were the belly and thighs of the statue in Nebuchadnezzar's dream made of?

14. According to Revelation 8 what does John hear when the seventh seal is opened?

15. In which chapter of his prophecy is Ezekiel asked to cook?

Quiz # 12
DREAMS, VISIONS AND PROPHECIES

1. According to his dream in Genesis 41, where was Pharaoh standing?

2. How many years of captivity does the prophet predict in Jeremiah 25?

3. In the Old Testament the prophet Micah declares judgement against which two places?

4. Jesus compared his death and resurrection to the experience of which Old Testament prophet?

5. Which Old Testament prophet was an Elkoshite?

6. In Acts 16 Paul and his companions had a vision of a man from where?

7. According to the prophetic words of John the Baptist in Luke's Gospel, where was the ax?

8. In Daniel 7, what was the second beast seen in the dream?

9. In Revelation the third message John receives is for which Church?

10. Which chapter of the prophet Isaiah talks of the virgin having a child?

11. True or false? The prophesy of Nahum pronounced judgement against Nineveh.

12. True or false? In Acts 2, Peter, quoting Joel, says that all men will dream dreams.

13. In Nebuchadnezzar's dream what were the statue's legs made of?

14. In 1 Kings 18 how many stones did the prophet Elijah use to build his altar?

15. In which chapter of Jeremiah does the prophet see a boiling pot?

Answers

1. By the River Nile **2.** 70 **3.** Samaria and Jerusalem **4.** Jonah **5.** Nahum
6. Macedonia **7.** At the root of the trees **8.** A bear **9.** The Church at Pergamum
10. Chapter 7 **11.** True (Nahum 2:1) **12.** False. He says old men will dream dreams (Acts 2:17)
13. Iron **14.** 12 **15.** Chapter 1

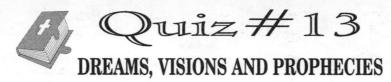

Quiz # 13

DREAMS, VISIONS AND PROPHECIES

1. According to 1 Kings 14, which prophet spoke against Jeroboam?

2. In Jacob's dream at Bethel, what was going up and down the ladder?

3. True or false? The statue in Nebuchadnezzar's dream had toes made of wood and clay.

4. According to Ezekiel 47 what flows from the temple?

5. In Daniel's dream concerning the four beasts what was the bear holding in his mouth?

6. According to Genesis, what was the first thing Pharaoh saw in his first dream?

7. What did the prophet John the Baptist say the man with two tunics was to do?

8. In Daniel's dream concerning the four beasts, how many ribs was the bear holding in its mouth?

9. According to Ezekiel, the word of the Lord came to him during the exile of which king?

10. True or false? Saul was still a long way away from Damascus when he had his vision of Jesus.

11. According to Joseph in Genesis 40, what did the three branches in the cup bearer's dream signify?

12. In John's vision, as recorded in Revelation 11, how many witnesses does he see?

13. What was the name of Bethel, before Jacob renamed it after his dream?

14. According to Jesus in Luke, which Old Testament prophet was killed between the altar and the sanctuary?

15. How many chapters are there in the prophecy of Hosea?

---

13. Luz **15.** 14

9. Jehoiachin **10.** False. He was nearly at the city (Acts 9:3) **11.** 3 days **12.** 2

4. A river **5.** Ribs **6.** 7 fat cows **7.** Share them with the person who had none **8.** 3

1. Ahijah **2.** Angels of God **3.** False, they were made of iron and clay (Daniel 2:33)

Answers

392

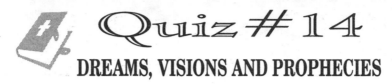

Quiz # 14

DREAMS, VISIONS AND PROPHECIES

1. In Genesis what does Jacob see in his dream while traveling to Haran?

2. True or false? Jeremiah has a vision of three baskets of figs.

3. In Genesis 41, how many animals does Pharaoh see in his first dream?

4. What personal tragedy strikes the prophet Ezekiel?

5. Which book comes immediately before the prophecy of Ezekiel?

6. According to Matthew, Joseph was told to take Mary and Jesus to which country in a dream?

7. How many chapters does the Old Testament prophecy of Haggai contain?

8. According to the book of Revelation, which church tolerated "that woman Jezebel"?

9. Which prophetic book contains the "Servant Songs"?

10. What did the seraph place on the lips of the prophet Isaiah?

11. In Genesis 28 Jacob has a dream while traveling to where?

12. Which Old Testament prophetic book contains the words, "But you, Bethlehem Ephrathah, though you are small among the clans of Judah..."?

13. What request did the man of Macedonia make to Paul when he appeared to him in a vision?

14. Who was the king of Israel when Amos received his prophecy?

15. According to 2 Kings 19 who prophesied the fall of Sennacherib?

Answers

1. A stairway or ladder from heaven to earth **2.** False. There are only 2 baskets of figs (Jeremiah 24:1) **3.** 14: seven fat cows and seven thin ones **4.** His wife dies **5.** Lamentations **6.** Egypt **7.** 2 **8.** The Church at Thyatira **9.** Isaiah **10.** A live coal **11.** Haran **12.** Micah **13.** "Come to Macedonia and help us" **14.** Jehoash **15.** Isaiah

Quiz # 15

DREAMS, VISIONS AND PROPHECIES

1. Fill in the missing word: "Only in his home town... is a prophet without ___"?

2. Where does Elijah flee to after his ordeal on Mount Carmel?

3. In the Old Testament, what were the seven fat cows doing in Pharaoh's first dream?

4. What is the third beast seen in Daniel 7?

5. According to Jeremiah 7 what will be the new name of the valley of Ben Hinnom?

6. In Daniel's vision concerning the four beasts how many wings does the leopard have?

7. In the Old Testament what did Jacob promise to give God after his dream at Bethel?

8. How many days was Ezekiel told to lie on his right hand side for the sin of Judah?

9. Whose prophecy is placed first in the Bible, that of Haggai or that of Zechariah?

10. Which Old Testament prophet was the son of Buzi?

11. How many shepherds are mentioned in Zechariah 11?

12. In which chapter of Revelation does John see a beast emerge from the sea?

13. Which prophetic book is placed immediately after Song of Songs?

14. After his vision on the road to Damascus for how long was Saul unable to see?

15. What strikes the statue in Nebuchadnezzar's dream in Daniel 2?

Quiz # 16
DREAMS, VISIONS AND PROPHECIES

1. In which chapter of his prophecy does Jeremiah speak of a Righteous branch?

2. Which two prophets does Mark quote at the beginning of his Gospel?

3. True or false? Jeremiah 31:1 reads: "Woe to those who go down to Egypt for help."

4. In the Old Testament which group of prophets cut themselves during a competition between rival gods?

5. How many chapters does the Old Testament prophecy of Micah have?

6. In the New Testament, how many of Joseph's dreams are recorded?

7. According to Revelation there were followers of the Nicolaitans in which Church?

8. Which Old Testament book lies between Habakkuk and Haggai?

9. According to Isaiah 61, the Spirit of God was on the prophet to preach good news to whom?

10. When Jacob had his famous dream in Genesis 28 he was traveling from which city?

11. In his vision in Acts 9, Ananias was told that Saul would appear before which three groups of people, for the sake of God?

12. The word of the Lord came to the prophet Haggai in which year of Darius' reign?

13. According to Peter in Acts 2 what will happen to the sun?

14. True or false? The prophet Haggai called for the house of the Lord to be built.

15. On the night of his famous dream what did Jacob use as a pillow?

Answers

1. Chapter 23 **2.** Isaiah and Malachi **3.** False, it appears in Isaiah 31:1
4. The prophets of Baal **5.** 7 **6.** 4 **7.** The Church at Pergamum **8.** Zephaniah **9.** The poor
10. Beersheba **11.** The Gentiles, their kings and the people of Israel **12.** The second
13. It will be turned to darkness **14.** True (Haggai 1:4) **15.** A stone

Quiz # 17

DREAMS, VISIONS AND PROPHECIES

1. In the Revelation of John, which Church receives the penultimate message?

2. In which chapter of Isaiah does the servant of the Lord first appear?

3. What bird descended on Jesus immediately after his baptism?

4. In chapter 31 of his book Ezekiel sees a cedar tree in which country?

5. According to 1 Corinthians 14 what is the purpose of a prophet?

6. In Genesis, Pharaoh's baker had a dream in which he saw baskets containing what?

7. Jeremiah puts on a belt made of which material?

8. True or false? God comforted Elijah by telling him there were 2,000 prophets in Israel still loyal to him.

9. According to Acts 10, where was Peter when he had his vision?

10. According to Ezekiel, what rested in the cedars of Lebanon?

11. According to Genesis, which animals came out of the Nile after the fat cows?

12. Ezekiel the prophet was bound up with ropes. What did this represent?

13. In the New Testament, which inhabitant of Damascus was told in a vision to go and visit Saul?

14. Before the apostles select a replacement for Judas, Peter quotes two prophecies from which Old Testament book?

15. In Revelation 16, John sees a vision of seven bowls. What do they contain?

---

13. Ananias **14.** Psalms **15.** God's wrath

9. Joppa **10.** All the birds of the air **11.** 7 thin cows **12.** The siege of Jerusalem

5. To edify the Church **6.** Bread **7.** Linen **8.** False, he said there were more than 7,000 (1 Kings 19:18)

1. The church at Philadelphia **2.** Chapter 42 **3.** A dove **4.** Lebanon

Answers

Quiz # 18

DREAMS, VISIONS AND PROPHECIES

1. Isaiah makes a poultice of what?

2. Why does Isaiah make this poultice?

3. Which king asked Jeremiah to enquire of the Lord about Nebuchadnezzar attacking Jerusalem?

4. According to Revelation 16 who gathers together at Armageddon?

5. Which builder's item is seen by Amos?

6. In Ezekiel's prophecy, what does the cedar in Lebanon represent?

7. In Joseph's second dream what bows down to him?

8. In the Old Testament, whose prophecy comes after the book of Zechariah?

9. John the Baptist prophesied that Jesus would baptize with the Holy Spirit and with what?

10. In Acts, Ananias was told in a vision to go to whose house?

11. In Daniel how many horns does the fourth beast of Daniel's dream have?

12. Who ordered the execution of the prophet John the Baptist?

13. Which Roman centurion had a vision in Acts 10?

14. What was the significance of placing the live coal on Isaiah's lips?

15. According to Daniel 2, what does the rock in Nebuchadnezzar's dream become?

Quiz # 19

DREAMS, VISIONS AND PROPHECIES

1. What name did Pharaoh give to Joseph after he had interpreted his dreams?

2. According to Mark, which Old Testament prophets did Andrew see at Jesus' transfiguration?

3. In which chapter of his book does Ezekiel prophesy against the mountains of Israel?

4. In which chapter of the book of Daniel does "one like a son of man" appear?

5. The words "Prepare the way for the Lord, make straight paths for him," were fulfilled by the ministry of whom?

6. In what chapter of his prophecy does Ezekiel speak of a watchman?

7. In which Old Testament book does it say, "The Lord your God will raise up for you a prophet like me from among your own brothers"?

8. Where is Jeremiah told to go in chapter 18 of his prophecy?

9. In which chapter of Revelation does John record a vision of the fall of Babylon?

10. Daniel has a vision in which he is in which citadel?

11. Which king was on the throne in Judah when Amos began prophesying?

12. True or false? In Acts, Ananias had a vision telling him to go the house of Judas who lived in Narrow Street.

13. True or false? According to 2 Corinthians 12 Paul knew of a man who was caught up to the seventh heaven.

14. In Daniel 8 there is a vision of a ram with how many horns?

15. In the New Testament, where was the Roman centurion Cornelius when he had his vision?

Answers

1. Zaphenath-Paneah **2.** None. Andrew was not present **3.** Chapter 6
4. Chapter 7 (7:14) **5.** John the Baptist **6.** Chapter 33 **7.** Deuteronomy **8.** The potter's house
9. Chapter 18 **10.** Citadel of Susa **11.** Uzziah **12.** False. It was in Straight Street (Acts 9:11)
13. False. He was caught up to the third heaven (2 Corinthians 12:2) **14.** 2 **15.** Caesarea

398

Quiz #20

DREAMS, VISIONS AND PROPHECIES

1. The words "Comfort, comfort my people," appear in which chapter of Isaiah?

2. According to Jeremiah 20, which priest ordered the prophet to be beaten?

3. According to Genesis, why were the cup bearer and the baker in prison with Joseph?

4. What was the one-horned animal in Daniel's vision in chapter 8 of his book called?

5. In Acts, to whom did Philip explain the meaning of a passage in Isaiah's prophecy?

6. To what position did Nebuchadnezzar exalt Daniel after he had interpreted his dream of the statue?

7. In the book of Revelation, which is the second Church to receive a message?

8. In the Old Testament, how many prophets did Elijah defeat on Mount Moriah?

9. Ezekiel 34 contains prophecy against which group of people?

10. In his Pentecost speech, what does Peter say the moon will turn into?

11. According to Ezekiel 15, Jerusalem is a useless what?

12. Which Old Testament prophet was the son of Amoz?

13. According to his vision in Acts, Ananias was to go to a house and ask for whom?

14. Which New Testament book contains prophecy concerning the man of lawlessness?

15. How many chapters are there in the prophecy of Isaiah?

Answers

1. Chapter 40 2. Pashhur 3. They had offended Pharaoh 4. Goat
5. Ethiopian eunuch 6. Ruler of the province of Babylonia 7. The Church at Smyrna
8. None, they were defeated on Mount Carmel 9. Shepherds of Israel 10. Blood 11. Vine
12. Isaiah 13. A man from Tarsus 14. 2 Thessalonians 15. 66

Quiz #21

DREAMS, VISIONS AND PROPHECIES

1. Which North American city has the same name as one of the Churches mentioned in the book of Revelation?

2. In 1 Kings 22 Micaiah prophesies against which wicked king of Israel?

3. Which Old Testament prophet records the words, "Be ever hearing, but never understanding"?

4. In the Old Testament, how many false prophets of Baal did Elijah defeat on Mount Carmel?

5. Which New Testament book contains prophetic messages for seven Churches?

6. Where did Jesus prophesy he would go after his resurrection?

7. In what chapter of Genesis does Joseph first tell his family of his dreams?

8. True or false? In Acts Saul had a vision telling him that Ananias was going to come to him.

9. According to Peter, speaking on the day of Pentecost, what gift was prophesied by Joel?

10. Anna, the prophetess who greeted baby Jesus in the temple, was the daughter of whom?

11. In addition to being a prophet, what else did Jeremiah do?

12. Isaiah prophesied the downfall of which Assyrian king?

13. According to John the Baptist's prophetic words, what did Jesus hold in his hand?

14. In chapter 20 of Revelation, John has a vision about which city?

15. Who is the first person to make a prophecy in Luke's Gospel?

Answers

1. Philadelphia **2.** Ahab **3.** Isaiah **4.** 450 **5.** Revelation **6.** Galilee
7. Chapter 37 **8.** True **9.** The Holy Spirit **10.** Phanuel **11.** He was a priest
12. Sennacherib **13.** A winnowing fork **14.** The new Jerusalem **15.** Zechariah

Facts 1

DREAMS, VISIONS AND PROPHECIES

Genesis 3:15 is the first verse in the Bible which is sometimes understood as a prophecy about Jesus' life.

Abraham is the first person in the Bible to be called a prophet (Genesis 20:7).

The wife of Isaiah was called the prophetess, probably by association with her husband (Isaiah 8:3).

The ministry of the prophet Jeremiah spanned the reigns of five kings: Josiah, Jehoahaz, Jehoiakim, Jehoiachin and Zedekiah.

The name of Micah the prophet means "Who is like Yahweh?"

The transfiguration of Jesus is mentioned only in the synoptic Gospels (Matthew, Mark and Luke).

Isaiah, Jeremiah, Ezekiel and Daniel are called the Major Prophets.

In his gospel Matthew mentions 22 times that Old Testament prophecies have been fulfilled.

The first two kings of Israel, Saul and David, were both prophets. The combination of the roles of king and prophet did not continue beyond them.

The name of the prophet Zephaniah means "Yahweh has hidden."

Isaiah is sometimes called the evangelical prophet because the word *"euangelizomai"* meaning "to proclaim good news", appears in Greek translations of Isaiah 40:9.

Facts 2

DREAMS, VISIONS AND PROPHECIES

Moses was considered the archetypal prophet with whom Jesus himself would be compared (Deuteronomy 18:15-19).

Daniel, Ezekiel, Obadiah and Nahum all prophesied during the period of exile in Babylon.

The first dream recorded in the Bible is that of Abimelech which warned him that Sarah and Abraham were really husband and wife (Genesis 20:3).

Joseph's brothers nicknamed him "dreamer" because of the dreams he had which implied he would become their superior (Genesis 37:19).

God spoke to Joseph, the father of Jesus, four times through dreams.

Philip's four unnamed daughters were all prophetesses (Acts 21:9).

Matthew's Gospel refers to the Old Testament prophet Jeremiah on three occasions (Matthew 2:17; 6:14; 27:9).

The name of the prophet Ezekiel appears only twice in the Bible (Ezekiel 1:3; Ezekiel 24:24).

The god against which the prophet Elijah fought and spoke was Baal-melqart, the protective god of Tyre.

Only two passages from the book of Amos are quoted directly in the New Testament. Amos 5:25-27 is quoted in Acts 7:42-43, and Amos 9:11-12 is quoted in Acts 15:16-17.

The prophecy of Obadiah is the shortest book in the Old Testament having only 21 verses.

Facts 3

DREAMS, VISIONS AND PROPHECIES

In Judges 7 a Midianite soldier interprets the dream of his friend and fellow soldier. It is the only one occasion in the Bible where the correct interpretation of a dream is given by a non-Israelite.

The only dream given to a woman in the New Testament is the dream of Pilate's wife (Matthew 27:19).

According to Jewish tradition the prophet Isaiah was sawn in two during the reign of king Manasseh.

The oldest surviving complete copy of Isaiah was found in Cave 1 at Qumran near the Dead Sea.

In the 1st Century A.D. there were attempts to ban the book of Ezekiel from public use partly because of the unsavory contents of chapter 16.

Daniel 2:4-7:28 is written in Aramaic, but the rest of the book is written in Hebrew.

Joshua, Judges, 1 and 2 Samuel and 1 and 2 Kings are sometimes known as the Former Prophets.

Although the prophet Amos lived in the kingdom of Judah he preached to the northern kingdom of Israel.

The first instance of Jesus reading a passage of the Old Testament is recorded in Luke 4:17 where he is reading from Isaiah 61:12.

The Greek word "*apokalypto*" from which the English word "apocalyptic" is derived, means "unfolding" or "revealing."

Facts 4

DREAMS, VISIONS AND PROPHECIES

God is called "The Holy One of Israel" more than 25 times in the book of Isaiah.

The Israelites were warned to beware of false prophetesses as well as false prophets (Ezekiel 13:17).

The name "Daniel" means "God is my judge."

The Hebrew word *"ro'eh"*, is translated as "seer" and is derived from the root of the verb "to see".

Two dreams in the Old Testament concern bread: that of Pharaoh's baker, and that of a Midianite soldier (Genesis 40 and Judges 7). They both had unfavorable interpretations.

In the Old Testament both Joseph and Daniel acknowledged that their ability to interpret dreams was a God given one (Genesis 40:8; Daniel 2:28).

The first vision mentioned in the Bible came to Abram (Genesis 15:1).

The last twelve prophetic books of the Old Testament are known as the Minor Prophets, not because their message was unimportant, but because of the brevity of their prophecies.

According to Numbers, Moses was different from other prophets because the Lord did not speak to him in dreams, but face to face (Numbers 12:8).

In the Old Testament, Joseph is credited with interpreting four dreams, that of the cup bearer, one of the baker and two of Pharaoh.

With some notable exceptions (e.g. Jacob, Solomon and Joseph, the foster-father of Jesus), the majority of those who received God-inspired dreams in the Bible do not belong to God's chosen people.

Dr. Luke is the only Gospel writer who specifically uses the word "vision". He uses it twice, in Luke 1:22 and 24:23.

Facts 5

DREAMS, VISIONS AND PROPHECIES

Obadiah means "servant of Yahweh" or "worshipper of Yahweh".

In addition to "foretelling" the future, the role of the Old Testament prophet was to "forth-tell" the word of God as it applied to the immediate situation.

The name of the prophet Elisha means "God is salvation."

According to Jewish tradition the prophet Isaiah was of royal blood.

Jesus identified John the Baptist as the Old Testament Elijah who was to come (Matthew 11:14).

The books of Isaiah, Obadiah, Micah and Nahum all begin with the assertion that the writer had a vision.

In the New Testament Luke shows great interest in visions. He records the visions of Zechariah (Luke 1:22), Ananias (Acts 9:10), Cornelius (Acts 10:3), Peter (Acts 10:10) and Paul (Acts 18:9).

Jeremiah is directly quoted forty times in the New Testament, half of these quotations coming in the book of Revelation.

The name of Jonah the prophet means "dove".

Jacob is the first of God's chosen people in the Bible who has a dream (Genesis 28).

Miriam, the sister of Moses, was called a prophetess (Exodus 15:20).

Facts 6

DREAMS, VISIONS AND PROPHECIES

Samuel is sometimes called the "last of the judges and the first of the prophets of Israel."

The last mention of prophets in the Bible occurs in the final chapter of Revelation (Revelation 22:9).

The name of the prophet Elijah means "Yah is El" or "Yahweh is God."

The apostle Paul had many visions and revelations which he did not speak about in detail.

Ten times in his Gospel Matthew uses the formula, "This was to fulfil what was spoken by the prophet, saying..."

According to the writer of Ecclesiastes the person who spends too much time dreaming is as bad as the person who talks too much (Ecclesiastes 5:7).

The book of Daniel and the book of Revelation are examples of apocalyptic literature, in which vivid symbolism and imagery abound.

The name Isaiah means "Yahweh is salvation."

Only four women are called prophetess in the Old Testament: Miriam (Exodus 15:20); Deborah (Judges 4:4); Huldah (2 Kings 22:14); and Noadiah (Nehemiah 6:14).

Only one person is identified by name in the New Testament as being a prophetess: Anna (Luke 2:36). However, Philip had four daughters who prophesied (Acts 21:8-9).

In Ezekiel's famous vision of the valley of dry bones, Ezekiel 37, the dry bones symbolize Israel's apparently hopeless condition in exile.

Earth, Wind and Fire

Quiz # 1

EARTH, WIND AND FIRE

1. According to Genesis, what did God create on the first day?

2. In 1 Kings 17, who did the prophet Elijah inform that there would be no rain for three years?

3. In the Sermon on the Mount, who did Jesus say rain fell upon?

4. True or false? According to Exodus, the quail appeared each morning.

5. In Acts, at which city did Paul draw attention to God's kindness in sending rain?

6. Ezekiel prophesies an earthquake when Israel is attacked by whom?

7. What was the first plague with which Moses struck Egypt?

8. According to Zechariah 14:17, why will God withhold rain?

9. What did God send to make the waters recede after the flood?

10. According to Psalm 1, what does the wind blow away?

11. In the first chapter of Ecclesiastes the writer says that generations come and go, but something endures for ever. What is it?

12. What, according to the vision in Daniel 2, was swept away by the wind?

13. Jesus says that a cloud rising in the west means what is coming?

14. In which Old Testament prophetic book do we find the words, "Your love is like the morning mist, like the early dew that disappears"?

15. How many times did God call Moses' name from the burning bush?

Answers

1. Light 2. Ahab 3. The righteous and the unrighteous 4. False. They appeared in the evening (Exodus 16:13) 5. Lystra 6. Gog 7. The Nile turning to blood 8. If people fail to go to Jerusalem to worship 9. A wind 10. Chaff 11. The earth 12. Fragments of the statue 13. Rain 14. Hosea 15. Twice

Quiz #2

EARTH, WIND AND FIRE

1. In which chapter of the Gospel of John does Jesus say that the wind blows where it pleases?

2. On which day was the sky created?

3. When Moses saw the burning bush what was he forbidden to do?

4. According to Song of Songs, what burns like blazing fire?

5. What, according to Jesus, is clothed one day and thrown into the fire the next?

6. Which New Testament book refers to Elijah praying that it would not rain?

7. According to Revelation 9, what proportion of mankind is killed by plagues of fire, smoke and sulfur?

8. According to Exodus, what did the Israelites see each morning in the desert?

9. What did the Israelites set up to mark the place where they had crossed the river Jordan?

10. When the Lord descended to Mount Sinai, what was it covered with?

11. Fill in the missing word: "They sow the wind and reap the ___"

12. According to Amos 5, what should "roll on like a river"?

13. True or false? The top of mount Sinai was not visible from the plain below.

14. According to Exodus, what was the second plague suffered by the Egyptians?

15. According to Joshua 10 the moon stood still over which valley?

Answers

1. Chapter 3 **2.** Day 2 **3.** Come any closer **4.** Love **5.** Grass **6.** James **7.** One third **8.** A layer of dew **9.** 12 stones **10.** Smoke **11.** Whirlwind **12.** Justice **13.** False. It was visible (Exodus 19:16) **14.** Frogs **15.** Aijalon

Quiz #3

EARTH, WIND AND FIRE

1. In the Old Testament, on which day were the Israelites forbidden to light fires?

2. In Judges, who fastened torches to foxes' tails?

3. As recorded in Genesis what did God create on the third day?

4. According to the book of Esther, why was King Xerxes angry with Vashti?

5. According to Jesus, what is more important than burnt offerings and sacrifices?

6. How many times did Elijah call down fire on messengers sent by king Ahaziah?

7. According to the Old Testament, what was the name of the ravine where Elijah was miraculously fed by ravens?

8. In Acts, who went to the river outside Philippi expecting to find a place of prayer?

9. According to Genesis 41, what was scorched by an east wind?

10. As recorded in 1 Samuel 5 which towns were afflicted with plagues of tumors?

11. In Revelation 15 John sees fire mixed in a sea made of what material?

12. In which prophetic book does God send rain on one town but not on another?

13. Which Old Testament character had to choose a punishment from three years famine, three months of military defeats or three days of plague?

14. Which form of punishment listed in the previous question was choosen?

15. The greatest earthquake known to man is prophesied in which chapter of Revelation?

Answers

1. The Sabbath 2. Samson 3. Dry land, the sea and vegetation
4. She refused to go to him 5. Loving God and one's neighbor 6. Twice 7. Kerith
8. Paul and his companions 9. Ears of corn in Pharaoh's dream 10. Ekron and Ashdod 11. Glass
12. Amos 13. David 14. 3 days of plague 15. Chapter 16

Quiz #4
EARTH, WIND AND FIRE

1. According to Hosea 12, who feeds on the wind?

2. In Joshua 8 a covenant of renewal takes place upon which mountain?

3. During Paul's sea journey mentioned in Acts 27 what was not seen for many days?

4. What did God create on the fourth day?

5. In Revelation 8 a star is given a name. What is it?

6. Which chapter of Isaiah's prophecy makes ironic comparisons between an idol and firewood?

7. According to Jesus in Luke 17, sulfur and fire rained down upon which city?

8. What did the voice from the burning bush command Moses to do?

9. Which Old Testament commander was lured to the Kishon river in Judges?

10. Jesus, speaking in Matthew 7, says that something is thrown on the fire. What is it?

11. According to Exodus, what happened to the manna when the sun grew hot?

12. In the book of Numbers, who made an offering of unauthorized fire?

13. In John's account of Jesus walking on water, where does he say the disciples were heading in their boat?

14. According to Judges 19 whose companions threatened to burn his house if he did not explain a riddle to them?

15. Which Old Testament prophetic book begins with what the prophet saw two years before an earthquake?

Answers

1. Ephraim **2.** Ebal **3.** The sun and the stars **4.** The sun, moon and stars **5.** Wormwood
6. Chapter 44 **7.** Sodom **8.** Remove his sandals **9.** Sisera **10.** A tree bearing bad fruit
11. It melted away **12.** Nadab and Abihu **13.** Capernaum **14.** Samson's **15.** Amos

Quiz #5

EARTH, WIND AND FIRE

1. According to Exodus the Israelites could collect double the usual amount of manna on which day?

2. What was the origin of the wind on the day of Pentecost?

3. By what name is the lake of fire of Revelation 20 also known?

4. Which king did David defeat when he restored his control along the Euphrates?

5. True or false? On the fifth day God created all creatures.

6. In Genesis, which flaming object guarded the way to the tree of life?

7. Which was the only northern city Joshua burnt to the ground?

8. In the book of Hosea who says, "I will be like the dew to Israel"?

9. In Genesis 19 who sees smoke rising from the destroyed cities of Sodom and Gomorrah?

10. According to Exodus 10 what was brought to Egypt by an east wind?

11. As specified in Numbers 28, how many lambs were to be prepared as burnt offerings each day?

12. In the New Testament why couldn't Jesus' disciples heal the boy who kept on falling into fire and water?

13. What, according to Jeremiah 10, does God send with rain?

14. Which king of Judah burnt incense at the altar when he should not have done so?

15. True or false? According to Passover regulations the meat was to be boiled and eaten.

---

10. Locusts 11. 2 12. They lacked faith 13. Lightning 14. Uzziah 15. False. It was to be roasted (Exodus 12:9)

5. False, he created only the fish and the birds 6. A sword 7. Hazor 8. God 9. Abraham

1. Sixth day 2. Heaven 3. The second death 4. Hadadezer

Answers

Quiz #6

EARTH, WIND AND FIRE

1. On which island did the apostle Paul and his companions receive a warm welcome because of the rain?

2. According to Acts, who did Paul meet by the river outside Philippi?

3. In the words of Psalm 11 a scorching wind will be whose lot?

4. King Saul and his sons died on which mountain?

5. How many times a day was Elijah fed by ravens?

6. Whose armies were defeated by hailstones according to the book of Joshua?

7. Which Old Testament king threw Jeremiah's scrolls onto a fire?

8. Zechariah 14 records an earthquake that took place during the reign of which king?

9. In the Old Testament how many of Korah's rebellious followers were devoured by fire?

10. Which disciple warmed himself by a fire after Jesus' arrest?

11. What did God create on the sixth day?

12. According to Exodus 16 for how long did the Israelites eat manna?

13. In the Old Testament, what guided the Israelites by day during the Exodus?

14. What insect plagued the Egyptians after the mosquitoes had gone?

15. In the book of Jonah how did the sailors calm the fierce storm?

Answers

1. Malta 2. Lydia 3. The wicked 4. Gilboa 5. Twice 6. The armies of the Amorite kings
7. Jehoiakim 8. Uzziah 9. 250 10. Peter 11. Land animals and man 12. 40 years
13. A pillar of cloud 14. Flies 15. They threw Jonah overboard

Quiz #7

EARTH, WIND AND FIRE

1. According to Exodus the locusts that plagued Egypt were carried away by the wind. Where did it take them?

2. A fiery furnace is mentioned in which chapter of the book of Daniel?

3. Who burnt their possessions in Acts 19?

4. Which chapter of 2 Kings records Elijah being transported to heaven in a fiery chariot?

5. What precisely did the repentant sorcerers at Ephesus burn?

6. According to Genesis, what material did God use to create man?

7. In the Old Testament, how old did the lambs that were sacrificed daily have to be?

8. What does the Hebrew word "manna" mean?

9. According to Job 41 smoke pours from the nostrils of which animal?

10. What guided the Israelites by night during their Exodus from Egypt?

11. According to Numbers at what time of day were the daily lamb offerings to be burnt?

12. In Revelation 9 four angels are bound by which river?

13. According to Exodus 24, for how many days did a cloud cover Sinai?

14. Why did the sailors choose to leave Crete against the advice of the apostle Paul?

15. According to Judges the men of Ephraim wanted to burn whose house?

Answers

1. To the Red Sea 2. Chapter 2 3. Sorcerers 4. Chapter 2 5. Scrolls
6. Dust 7. 1 year old 8. What is it? 9. Leviathan 10. A pillar of fire
11. Morning and twilight 12. Euphrates 13. 6 days
14. Because of a favorable south wind 15. Jephthah's

Quiz #8

EARTH, WIND AND FIRE

1. Which Old Testament prophet made an ax head float on water?

2. What enveloped Jesus and his disciples on the mount of transfiguration?

3. According to Proverbs, "As a north wind brings rain so a sly tongue brings" what?

4. True or false? When the prophet Jonah admitted the storm was his fault the sailors threw him overboard immediately.

5. In Acts, what was the value of the scrolls burnt at Ephesus?

6. On which mountain did Elijah do battle with the priests of Baal?

7. Where was the garden God made for Adam?

8. According to the book of Joshua, who was stoned and then burnt for taking booty from Jericho?

9. In Daniel, who were thrown into a fiery furnace?

10. According to Numbers what animals were to be burnt for the monthly offerings?

11. How many times did Elisha tell Naaman to wash in the Jordan?

12. What names did Moses give to the place where he obtained water from a rock?

13. Which two disciples of Jesus wished to call down fire from heaven on a village?

14. According to Leviticus, when the priests removed the ashes of the burnt offerings they were to wear undergarments made of which material?

15. Jesus, speaking in Matthew 24, says that earthquakes will be accompanied by what?

Answers

1. Elisha 2. A cloud 3. Angry words 4. False. They tried to row to land (Jonah 1:13)
5. 50,000 drachmas 6. Carmel 7. Eden 8. Achan 9. Shadrach, Meshach and Abednego
10. 2 young bulls, 1 ram and 7 male lambs 11. 7 12. Massah and Meribah
13. James and John 14. Linen 15. Famines

415

Quiz #9

EARTH, WIND AND FIRE

1. Moses gave the name "Massah" to the place where he obtained water from the rock. Why?

2. In Acts 27, Paul and his companions were propelled by a storm to the lee of which small island?

3. In Revelation 12, what swallows the river spewed out by the dragon?

4. In the Old Testament, which animals were to provide the burnt offering at the Passover?

5. The writer of which book continually laments that life is like chasing after the wind?

6. According to Luke 16, who told Abraham that he was in agony in the fire?

7. What, according to the Psalmist, vanishes like smoke?

8. In which direction could the Garden of Eden be found?

9. In the book of Joshua who looked back to see their city on fire?

10. In the Old Testament what was the sixth plague brought upon the Egyptians by God?

11. Whose hearts burned within them when Jesus opened the scriptures to them?

12. Which king ordered three Israelites to be thrown into a fiery furnace when they disobeyed his command?

13. Which king of Judah was punished with leprosy for burning incense in the temple?

14. In the book of Job, who asks, "Who fathers the drops of dew?"?

15. How many people were on the mount of transfiguration altogether?

Answers

1. It means "testing", because the Israelites tested the Lord **2.** Cauda **3.** The earth **4.** 2 young bulls, 1 ram and 7 male lambs **5.** Ecclesiastes **6.** The rich man **7.** The Psalmist's days **8.** East **9.** The men of Ai **10.** Boils **11.** Cleopas and his friend **12.** Nebuchadnezzar **13.** Uzziah **14.** The Lord **15.** 6

Quiz # 10

EARTH, WIND AND FIRE

1. According to Psalm 18 who "soared on the wings of the wind"?

2. The prophet Amos denounces the "cows of Bashan" who live on which mountain?

3. According to Micah, what will be like "dew from the Lord, like showers on the grass"?

4. The apostle Paul says that it is better to do what than to burn with passion?

5. According to Jesus, in Mark 13, earthquakes are the beginnings of what?

6. In Numbers, one animal was to be added to the burnt offerings at Passover as an atonement for sin. Which animal was it?

7. In Isaiah 11 God promises to break the Euphrates into how many streams?

8. Complete the proverb. "As ____ to the teeth and smoke to the eyes, so is a sluggard to those who send him."

9. According to the account in Genesis, how did God bring Adam to life?

10. Which Old Testament prophet was protected by hills full of horses and chariots of fire?

11. According to Leviticus 6 when was the priest to add firewood to the altar of burnt offerings?

12. In Matthew 28 what causes the violent earthquake?

13. In the Old Testament, how many additional animals were to be sacrificed at the Feast of Weeks?

14. Who saw Peter in the firelight and accused him of being a follower of Jesus?

15. According to Job 24, who are drenched by the mountain rains?

---

13. 2 young bulls, 1 ram, 7 male lambs plus 1 goat for sin 14. A servant girl 15. The poor
9. He breathed into his nostrils 10. Elisha 11. Every morning 12. An angel
5. Birth pains or suffering (before the coming of the Messiah) 6. Goat 7. 7 8. Vinegar
1. God 2. Samaria 3. The remnant of Jacob 4. Marry

Answers

Quiz #11

EARTH, WIND AND FIRE

1. Complete the proverb: "Like clouds and wind without rain is a man who boasts of ___ ___ ___ ___ ___."

2. What was the nationality of the man told to wash in the Jordan by Elisha the prophet?

3. In Jeremiah 2 what animal sniffs the wind of the desert?

4. According to Genesis 38, who did Judah wish to burn?

5. According to Amos 5, what should be "like a never failing stream"?

6. In Luke's Gospel, chapter 21, Jesus says that earthquakes and famines will be accompanied by what?

7. On the Day of Atonement, how many bulls were to be presented as a burnt offering?

8. According to Acts 27 the sailors accompanying Paul feared they would run aground on which group of sand-bars?

9. According to John 15 what is thrown in the fire?

10. Which four rivers are named in the account of creation?

11. According to Acts, what prevented the disciples from seeing Jesus ascend into heaven?

12. In Daniel, the king ordered the fiery furnace to be how many times hotter than normal?

13. According to Zechariah which mountain will split in two?

14. Fill in the missing words: Jesus questioned the crowd asking, "What did you go out into the desert to see? A ___ swayed by the ___?"

15. According to Revelation 22, what stands either side of the river of the water of life?

Quiz # 12

EARTH, WIND AND FIRE

1. For how many nights were Paul and his companions caught in the storm of Acts 27?

2. According to Genesis, what geographical feature is found in the valley of Siddim?

3. According to James, what virtue helps a farmer wait for the autumn and spring rains?

4. In Exodus 32, what made Moses burn with anger when he approached the Israelite camp?

5. After his resurrection Jesus prepared a fire for which meal?

6. True or false? The seventh plague consisted of locusts.

7. In the Old Testament how many bulls were to be presented as a burnt offering on the first day of the Feast of Tabernacles?

8. Which Psalm contains the line "He hurls down hail like pebbles. Who can withstand his icy blast?"?

9. In 1 Kings 18 how many times did Elijah go and tell his servant to go and look towards the sea?

10. Which ingredient did Jesus use to heal a blind man according to John 9?

11. Which raw material did God use to create woman?

12. According to Leviticus 1, which two birds could be presented as a burnt offering?

13. What did the disciples see on the Day of Pentecost?

14. According to 2 Kings 25 which invader set fire to Jerusalem?

15. In Acts 16 a violent earthquake caused the prison doors to do what?

Answers

1. 14 **2.** The Salt Sea **3.** Patience **4.** The golden calf **5.** Breakfast
6. False. It was a hailstorm (Exodus 9:18) **7.** 13 **8.** Psalm 147:17) **9.** 7 times
10. Mud **11.** Adam's rib **12.** Dove or pigeon **13.** Tongues of fire **14.** Nebuchadnezzar **15.** To fly open

Quiz # 13
EARTH, WIND AND FIRE

1. What did Jesus' disciples think they saw during the storm recorded in Matthew 14?

2. When God promised Abraham land in Genesis 15 which two rivers were included in the boundaries?

3. In which two rivers would Naaman have preferred to wash?

4. In the book of Job who asks, "Does the rain have a father?"?

5. By which sea was Jesus walking when he called Peter and Andrew?

6. In Leviticus 4 which animal was to be burnt as an offering for a priest's sin?

7. According to Jeremiah 22, who will be driven away by the wind?

8. Which creature that plagued Egypt suddenly died?

9. How many years after the flood did Noah live?

10. Where was the tower which was set on fire by Abimelech?

11. Roughly, how many people were killed by the fire started by Abimelech?

12. According to Genesis 2 the river Pishon flowed through which land?

13. What did Moses burn and grind to powder in Exodus 32?

14. What, according to 1 Kings 18, did Elijah's servant see rising from the sea?

15. According to Proverbs 16:15 whose "favor is like a rain cloud in spring"?

Quiz # 14

EARTH, WIND AND FIRE

1. According to Exodus 17, what essential substance did the Israelites lack at Rephidim?

2. What was the fate of the soldiers escorting Shadrach, Meshach and Abednego to the fiery furnace?

3. According to Leviticus 4, what burnt offering could be presented for a leader's unintentional sin?

4. In Pharaoh's dream cows emerged from which river?

5. When he healed a blind man, what did Jesus do to make mud?

6. How old was Noah when the flood waters came?

7. Which disciples accompanied Jesus when he was transfigured?

8. What happened on Malta when the apostle Paul put wood on a fire?

9. According to Judges 20, the Israelites set fire to the towns of which tribe?

10. Locusts were sent by God upon Egypt in which plague?

11. According to Joshua, the Jordan was in flood in which period of the year?

12. In 1 Chronicles King David orders whose gods to be burned?

13. True or false? According to Genesis 8 the flood waters covered the mountains by more than 20 feet.

14. According to Jesus, where can true faith cast a mountain?

15. On the final part of his sea journey to Rome a south wind blew Paul from Regium to which city?

Answers

1. Water 2. They were killed 3. Male goat 4. The river Nile
5. He spat on the ground 6. 600 7. Peter, James and John 8. A snake emerged from it
9. Benjamin 10. Eighth 11. Harvest 12. Philistine 13. True (Genesis 7:20) 14. Into the sea 15. Puteoli

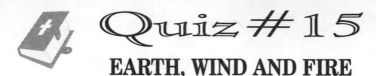

Quiz #15

EARTH, WIND AND FIRE

1. In Ezekiel 5, what is the prophet told to scatter to the wind?

2. At what time of the day did the waters of the Red Sea return to normal?

3. "It is as if the dew of Hermon were falling on Mount Zion," is a quotation from which Psalm?

4. Which tribe did Moses bless saying, "may the Lord bless his land with the precious dew from heaven above"?

5. According to 2 Peter 2 what returns to wallow in the mud?

6. In the book of Job who was killed by a mighty wind striking a house?

7. Where was Jesus when he turned water into wine?

8. By what name is the Sea of Galilee also known?

9. Which Old Testament book records a public gathering thrown into confusion by rain?

10. According to the curse of Genesis which creature will eat dust all the days of its life?

11. Psalm 48 says that something is shattered by an east wind. What is it?

12. What type of snake emerged from a fire and bit the apostle Paul?

13. In Revelation 6 the moon turns to what?

14. According to Genesis 8, when did the mountain tops become visible during the flood?

15. At his transfiguration the face of Jesus shone like what, according to Matthew?

Answers

1. His hair **2.** Daybreak **3.** Psalm 133 **4.** Joseph **5.** A sow
6. Job's sons and daughters **7.** Cana **8.** Tiberias **9.** Ezra **10.** Serpent **11.** The ships of Tarshish
12. A viper **13.** Blood **14.** The first day of the tenth month **15.** The sun

Quiz #16

EARTH, WIND AND FIRE

1. According to Genesis, what happened on the 17th day of the second month of Noah's 600th year?

2. In Daniel, how many people could the king see in the fiery furnace?

3. What did the fourth person in the fiery furnace look like?

4. In the book of Job which of his "friends" calls Job's words a "blustering wind"?

5. As recorded in the Gospel of John, what was Jesus' first miracle?

6. According to Psalm 11, what will rain on the wicked?

7. When Jesus turned water into wine how many jars were filled?

8. According to Revelation 7, how many angels held back the four winds?

9. In the book of Judges who looked for a sign involving dew?

10. According to 1 Corinthians 3, fire will test the quality of each man's what?

11. In Revelation 6 an earthquake occurs after which seal is broken?

12. According to 2 Chronicles 16 a huge fire was burnt in honor of which deceased king?

13. After Jesus had calmed the storm, what question did the disciples ask each other?

14. Which heavenly bodies are struck after an angel sounds a trumpet in Revelation 8?

15. According to the Old Testament, what does the sign of the rainbow mean?

Answers

1. It began to rain **2.** 4 **3.** A son of the gods **4.** Bildad
5. He turned water into wine **6.** Fiery coals and burning sulfur **7.** 6 **8.** 4
9. Gideon **10.** Work **11.** Sixth **12.** Asa **13.** "Who is this?"
14. The sun, moon and the stars **15.** Never again will God flood the whole earth

Quiz #17

EARTH, WIND AND FIRE

1. How many of Pharaoh's army survived their encounter with the Red Sea?

2. In Judges did Gideon ask for the dew to be on the fleece or the ground for his first sign?

3. According to Exodus the baby Hebrew boys were to be thrown into which river?

4. When Jesus changed water into wine what was the approximate capacity of the jars?

5. Complete the proverb, "He who brings trouble on his family will inherit only ____."

6. True or false? Peter wished to build two shelters during Jesus' transfiguration.

7. In which chapter of his book was the prophet Jeremiah given a word concerning a drought?

8. According to Proverbs 27:14, what is like constant dripping on a rainy day?

9. In 2 Samuel 13, which distraught woman put ashes on her head?

10. According to Ezekiel 19, what is destroyed by an east wind?

11. In Revelation 12, who wears a crown of twelve stars?

12. According to Psalm 46 there is a river whose streams make glad what?

13. What was the ninth plague to strike Pharaoh and Egypt?

14. According to Acts 10 whose house was by the sea?

15. Why were Shadrach, Meshach and Abednego thrown into the fiery furnace?

Answers

1. None 2. The fleece 3. Nile 4. 20-30 gallons 5. Wind
6. False. He wished to build three (Matthew 17:4) 7. Chapter 14 8. A quarrelsome wife
9. Tamar 10. A vineyard 11. The woman who was about to give birth 12. The city of God 13. Darkness
14. Simon the Tanner's 15. They refused to bow down and worship the image of gold

Quiz # 18
EARTH, WIND AND FIRE

1. In the first chapter of Job, he is told that fire fell from the sky burning what?

2. According to John the Baptist, Jesus would baptize with fire and what else?

3. Which Old Testament leader commanded the sun to stand still?

4. In Exodus, God promised to rain down what from heaven?

5. What is the biblical reference for "Do not put out the Spirit's fire"?

6. In the plagues of Egypt which creature came from the dust?

7. What was Jesus doing during the storm on the lake, according to Mark?

8. How many times was the apostle Paul shipwrecked at sea?

9. Which Old Testament prophet was thrown into a cistern and sank into the mud?

10. According to 1 Kings 19, what did Elijah experience after the powerful wind on the mountain of God?

11. What did Aaron claim emerged from the fire after he threw jewelry onto it?

12. 2 Samuel records that Absalom set fire to whose barley field?

13. The pregnant woman in the vision of Revelation 12 was clothed with what?

14. To whom did the prophet Elijah say, "Go, eat and drink, for there is the sound of a heavy rain"?

15. Which river did the Israelites have to cross before entering the Promised Land?

Answers

1. Sheep and servants **2.** The Holy Spirit **3.** Joshua **4.** Bread
5. 1 Thessalonians 5:19 **6.** Gnats **7.** Sleeping **8.** 3 **9.** Jeremiah **10.** An earthquake
11. The golden calf **12.** Joab's **13.** The sun **14.** Ahab **15.** Jordan

Quiz #19

EARTH, WIND AND FIRE

1. In which chapter of Exodus are manna and quail first mentioned?

2. What was the name of the king of Judah who sacrificed his son in the fire?

3. According to Revelation 11, how many people will be killed by an earthquake?

4. True or false? The magicians of Egypt were able to replicate the plague of gnats Moses inflicted upon them.

5. In the Old Testament who stood in the river Jordan while the people crossed into the Promised Land?

6. On which mountain did Moses receive the ten commandments?

7. Which king received a sign in which a shadow went back ten steps?

8. According to Job 24, what do heat and drought snatch away?

9. According to 2 Kings 21, which wicked king sacrificed his son in the fire?

10. What was unusual about the darkness of the ninth plague to strike Egypt?

11. According to Judges 12, who wanted to burn down Jephthah's house?

12. In Daniel's vision of a river flowing from the Ancient of Days, what was the river composed of?

13. When Joshua commanded the sun to stop still, for how long did it remain so?

14. In the Song of Solomon, whose head was drenched with dew?

15. The pregnant woman in the vision of Revelation 12 had what under her feet?

Quiz #20
EARTH, WIND AND FIRE

1. Fill in the missing word: "Can a man scoop fire into his ___?"

2. According to Genesis, which wicked desert lies between Elim and Sinai?

3. According to Joshua 7, why did the Lord's anger burn against Israel?

4. In 2 Samuel 22 David says that smoke came from where?

5. According to Jesus, speaking in the sermon on the mount, what could make someone liable to the fires of hell?

6. In the Old Testament why did Samuel ask God to send thunder and rain upon the wheat harvest?

7. In the Old Testament Joshua commanded the sun to stay still over which city?

8. Who will be revealed from heaven in blazing fire according to 2 Thessalonians 1:7?

9. What could the Israelites see after the Lord had returned the waters of the Red Sea to their proper place?

10. Immediately before Elijah heard a whisper in 1 Kings 19, what had he encountered?

11. In which month of their journey did the Israelites arrive at Mount Sinai?

12. Who met an angel of God in a fiery bush?

13. In Daniel 10 the prophet had a vision when he was standing by which river?

14. During which watch of the night did Jesus walk to the disciples on the water?

15. What were the priests holding as the Israelites crossed the Jordan river?

Quiz #21

EARTH, WIND AND FIRE

1. According to James 3 what is set on fire by a small spark?

2. Fill in the missing word: "Without ____ a fire goes out."

3. As recorded in the Old Testament, on which day were the Israelites to receive a double portion of bread from heaven?

4. Which king of Israel committed suicide by setting fire to his palace?

5. According to Daniel, which king was to be covered in the dew of heaven?

6. In the book of Job who asks if a wise man can "fill his belly with the hot east wind"?

7. According to 1 Kings 19 which ruler had captured and set fire to Gezer?

8. Where did the Israelites travel to after they had miraculously crossed the Red Sea?

9. What was unusual about the burning bush Moses discovered?

10. According to David in 2 Samuel 23 who is "like the brightness after rain"?

11. In Luke 12 Jesus quotes from a proverb which says that a south wind signifies what?

12. Fill in the three missing words: According to Proverbs 27:16, "restraining ____ ____ ____ is like restraining the wind."

13. What was the final plague to strike the land of Egypt?

14. In the earthquake predicted in Revelation 11 how much of the city collapses?

15. In Isaiah 29 someone comes with thunder and earthquake. Who is it?

Facts 1

EARTH, WIND AND FIRE

Dew is mentioned 36 times in the Old Testament.

There is only one specific record of rain falling in the book of Acts (Acts 28:2).

"Matar", *"gesem"* and *"zarem"* are all Hebrew words used to signify violent rain.

The "west wind", *"ruah yam"*, was considered to be the father of rain (1 Kings 18:44-45).

Sun worship, although forbidden (Deuteronomy 4:19), was practised in Old Testament (2 Kings 23:11) times.

In the Bible, lightning is frequently associated with theophanies (that is, appearances of God). For example; Exodus 19:16; Ezekiel 1:13-14; Revelation 4:5.

There are four seas named in the Old Testament, the Red Sea, the Dead Sea, the Sea of Galilee and the Mediterranean Sea.

The lowest point on land mentioned in the Bible is the Dead Sea.

The first expression of God's holiness in the Bible occurs in the story of Moses and the burning bush (Exodus 3).

"Yarden", the Hebrew word for the river Jordan, means "descender".

The surface of the Dead Sea is an average of 1365 ft. below sea level.

Facts 2

EARTH, WIND AND FIRE

St. Catherine's Monastery is now situated below Jebel Musa, at the site traditionally regarded as being Mount Sinai of the Old Testament.

During the Feast of Tabernacles 71 bulls or young bulls were to be offered as burnt sacrifices (Numbers 29).

15 rams were burnt as sacrifices during the Feast of Tabernacles in the Old Testament (Numbers 29).

The first recorded earthquake in the Bible is mentioned in 1 Kings 19:11 when the Lord appears to Elijah.

In Hebrew the words *"rebibim"* and *"resisim"* are used to describe showers and gentle types of rainfall.

In the Bible thunder is frequently associated with the voice of God (Psalm 77:18; Psalm 104:7).

According to Genesis, after the flood reached its maximum, the waters receded for 74 days until the mountain tops became visible (Genesis 8:5).

The deepest point of the Dead Sea lies more than 2,600 feet below sea level.

Two kings in the Old Testament sacrificed their sons in fire: Ahaz and Manasseh.

The direct distance of 72 miles from Lake Hulah to the Dead Sea is doubled by the river Jordan's meander.

The Dead Sea is 44 miles long and nearly 9 miles wide at places.

Facts 3

EARTH, WIND AND FIRE

The mount of Olives is mentioned eleven times in the Gospels.

According to Numbers 29, 105 lambs were to be sacrificed during the Feast of Tabernacles.

Dew is mentioned five times in the book of Daniel.

In Israel thunder storms are most frequent during November and December.

Noah sent the raven out from the ark 264 days after the flood had begun.

In the Old Testament the mountains were often thought to be symbols of fertility (Deuteronomy 33:15).

The annual rainfall in the region of the Dead Sea is approximately two inches.

There are strange pillar formations in the south west corner of the Dead Sea known locally as "Lot's Wife".

According to Genesis, the first person born after the flood was Arphaxad (Genesis 11:10).

Eight goats were to be offered as burnt offerings during the feast of Tabernacles (Numbers 29).

Other than the book of Genesis a rainbow is mentioned on only one other occasion in the Old Testament (Ezekiel 1:28).

Facts 4

EARTH, WIND AND FIRE

There are eleven earthquakes recorded in the New Testament.

Hail is often known to accompany the violent thunder storms that usually strike Israel between December and March.

The Hebrew word "*mabbul*", used to describe the Flood in Genesis, occurs only once outside the flood narratives in the Bible (Psalm 29:10).

Noah sent the dove from the ark 264 days after the flood had first begun.

Mountains in the Bible were sometimes used as symbols denoting difficulty and obstacles (Matthew 21:21).

Mount Nebo, the site from which Moses viewed the promised land before his death, is 2,739 feet high.

The River Euphrates is the largest river in West Asia, being 1,510 miles long.

Of the Gospel writers, only Matthew and Mark mention John the Baptist's activity in the River Jordan (Matthew 3:6; Mark 1:5).

The Bible often describes the disease of leprosy as one which turns the skin white like snow (Exodus 4:6).

The word sun is mentioned most times in the book of Ecclesiastes where it appears 35 times.

Noah was the first person in the Bible to make a burnt offering (Genesis 8:20).

Facts 5

EARTH, WIND AND FIRE

Revelation is the only book in the New Testament to mention the word "rainbow" which it does on two occasions (Revelation 4:3; 10:1).

The Hebrew word for dew, "*tal*", means "sprinkled moisture".

The "north wind", "*ruah sapon*", was associated with cold weather conditions in the Old Testament (Job 37:9).

In the Old Testament the mountains were considered to be the oldest created objects (Job 15:7; Proverbs 8:25).

Mount Carmel, where Elijah triumphed over the prophets of Baal, is 1,740 feet high.

The headwaters of the River Jordan collect into Lake Hulah, which is 230 feet above sea level.

The Dead Sea is also called the Salt Sea (Genesis 14:3), the Eastern Sea (Ezekiel 47:18) and the sea of Arabah (Deuteronomy 4:49).

The New Testament book mentioning the sun most frequently is Revelation where it occurs twelve times.

Three constellations that are recognized today are mentioned in Job: The Bear, Orion and Pleiades (Job 38).

The earliest mention of rain occurs in Genesis 2:5.

"*Ruah sapon*", called the "whirlwind" or "south wind" in the Bible, could be either tempestuous (Isaiah 21:1) or gentle (Acts 27:13).

Facts 6

EARTH, WIND AND FIRE

In the Bible the whirlwind symbolizes divine judgement because of its suddenness (Psalm 18:10; Nahum 1:3).

The moon, like the sun, became an object of idolatrous worship in ancient Israel (Job 31:26), even though this was forbidden (Deuteronomy 4:19; 17:3; Ezekiel 8:16-17).

In Arabic the name for the Dead Sea means "Sea of Lot".

Mount Sinai, where Moses received the Ten Commandments, is also called Mount Horeb in the Old Testament.

The sun and the moon were created on the fourth day, although their names are not given.

In the Old Testament the whirlwind was often used to symbolize the sudden attack of an invading king or army (Isaiah 5:28; Jeremiah 4:3).

The Mediterranean is also known as "The Great Sea" (Joshua 1:4), "The Western Sea" (Deuteronomy 11:24) and "The Sea of the Philistines" (Exodus 23:31).

According to Genesis 22:6, Abraham "carried" the fire for the sacrifice of Isaac, thus conforming to the ancient custom of preserving fire rather than taking the trouble of re-igniting it each time it was needed.

On the Day of Pentecost in Acts 2 a sound like the blowing of a violent wind was heard. "Breath" or "wind" is used as a symbol of the Spirit of God (Ezekiel 37:9, 14; John 3:8).

Tongues of fire were seen on the Day of Pentecost in Acts 2, resting on each of the people present. Fire was a symbol of God's presence (Exodus 3:2) as well as of God's judgment (Matthew 3:12).

God appeared to Moses in the burning bush which was on fire but did not burn up. Fire often accompanies God when he reveals himself in the Old Testament (Exodus 13:21; 19:18; 1 Kings 18:24, 38).

Elijah challenged the supporters of Baal to a contest in 1 Kings 18. As both Baal and the Lord were said to thunder (Psalm 29:3-9) and use lightning as their weapon (Psalm 18:14), Elijah said that everyone would know that the true God would be "the god who answers by fire."

All Creatures Great and Small

Quiz # 1

ALL CREATURES GREAT AND SMALL

1. According to Genesis, on which day did God create birds and sea creatures?

2. Where in the Bible is goat's milk referred to as feeding a family as well as nourishing servant girls?

3. Who did the Lord keep reminding about what he had done in Egypt and how he had carried his people on eagles' wings?

4. In the account in Genesis, who named the animals?

5. Which animal persuaded Eve to eat fruit from the tree of knowledge?

6. Where is the only place in the Bible that a chameleon is mentioned?

7. In the book of Genesis, what punishment did God deal to the serpent for tempting Eve?

8. Which people did Balaam describe as people who are "like a lion that does not rest till he devours his prey"?

9. According to the book of Genesis, how did Abel make his living?

10. In the book of Genesis, what offering did Abel make to God?

11. Who escaped the great flood in an ark full of animals?

12. In which book of the Bible does the story of Noah's ark appear?

13. What was the first bird that Noah sent out from the ark to find dry land?

14. Who does the prophet Zephaniah liken to roaring lions?

15. According to Genesis, how many times did Noah send the dove out from the ark?

Answers

1. On the fifth day 2. Proverbs 27:27 3. The Israelites 4. Adam 5. The serpent 6. Leviticus 7. It must crawl on its belly and eat dust 8. Israel 9. He kept flocks 10. Fat portions from the firstborn of his flock 11. Noah and his family 12. The book of Genesis 13. A raven 14. The officials of Jerusalem 15. 3

Quiz #2

ALL CREATURES GREAT AND SMALL

1. In the book of Genesis, God stopped Abraham sacrificing his son, Isaac. What did Abraham sacrifice instead?

2. Which bird is described in the Bible as stretching out its wings and catching its young?

3. Who in the New Testament described himself as being delivered from the lion's mouth?

4. What animals did Abraham's servant take with him when he went looking for a bride for Isaac?

5. When Abraham's servant waited by a well, hoping to find a wife for Isaac, what test did he set for any prospective bride?

6. Who asked, "Which of you, if his son asks for a fish, will give him a snake?"?

7. According to the book of Genesis, what was Rachel doing when she met Jacob?

8. Who predicted that "in that day" a man would keep alive a young cow and two goats?

9. Which Old Testament character was tricked into working for his uncle, Laban, and was paid for his work in speckled and spotted sheep and goats?

10. The psalmist says that the Lord will provide food for young ravens. What must they do first?

11. In the book of Genesis, who had a dream about fat and skinny cows?

12. What do the following have in common: the weasel, the rat, the great lizard and the gecko?

13. Which Old Testament prophet was told by the Lord to tell a parable about two eagles and a vine?

14. Who was offered a piece of broiled fish to eat?

15. Which two brothers turned their staffs into snakes?

Answers

1. A ram 2. The eagle 3. Paul 4. Camels 5. He asked for water and waited to see whether she offered water to his camels too 6. Jesus 7. Bringing her father's sheep to the well for water 8. Isaiah 9. Jacob 10. Call 11. Pharaoh 12. They are all unclean 13. Ezekiel 14. The risen Jesus 15. Moses and Aaron

Quiz #3

ALL CREATURES GREAT AND SMALL

1. How long would it take for Daniel's vision of a ram and a goat to be fulfilled?

2. In Ezekiel's parable to which country did a great eagle with powerful wings, long feathers and full plumage of varied colors go?

3. According to the book of Exodus, what was the second of the ten plagues that hit Egypt?

4. Who said, "Pray to the Lord to take the frogs away from me and my people, and I will let your people go"?

5. In the Old Testament, which animal was the emblem of the tribe of Benjamin?

6. What was the answer to the riddle that Samson set for the guests at his wedding: "Out of the eater, something to eat: out of the strong, something sweet"?

7. Which bird is said to treat its young harshly, as if they did not belong to her?

8. Who spent three days and three nights inside a great fish?

9. Where will the falcons gather, according to the prophet Isaiah?

10. Who was sent to die in the lions' den?

11. According to the book of Exodus, what did God tell the Israelites to eat with lamb on the night of the Passover?

12. When the Israelites were very hungry in the desert what kind of birds did God send for them to eat?

13. While Moses was on Mount Sinai receiving the ten commandments, the Israelites made a golden idol in the shape of which animal?

14. Which Psalm is this quotation taken from: "The Lord is my shepherd, I shall not be in want. He makes me lie down in green pastures"?

15. In the Old Testament, which animal was the emblem of the tribe of Judah?

---

11. Bitter herbs and unleavened bread **12.** Quail **13.** A calf **14.** Psalm 23 **15.** The lion
5. The wolf **6.** Honey from a lion **7.** The ostrich **8.** Jonah **9.** Over Edom **10.** Daniel
1. 2,300 evenings and mornings **2.** Lebanon **3.** Frogs **4.** Pharaoh

Answers

Quiz #4

ALL CREATURES GREAT AND SMALL

1. In the book of Exodus, what was the third of the ten plagues?

2. In 2 Samuel, which prophet told King David the story of the rich man who stole a poor man's pet lamb?

3. In Revelation, who is described as the "lion of the tribe of Judah"?

4. In the book of Numbers, whose donkey saw an angel barring the path and refused to go on?

5. In the book of Judges, what bone did Samson use to kill 1,000 Philistines?

6. Who in the Old Testament said, "The lions may roar and growl, yet the teeth of the great lions are broken"?

7. Whose donkey was granted the power of speech and said, "Am I not your own donkey, which you have always ridden, to this day? Have I been in the habit of doing this to you?"?

8. Which city is being described: "They (the Israelites) destroyed with the sword every living thing in it—men and women, young and old, cattle, sheep and donkeys"?

9. At the siege of Jericho, the Israelite priests marched round the city blowing their trumpets. What were the trumpets made from?

10. What is a shophar?

11. Which Old Testament character tested God by leaving a sheep's fleece out overnight?

12. Who said, "I am the good shepherd. The good shepherd lays down his life for the sheep"?

13. In the book of Judges, who set fire to the Philistines' fields of crops using pairs of foxes with torches tied to their tails?

14. In the Old Testament, which animal was the emblem of the tribe of Dan?

15. Which Old Testament character "tore the lion apart with his bare hands as he might have torn a young goat"?

Quiz #5

ALL CREATURES GREAT AND SMALL

1. In the book of Judges, when Samson went back to look at the carcass of the lion he had killed, what did he find had nested there?

2. What was the fourth of the ten plagues described in the book of Exodus?

3. Which Old Testament character said, "I will place a sheep's fleece on the threshing floor. If there is dew only on the fleece and all the ground is dry, then I will know that you will save Israel by my hand"?

4. As a sign of God's judgment which place is going to be so desolated that owls will nest there, lay their eggs, hatch their eggs and care for their young?

5. Who told Saul that he would find a man carrying three young goats?

6. Which place did Ezekiel prophesy would become pasture for camels?

7. Who longed for the wings of a dove?

8. In 1 Samuel, who captured the Ark of the Covenant but sent it away on a cart pulled by two untrained cows?

9. Which Old Testament prophet said that when Nineveh fell its slave girls would moan like doves?

10. Whose large herds did Jeremiah say would become booty?

11. How did Jonah get out of the great fish that swallowed him?

12. Jesus said that Peter would deny him three times before which bird crowed?

13. Which animal that only needs poor pasture is sometimes called "the poor man's cow"?

14. In 1 Kings, what kind of birds did God send to feed Elijah when he was in the wilderness?

15. In the Old Testament, which animal was the emblem of the tribe of Issachar?

Quiz #6

ALL CREATURES GREAT AND SMALL

1. The account of the shepherds who went to visit the baby Jesus appears only in one Gospel. Which one?

2. What is the only animal mentioned as a pet in the Old Testament?

3. Four of the ten plagues that are described in the book of Exodus involve animals. Frogs, gnats, and flies are three of them—what is the fourth?

4. What was David's job before he was chosen to become the next king of Israel?

5. Where was Jonah traveling to when he was swallowed by a great fish?

6. Which dangerous animal was well-known for inhabiting "Jordan's thickets"?

7. In Exodus, what did God tell the Israelites to do with the blood of the lambs they were to eat on the night of the Passover?

8. How did Daniel explain the fact that he had not been eaten by the lions?

9. How many more camels did Job have at the end of his suffering than he had before the calamities hit him?

10. Referring to his enemies, who wrote" "Dogs have surrounded me"?

11. In Luke's account of the birth of Jesus, what were the shepherds doing when the angel of the Lord appeared to them?

12. Who announced that Judah would be attacked by an army which had horses that were swifter than eagles?

13. In which book of the Old Testament does the story of Gideon and the sheep's fleece appear?

14. When Jesus was a baby his parents took him to the Temple in Jerusalem to present him to the Lord. What sacrifice did they offer?

15. Which insect teaches lazy people, according to the book of Proverbs?

Answers

1. Luke's Gospel **2.** A lamb **3.** Locusts **4.** He kept his father's sheep **5.** Tarshish **6.** The lion **7.** Put it on the top and both sides of their door frames **8.** He said God sent an angel to stop their mouths **9.** 3,000 camels. (Job owned 3,000 camels in Job 1:3, but in Job 42:12 he had 6,000 camels) **10.** The psalmist **11.** Keeping watch over their sheep at night **12.** Jeremiah **13.** Judges **14.** 2 birds **15.** The ant

Quiz #7

ALL CREATURES GREAT AND SMALL

1. Which Old Testament prophet pictures a man-eating lion trapped in a pit?

2. In which Old Testament book is it said that animals should be "asked" because they are capable of teaching?

3. In which book of the Bible is the camel first mentioned?

4. In his oracle about the animals of the Negev what are the first animals mentioned by Isaiah?

5. Which king had apes and baboons imported every three years?

6. Which prophet said that because of Israel's unfaithfulness to God, beasts of the field, birds of the air and fish of the sea were dying?

7. True or false? When Adam and Eve lived in the Garden of Eden, they were vegetarians – they did not eat meat.

8. For how many days and nights was Jonah inside a great fish?

9. After Daniel had been saved from the lions' den, who were thrown to the lions?

10. Which Old Testament prophet described a land of hardship as one where lions and lionesses were present?

11. Who complained that he had become a companion of owls?

12. Who met Elisha with a gift of forty camel-loads of the finest wares of Damascus?

13. What words does the book of Job use to indicate that the additional sheep, camels, oxen and donkeys Job had after he suffered were a sign of God's blessing?

14. Which Old Testament prophet wrote, "You have made men like fish in the sea, like sea creatures that have no ruler"?

15. Which prophet warned about a coming destruction in which the Lord will "sweep away the birds of the air and the fish of the sea"?

Answers

1. Ezekiel **2.** Job **3.** Genesis **4.** Lions **5.** King Solomon **6.** Hosea
7. True **8.** 3 **9.** The officials who had falsely accused Daniel **10.** Isaiah **11.** Job
12. Hazael **13.** "The Lord blessed the latter part of Job's life more than the first"
14. Habakkuk **15.** Zephaniah

Quiz #8

ALL CREATURES GREAT AND SMALL

1. Which Old Testament writer mentions three methods of trapping animals, a "net", a "trap", and a "noose", in successive verses?

2. How many horses returned with Nehemiah to Jerusalem?

3. Who knows every bird of the mountains, according to the psalmist?

4. As he acted out the siege of Jerusalem, who was allowed to bake his bread over cow manure rather than human excrement?

5. How many female goats did Jacob select as a gift for his brother Esau?

6. Who in the Old Testament was asked by the Lord, "Does the eagle soar at your command and build his nest on high?"?

7. About whom was Ezekiel lamenting when he said, "What a lioness was your mother among the lions"?

8. What did Jesus say the hired hand would do when he saw the wolf about to attack the sheep?

9. Whose men and camels was it impossible to count?

10. How many donkeys returned with Nehemiah to Jerusalem?

11. In Jesus' Parable of the Net, what was caught when the net was let down into the lake?

12. Which Old Testament prophet said that an invading army would have teeth like a lion?

13. Who said that he would send his disciples as lambs among wolves?

14. In Daniel's vision of a ram and a goat what came from one of the goat's four new horns?

15. In Daniel's dream about four beasts, how many horns did the fourth great beast have?

Answers

1. Job 2. 736 3. God 4. Ezekiel 5. 200 6. Job
7. The princes of Israel 8. "Abandon the sheep and run away" 9. The Midianites 10. 6,720
11. All kinds of fish 12. Joel 13. Jesus 14. Another horn 15. 10 horns

Quiz #9

ALL CREATURES GREAT AND SMALL

1. Which Old Testament prophet refers to rod and line fishing in the river Nile?

2. Who murdered whom during the festivities surrounding sheep shearing?

3. How many sheep did Solomon sacrifice at the dedication of the temple?

4. Which New Testament pool was used to bathe sheep in?

5. How many goats and sheep did Nabal have?

6. Who did Jesus accuse of being guilty of swallowing, figuratively speaking, a camel?

7. Which Old Testament prophet never died?

8. Who had 50,000 camels?

9. Who said to Job, "The wild animals will be at peace with you"?

10. How many mules returned with Nehemiah to Jerusalem?

11. How many male goats did Jacob select as a gift for his brother Esau?

12. In his oracle about the animals of the Negev what are the second animals mentioned by Isaiah?

13. Who predicted that one of his sons would "tether his donkey to a vine"?

14. Who likened Israel's destruction to the ravaging of boars from the forest?

15. What question about mountain goats did the Lord ask Job?

---

1. Isaiah *2.* Absalom killed Amnon *3.* 120,000 sheep *4.* The Pool of Bethesda
5. 1,000 goats and 3,000 sheep *6.* Teachers of the law *7.* Elijah *8.* The Hagrites *9.* Eliphaz
10. 245 *11.* 20 *12.* Lionesses *13.* Jacob *14.* The Psalmist *15.* "Do you know when they give birth?"

Answers

Quiz # 10

ALL CREATURES GREAT AND SMALL

1. Which Old Testament judge prepared a meal of a young goat for an angel?

2. According to the account in Genesis 1, on which day did God create land animals?

3. Which Old Testament prophet mentions two types of fishing, rod and line and the drag net, in one verse?

4. True or false? There are about 80 mammals mentioned in the Bible.

5. What animals did the Queen of Sheba use to carry her baggage?

6. How many camels returned with Nehemiah to Jerusalem?

7. Which of his sons did Jacob liken to a "rawboned donkey"?

8. How many bears mauled 42 youths because they had been jeering at Elisha?

9. In his prophecy against which city does Ezekiel proclaim, "Out in the sea she will become a place to spread fishing nets"?

10. Who were called "cows of Bashan" by the prophet Amos?

11. Which Old Testament prophet described the Babylonians' horses as fiercer than wolves at dusk?

12. In Daniel's vision of a ram and a goat, what happened to the goat's horn after he fought with the ram?

13. In Jesus' Parable of the Net where were the bad fish put?

14. To which animal did the Lord give the salt flats as his habitat ?

15. What do a lion, a strutting rooster and a he-goat have in common with each other?

---

1. Gideon 2. On the sixth day 3. Habakkuk 4. True 5. Camels 6. 435 7. Issachar 8. 2 bears 9. Tyre 10. The women who oppressed the poor 11. Habakkuk 12. It was broken off 13. The bad fish were thrown away. 14. The wild donkey 15. They move with stately bearing

Answers

Quiz # 11

ALL CREATURES GREAT AND SMALL

1. In Ezekiel's vision of living creatures and the glory of the Lord what animal did the feet of the four living creatures look like?

2. Who warned against false prophets who would come in sheep's clothing but were really wolves?

3. What animal is mentioned in the Parable of the Good Samaritan?

4. In Daniel's vision of a ram and a goat where did Daniel find himself?

5. Which bird did the Lord describe in Jeremiah's prophecy as swooping down and spreading its wings over Moab?

6. Jeremiah said the same bird would spread its wings over another country. Which country?

7. What do the two daughters of the leech cry?

8. Some days after Jesus' resurrection, who said, "I am going out to fish"?

9. How many sheep were taken from the Hagrites?

10. In the miraculous catch of fish after Jesus' resurrection how many fish were caught?

11. What were the Israelites commanded not to do if they came across a mother bird sitting on its young in its nest?

12. In Ezekiel's vision of living creatures and the glory of the Lord, what did the right hand side of each face look like?

13. Which Psalm states, "He will cover you with his feathers, and under his wings you will find refuge"?

14. How many sheep did the Israelites take as plunder from the Midianites?

15. Which king lived with wild donkeys as a divine punishment?

Quiz # 12

ALL CREATURES GREAT AND SMALL

1. Who wrote, "Every animal of the forest is mine"?

2. Who said, "Look at the birds of the air; they do not sow or reap or store away in barns, and yet your heavenly Father feeds them"?

3. Which bird's wings are said to flap joyfully but cannot be compared with the pinions and feathers of the stork?

4. Of which two friends was it said, "in life they were loved and gracious, and in death they were not parted. They were swifter than eagles, they were stronger than lions"?

5. Which of his sons did Jacob liken to "a ravenous wolf"?

6. Who had a vision about a ram and a goat?

7. Which Old Testament prophet said that an invading army would have fangs like a lioness?

8. How many ewes did Jacob select as a gift for his brother Esau?

9. In his oracle about the animals of the Negev, what are the third animals mentioned by Isaiah?

10. In which Psalm did the Psalmist pray, "Rescue me from the mouth of the lions"?

11. Whose camels did Jeremiah say would become plunder?

12. In one of the visions in the book of Revelation, what did the beast that came out of the sea resemble?

13. In Ezekiel's vision of living creatures and the glory of the Lord what did the left hand side of each face look like?

14. What is the first profession mentioned in the Bible?

15. In one of the visions in the book of Revelation what did the feet of the beast that came out of the sea resemble?

---

12. A leopard 13. An ox 14. A keeper of sheep 15. Bear

5. Benjamin 6. Daniel 7. Joel 8. 200 9. Adders 10. Psalm 22 11. Those of Kedar and the kingdoms of Hazor

1. The Psalmist 2. Jesus 3. The ostrich 4. Saul and Jonathan

Answers

Quiz # 13

ALL CREATURES GREAT AND SMALL

1. How much did Jesus say five sparrows were sold for?

2. In his teaching about the resurrection body who wrote that all flesh is not the same: that men have one kind of flesh, animals have another and birds another?

3. In one of the visions in the book of Revelation what did the mouth of the beast that came out of the sea resemble?

4. Which bird dwells on a cliff and stays there at night and has a rocky crag as his stronghold?

5. In Daniel's vision of a ram and a goat how many horns did the ram have?

6. True or false? In Daniel's vision of a ram and a goat no animal could withstand the attacks of the ram.

7. The first of the four living creatures mentioned in Revelation 4 was like which animal?

8. Who is described as being like a lioness?

9. Who told his readers to be certain that they knew about the condition of their flocks?

10. Who asked, "Does a wild donkey bray when it has grass?"?

11. In Daniel's vision of a ram and a goat who won the fight between the two animals?

12. In Jesus' Parable of the Net where were the good fish put?

13. Jesus told his disciples to be as shrewd as what?

14. From where will the wolf come which Jeremiah pictures attacking the people of Jerusalem?

15. Who sacrificed sheep, cattle and fattened calves at the Stone of Zoheleth?

Quiz # 14
ALL CREATURES GREAT AND SMALL

1. How many cattle did the Israelites take as plunder from the Midianites?

2. In Daniel's vision of a ram and a goat which two nations did the ram represent?

3. Who asked King Saul why he was pursuing him—as if he was a flea?

4. How many rams did Jacob select as a gift for his brother Esau?

5. In Daniel's vision of a ram and a goat what country did the goat represent?

6. How many bulls did Jacob select as a gift for his brother Esau?

7. Which two owls are mentioned by Zephaniah?

8. Who did Amos say dined on choice lambs and fattened calves?

9. Although the Son of Man has nowhere to rest, what did Jesus say foxes and birds have?

10. In Daniel's vision of a ram and a goat, what did the four horns which grew on the goat, and replaced the broken off horn, represent?

11. Who prayed, "Save me from the horns of the wild oxen"?

12. Which Old Testament prophet wrote, "Their roar is like that of a lion, they roar like young lions"?

13. Who described Israel as a scattered flock which had been chased away by lions?

14. Who replied to one of his so-called comforters, "Let the fish of the sea inform you"?

15. In Ezekiel's vision of living creatures and the glory of the Lord, what kind of bird did each living creature have a face like?

Quiz # 15

ALL CREATURES GREAT AND SMALL

1. Which prophet said that an eagle was over the house of the Lord because Israel had broken God's covenant?

2. In Daniel's dream about four beasts what was the first great beast like?

3. What kind of person, according to the book of Proverbs, cares for the needs of his animal?

4. How many female camels with their young did Jacob select as a gift for his brother Esau?

5. Which five Old Testament prophets mention a swarm of locusts?

6. In Daniel's dream about four beasts what was very unusual about the mouth of the second great beast?

7. Which king was called a fox by Jesus?

KING HEROD

8. Which animal, used to describe Jesus in Revelation, was slain from the beginning of the world?

9. In his oracle about the animals of the Negev what are the fourth animals mentioned by Isaiah?

10. In the book of Revelation, after the fourth angel sounded his trumpet, what did John see flying in mid-air?

11. In the book of Revelation, what were the first three words which John heard the creature say from mid-air?

12. Who mentions the desert owl, the screech owl and the great owl in a single verse?

13. Which Old Testament prophet warned that a leopard would tear in pieces anyone who came out of the city?

14. In Daniel's dream about four beasts, what kind of teeth did the fourth great beast have?

15. How many times does the prophet Isaiah picture the wolf and the lamb together?

---

13. Jeremiah **14.** Iron teeth **15.** Twice

9. Darting snakes **10.** An eagle **11.** "Woe! Woe! Woe!..." **12.** Isaiah

6. It had 3 ribs between its teeth **7.** King Herod **8.** The Lamb

1. Hosea **2.** A lion **3.** A righteous person **4.** 30 **5.** Isaiah, Jeremiah, Joel, Amos, Nahum

Answers

Quiz #16

ALL CREATURES GREAT AND SMALL

1. Who is the only person to write about ravens in the New Testament?

2. In Daniel's dream about four beasts, what kind of wings did the first great beast have?

3. In Daniel's vision of a ram and a goat, what feature about the coat of the goat is mentioned in the interpretation of the vision?

4. Whose houses are going to be filled with jackals according to one Old Testament prophet?

5. Which Old Testament book says, "His hair is wavy and black as a raven"?

6. What is going to be pecked out by the ravens of the valley, according to the book of Proverbs?

7. In which Old Testament book is there a reference to fish being caught in a cruel net?

8. How many donkeys did the Israelites take as plunder from the Midianites?

9. Which country did Jeremiah say would hiss like a fleeing serpent?

10. In which famous Egyptian river did the Lord say he would put hooks into the jaws of the Egyptians, as if they were fish?

11. Who, according to Isaiah, will soar on wings like eagles and run and not grow weary?

12. Who was thrown into the lions' den in which Daniel had survived a night?

13. In Daniel's vision of a ram and a goat, what replaced the goat's single horn?

14. Who did Jesus tell his disciples to be as innocent as?

15. To which wild animal, according to the Psalmist, do the mountains belong?

Quiz # 17

ALL CREATURES GREAT AND SMALL

1. How many cows did Jacob select as a gift for his brother Esau?

2. Which Old Testament prophet spoke of a people who moaned like a mourning dove?

3. Which Old Testament prophet described survivors who escaped to the mountains as moaning like doves?

4. Who complained to his father that he had never been given a young goat so he could have a celebration?

5. Who did not enter the tabernacle by means of the blood of goats and calves?

6. True or false? Jesus was the first person to say, "One swallow does not make a summer."

7. Who used some goat's hair to fool people that David was in bed?

8. Who, according to the letter of Hebrews, went about in sheepskins and goatskins?

9. Who said that wild goats would bleat to each other?

10. For lack of what, according to the book of Job, may a lion perish?

11. Who is described as being like a lion which crouches and lies down?

12. In Daniel's vision of a ram and a goat, how many horns did the goat have?

13. Which Old Testament prophet asked the question, "Who are these that fly along like clouds, like doves to their nests"?

14. Complete this saying from the book of Proverbs, "Like a fluttering sparrow or a darting swallow..."

15. In Daniel's dream about four beasts what was the second great beast like?

---

1. 40 2. Isaiah 3. Ezekiel 4. The elder son in Jesus' Parable of the Prodigal Son
5. Jesus 6. False. Jesus never said any such thing. 7. Michal
8. Old Testament followers of God who were persecuted 9. Isaiah 10. Prey 11. Judah
12. 1 13. Isaiah 14. "an undeserved curse does not come to rest" 15. A bear

Answers

452

Quiz # 18

ALL CREATURES GREAT AND SMALL

1. In Daniel's dream about four beasts what was the third great beast like?

2. According to the Psalmist to whom does every animal of the forest belong?

3. As a punishment from God which king would have nails like the claws of a bird?

4. Who wrote in his prophetic book, "Like cages full of birds, their houses are full of deceit"?

5. In Jesus' parable about 100 sheep, how many sheep got lost?

6. In Daniel's vision of a ram and a goat, who was represented by the first horn on the goat?

7. Who asked, "Does... an ox bellow when it has fodder?"?

8. Who did Jeremiah say were like fattened calves?

9. Who asked a king why he was being treated like a dead dog?

10. The lazy are told to consider the ant and be what?

11. Who pictured a large number of fish at the point where the river flowing from the temple emptied into the sea?

12. True or false? More than 20 wild animals are mentioned in the Bible.

13. In Daniel's dream about four beasts what did the third great beast have on its back?

14. True or false? No more than 15 of the Bible books mentions birds.

15. True or false? The Bible mentions about 50 species of birds.

Quiz # 19

ALL CREATURES GREAT AND SMALL

1. What, according to the book of Proverbs, sprout wings and fly off into the sky like eagles?

2. What, according to the Psalmist, will be renewed like the youth of an eagle?

3. Who was described as being like a lion's cub?

4. When Jesus cleansed the temple, what was being sold from benches?

5. When Jesse allowed David to go to Saul, what animal did David take with him?

6. Who in the Old Testament describes himself as one who was shaken off like a locust?

7. In the book of Revelation, what came out of the smoke?

8. What will hyenas do in the strongholds of Babylon?

9. True or false? Cats are mentioned as pets six times in the Old Testament and six times in the New Testament.

10. Who mentions the speed of a camel?

11. Who made two golden calves?

12. What animal did Samson take with him when he visited his wife?

13. Who said, in his second oracle, "The people rise like a lioness"?

14. Who in the New Testament likened false teachers to dogs?

15. When did the Spirit descend on Jesus like a dove?

Answers

1. Riches **2.** Your youth (Psalm 103:5) **3.** Dan **4.** Doves **5.** A young goat **6.** The Psalmist **7.** Locusts **8.** Howl **9.** False. Domestic cats are not mentioned in the Bible. **10.** Jeremiah **11.** Jeroboam **12.** A young goat **13.** Balaam **14.** Paul **15.** When Jesus was baptized.

Quiz #20
ALL CREATURES GREAT AND SMALL

1. How many female donkeys did Jacob select as a gift for his brother Esau?

2. Who wrote, "There are three things that are too amazing for me... the way of an eagle in the sky, the way of a snake on a rock..."?

3. What stood on twelve bulls?

4. When the Israelites were in Samaria why did the Lord send lions among them?

5. Who in the New Testament wore clothes made from camel hair?

6. Whose throne had six steps and two lions on each step?

7. As a result of Jonah's preaching many of which group of animals were spared God's judgment?

8. Who asked why God allowed evil men to drive away an orphan's donkey and take a widow's ox In pledge?

9. Which place did Ezekiel prophesy would become a resting place for sheep?

10. Which Old Testament prophet wrote that owls moaned?

11. When Abraham was told to go and sacrifice his son what animal did he saddle up?

12. Which of his sons did Jacob liken to "a lion's cub"?

13. In Daniel's vision of a ram and a goat, where did the goat appear from?

14. The second of the four living creatures mentioned in Revelation 4 was like which animal?

15. What color were ram skins dyed in Exodus 25:5?

---

8. Job 9. Ammon 10. Micah 11. A donkey 12. Judah 13. The west 14. An ox 15. Red
4. Because they did not worship the Lord 5. John the Baptist 6. Solomon's throne 7. Cattle
1. 20 2. The writer of the book of Proverbs 3. A metal basin symbolising the sea in Solomon's Temple

Answers

Quiz #21

ALL CREATURES GREAT AND SMALL

1. Who said he was like an owl among ruins?

2. In Daniel's vision of a ram and a goat the goat's last horn grew until it reached where?

3. Which New Testament writer referred to Balaam as the man who was "rebuked for his wrongdoing by a donkey"?

4. Who said, "I will make you fishers of men"?

5. Which Old Testament prophet pictured Israel as a wild donkey wandering alone?

6. Which Old Testament prophet asked the question, "Where now is the lions' den...?"?

7. Who, according to the book of Lamentations, were swifter than eagles in the sky, as they chased the Israelites over the mountains?

8. Whose unborn son did an angel foretell would be "a wild donkey of a man"?

9. Who in the New Testament referred to non-Jews as dogs?

10. Against which country did Isaiah prophecy by saying that "no shepherd will rest his flocks there"?

11. Which Old Testament book mentions that camels wore ornaments around their necks?

12. How many male donkeys did Jacob select as a gift for his brother Esau?

13. The fourth of the four living creatures mentioned in Revelation chapter four was like which animal?

14. Who, in the Old Testament, said, "Their bulls never fail to breed; their cows calve and do not miscarry"?

15. Which country did Obadiah say would be brought down even though he soared like an eagle and made his nest among the stars?

---

12. 10 13. A flying eagle 14. Job 15. Edom

6. Nahum 7. Our pursuers 8. Hagar's 9. Jesus 10. Babylon 11. The book of Judges

1. The Psalmist 2. Until it reached the hosts of the heaven 3. Peter 4. Jesus 5. Hosea

Answers

Facts 1

ALL CREATURES GREAT AND SMALL

In the Bible, the serpent is often a symbol of evil, as it is in the story of the Garden of Eden.

In the time of Abraham and the other Patriarchs, a man's wealth was measured by the number of sheep and other animals he owned.

Moses and Aaron turned their staffs into serpents to impress Pharaoh. The serpent was a symbol of Pharaoh's power and appeared on his head-dress and other regalia.

There are more references to sheep in the Bible than to any other animal. Sheep are mentioned over 400 times.

The Bible says that Jonah was swallowed by a "great fish". This may have been a sperm whale, as these creatures are found in the Eastern Mediterranean and can swallow a man whole.

Popular imagery has oxen and asses around Jesus' crib, but the Bible doesn't mention any animals, but simply says that Mary, "placed him in a manger, because there was no room for them in the inn" (Luke 2:7).

According to Leviticus 17:14, "You must not eat the blood of any creature, because the life of any creature is its blood." Life and blood are seen as synonymous with each other. In Old Testament theology all life belongs to God.

The early Christians were told to follow the Jewish food laws about the draining of the blood from animals (Acts 15:29). This may have been as a protection against blood disease and infections.

Noah was told to take seven of every kind of clean animal, but only two of every kind of unclean animal, into the ark. More ceremonially clean animals than unclean animals were needed as the former were used in Noah's sacrifices of burnt offerings.

Goats were important in the Old Testament for their hair. Goat hair was woven into sackcloth and used for making tents. The hangings in the tabernacle were made of goat hair (Exodus 26:7; 35:23, 26).

Facts 2

ALL CREATURES GREAT AND SMALL

It may seem strange that Numbers 32:16 says that Gad and Reuben planned to "build sheepfolds" for cattle. But in the Bible "cattle" was a broad term which included many types of livestock.

Among the different breeds of sheep found in the Bible there was at least one which had a plump tail prized for its fat (Exodus 29:22). This large tail was fried and eaten.

Pharisees went to extreme lengths to make sure that they never ate anything that was unclean. They used to strain their drinking water through a cloth to ensure they didn't swallow a gnat.

Queen Jezebel was thrown into the street and her corpse was eaten by scavenging dogs (2 Kings 9:35-37). A more disgraceful end to one's life could not be imagined.

Goats, unlike sheep, had their drawbacks: they smelled a great deal, were very lively and were very willful. In Jesus' parable it was the goats, not the sheep, who were put on the left hand side, the side of disfavor.

Jerome suggested that the 153 fish of John 21:11 represented one fish of every kind. This is highly conjectural.

Augustine conjectured that the 153 fish of John 21:11 referred to the Ten Commandments and the seven gifts of the Spirit. Add the numerals of ten (1+2+3+4+5+6+7+8+9+10=55) and seven (1+2+3+4+5+6+7=28) - a total of 83 - to the sum of 7 times 10 (70) and the sum is 153!

David says he protected his sheep from lions and bears (1 Samuel 17:34-36). Hyenas and jackals were also a constant danger to the flocks.

When Paul was gathering some brushwood for a fire in Acts 28:1-6 a viper fastened itself to his hand. The islanders must have known that this snake was poisonous because they expected Paul to die.

Facts 3

ALL CREATURES GREAT AND SMALL

Luke 5:4 refers to seine net fishing when they "let down their nets for a catch." This consisted of a large net, about eight feet wide and up to hundreds of feet long, hanging vertically, with floats at the top and weights at the bottom.

The Philistines suffered from "an outbreak of tumors" (1 Samuel 5:9). The symptoms fit those of the bubonic plague which was carried by the flea of black rats, possibly the type of rat in 1 Samuel 6.

The prophet Isaiah is the only prophet to mention a bat. Isaiah says that people will discard their idols to bats as this unclean animal mirrors their desolation (Isaiah 2:20).

The word "behemoth" came into the English language when translators of the Bible were unable to identify the animal mentioned in Job 40:15. "Look at the behemoth, which I made... and which feeds on grass."

Owls are mentioned eight times in the Old Testament. As four different Hebrew words are used for owls it probably means that different species are implied.

According to Jeremiah 8:7, "Even the stork in the sky knows her appointed seasons." The white stork is a striking migratory bird which travels north along the Jordan valley in March and April.

White donkeys were special. Only high-ranking people, such as governors or nobles, could afford them (see Judges 5:10).

The word used by Jesus in Matthew 10:29, translated "sparrows," may imply assorted small birds which were, and still are, killed and sold in Palestine.

Quails are mentioned in Exodus 16:13. These migratory birds only fly a few feet above the ground. One of their routes takes them across the route used by the Israelites after the Exodus.

Facts 4

ALL CREATURES GREAT AND SMALL

The Israelites were not allowed to eat pigs (Leviticus 11:7). Pigs are scavengers and so easily picked up diseased material and became infected.

There was a further hygienic reason for not eating pigs. Pigs were often hosts to tapeworms that cause trichinoisis. These tapeworms could only be transmitted when a pig was eaten.

The elephant is never directly mentioned in the Bible, but there are 12 references to ivory which came from the African elephant and the Asian elephant.

In the Bible the word "lion" or "water lion" occurs over 100 times, translating nine different Hebrew words. This rich vocabulary suggests how common lions were.

All the few references to leopards in the Bible are figurative. The most famous one concerns a question that is expecting a negative answer: "Can a leopard change his spots?"

Half the references to wolves in the Bible refer to people in authority who misuse their position (e.g. Zephaniah 3:3).

Locusts are one of the most important insects mentioned in the Bible, making 56 appearances.

Locusts do not migrate according to a set route as their swarms are largely wind-driven. Hence in Exodus 10 it is "the wind" that brings the locusts.

Joel 1:4 mentions the devastation to crops caused by locusts. In 1889 a desert swarm of locusts crossed the Red Sea and destroyed crops over an area of over 3,000 square miles.

Facts 5

ALL CREATURES GREAT AND SMALL

In biblical times donkeys were important as beasts of burden. They could exist on very poor diets, provided a useful means of transport and were used to plow fields.

Care for animals was endorsed in the laws of the Old Testament. It was permitted for cattle to be watered on the Sabbath. Hence Jesus asked, "Doesn't each of you on the Sabbath... give it [his ox or donkey] water?" (Luke 13:15)

Isaiah describes God's care for his people as a shepherd carrying lambs and not pushing ewes too hard during the time of lambing. "He gathers the lambs in his arms... he gently leads those who have young" (40:11).

Camels are well suited to survive desert conditions. Their long legs keep their bellies well away from the blazing sand. They can survive long periods without food and water and can gulp 25 gallons of water in ten minutes.

The thick woollen coat of camels are perfect insulation enabling them to conserve water. Abraham and Job counted camels among their possessions (Genesis 22:16; Job 1:3; 42:12).

Bears are rarely mentioned in the Bible, but they are used in visions which were given to Isaiah (11:7), Daniel (7:5) and John (Revelation 13:2).

King Darius should not be thought eccentric for keeping a den of lions (Daniel 6:16-23). Lion-hunting was a favorite sport of kings.

The Israelites were told to be considerate and kind even to those who were hostile towards them. If they saw their enemy's donkey collapse under its load they were told, "be sure to help him with it" (Exodus 23:5).

The quails the Lord provided for the Israelites in the desert were a small game bird which flew in large flocks close to the ground. They often become exhausted and when they land can easily be caught by hand.

Facts 6

ALL CREATURES GREAT AND SMALL

Exotic animals were imported by Solomon (1 Kings 10:22). Countries such as Assyria had public zoos and bred lions which were used in royal hunts.

"You anoint my head with oil" (Psalm 23:5) is perhaps explained by the fact that if a sheep was cut a shepherd would apply some of the olive oil he always carried with him for this purpose.

The Old Testament teaches that animals should be cared for and well-treated. This attitude was not taken up in the West until the nineteenth century.

In the Bible horses are often linked with war. Deuteronomy 17:16 and Isaiah 31:1 warn Israel against equipping themselves with horses. In the book of Revelation (6:1-8) horses are still linked with war.

In addition to birds only three kinds of animals were offered in Jewish sacrifices; goats, sheep and bullocks. Priests who sinned offered a young bull, rulers offered a goat and ordinary people a lamb or goat.

The donkey was a symbol of patient service and humility and it is perhaps for this reason that Jesus chose to ride into Jerusalem on a donkey on the Sunday before his death.

In Lake Galilee the "St. Peter's fish", tilapa, often pick up bright objects in their mouths to prevent their young fish from returning to their mouths for protection. This may shed light on the coin mentioned in Matthew 17:24-27.

Jesus says he is "the gate" for sheep (John 10:7). At night the shepherd himself would lie across the opening of the cave to protect his sheep. The shepherd became the door or gate for the sheep to pass through to the pasture.

Nearly every sacrifice the Israelites made involved sprinkling or smearing the blood of an animal on the altar in the tabernacle. This emphasised that one life was being given on behalf of another.

Elijah, Your Chariot Is Waiting

Quiz # 1

ELIJAH, YOUR CHARIOT IS WAITING

1. Who escaped, by night, in a basket down a city wall when he heard that the Jews plotted to kill him?

2. Who was in danger of being killed by fire and water by his convulsions?

3. What name does Revelation 6:8 give to the rider of the pale horse?

4. Which godly man, in the middle of great suffering, cursed the day he was born?

5. After David had killed Goliath, the Shaaraim Road from Gath to Ekron was lined with the dead bodies of which people?

6. Everyone in Israel mourned for their king-maker and buried him in his home town of Ramah. Who was he?

7. In the New Testament who did some Jews seize in the temple courts and nearly kill?

8. Which Old Testament book says that there is a time to kill and a time to heal?

9. How did Hazael assassinate the sick Ben-Hadad and so become king?

10. Which two brothers murdered Abner?

11. Who falsely claimed that he killed Saul in accordance with Saul's request?

12. In which valley did David strike down 18,000 Edomites?

13. Who said of the people of Gog that every man's sword would be against his brother?

14. Who killed Solomon's brother Adonijah on Solomon's orders?

15. Who said that if anyone killed Cain he would suffer vengeance seven times over?

Answers

1. Paul 2. The deaf, mute boy who was brought to Jesus for healing 3. Death
4. Job 5. The Philistines 6. Samuel 7. Paul 8. Ecclesiastes 9. He suffocated him with a thick wet cloth
10. Joab and Abishai 11. An Amalekite young man 12. The Valley of Salt
13. Ezekiel 14. Benaiah 15. The Lord

Quiz #2
ELIJAH, YOUR CHARIOT IS WAITING

1. What did Sennacherib's two sons, Adrammelech and Sharezer, do while he was worshiping his god Nisroch?

2. Who saved Israel by killing 600 Philistines with an ox-goad?

3. How many of the Arameans who helped Hadadezer were killed by David's army?

4. Which judge "on one stone murdered his seventy brothers"?

5. Who killed thirty men at Ashkelon?

6. Who with ten men assassinated Gedaliah?

7. Which army had more people killed by large hailstones than by the swords of the Israelites?

8. For how long did the Israelites mourn Aaron?

9. Who was killed by being stabbed in the stomach while he was lying down at midday?

10. When Saul's armor-bearer saw that Saul was dead after falling on his own sword, what did he do?

11. Who told his wife to say that she was his sister because he feared that Pharaoh might kill him?

12. Who plotted to arrest Jesus and in some underhand way to kill him?

13. Who did God tell in a dream that he was as good as dead because he had taken a woman who was married?

14. Who died at Kiriath Arba and was wept over by Abraham?

15. Who was dead but is now alive for ever?

Answers

1. Killed him with swords 2. Shamgar 3. 22,000 4. Abimelech
5. Samson 6. Ishmael 7. The Amorites 8. 30 days 9. Ish-Bosheth 10. He fell on his own sword
11. Abraham 12. The chief priests and the elders of the people
13. Abimelech 14. Sarah 15. The risen Lord Jesus Christ

Quiz #3

ELIJAH, YOUR CHARIOT IS WAITING

1. How many suicides are recorded in the Bible?

2. Who predicted that brothers would betray brothers to death and that children would even rebel against their parents and have them put to death?

3. True or false? In the Old Testament someone convicted of murder could offer a ransom in return for his death sentence being commuted.

4. Who slaughtered 80 men and then threw their bodies into a cistern in Jerusalem?

5. Which prophet records that God compared the unfaithful officials in Jerusalem to wolves tearing their prey and shedding blood in order to make money?

6. Who, according to one of God's commands, had to be stoned or shot with arrows but couldn't have a hand laid on him?

7. Which person who had eleven brothers was embalmed and put in a coffin in Egypt?

8. According to Psalm 116:15, what is precious about God's saints?

9. Where did Moses say a blasphemer should be stoned?

10. Where in the Bible does it say that nobody has power concerning the day of their death?

11. Who committed his spirit into God the Father's hands as he died?

12. Which woman said to her mother-in-law that she would die where she died and would be buried where she was buried?

13. Where, according to the book of Revelation 21:1-4, will there be no more death?

14. Who warned his hearers to be more concerned about the one who could kill the soul than about those who could kill the body?

15. Which Old Testament prophet records the words, "I will destroy her ruler and kill all her officials"?

Quiz #4

ELIJAH, YOUR CHARIOT IS WAITING

1. True or false? Two brothers had all the people of Shechem killed for the sake of one woman whose name was Esther.

2. Which king of Judah sacrificed his own children by burning them before pagan gods?

3. Which of Joseph's brothers did not want to kill him?

4. Which of Jesus' disciples said that the disciples should go with Jesus and die with him?

5. After the downfall of Haman, who became second in rank to King Xerxes?

6. Which Israelite commander was killed at the gates of Hebron?

7. When Pharaoh heard that Moses had killed an Egyptian, what did he try to do to Moses?

8. True or false? The Israelites were given a law by God stating that murderers should be put to death.

9. Which woman murdered her whole family, except one grandson?

10. Which king of Israel was burned to death after he set fire to his own palace?

11. What were the four kinds of destroyers God promised he would send on the unrepentant people of Jerusalem?

12. Who said, "Don't kill us! We have wheat and barley, oil and honey, hidden in a field"?

13. Which Old Testament book opens with the words, "After the death of Moses the servant of the Lord..."?

14. Who described himself to Saul as "a dead dog"?

15. To whom did Elijah send a letter which said, "You have murdered your own brothers, men who were better than you"?

Quiz #5

ELIJAH, YOUR CHARIOT IS WAITING

1. Who was assassinated at Beth Millo?

2. Who rashly promised that if he won his battle against the Ammonites he would sacrifice the first living thing that came out of his property, and then did so when his daughter came out to greet him?

3. Who gave orders that all Hebrew baby boys should be killed while girls were allowed to live?

4. Who ordered a baby to be cut in two so that one half of the baby could be given to two women?

5. Who did Shemaiah tell to hide in the temple because men were planning to kill him at night?

6. In which poetic book of the Old Testament is the verse, "Bloodthirsty men hate a man of integrity and seek to kill the upright"?

7. Which of David's sons was murdered at a party?

8. Which Old Testament prophet asked God not to forgive the crimes of those who sought to kill him?

9. Who told Moses to say to Pharaoh that his firstborn son would be killed?

10. In which Old Testament book is it written, "Cursed is the man who accepts a bribe to kill an innocent person"?

11. Who prevented soldiers from killing Paul and other prisoners on board a boat?

12. After he had been killed in battle who had his head and his body attached to the wall of a town called Beth Shan?

13. A tornado killed whose ten children?

14. Which biblical book pictures all of the dead, both great and small, standing before God's throne as books are opened?

15. Who is going to end up by being thrown into a lake of burning sulfur?

Answers

1. Joash 2. Jephthah 3. The King of Egypt 4. Solomon
5. Nehemiah 6. Proverbs 7. Amnon 8. Jeremiah 9. The Lord God 10. Deuteronomy
11. A centurion 12. King Saul 13. Job's 14. The book of Revelation 15. The devil

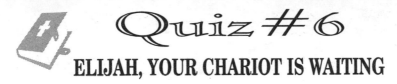

Quiz #6

ELIJAH, YOUR CHARIOT IS WAITING

1. In the book of Genesis, who killed his brother, Abel?

2. In the book of Genesis, how did God destroy the cities of Sodom and Gomorrah?

3. True of false? In the Old Testament, God destroyed the cities of Sodom and Gomorrah because he could not find even ten good people living there.

4. Which Old Testament character was turned into a pillar of salt?

5. In the book of Genesis, who narrowly escaped death when Abraham was about to sacrifice him?

6. Whose brothers hoped he would meet a sticky end when they threw him into a well and abandoned him?

7. Joseph's brothers showed Jacob Joseph's blood-stained coat. What did Jacob think had happened to Joseph?

8. In the book of Genesis, what happened to Pharaoh's baker, who was imprisoned with Joseph and told him his dream?

9. In the book of Genesis, what dream did the baker tell Joseph that he had?

10. In the book of Exodus, what fate did Pharaoh decree for every male child born to a Hebrew woman?

11. Which Old Testament character was saved from a certain death because his mother hid him among the bulrushes on the banks of the Nile?

12. Who rescued baby Moses from the river Nile?

13. In Exodus, who met their deaths in the tenth plague?

14. How did the Israelites escape the angel of death?

15. In the book of Exodus, who was drowned in the Red Sea?

Quiz #7

ELIJAH, YOUR CHARIOT IS WAITING

1. Why didn't the Israelites starve as they wandered in the desert?

2. Which Old Testament city was destroyed when its walls fell to the ground?

3. When Joshua destroyed the city of Jericho, he cursed any man who might try to rebuild it. In the book 1 Kings, who unwisely rebuilt the city?

4. In the book of Judges, who killed Sisera by driving a tent peg through the temple of his head?

5. At which cave did 3,000 men try to kill Israel's most famous judge?

6. Which Old Testament character met his death when he single-handedly destroyed a Philistine temple?

7. In which book of the Bible does the account of Samson's death appear?

8. True or false? When Samson's hair was cut off he lost his strength for ever.

9. In the book 1 Samuel, who died suddenly when he heard the news that the Ark of the Covenant had been captured by the Philistines?

10. What were the names of Eli's two sons who were killed in battle against the Philistines?

11. Which Old Testament character died when he was hit on the forehead by a stone from a sling?

12. Who narrowly escaped being killed when King Saul threw a spear at him?

13. In 1 Samuel, how did King Saul die?

14. Which Old Testament king was warned of his imminent death by the witch of Endor?

15. Who was a close friend of David and died with his father Saul in a battle against the Philistines?

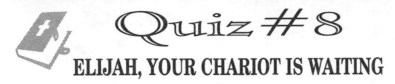

Quiz #8

ELIJAH, YOUR CHARIOT IS WAITING

1. In 2 Samuel, what was the name of Bathsheba's husband whose death in battle King David arranged?

2. To whom did the prophet Nathan say, "The Lord says: 'Out of your own household I am going to bring calamity on you' "?

3. Which Old Testament character came to a sticky end when he was caught by his head in the branches of an oak tree?

4. Who killed a man hanging from the branches of a tree?

5. In 1 Kings, who was stoned to death after he refused to sell his vineyard to King Ahab?

6. Which infamous Old Testament queen died when she was pushed out of a window?

7. According to the book of Jeremiah, what happened to many of the people of Jerusalem after the city was defeated by Nebuchadnezzar, king of Babylon?

8. Which prophet falsely said that Nebuchadnezzar's grip on Jerusalem would be broken?

9. Which three people escaped death when they were thrown into Nebuchadnezzar's fiery furnace?

10. Which Old Testament character saw a hand writing on the wall and was slain later that night?

11. Who was saved from being mauled to death in the lions' den?

12. Why was Daniel condemned to death in the lions' den?

13. What happened to King Darius' wicked officials who had plotted against Daniel?

14. In the book of Esther, what was the name of the chief minister who plotted to have all Jews put to death?

15. Which Old Testament character's sticky end is described thus: "But when they went out to bury her, they found nothing except her skull, her feet and her hands"?

Answers

1. Uriah the Hittite 2. King David 3. Absalom 4. Joab, commander of David's army 5. Naboth 6. Queen Jezebel 7. They were taken into exile 8. Hananiah 9. Shadrach, Meshach and Abednego 10. King Belshazzar 11. Daniel 12. Because he continued to worship God and not King Darius 13. They were thrown to the lions themselves 14. Haman 15. Jezebel

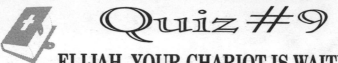

Quiz #9

ELIJAH, YOUR CHARIOT IS WAITING

1. True or false? Jonah met his death when he was swallowed by a giant fish.

2. True or false? The people of Nineveh did not listen to the prophet Jonah's warning that they should repent, so their city was destroyed.

3. Whose head was presented to Salome on a platter?

4. How had John the Baptist offended Herod and his wife?

5. In the New Testament, who ordered that all baby boys in Bethlehem under the age of two should be killed?

6. According to tradition, which of the disciples died by being crucified upside down?

7. Which group of animals rushed into the lake and were drowned when Jesus healed a man who was possessed by demons?

8. Which of Jesus' parables features a traveler who was attacked and left half-dead on his way to Jericho?

9. True or false? In Jesus' Parable of the Good Samaritan, three men passed by the injured traveler before the Samaritan stopped to help him.

10. In Jesus' story of the rich man and the beggar Lazarus, what happens to the rich man when he dies?

11. In Jesus' Parable of the Talents, why did the master take the third servant's one talent away and throw him out of the house?

12. Which New Testament character said, shortly before his death, "I have sinned... for I have betrayed innocent blood"?

13. What was the name of the first Christian martyr whose death is described in Acts?

14. According to the book of Acts, which disciple, brother of John, was "put to death with the sword" by King Herod?

15. In the book of Acts, who fell out of a window to his death, but was brought back to life by Paul?

Answers

1. False. Jonah was swallowed by a fish, but didn't die (Jonah 1:17)
2. False. They repented and God spared their city (Jonah 3:10) **3.** John the Baptist **4.** John the Baptist said in public that they had married unlawfully **5.** King Herod **6.** Peter **7.** Pigs **8.** The Parable of the Good Samaritan **9.** False. Only two men passed by (Luke 10:31-32) **10.** He is sent to hell **11.** Because he had not done anything with the money **12.** Judas **13.** Stephen **14.** James **15.** Eutychus

Facts 1

ELIJAH, YOUR CHARIOT IS WAITING

When Joseph died the Egyptians mourned for him for seventy days. The length of the mourning period depended on the importance of the person who had died. The Egyptians treated Joseph like royalty by observing such a long time of mourning for him.

The Bible does not say that Enoch "died", but that he was "taken". The implication is that he was taken to heaven, to God's presence, without experiencing death.

When Ahithophel realized that his advice was not going to be taken, he went home and took his own life by hanging himself. He probably thought that the rebellion he had conspired in would fail and he would be branded a traitor.

Pilate allowed Jesus to be crucified even though he knew that Jesus was innocent. In both John's Gospel and in Luke's Gospel the fact that Pilate found no basis for any charges against Jesus is recorded three times.

The risen Jesus told Peter that when he was old he would stretch out his hands, be dressed by somebody else and go where he did not want to go (John 21:18). From the days of the early church this has been taken as a reference to Peter's own martyrdom by crucifixion.

Joab stabbed Abner to death. He did this to avenge the death of his brother Asahel. But as Abner had killed Asahel in a battle, Joab's action can hardly be classed as justifiable blood revenge. It was murder.

When Jesus told his would-be followers that they had to take up their crosses if they wanted to be his disciples, it was no mere figure of speech. Jesus was saying that being his follower could lead to being put to death, since the cross was an instrument of death.

Ebed-Melech heard that Jeremiah had been left to die in a muddy cistern. Ebed-Melech went and told King Zedekiah about this as the king was sitting in the Benjamin Gate. This gate served as a courtroom and Zedekiah may have been dealing with legal cases when Ebed-Melech arrived.

"Thou shalt not kill" (Exodus 20:13 KJV) is one of the Ten Commandments. The NIV has "You shall not murder" because the Hebrew verb implies a deliberate and premeditated act.

Facts 2

ELIJAH, YOUR CHARIOT IS WAITING

Amos condemned the Moabites for burning the bones of the king of Edom (Amos 2:1). This prevented the spirit of the king ever finding rest as it was then believed that bodies decently buried found rest.

Jesus saved an adulterous woman from being stoned (John 8:1-11). The teachers of the law and the Pharisees had conveniently forgotten that the law stated that both parties, the man and the woman, should be executed.

The Israelites were told that they would die if they walked up Mount Sinai or even touched it. This was to teach them about God's holiness. Mount Sinai was holy because of God's presence there.

Joshua 7:25 says that "all Israel" stoned Achan and then burned his body. God had ordered anyone who broke his covenant to be stoned. His body was burned as a sign that the land was being purged of evil.

The Bible states that Joseph was 110 years old when he died (Genesis 50:26). Some very old Egyptian records reveal that 110 years was considered to be an ideal life span. The Egyptians would have thought that Joseph was greatly blessed to have lived to that exact age.

Two of Aaron's sons, Nadab and Abihu, fell dead because they made an offering of unauthorized fire. In some unexplained way they used fire in a way not permitted by God. This incident illustrates the dire consequences of disobeying God.

Some parts of the Bible appear to teach that the wicked will be annihilated. However, Revelation 14:11 does not seem to support this . "And the smoke of their torment ascendeth up for ever and ever: and they [those who worship the beast] have no rest day or night" (KJV).

The Bible does not say that Elijah died but that he was carried into heaven by a whirlwind. Elijah never experienced physical death but was taken bodily into heaven.

Jeroboam's wife was told by Ahijah that her son would die as soon as she returned to her house. This did indeed take place. However, her son was spared the utter disgrace which befell his father's house.

According to the book of Genesis everyone is made of dust and after death will return to being dust. In the Bible dust often stands for human frailty.

Facts 3

ELIJAH, YOUR CHARIOT IS WAITING

The phrase "a second death" is mentioned only in the book of Revelation. It is defined as the "Lake of Fire".

2 Samuel 12:14 states that because of David's sin the baby son born to Bathsheba would die. David was disciplined in this way by God, but was himself spared the usual death penalty for murder and adultery.

Adoniram, who was in charge of forced labor in King Rehoboam's time, was stoned to death by the Israelites (1 Kings 12.18). But he was in this post under both David and Solomon and the people really only vented their fury on him because Rehoboam escaped.

Hebrews 11:37 says that some of God's faithful followers in the Old Testament were martyred by being sawn in two. While the Bible does not say who this refers to there is an old tradition that it alludes to the way Isaiah was killed, by order of wicked King Manasseh.

When Josiah died, Jeremiah composed laments for him (2 Chronicles 35:25). This is one of the arguments for supporting Jeremiah's authorship of the book of Lamentations.

The Israelites had a law that anyone accused of murder could not be convicted on the evidence of a single witness (Numbers 35:30). There had to be 2 or 3 witnesses before anyone could be put to death for murder.

Hebrews 11:37 mentions that some of God's people were stoned to death in the Old Testament. One such faithful prophet was Zechariah who was stoned to death by order of King Joash in the courtyard of the temple.

Some valiant men from Jabesh Gilead retrieved Saul's dead body from Beth Shan and burned it. Cremation was not a normal practice among the Jews, but was probably done in this instance to prevent Saul's corpse being further abused.

Aaron died on top of Mount Hor in full view of all the Israelites. Just before he died, Moses placed Aaron's priestly garments on his son Eleazar. Aaron's death marked the passing of a generation.

Facts 4

ELIJAH, YOUR CHARIOT IS WAITING

1 Kings 13 records the death of an old man of God. A lion killed him as he traveled by donkey. God's hand is seen here because when a prophet arrived on the scene he found that the donkey had not run off and the body had not been mauled.

The Living One holds the keys of death and Hades (Revelation 1:18). This emphasizes Christ's complete control over the domain of life and death.

Ecclesiastes 3:2 says there is a time to be born and a time to die. This teaches that birth and death are ultimately in God's hands and are by divine appointment.

Jesus promised one of the dying criminals beside him on the cross that he would be with him in paradise. The word "paradise" only occurs three times in the New Testament and refers to a state of rest and a time of bliss between death and resurrection.

Paul states in 1 Corinthians 15:26 that death is the last enemy that will be destroyed. This will happen at Jesus' return when all his enemies will be conquered.

The church at Smyrna are encouraged to be faithful to God even if this involves martyrdom (Revelation 2:10). They are promised the "crown of life," a reference to the garland or wreath won for endurance at athletic contests.

Eliphaz, one of Job's so-called comforters, maintains that resentment kills a fool (Job 5:2). By this he was implying that Job faced his difficulties because of his resentment against God.

Jesus warned his disciples that the day would come when they would be killed for being his followers and that those who did this would think that they were serving God. Throughout history this has been proved true as religious people have often been the greatest persecutors of Christians.

Jesus said Old Testament martyrs ranged from Abel to Zechariah. Abel's murder comes in Genesis, but Zechariah's murder is recorded in 2 Chronicles. The Jews placed 2 Chronicles last in the Old Testament.

Gideon ordered his son Jepher to kill Zebah and Zalmunna. Jepher refused because he was only a boy and was afraid to do this (Judges 8:20). It was probably considered a great disgrace to be killed by a child.

Facts 5

ELIJAH, YOUR CHARIOT IS WAITING

Ishmael assassinated Gedaliah (Jeremiah 41:1). As Gedaliah had been left in charge of Jerusalem as a puppet ruler controlled by the Babylonians, and since Ishmael was himself of royal blood and had been one of King Zedekiah's officers, Ishmael may have acted out of loyalty to Zedekiah.

While Jesus was eating in the home of Simon the Leper a woman poured very expensive perfume on him which the guests said was a waste (Mark 14:3-9). Jesus said that it was in preparation for his burial. Jews anointed their corpses with aromatic oil as part of their funeral preparation.

Methuselah was 969 years old when he died (Genesis 5:27). He had "lived 187 years" when his son Lamech was born; Lamech had "lived 182 years" when Noah was born; and Noah was 600 years old when the flood came. So Methuselah died in the year of the flood.

Job asked the question, "If a man dies, will he live again?" (Job 14:14) In the Old Testament there appears to have been less certainty about resurrection life than there is in the New Testament.

Herod, grandson of Herod the Great, died by being struck down by God's angel and then being eaten by worms. Acts 12:23 indicates that this happened suddenly, just after people had hailed him as a god.

Isaiah prophesied that the Lord Almighty would swallow up death for ever. So, death, which has been called "the great swallower" will itself be swallowed up. Paul uses this verse to great effect in 1 Corinthians 15:54.

Jeremiah, personifying death, talked about death climbing in through their windows (Jeremiah 9:21). In a similar way Habakkuk says that death is never satisfied (Habakkuk 2:5).

The book of Lamentations records instances of mothers cooking their own children for food (4:10). When all the food in Jerusalem ran out during the Babylonian siege of 586 B.C. people were driven to cannibalism.

Apocalypse Now

Quiz # 1

APOCALYPSE NOW

1. Name the final battle between the forces of good and evil to take place at the end of the world.

2. When Jesus said that there will be no marriage in heaven, who was he talking to?

3. To what assembly did Paul say, "He [God] has set a day when he will judge the world with justice"?

4. How many horsemen are there in Revelation 6 ?

5. True or false? Jesus said that he would return in the same way in which he ascended into heaven.

6. In the light of God's coming judgment, who wrote that Christians live as "strangers" in "reverent fear"?

7. From where will people come to take their places at the feast in the kingdom of heaven?

8. Which book of the Bible says that the dead "were judged according to what they had done as recorded in the books"?

9. In Jesus' parable about all the nations being collected together and separated into two groups, the sheep were separated from what other animal?

10. True or false? In Mark 13, Jesus said that before the end of the world there would be an outbreak of unprecedented global peace between the nations.

11. What is the name of the city where, according to the author of Hebrews, there will be "thousands upon thousands of angels in joyful assembly"?

12. In John's apocalyptic vision, who sang, "Worthy is the lamb who was slain"?

13. When did Jesus say, "You will see the Son of Man sitting at the right hand of the Mighty One, and coming on the clouds of heaven"?

14. What was written on the foreheads of the 144,000?

15. In the face of what threatened destruction did Abraham ask, "Will not the Judge of all the earth do right?"?

Answers

1. Armageddon 2. The Sadducees 3. To a meeting of the Areopagus in Athens
4, 4 5. False. The angels said this (Acts 1:11) 6. Peter 7. From all 4 points of the compass
8. The book of Revelation 9. Goats 10. False. He spoke of wars and rumors of wars (Mark 13:7) 11. Heavenly
Jerusalem, the city of the living God 12. Thousands upon thousands of angels 13. When he was on trial before the
Sanhedrin 14. The name of the Lamb and of the Father 15. The destruction of Sodom and Gomorrah

Quiz #2

APOCALYPSE NOW

1. Supply the missing word from this verse in Psalm 58: "Surely the righteous still are rewarded; surely there is a God who ___ the earth."

2. Which New Testament book is sometimes called the Apocalypse?

3. Who, according to Revelation 20, is going to be bound by an angel for 1,000 years?

4. In Revelation 21, John records that God will wipe away every tear. He lists four things that will be "no more." Name one of the four.

5. In Isaiah's prophecy of peace in nature, who will live with the lamb?

6. Which New Testament author wrote that Jesus "would appear a second time, not to bear sin, but to bring salvation"?

7. True or false? Jesus taught that God the Father would not judge anyone as all judgment has been entrusted to the Son.

8. At Jesus' return, what will happen to the person who is ashamed of Jesus and his words?

9. Fill in the missing two words from Paul's second letter to the Corinthians: "For we must all appear before the ___ ___ of Christ."

10. True or false? The one thing that is not found in the sermons of the first Christians is any mention of God's judgment.

11. According to Isaiah's prophecy, in the year of the Lord's favor, what will happen to the ancient ruins?

12. In which of his letters does Paul write that at Jesus' second coming, God "will pay back trouble to those who trouble you"?

13. In Jesus' parable, why was the rich farmer exceedingly foolish?

14. Supply the missing word in this song sung by the great multitude in heaven: "Hallelujah! For our Lord God Almighty ___."

15. Who saw a vision of Jesus and wrote that from the waist up he looked like glowing metal, from the waist down he looked like glowing fire, and brilliant light surrounded him?

Quiz #3

APOCALYPSE NOW

1. Who said that Jesus' second coming would be as visible as lightning which comes from the east but is also seen in the west?

2. According to Isaiah, in the last days, which mountain will be chief among the mountains?

3. Who wrote, "He will judge the world in righteousness and the peoples with his truth"?

4. In the symbolic imagery used by John in Revelation 21, what is the bride of the Lamb?

5. The bride of the Lamb is bedecked with jewels, and given fine linen to wear. According to Revelation 19, what does the fine linen stand for?

6. Wide is the gate and broad the road that leads where?

7. Give the color of the first horse mentioned in Revelation 6.

8. The rider of the first horse mentioned in Revelation 6 had what in his hand?

9. What, according to Revelation 13, is going to be limited to 42 months?

10. In Revelation 20:4, what has been given to the souls of beheaded Christian martyrs?

11. In whose house did Peter say, "He [Jesus] is the one whom God appointed as judge of the living and the dead"?

12. According to Paul, when the Lord Jesus is revealed from heaven in blazing fire, who will be with him?

13. True or false? Jesus said that the righteous would live in heaven for 10,000 years.

14. Which New Testament author says that his readers should be patient and stand firm because the Lord's coming is near?

15. In the last days, when there is peace among the nations, what, according to Micah, will be beaten into pruning forks?

---

12. Powerful angels **13.** False. They will live for ever (Matthew 25:46) **14.** James **15.** Spears
9. The reign of the Beast (Antichrist) **10.** The authority to judge **11.** Cornelius, the Roman centurion
4. The holy city, Jerusalem **5.** The righteous acts of the saints **6.** To destruction **7.** White **8.** A bow
1. Jesus **2.** The mountain of the Lord's temple (Mount Zion) **3.** The Psalmist

Answers

Quiz #4

APOCALYPSE NOW

1. Which Old Testament prophet told the people to go into their rooms, close the doors and hide until God's wrath had passed?

2. Paul wrote to the Romans that on judgment day it will be revealed that some people, who do not have the written law, nevertheless obey the law written where?

3. True or false? Jesus said that one of the signs of the end of the age would be an increase in wickedness.

4. What is the first name given to the child-ruler mentioned in Isaiah 9:6?

5. Which prophet rebuked his hearers for longing for "the day of the Lord" warning that it would not be a day of deliverance but a day of judgment, as though a man fled from a lion only to meet a bear?

6. What was given to the rider of the first horse mentioned in Revelation 6?

7. True or false? The rider of the first horse was intent on planting seeds.

8. Which wise man thought, "God will bring to judgment both the righteous and the wicked"?

9. According to Mark 13, what will the false Christs do?

10. Name two things that, according to Mark 13, are the beginning of birth-pains marking the end of the present age.

11. What, according to Paul's second letter to Timothy, will be awarded to everyone who longs for the appearing of Jesus?

12. Why should Christians at Rome not look down on or judge a brother?

13. Where in the New Testament is the final reference to Jesus' return?

14. Where does Paul explain God's plan for the future of the nation of Israel?

15. Name the only New Testament author to use the word "antichrist."

---

13. Revelation 22:10, the penultimate verse of the Bible **14.** Romans chapters 9 to 11 **15.** John
9. Perform signs and miracles to deceive the elect **10.** Wars, false Christs, earthquakes, famine
5. Amos **6.** A crown **7.** False. He was intent on conquest (Revelation 6:2) **8.** The author of Ecclesiastes
11. A crown of righteousness **12.** Because everyone will stand before God's judgment seat
1. Isaiah **2.** On their hearts **3.** True (Matthew 24:12) **4.** Wonderful Counselor

Answers

483

Quiz #5

APOCALYPSE NOW

1. In Jesus' Parable of the Sheep and the Goats, where are the sheep and goats standing?

2. The prophet Joel pictured the day of God's judgment as a day of darkness and gloom, like what sort of terrible plague?

3. What is the second name given to the child ruler in Isaiah 9?

4. According to Paul in 2 Thessalonians, why do people perish?

5. True or false? Jesus said that one of the signs of the end of the age would be that America would be defeated in a battle by Russia.

6. Where, according to Jesus, do moth and rust not destroy?

7. Supply the missing word from Paul's words to the Corinthians: "Wait till the Lord comes. He will bring to ____ what is hidden in darkness."

8. Just before Stephen was martyred, what did he see as he looked up to heaven?

9. Who promised his readers that when the Chief Shepherd appears they would receive a never-fading crown of glory?

10. True or false? Jesus never spoke about eternal punishment.

11. Which Old Testament prophet wrote, "The sun will be turned to darkness and the moon to blood before the coming of the great and dreadful day of the Lord"?

12. In John the Baptist's prophecy of the coming of the Messiah, he used an image of a farmer. What does the Messiah have in his hand?

13. In John the Baptist's prophecy, what does the Messiah do with the wheat?

14. According to Isaiah, what will come up from the stump of Jesse (King David's father)?

15. True or false? Among the marks of godlessness in the last days (listed in 2 Timothy 3) people will be unforgiving.

Quiz #6

APOCALYPSE NOW

1. With reference to God's judgment, which Old Testament prophet said, "Not a root or branch will be left to them [the arrogant and evildoers]"?

2. Supply the missing four words from Malachi's prophecy: "For you who revere my name, the sun of righteousness will arise with ___ ___ ___ ___."

3. Paul does not use the word "Antichrist" but has another name for the same person. What is this name?

4. What is the name used in Revelation for the Antichrist?

5. When Jesus spoke to the Sadducees, he said that those who take part in the resurrection of the dead will not marry. What else will they not do?

6. What is the color of the second horse mentioned in Revelation 6?

7. In the vision in Revelation 6, what was given to the rider of the second horse?

8. The rider of the second horse was given power to do what?

9. True or false? Jesus said that anybody who said, "You fool," would be liable to the fire of hell.

10. To which of his friends did Paul write: "There will be terrible times in the last days"?

11. In Isaiah's prophecy of peace in nature, the lion will eat straw like what animal?

12. In Jude's account of the day of judgment, what sin had been committed by the angels chained up in darkness?

13. True or false? Peter wrote that when Jesus returns he will expose the motives of people's hearts.

14. Paul wrote that in the last days people will be lovers of themselves and what else?

15. Paul wrote that in the last days people will always be learning, and yet what will they not acknowledge?

---

14. Money **15.** The truth

their own home (heaven) **13.** False. Paul wrote this to the Corinthians (1 Corinthians 4:5)

9. True (Matthew 5:22) **10.** Timothy **11.** The ox **12.** They did not keep their positions of authority but abandoned

4. The Beast **5.** Die **6.** Fiery red **7.** A large sword **8.** To take peace from the earth and to make men kill each other

1. Malachi **2.** Healing in its wings **3.** The Man of Lawlessness

Answers

485

Quiz #7

APOCALYPSE NOW

1. In Isaiah's prophecy of peace in the new creation, what animal will the leopard lie down with?

2. Fill in the missing word from the Sermon on the Mount: "But I tell you that anybody who is ____ with his brother will be subject to judgment."

3. To which Christian minister did Paul say that Jesus' second coming should be a spur to his work?

4. Paul wrote to the Thessalonians that for non-believers the day of the Lord will come like what in the night?

5. In Revelation 20, the devil is called Satan, and he is also given the name of what mythological animal?

6. According to the prophets, in the future age, God's chosen king will be a descendant of which king of Israel?

7. Which New Testament writer wrote, "Dear children... as you have heard that the antichrist is coming, even now many antichrists have come"?

8. From the Sermon on the Mount, why should those who are persecuted and maligned for the sake of Jesus nevertheless be happy?

9. Supply the missing four words from chapter 12 of Hebrews: "[Jesus] for the ____ ____ ____ endured the cross, scorning its shame, and sat down at the right hand of the throne of God."

10. True or false? In the Parable of the Vineyard Workers, the workers who worked all day were paid more than the workers who worked for only one hour.

11. Fill in the missing word from Daniel's prophecy: "Those who are wise will shine like the brightness of the heavens, and those who lead many to righteousness like the ____ for ever and ever."

12. Who wrote that scoffers would come in the last days?

13. What is the third name given to the child-ruler mentioned in Isaiah 9:6?

14. True or false? Jesus said that anybody who said to him, "Lord, Lord," would enter the kingdom of heaven.

15. In Revelation 6, what did the rider of the black horse have in his hand, symbolizing famine?

Quiz #8
APOCALYPSE NOW

1. In the book of Revelation, who has the number 666?

2. True or false? The Bible never speaks about "rewards" in heaven.

3. In order to stress the importance of obedience to God, who taught that it is better to tear out an eye than have two eyes but go to hell?

4. According to Mark 13, as well as false Christs, what other group of false people will appear in the lead up to the end times?

5. Who appealed to his readers as a fellow elder, a witness of Jesus' sufferings and as one who was going to share in the future glory?

6. True or false? When Jesus said to the repentant thief, "Today you will be with me in paradise," the thief replied, "Then save me from dying on this cross."

7. Which Old Testament prophet said that a time would come when the earth would no longer conceal her slain?

8. When Martha said to Jesus, "I know he will rise in the resurrection at the last day," who was she talking about?

9. In Isaiah's prophecy of future peace, who will lead the wild and tame animals?

10. Who wrote that at the Lord's coming the ungodly would be convicted of all the harsh words they had spoken against the Lord?

11. Matthew 24 records Jesus' warning that he would come again when his disciples were not expecting him. What did Jesus therefore tell them to do?

12. True or false? Peter wrote that he would prefer to be away from the body and at home with the Lord.

13. Supply the missing words from Paul's first letter to the Corinthians: "Therefore you do not lack any spiritual gift as you eagerly wait for ___ ___ ___."

14. In Jesus' Parable of the Wedding Banquet, why was one of the guests thrown out?

15. When did Jesus pray, "Father, I want those you have given me to be with me where I am and to see my glory"?

Quiz #9

APOCALYPSE NOW

1. In which Gospel are these words of Jesus recorded: "There is a judge for the one who rejects me and does not accept my words"?

2. True or false? Paul taught that at Jesus' second coming the Christians who are still alive will be raised up to meet Jesus in the air.

3. How many apocalyptic visions are recorded in the book of Zechariah?

4. What was seen in the first vision in the book of Zechariah?

5. What was the meaning of Zechariah's first vision?

6. Which Old Testament prophet spoke about God creating new heavens and a new earth and a time when "the former things will not be remembered"?

7. What did Paul pray for in connection with the coming of Jesus for the spirits, souls and bodies of the Christians in Thessalonica?

8. According to Isaiah, who will have good news preached to them in the year of the Lord's favor?

9. What is the color of the third horse mentioned in Revelation 6?

10. In Joel's prophecy of the day of the Lord, what will the sons and daughters do?

11. According to Peter, there will be a new heaven and a new earth which will be the home of what?

12. How many times is Jesus' return mentioned in the New Testament?

13. Who said that at the end of the age the wicked would be thrown into a "fiery furnace" where there would be "weeping and gnashing of teeth"?

14. What percentage of the Bible is made up of predictions about the future?

15. In the Parable of the Great Banquet, when the banquet was ready, the guests made excuses. Name one of the three excuses given.

Quiz # 10

APOCALYPSE NOW

1. Who told Timothy "to keep this command without spot or blame until the appearing of our Lord Jesus Christ"?

2. Supply the missing word from Isaiah's prophecy of the end times: "For the earth will be full of the _____ of the Lord as the waters cover the sea."

3. According to Peter, which cities did God make "an example of what is going to happen to the ungodly"?

4. Who is going to be thrown into the lake of burning sulfur with the Beast and the false prophet?

5. Zechariah said that when the Lord comes to reign, Israel would have to flee from the earthquake like they had to previously in whose reign?

6. According to Paul's letter to Timothy, in the last days, instead of loving God, what will people be lovers of?

7. True or false? Paul lists the wickedness of the last days and tells Timothy to do all he can to convert people who have only a form of godliness.

8. What is the fourth name given to the child-ruler mentioned in Isaiah 9:6?

9. Supply the missing word from Paul's letter to Titus: "While we wait for the blessed _____ the glorious appearing of our great God and Savior, Jesus Christ."

10. Jesus said that the coming of the Son of Man would overtake people suddenly and shockingly, just as in what Old Testament period?

11. True or false? Jesus said that only he and God the Father knew when the "day" would come?

12. Which New Testament writer wrote that his readers should continue in Jesus so that when Jesus comes they will be confident and unashamed?

13. In Zechariah's second vision, what symbolized that the nations which destroyed Israel would be destroyed?

14. According to Isaiah, in the year of the Lord's favor, who will be released from darkness?

15. When Jesus talked of hell as a place where "their worm does not die, and the fire is not quenched", which prophet was he quoting from?

Quiz # 11

APOCALYPSE NOW

1. In Zechariah's third vision, forecasting full restoration for God's people, Zechariah saw a man with a measuring line: what was he measuring?

2. In Revelation 19 John records a vision of a great white horse. The rider is called Faithful and True. What further name is he given?

3. The armies of the rider on the white horse are also on white horses. What are they wearing?

4. According to Jesus, what is it, that, if given to one of his little ones, will earn someone a reward in heaven?

5. Supply the missing word from Jeremiah's prophecy in chapter 23: "'The days are coming,' declares the Lord, 'when I will raise up to David a righteous ____.'"

6. According to Revelation 13, who gives the Beast his power?

7. How long will the child-ruler of Isaiah 9:6 reign?

8. Who, in torment in hell, saw Abraham?

9. What, according to the apostle Paul, are our light and passing troubles going to achieve for us?

10. What is the meaning of Zechariah's fourth vision in which the high priest's dirty clothes are replaced by rich, clean clothes?

11. Who predicted that Zion's future king would take away the war-horses from Jerusalem?

12. Paul wrote to Timothy that in the last days people would have a form of godliness, but what would they lack?

13. Supply the missing two words from the promise Jesus gave to his followers: "In my Father's house are many ___; if it were not so, I would have told you. I am going there to prepare a ___ for you."

14. According to Paul, where is our citizenship?

15. To whom did Paul write, "We eagerly await a Savior from there [heaven], the Lord Jesus Christ"?

Quiz # 12

APOCALYPSE NOW

1. From Jeremiah chapter 23, complete the name given to the future King who reigns wisely: "This is the name by which he will be called: The Lord Our ___."

2. True or false? Jesus compared heaven to a wedding banquet which a Pharisee prepared for his son.

3. In which of his letters does Paul say that Christians must not mind if their earthly bodies are destroyed because they have "a building from God, an eternal house in heaven"?

4. What does Paul say is a guarantee that Christians have an eternal house in heaven?

5. Who said that the day of the Lord would be like a launderer's soap?

6. What was the color of the fourth horse mentioned in Revelation 6?

7. According to Revelation 1, when Jesus returns, as well as all the peoples of the earth, who in particular will mourn because of him?

8. Who wrote that those who "do not obey the gospel of our Lord Jesus... will be... shut out from the presence of the Lord and from the majesty of his power when he comes again"?

9. Supply the missing word from Isaiah's prophecy about the child-ruler's reign: "Of the increase of his government and ___ there will be no end."

10. What symbols did Zechariah see in his fifth vision to remind him of God's mighty resources?

11. In Jesus' Parable of the Weeds, when will the weeds be separated from the wheat?

12. In Jesus' Parable of the Weeds, what do the weeds and wheat represent?

13. When Joel spoke of the day of the Lord, what did he say the young men would see?

14. According to John chapter 6, who will be raised up by Jesus at the last day?

15. Who, according to 1 Corinthians 15, are to be pitied more than all men?

---

14. Everyone who looks to the Son and believes in him 15. Christians if there is no resurrection
13. The young men will see visions
8. Paul 9. peace 10. The golden lampstand and two olive trees 11. At the harvest 12. Genuine and false believers
4. The Holy Spirit, who is a deposit given by God 5. Malachi 6. A pale horse 7. Those who pierced him
1. Righteousness 2. False. It was a king (Matthew 22:2) 3. 2 Corinthians

Answers

491

Quiz #13

APOCALYPSE NOW

1. What name did Ezekiel give to the shepherd who would tend Israel?

2. When Paul wrote to the Philippians that by his power Jesus would transform our lowly bodies, what did he say the new bodies would be like?

3. What, according to James, is set on fire by hell?

4. When Paul wrote to Timothy that Hymenaeus and Philetus had wandered from the truth and destroyed the faith of some, to what wrong teaching was he referring?

5. Who, in the New Testament, describes evil men as "wild waves of the sea, foaming up their shame" saying they will be judged when the Lord comes with thousands of holy ones?

6. True or false? Jesus told a story about the owner of a house, who sold his house and left the country.

7. King Nebuchadnezzar had a dream of an enormous statue made of different substances. Its head was made of gold, what were its feet made of?

8. What did King Nebuchadnezzar's statue represent?

9. Who had the wisdom to describe and interpret King Nebuchadnezzar's dream?

10. Who in the Old Testament said that the day of the Lord would "burn like a furnace"?

11. Complete Paul's "trustworthy saying": "If we disown him he will also ____us."

12. To whom did Paul write these words, "When Christ, who is your life, appears, then you also will appear with him in glory"?

13. Supply the missing word from these words spoken by God at the end of Zechariah's fifth vision: "'Not by might nor by power, but by my ____,' says the Lord."

14. Name two of the three disciples who were with Jesus on the mountain when he revealed his glory

15. Who said that the day of the Lord would be like a refiner's fire?

Quiz # 14

APOCALYPSE NOW

1. True or false? Paul wrote to Timothy that in the last days people would worm their way into homes and gain control of weak-willed women.

2. In the year of the Lord's favor, what, according to Isaiah, will replace ashes?

3. Which Old Testament prophet wrote of the future restoration: "I will make a covenant of peace with them and rid the land of wild beasts...I will send down showers in season; there will be showers of blessing"?

4. To encourage persecuted Christians, which writer said that at the return of Jesus, "You will receive the crown of glory that will never fade away"?

5. According to Hebrews, why did Moses choose disgrace rather than enjoy the treasures of Egypt?

6. Fill in the missing words from Paul's letter to the Romans: "This will take place on the day when God will judge men's ____ through Jesus Christ."

7. In Joel's prophecy of the day of the Lord, the Spirit will be poured out on all people, even on whom?

8. Zechariah's sixth vision of a large flying scroll was a condemnation of everyone who swears falsely, and of what other group of people?

9. Fill in the missing three words from Zephaniah's song of joy for a restored Jerusalem: "The Lord your God is with you, he is ____ ____ ____."

10. According to Zechariah, when the Lord comes to reign, the words HOLY TO THE LORD will be inscribed on the bells on which animals?

11. In King Nebuchadnezzar's dream, the statue was destroyed by a rock not made with hands. What then happened to the rock?

12. In King Nebuchadnezzar's dream, what did the rock represent?

13. What, according to John's first letter, is the Christian's motive for living a pure life?

14. Who referred to Jesus' return as the time "when the Chief Shepherd appears"?

15. In Zechariah's seventh vision of a woman in a basket, all iniquity in the land was removed to what more suitable place?

Quiz #15

APOCALYPSE NOW

1. What was Paul's reason for writing that the Corinthians should not judge people before the appointed time, but wait until the Lord returns?

2. In Revelation 6, what was the name of the rider on the pale horse?

3. True or false? According to the book of Revelation, when Jesus returns, only his disciples will see him.

4. Supply the missing word from Jesus' declaration in Revelation 1: "Behold I am alive for ever and ever! And I hold the ____ of death and Hades."

5. What did Zechariah see in his eighth vision symbolizing worldwide divine judgment?

6. In Zechariah's prophecy of future restoration, what name will be given to Jerusalem?

7. In Jesus' words about future destruction, where will the Abomination of Desolation stand?

8. Who said that Israel could look forward to a time when their land would be renowned for its crops, and they would no longer be victims of famine?

9. According to Jesus, when nations see the Son of Man appear in the sky with power and great glory, what will they do?

10. In the year of the Lord's favor, instead of a spirit of despair, what will the people have?

11. In Jesus' Parable of the Rich Man and Lazarus, when the rich man was in hell, why did he want Lazarus to come to him?

12. True or false? In Jesus' Parable of the Rich Man and Lazarus, Abraham said that a great chasm had been fixed between the rich man and Lazarus and no one could cross it.

13. In the book of Revelation, John is shown a series of seven seals followed by two other series of seven things. Name one of them.

14. What followed closely behind the rider of the fourth horse mentioned in Revelation 6?

15. According to Hebrews chapter 9, human beings are destined to die once, and what comes after that death?

---

13. Trumpets and bowls 14. Hades 15. The judgment
11. The rich man wanted Lazarus to cool his tongue with water 12. True (Luke 16:26)
7. "where it does not belong," in the holy place, in God's temple 8. Ezekiel 9. Mourn 10. A garment of praise
(Revelation 1:7) 4. Keys 5. Four chariots drawn by red, white, black, and dappled horses 6. The City of Truth
1. Because God will reveal hidden motives, and expose what is hidden 2. Death 3. False. Every eye will see him

Answers

Quiz # 16

APOCALYPSE NOW

1. Who, according to Jesus, are going to shine like the sun in the kingdom of their Father?

2. Which two Old Testament people talked with Jesus during his transfiguration?

3. Who in the Old Testament stated that the Lord would guide him with his counsel and afterwards would take him into glory?

4. Whose words is Paul alluding to when he states in 1 Corinthians 15:54 that "death has been swallowed up in victory"?

5. Which Old Testament prophet was told to take two sticks, one for Judah and one for Ephraim [Israel], and join them together to symbolize future unity?

6. What, according to Paul, is the perishable going to be clothed with?

7. The prophet Jeremiah looked forward to the day when God's laws would be written—where?

8. Supply the missing word from 2 Corinthians 3: "You show that you are a letter from Christ," written "not on tablets of ____ but on tablets of the human heart."

9. Who describes evil men as wandering stars?

10. If we share in Christ's sufferings now, what, according to Romans 8, will we also share in?

11. Who promised his readers that at Christ's return they would be like Jesus and would see him as he is?

12. In Jesus' Parable of the Tenants, why did the owner of the vineyard send his own son to collect the harvest?

13. What happened to the son of the vineyard owner in the Parable of the Tenants?

14. What did Jesus' listeners say should happen to the tenants?

15. In Jesus' Parable of the Tenants of the Vineyard, the servants were the prophets, and the son was Jesus. Who did the tenants represent?

Answers

1. The righteous 2. Moses and Elijah 3. The Psalmist in Psalm 74 4. Isaiah 5. Ezekiel 6. With the imperishable 7. On people's hearts 8. stone 9. Jude 10. Christ's glory 11. John 12. Because the tenants had beaten up, killed, or stoned the servants, and he said, "They will respect my son." 13. The tenants killed him 14. The vineyard should be taken from them and they should "come to a wretched end" 15. The leaders of the Jews who rejected Jesus

Quiz # 17

APOCALYPSE NOW

1. After Judas Iscariot committed suicide, who said of him that he had gone "to where he belongs"?

2. True or false? Jesus said that a time was coming when those who were in their graves would hear his voice and come out; and those who had done good would live.

3. In the future time when the dead heard the voice of Jesus, what did Jesus say would happen to those who had done evil?

4. What do the following Old Testament passages have in common: Isaiah 24–27; Joel 1–3; Zechariah 9–14?

5. When Jesus said to the crowd, "When you see a cloud, you know it will rain," why did he go on to condemn his listeners?

6. Which Old Testament prophet wrote, "I will make a covenant of peace with them; it will be an everlasting covenant"?

7. In Daniel's vision of the four great beasts, representing world empires, what symbolizes the antichrist who wages war against the saints?

8. In Daniel's vision in chapter 7, what name is given to the one who comes with the clouds of heaven, and is given glory and sovereign power?

9. Who predicted that Zion's coming king would free prisoners from the waterless pit?

10. Supply the missing word from chapter 15 of 1 Corinthians: "The last enemy to be destroyed is ___."

11. Who, according to Jesus, has crossed over from death to life?

12. Which Old Testament prophet made this reference to the resurrection of the dead, "You who dwell in the dust, wake up and shout for joy"?

13. Paul writes in 1 Corinthians that Christians are sacred because they are God's temple. What will happen to people who destroy God's temple?

14. True or false? There will be no temple in God's new Jerusalem.

15. About what did Jesus say to the Sadducees, "You are badly mistaken"?

Answers

1. Peter **2.** True (John 5:28-29) **3.** They would be condemned **4.** They are all apocalyptic in nature. **5.** Because they could understand the signs for good or bad weather, but could not read the signs of the times (the historic events that meant Jesus was the Messiah). **6.** Ezekiel **7.** The little horn with human eyes and a boastful mouth **8.** The son of man **9.** Zechariah **10.** death **11.** Whoever has Jesus' word and believes the one who sent Jesus **12.** Isaiah **13.** God will destroy them. **14.** True (Revelation 21:22) **15.** Their refusal to believe in the resurrection

Quiz # 18

APOCALYPSE NOW

1. Who predicted that the Lord's coming would be "a unique day, without daytime or night-time"?

2. Who wrote, "How much more severely do you think a man deserves to be punished who has trampled the Son of God underfoot...?"?

3. How did Jesus prove to the Sadducees that there is a resurrection?

4. According to Daniel 7, when the last and most powerful king is overthrown, who will be given the kingdom to enjoy its benefits for ever?

5. True or false? Jesus said that anybody who gave 2,000 shekels to the temple treasury would gain eternal life.

6. In which New Testament letter are the words, "After that, we who are still alive and are left will be caught up together with them in the clouds to meet the Lord in the air"?

7. About whom did Jesus say: "He will cut him to pieces and assign him a place with the hypocrites, where there will be weeping and gnashing of teeth"?

8. What, according to Isaiah, do the following have in common with each other: Assyria, Lower Egypt, Upper Egypt, Cush, Elam, Babylonia, Hamath and the islands of the sea?

9. In John 5, on what grounds did Jesus state, "my judgment is just"?

10. Complete this "trustworthy saying" of Paul: "If we endure, we will also ____ with him."

11. True or false? Jesus said that one of the signs of the end of the age would be that most people's love for God would remain strong.

12. Fill in the missing word from the angel's words in Revelation: "For the Lamb at the center of the throne will be their ____."

13. When Jesus was talking about the end times, he said that heaven and earth would pass away, but what would not pass away?

14. Who in the Old Testament had a vision of Jesus, and wrote that "his face [was] like lightning, his eyes like flaming torches"?

15. Fill in the missing words from Isaiah's prophecy of the year of the Lord's favor: "They will be called ____ of righteousness."

Quiz # 19

APOCALYPSE NOW

1. Which Old Testament prophet wrote that silver and gold would not be able to deliver people from God's wrath?

2. In Joel's prophecy of the day of the Lord, who will be saved?

3. In Revelation 7, who washed their robes in the blood of the Lamb so that the robes became white?

4. Which Old Testament prophet said that arrogant and evil people were like stubble who would be set on fire when the day of the Lord came?

5. Fill in the missing word from Job's affirmation that God will vindicate him: "I know that my Redeemer ___."

6. According to Paul in Romans 1, what is being revealed from heaven against godlessness and wickedness?

7. To whom did Jesus say, "You snakes! You brood of vipers! How will you escape being condemned to hell?"?

8. Who wrote these words to encourage his Christian friends at Thessalonica: "And so we will be with the Lord forever"?

9. What, according to Paul in Romans 8, has been groaning with pain, as a mother in childbirth, waiting for the final deliverance?

10. Who heard a voice from heaven telling him: "Write: Blessed are the dead who die in the Lord from now on"?

11. Fill in the missing words, the same word each time, from Paul's letter to the Romans: "Now if we are children, then we are ___ — ___ of God and co-___ with Christ."

12. Fill in the missing word from Ezekiel's vision: "Like the appearance of a ___ in the clouds on a rainy day, so was the radiance around him."

13. Which prophet wrote: "Multitudes who sleep in the dust of the earth will awake: some to everlasting life, others to shame and everlasting contempt"?

14. In Isaiah's prophecy of peace in nature, who will the cow feed with?

15. Name one of the two men, about whom Paul wrote to Timothy when he said, that in the last days, men will oppose the truth just as these two men opposed Moses.

Quiz #20

APOCALYPSE NOW

1. To stress the horror of the coming destruction of Jerusalem, Jesus said that when it was imminent no one in the field should go back for his cloak. What other illustration did he use?

2. According to Revelation 12, why is the devil filled with fury?

3. In Jesus' Parable of the Net, what kinds of fish were caught in the net?

4. In Jesus' Parable of the Ten Virgins, what happened to the five foolish virgins?

5. How are the present earth and heavens going to be destroyed, according to Peter?

6. In the teaching of Jesus in Matthew 16, the Son of Man will come in his Father's glory, and then reward everyone: according to what?

7. Which New Testament writer wrote that the Father judges a person's works impartially?

8. Name one of the two Old Testament prophets who used the image of sitting under a vine and figtree as a symbol of future peace.

9. At the end of the Parable of the Ten Virgins, why does Jesus tell his listeners to keep watch?

10. Who, according to the writer of Hebrews, looked forward to a city which had foundations which were designed by and built by God?

11. According to Revelation 7, what were the great multitude which could not be counted wearing?

12. In Revelation 7, what were the countless multitudes carrying?

13. What question did the rich young ruler ask Jesus?

14. What did Jesus tell the rich young ruler to do in order to have treasure in heaven?

15. The rich young ruler thought he had obeyed all the commands, but which command had he not kept?

Facts 1

APOCALYPSE NOW

God's goal for his people is eternal life in his kingdom (Matthew 25:34). Hell was "prepared for the devil and his angels" (Matthew 25:43). To choose hell is to reject God's intended destiny.

In Old Testament times it was understood that at death people went to "Sheol," which meant "the place of shades." It was a place of waiting, rather than a place of punishment.

The New Testament translation of "Sheol" is "Hades." Jesus spoke of the unrepentant city of Capernaum which would "go down to the depths " (Matthew 11:23). Hades is not usually the place of final judgment.

Jesus said that "the gates of Hades will not overcome it [my church]" (Matthew 16:18). These "gates of Hades" represent the rallying point for Satan's armies, as city gates were rallying centers for a city's army.

The Jews believed that there were two compartments to Hades. The wicked dead went to one part of Hades, while the righteous dead went to another part of Hades, called Paradise.

The word "Gehenna" comes from the Greek meaning "Valley of Hinnom." This was the garbage dump outside Jerusalem, where children were once sacrificed by fire (Jeremiah 7:31).

In New Testament times, there were always fires in the Valley of Hinnom, burning up the rubbish left there. It became a metaphor for hell (e.g. Matthew 5:22; 25:41).

In the Bible, the phrase "the day of the Lord" refers to a time when God will act decisively in human history to implement the final stage of his redemptive plan for humankind.

The Old Testament speaks about God's judgment in terms of "the day of the Lord." On "that day" God will judge all peoples and nations, including Israel (Zephaniah 1:15).

In the Old Testament (Zechariah 14) and the New Testament, the day of the Lord refers to the second coming of Jesus. It has been calculated that the second coming is foretold 319 times in the New Testament.

"The day of the Lord" in 2 Peter 3:10-13, refers to a future climactic time when earth will be destroyed by fire. This will also be the moment that the new earth and new heavens are ushered in.

Facts 2

APOCALYPSE NOW

The New Testament uses three words for the return of Jesus, each with a slightly different emphasis. In classical Greek "parousia" referred to the arrival of someone of high rank. This is the usual word for the return of Jesus (Acts 1:11).

"Epiphaneia" means "appearance", and was used in Greek mythology of the appearance of a god, or of an emperor coming out before his people (2 Thessalonians 2:8).

"Apocalypse" means "uncovering," in the sense of revealing a hidden glory or splendor (2 Thessalonians 1:7). Apocalyptic writings describe mystical revelations from God. They are characterized by the use of codes, numbers and symbols.

Heaven is pictured as a place where there will be no sin (Revelation 21:27), no evil people (Revelation 21:8), no darkness and no sadness of any kind (Revelation 21:4).

There is an important division in Mark chapter 13. Verses 1-23 refer to events that will occur before Jesus' return, while verses 14-27 refer to events that will take place at Jesus' return.

"Paradise" is used metaphorically three times in the New Testament and describes the place where the spirits of God's people go when they die (Luke 23:43).

The New Testament talks of death as "sleep" (Acts 7:59-8:1), but does not teach that the spirit is unconscious until Jesus' return. It may be said that the body "sleeps," waiting to be reunited with the spirit.

The Westminster Confession refers to the "intermediate state" as a state in which "souls of the righteous [are]... received into the highest heaven where they behold the face of God... waiting for the full redemption of their bodies."

John teaches that the "Antichrist" is an evil person. His chief characteristics are the denial that Jesus is from God (1 John 4:3), and self-exaltation.

The spirit of antichrist is at work in the world, causing many "antichrists" to arise. But in the last days this spirit will be fully expressed in one final evil figure.

In Revelation the Antichrist is referred to as the Beast (Revelation 13), and in Paul's writings as the Man of Lawlessness (2 Thessalonians 2:3). He will be decisively destroyed by the coming of Jesus (2 Thessalonians 2:8).

Facts 3

APOCALYPSE NOW

Apocalyptic literature appeared in Judaism between 200 B.C. and A.D. 100 when Jews felt pessimistic about their position in the world. Much Jewish apocalyptic writing is anonymous.

In addition to the genre of apocalyptic literature, one may distinguish an "apocalyptic view" of the future in which history is not seen as a cycle of endless repetition, but has a final, divine resolution.

In the Bible examples of writings with an apocalyptic viewpoint are Isaiah 56 to 65, Zechariah 9 to 14, Daniel 11 to 12, Matthew 24 and 2 Thessalonians 1 and 2.

2 Peter 3:10 states that "the heavens will disappear with a roar." This can be interpreted as apocalyptic language, similar to that found in Daniel and Revelation and need not be interpreted literally.

Jesus taught that only God knows the date of the Parousia (Matthew 24:36). It would catch non-Christians completely unawares. Christians, however, should be on the look-out and not be found unprepared.

From the words "the stars will fall from the sky" (Mark 13:25), some have concluded that the universe will break up at the end of the age. Such language, however, is common in the Bible, and stands for God's judgment.

Many different judgments are mentioned in the Bible. There is the judgment of the cross. This is Jesus' judgment on sin which took place as he died and cried out, "It is finished" (John 19:30).

A judgment called the "judgment of believers" takes place in this life and is God's correction of his followers (1 Corinthians 11:31-32).

A judgment, sometimes called "the judgment of self," refers to a Christian's stern criticism of his own deeds and motives so that he confesses his sin to God and turns away from known sin (1 Corinthians 11:31-32).

There will be a final judgment at the end of the world, when all humanity, living and dead (Acts 10:42), Christian and non-Christian (Romans 14:10-12) will be divided into two groups.

Facts 4

APOCALYPSE NOW

The New Testament teaches that the Judge at the end of the world will be Jesus himself (Acts 10:42), and the deciding issue will be a person's relationship to Christ (John 3:18).

At death, a believer's deeds are also said to be "judged." This is God's appraisal and results in a reward or the loss of reward (1 Corinthians 3:11-15; 2 Corinthians 5:10).

Jehovah's Witnesses teach that only 144,000 people will be members of God's kingdom. However, most Christians suggest that this number is symbolic and does not refer to the exact sum of God's faithful followers.

The idea that those who reject Jesus will be punished for ever in hell is hard for many to accept, and alternative interpretations of the biblical teaching have been put forward.

Some Christians suggest that the biblical image of "the fires of hell" indicates that those who reject God are completely destroyed, as fire destroys. This may happen at death, or after a period of realization and consequent suffering.

Other Christians believe that all people will acknowledge the sovereignty of God, and enter heaven. This may happen at death, or after a period in Purgatory.

Jesus said that one of the signs of the end of the age would be toppling of the massive stones of the temple (Mark 13:1). The historian Josephus records that some of these stones were 37 feet long, 18 feet wide and 12 feet high.

In Matthew 24:34 Jesus said that this "generation" would not pass away until the events he predicted took place. Usually "generation" meant Jesus' contemporaries, but it can also refer to the nation of Israel.

God's wrath should not be confused with human anger but is his active opposition to every kind of evil. In that sense he shows his wrath every day (Psalm 7:11).

Jesus' second coming is confirmed in every section of the Old Testament. "Then the Lord my God will come, and all the holy ones with him" (Zechariah 14:5).